Funky Florals

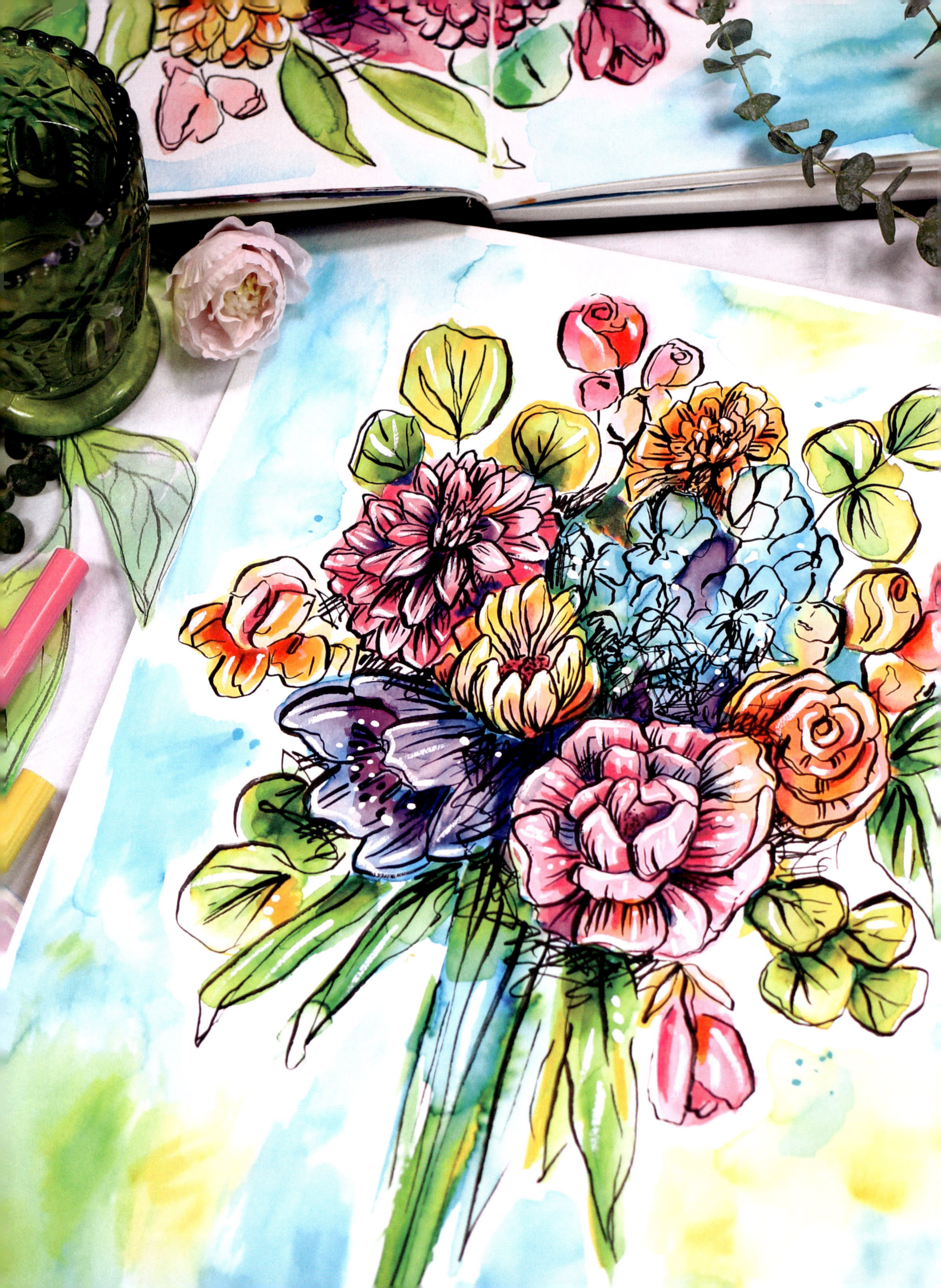

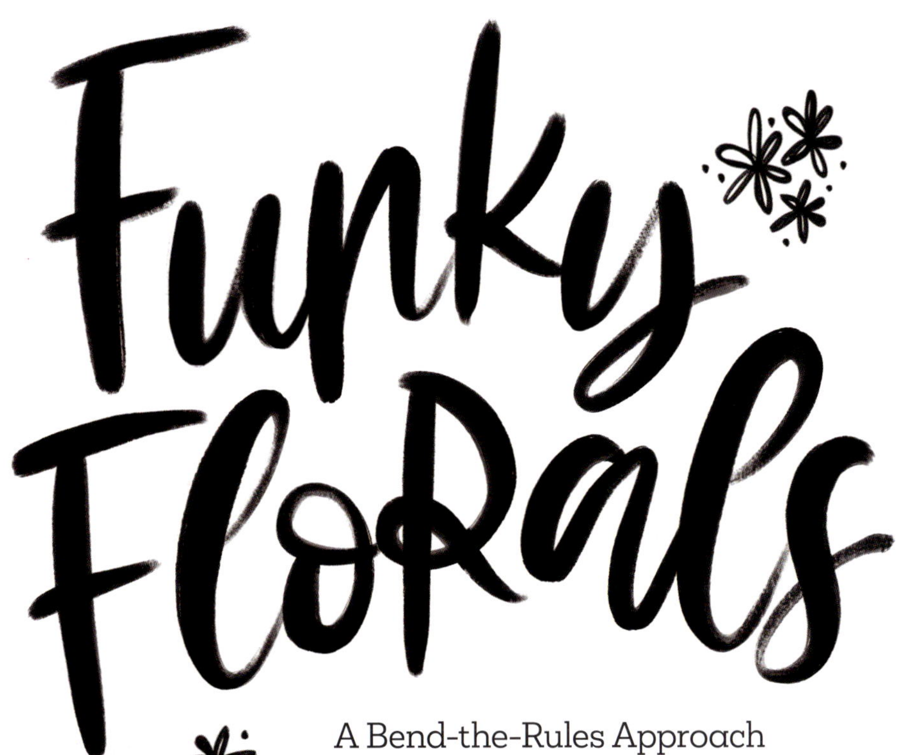

Funky Florals

A Bend-the-Rules Approach
to Making Bright,
Bold & Beautiful Flower Art
with Watercolor, Acrylics,
Markers & More

MEGAN WELLS

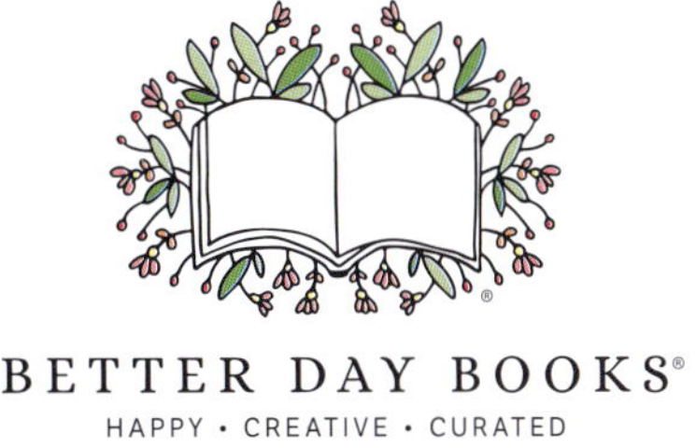

BETTER DAY BOOKS®

HAPPY · CREATIVE · CURATED

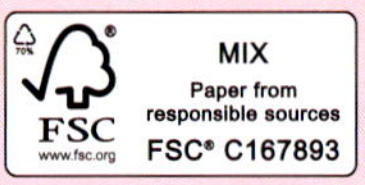

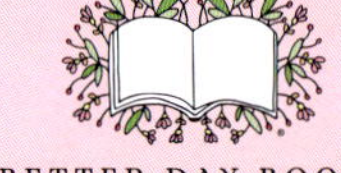

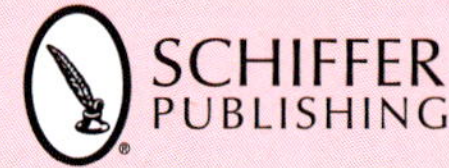

Better Day Books
Email: hello@betterdaybooks.com
Web: www.betterdaybooks.com
Visit us on Instagram!
@better_day_books

Schiffer Publishing
4880 Lower Valley Road
Atglen, PA 19310
Phone: 610-593-1777
Fax: 610-593-2002
Email: info@schifferbooks.com
Web: www.schifferbooks.com

For our complete selection of fine books on this and related subjects, please visit our website at www.betterdaybooks.com. You may also write for a free catalog.

Better Day Books titles are available at special discounts for bulk purchases for sales promotions or premiums. Special editions, including personalized covers, corporate imprints, and excerpts, can be created in large quantities for special needs. For more information, contact the publisher.

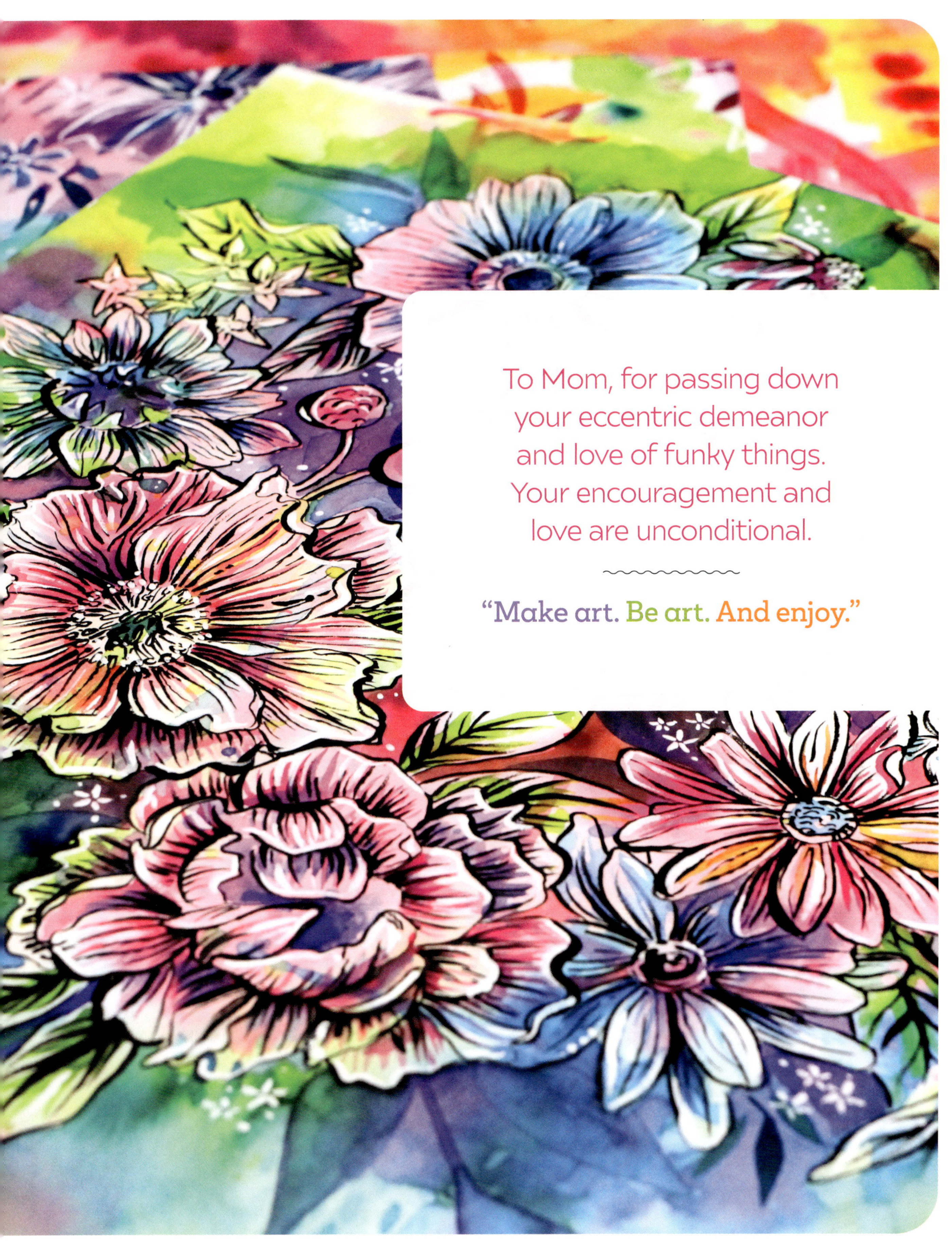
To Mom, for passing down
your eccentric demeanor
and love of funky things.
Your encouragement and
love are unconditional.

"Make art. Be art. And enjoy."

Contents

Getting Started

Creative Projects

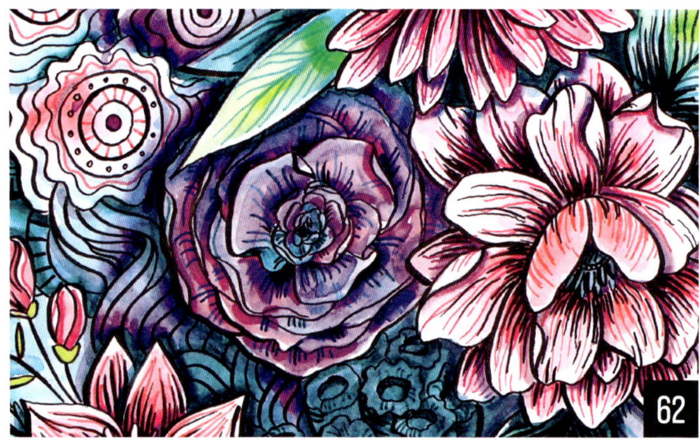

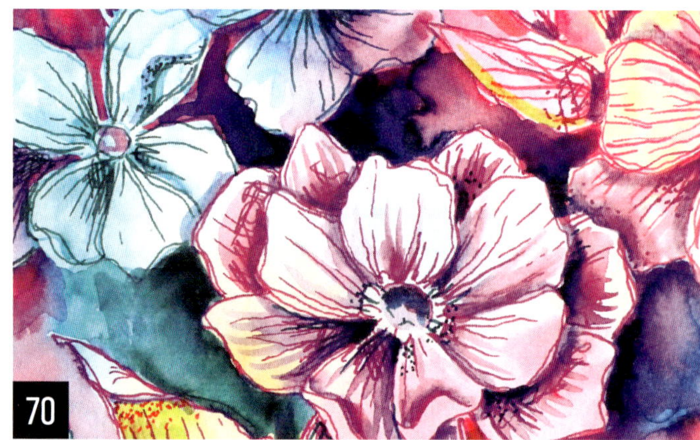

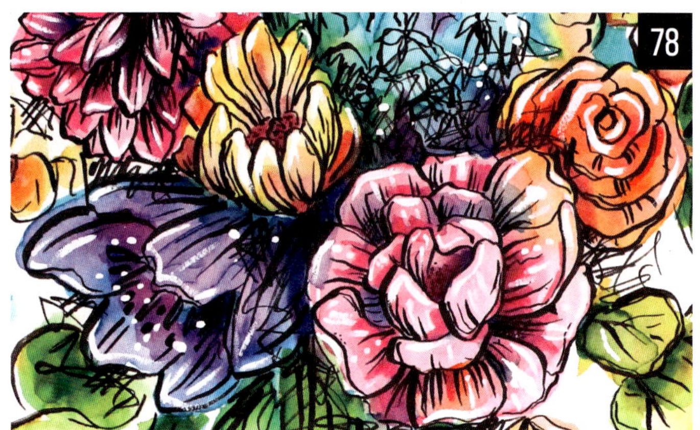

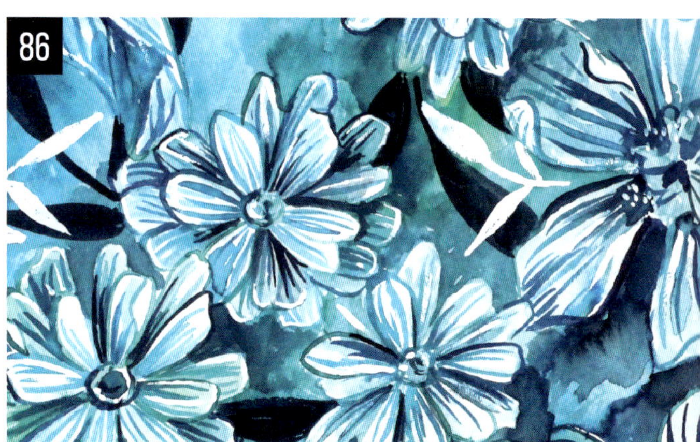

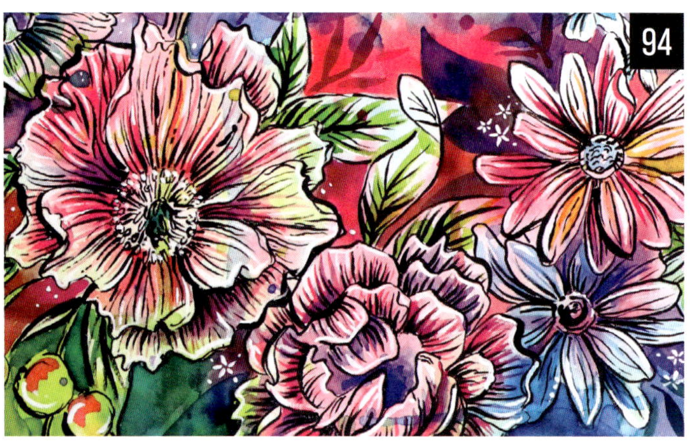

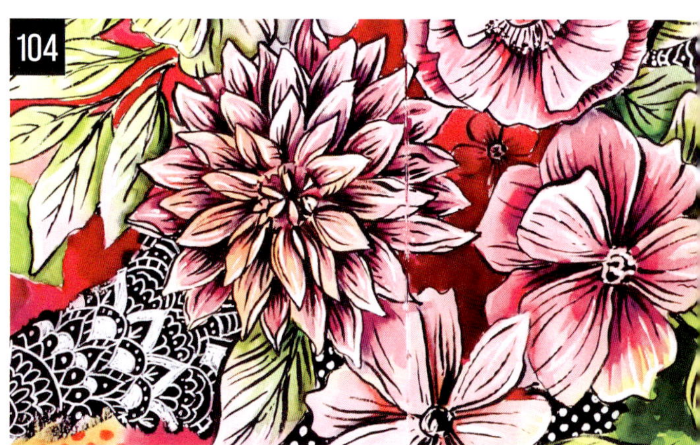

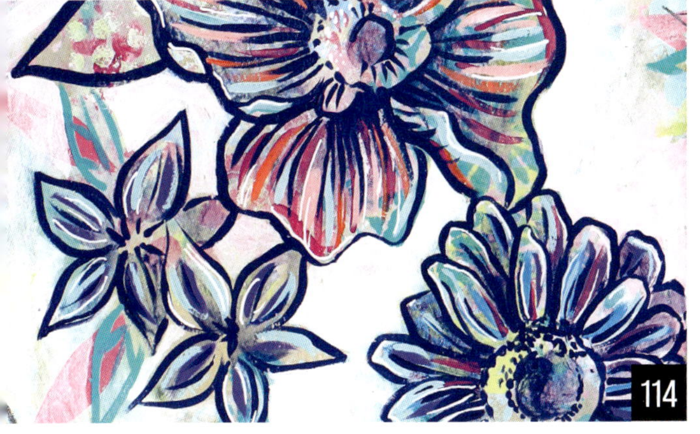

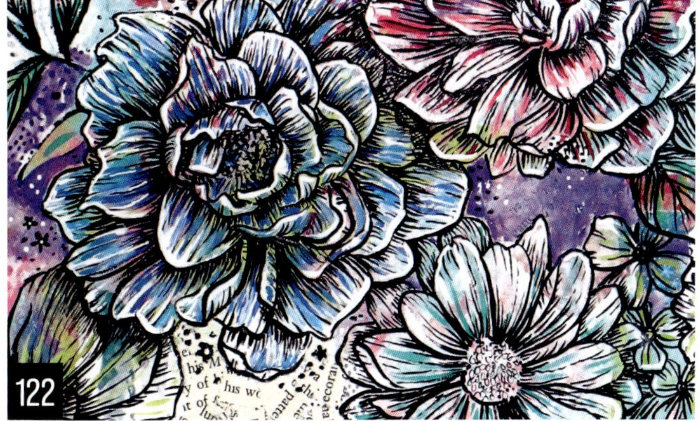

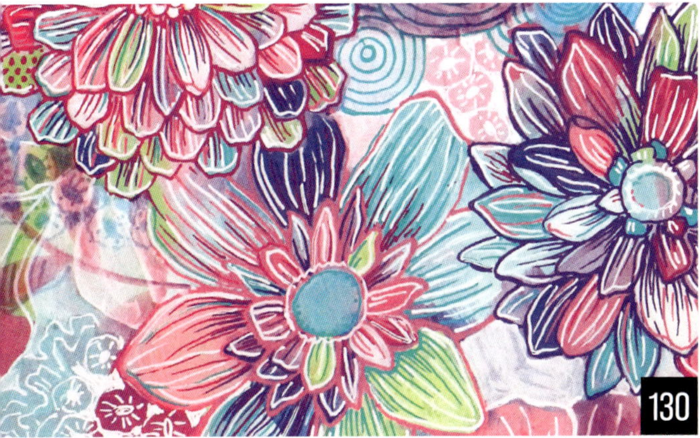

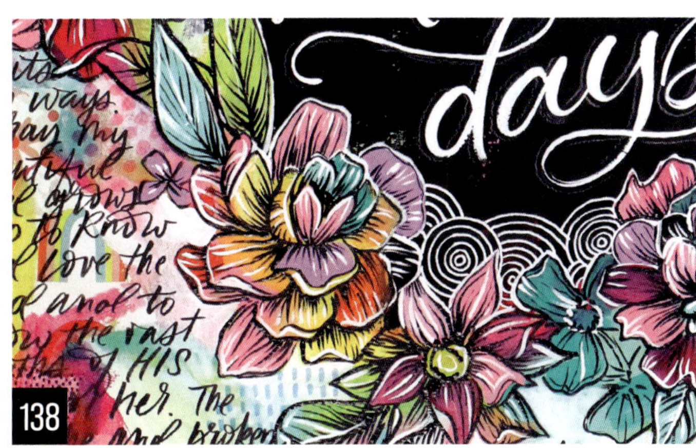

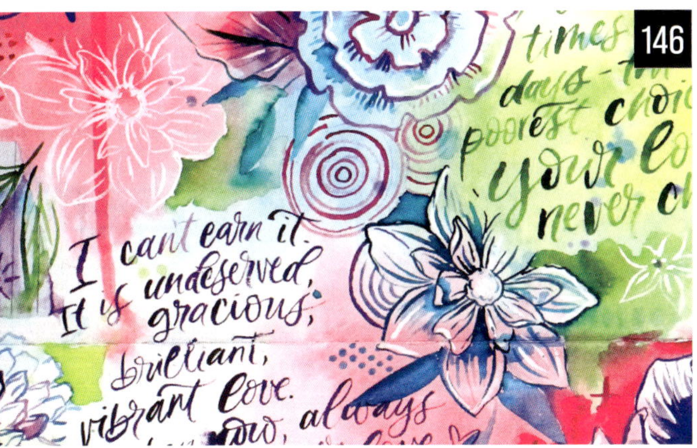

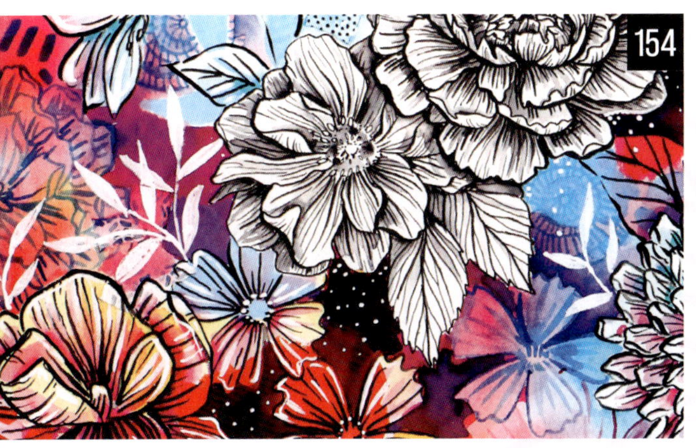

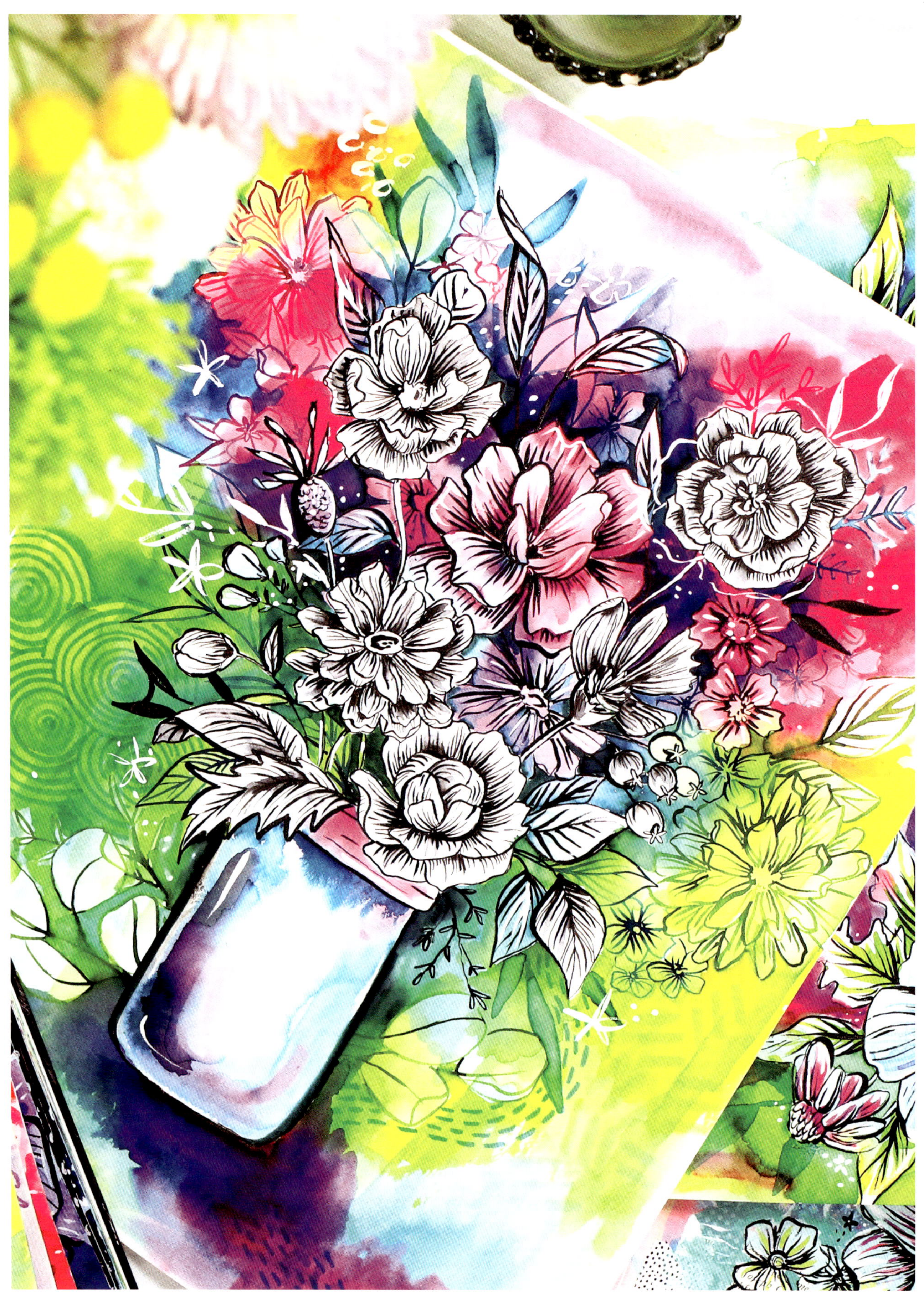

Welcome!

I am delighted you have found yourself here. Of the vast choices of books out there, you chose this one—thank you.

I want to begin this book with a note about what I hope and believe it will bring to you.

This book will help you let loose and let go of your creative fears: the fear of not being good and the fear of messing up (whatever that means). I want you to stop questioning every brushstroke or mark you make and just sink, confidently, into a new process of creating that will ultimately lead you to creating beautiful work.

See, that's the thing: I'm not naive to the fact that we all want to make pretty things. Believe it or not, you CAN make beautiful art that you are proud of and fully embrace the enjoyment of the process. You CAN let go and be free and also think through the choices you make as you create. You CAN get lost in your work yet remain keenly aware of what you are doing. You CAN embrace messing up and still make art that makes your heart sing.

You do not have to choose between process and product. You can have both.

This book is not a guidebook to how to draw or paint flowers. Flowers are the most widely interpreted subject matter out there. Just a few smooshes of color can be a flower. Flowers can be detailed and realistic or messy and whimsical, simple, intricate, soft, striking—there is no right or wrong way to paint or draw a flower.

I will walk you through a few step-by-step flowers, but only to get you going in the right direction. You will learn to take these basic floral shapes and combine them with flowers from your own imagination to create infinite works of art, all stemming from the 12 projects we will work through in this book.

I was initially hesitant to share my personal style and process with others because I was worried that my style would no longer be my own once my little secrets were let loose. But that hesitation was easily squashed by my desire to share the JOY I feel through my process of creating. How could I keep that to myself? It's too much fun, too rewarding, and too freeing not to spread it around.

So, enough jabbering—let's fuel up, dig in, and create some beautiful and FUNKY florals together. I can't wait to see what you make!

XO

Megan Wells

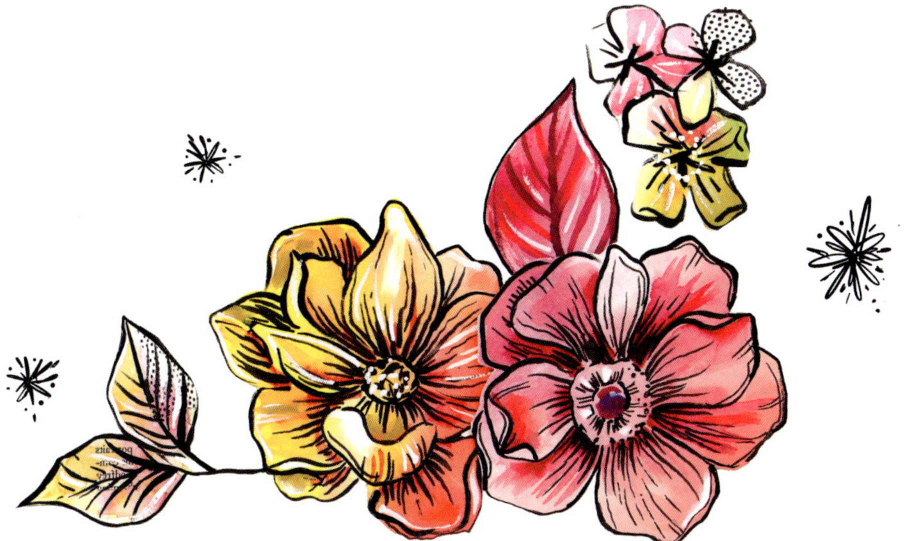

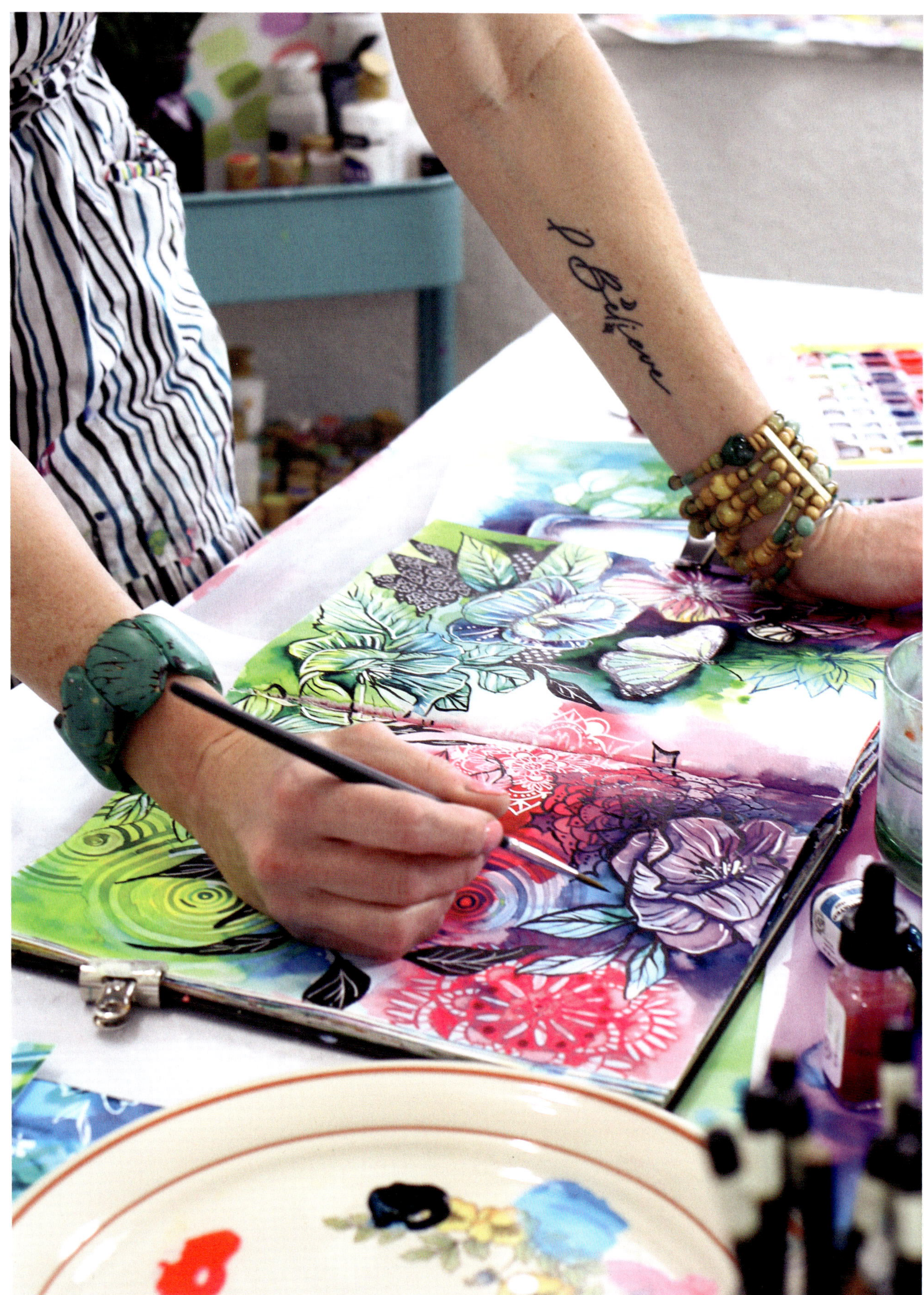

Meet the Author

When I tell someone I'm an artist, it's always followed by this question: "What type of art do you do?" That is harder for me to answer than Final Jeopardy. I blink and stare and open my mouth, and the first couple of words that come out are "Um . . . well . . . hmm . . . so . . . ," which eventually leads to "I paint mostly. And illustrate. I paint a lot of flowers. And do some lettering and design here and there. Oh, I also paint portraits. And pet portraits. I kind of do everything." Their next question, because they don't know what else to ask, is usually "What type of painting do you do? Oils? Watercolors?" And I blink, stare, and open my mouth again, and then I repeat the above.

I just make art! I just make stuff! I could say mixed media, sure, but does that really sum it up?

At one point in my 20s, I was going through a low time and a stressful situation that was consuming me. My mom texted me and told me to stop thinking about it. Her next words never left me. She said, **"Make art. Be art. Enjoy."** Those five words have summed up my creative process now for almost 20 years (thanks, Mom!), and those are also words I hope you can keep close to heart as you work through this book.

Now for the details:

I live and work in South Florida with my beautiful daughter and best-friend husband. I founded my company, Makewells, in 2012, after spending six years as a high school art teacher. Over the past 12 years, I've kinda done it all: murals, portraits, lettering, stationery, illustration, art journaling, creating online courses, licensing, and the list goes on.

There have been ups and downs, successes and failures. I've had opportunities I never dreamed of when starting out in my little basement apartment (writing five books is definitely in that category!), and I'm firm believer that God gives us all unique gifts we can use to glorify Him. I'm doing my best to use my gift in this little arena He's given me to shine. Creating and teaching art is my gift, and I seek to honor Him in all I make and do. It's a blessing, and I hope to never take it for granted.

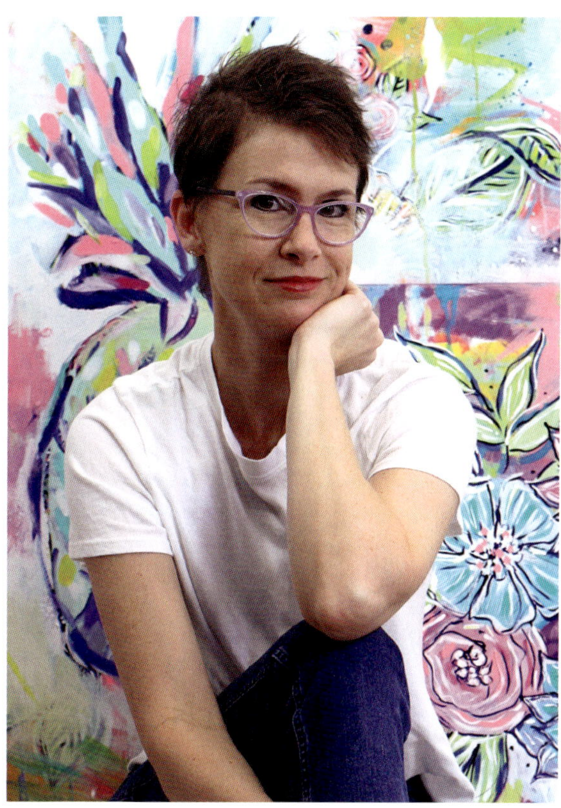

MEGAN WELLS is an artist, instructor, author, and the creative force behind Makewells design studio. She has authored 5 books, created 17 online classes, and had her work featured in retailers such as Pottery Barn Kids, Minted, Target, Michaels, Barnes and Noble, and more. A former high school art teacher, Megan loves colors, getting her hands messy, and teaching others the joy of expressing their creativity. She lives and works in Delray Beach, Florida. Learn more at www.makewells.com and @makewells on Instagram.

Let's Chat with Megan

We sat down with Megan to learn a little more about her and her artistic journey. Join us!

You were a high school art teacher for six years! Tell us about that time of your life.

Well, this was a lot of fun. I began teaching at the age of 24, so I had a great connection with my students and still keep in touch with many of them. I really enjoyed turning students who couldn't care less about art and only needed an elective into students who would call my class their favorite. I also began an AP program at the school I taught at, and many of the students in those classes have gone on to careers in art, which has been really rewarding to see.

The itch to be able to be a full-time artist was always there in me, though, and little things like lunch duty, dealing with discipline issues, grading, and having a constricted schedule really contributed to pushing me to make a change.

How did you develop your personal design style?

Making, making, making. I have spent a lot of time creating and I've created a lot of different kinds of art, but I'm constantly pulled back to funky florals. I think it's the thing that you start painting first when you don't know what to create that leads you to find your personal style.

What is your favorite flower (in general and your favorite to paint)?

A peony is both my favorite flower and my favorite flower to paint. They do not grow down here in South Florida, so they are a rare and special find. I also love succulents, although they aren't technically flowers.

Are you much of a gardener?

I am NOT. Sadly, I'm very talented at killing plants. I do well with succulents, but that's about it. I would make a good gardening assistant because I really enjoy pulling weeds, but keeping flowers alive is not one of my strong suits.

In addition to being a busy artist and entrepreneur, you are a mother. How do you balance it all?

Well, it's a busy life, but I love it. I squeeze as much work time as I can into school hours and do a lot of creative things with my six-year-old daughter—we love to color, build LEGO, and collect seashells together, and it's so special to share these hobbies.

What other passions and hobbies do you have in life, outside of your art?

I am in love with the ocean. We spend a lot of time at the beach, swimming and collecting seashells. You'll never find me just sitting on a towel. I grew up snorkeling, fishing, and diving, so the ocean feels like home to me.

I'm into anything that gets me outside in nature, so we love to go to nature trails and enjoy creation. If I lived near the mountains, I'd be a hiker. But in flat Florida, I'm an evening walker.

I am also very passionate about my faith. I love to study my Bible and pray and then incorporate many of these things into my art journaling.

Lately, and I say this with all seriousness, I am really into LEGO! My daughter and I love building sets together and our own creations, and I may be surpassing her in it being a favorite way to play and spend time together.

What's a perfect day for you?

A perfect day involves a few things: snorkeling to look for shells with my daughter on a hot summer morning when the ocean is clear and flat, a good chunk of time creating, and a nice dinner with our little family where I don't have to cook.

What do you struggle with as an artist?

I think most artists struggle with comparison—and that is definitely where I hop on the struggle bus. With social media in your face day in and day out, it's easy to see what other artists are making, what clients they are working with, how many followers they have . . . and compare yourself to them. I often have to take steps back from social media to realign my thinking. I try to keep a focus on the opportunities I've been given and not the ones that seem out of my reach. I'm a very competitive and driven person, but I need to balance contentment with that part of my personality.

Also, being the sole employee of my company is a lot to manage. I am not gifted in the business and finance aspect of the job, and those are things that take a lot of my time. I just want to make stuff, but those duties are just part of the gig!

What's next for you?

I'm in a phase where I have too many ideas and not enough time. I much prefer this to the dry seasons where I feel uninspired and flat, but my list of ideas is a bit overwhelming right now.

Many of those ideas center around funky florals, so a coloring book is on the list, as well as quite a few more online courses. I am tossing around other ideas too, including a coloring subscription box. And I'd welcome any new collaborations with Better Day Books, because they are an amazing team to work with!

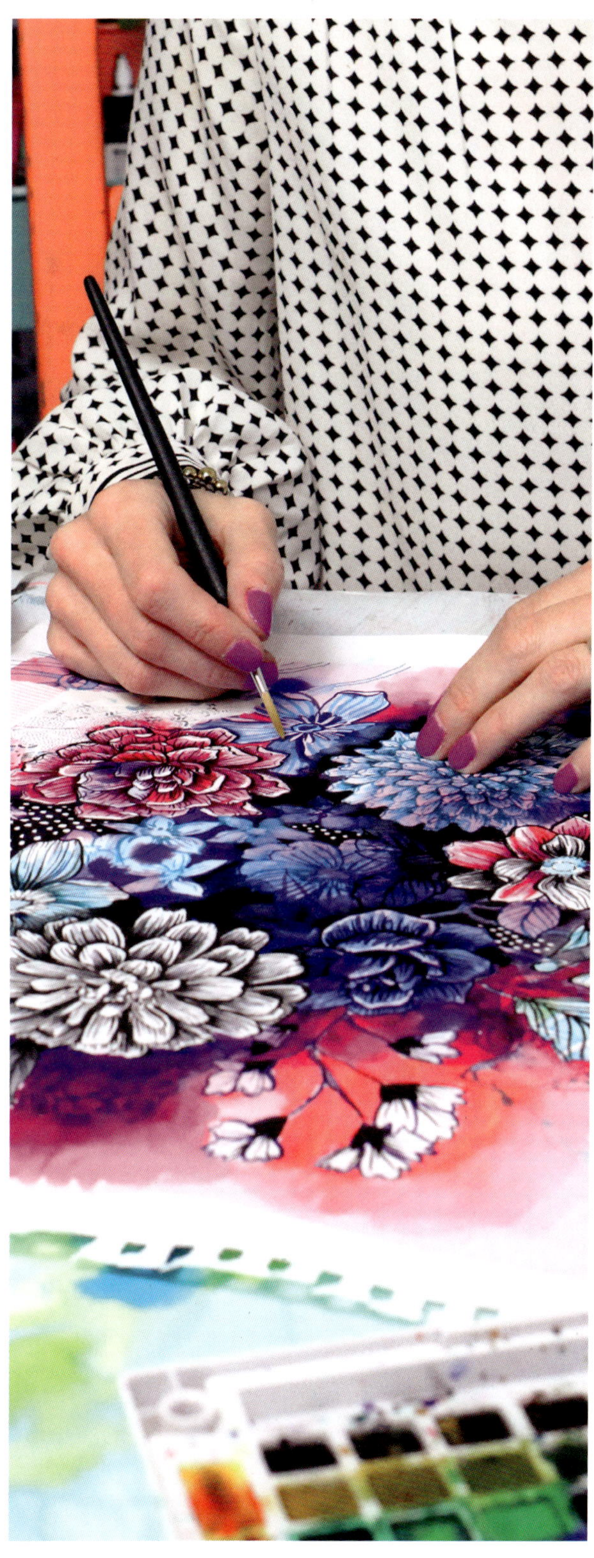

Creative Studio Space

Let's discuss your creative space. I know not everyone is able to have their own room for creating, or maybe not even their own table. But I do want to show you my little studio and give you a glimpse at my happy place (the one that's not the beach!). It's quite a small room, actually, but I've learned to maximize what I've been blessed with.

Depending on what I'm working on, my painting desk is usually set up looking directly out a large window at our little pond. I move things around if I'm filming a class. If possible, gravitate to a space with natural light. You can use smaller lights to supplement, of course, because you probably need to be able to paint when it's raining out or nighttime.

My inspiration board is in a place where I can freely look at it while I work. I change this up often with different color schemes, photos of florals, and other images that inspire me. **If you have an inspiration board, I recommend keeping it free of other artists' work** (for the

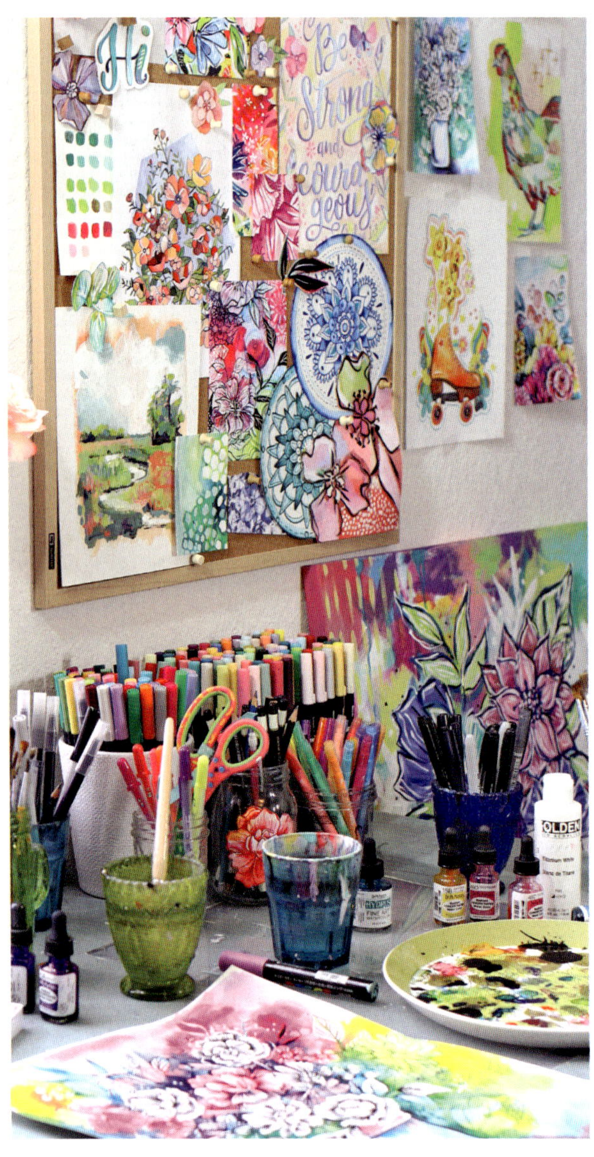

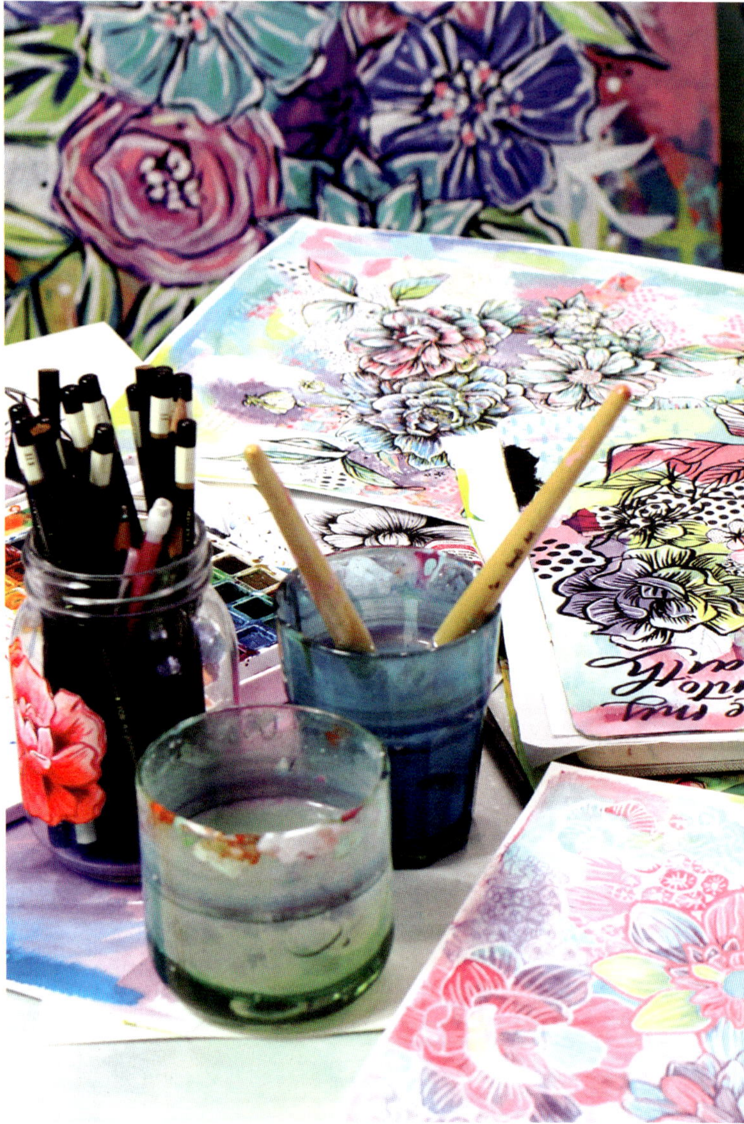

most part). If you are looking to embrace your own style and creativity, staring at another artist's work isn't going to take you there. When you look at and admire others' work, which is a fun and inspiring thing to do, set those images aside so that the impression is left in your mind but the images aren't right in front of you, stealing attention from the creativity already inside you.

My walls are filled with artwork, and it's mostly mine! Once again, this is to keep me focused on my own work and style. Once you've built up a large body of work, you can look back at your own pieces and inspire yourself with YOU.

I have carts full of paint, brushes, pens, and markers. I will confess, it's a bit tricky for me to keep my space neat and organized, but I do try. As an artist, I give myself quite a bit of leeway to create messes, but too much mess leaves me feeling overwhelmed. I try to tidy up regularly—but I don't manage to as often as my neat-freak husband would prefer!

If you aren't able to set aside a space of your own for art, here's what I recommend: have a cart to store your supplies so that it can easily be brought out and then put away again. Get creative with shelves and drawers and give yourself a protective table covering that can be easily rolled up and stored away. With some creativity and resourcefulness, even just a corner of your kitchen table can be transformed into your own private studio.

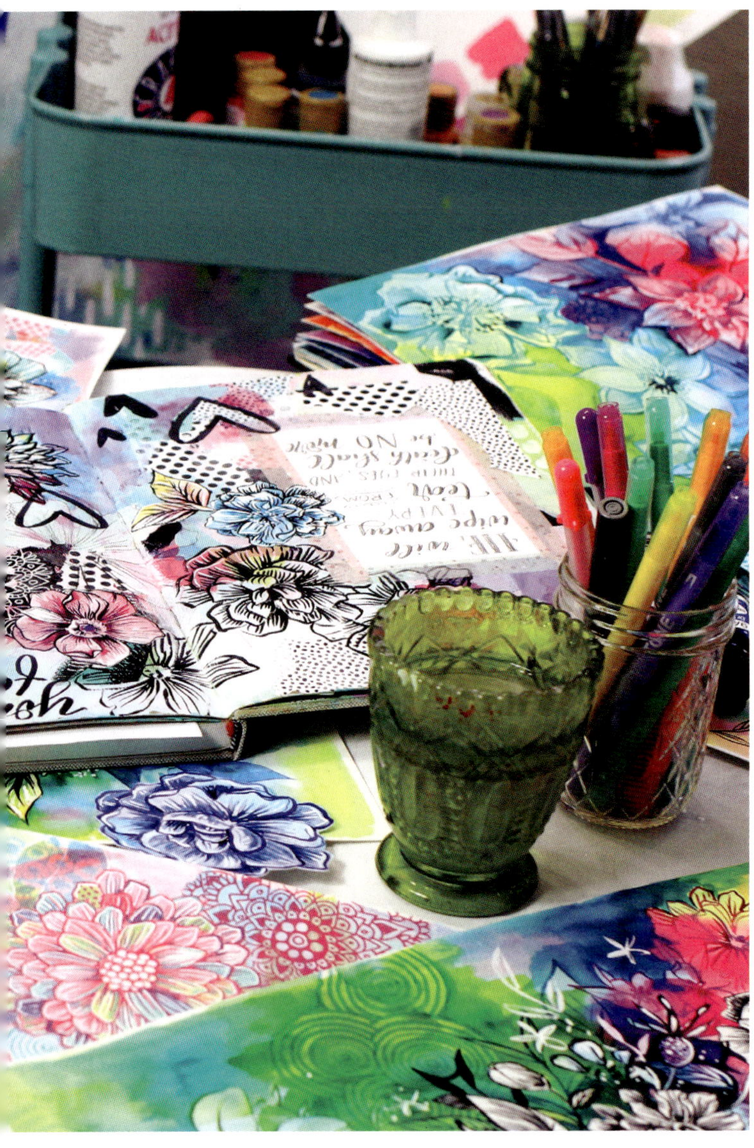

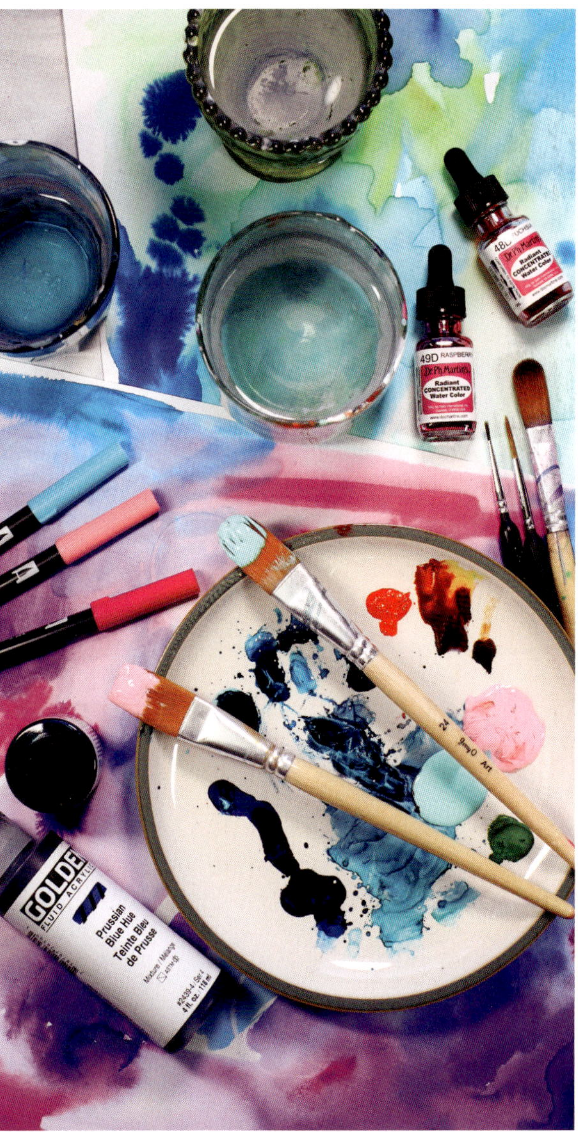

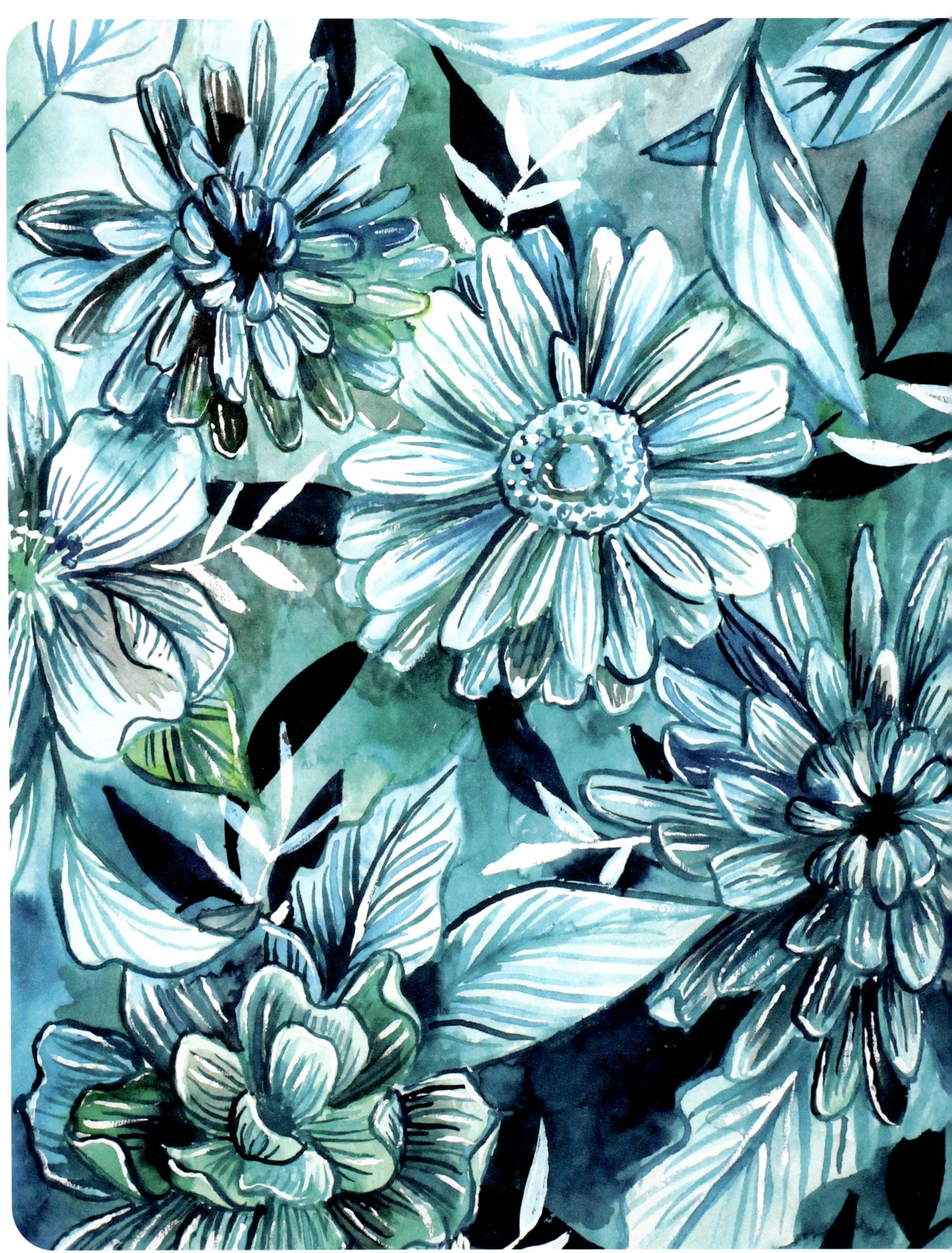

PART 1
Getting Started

Before you start tackling the projects later in the book and making your own funky floral compositions, let's take a minute to go over some basics. In this chapter, we'll discuss tools and supplies for mixed-media art, color theory fundamentals, a few step-by-step tutorials for getting you comfortable drawing flowers, and some tips for hand lettering. We'll also discuss the creative mindset—because all the right tools and technical know-how are nothing if you aren't in the right headspace for creative expression!

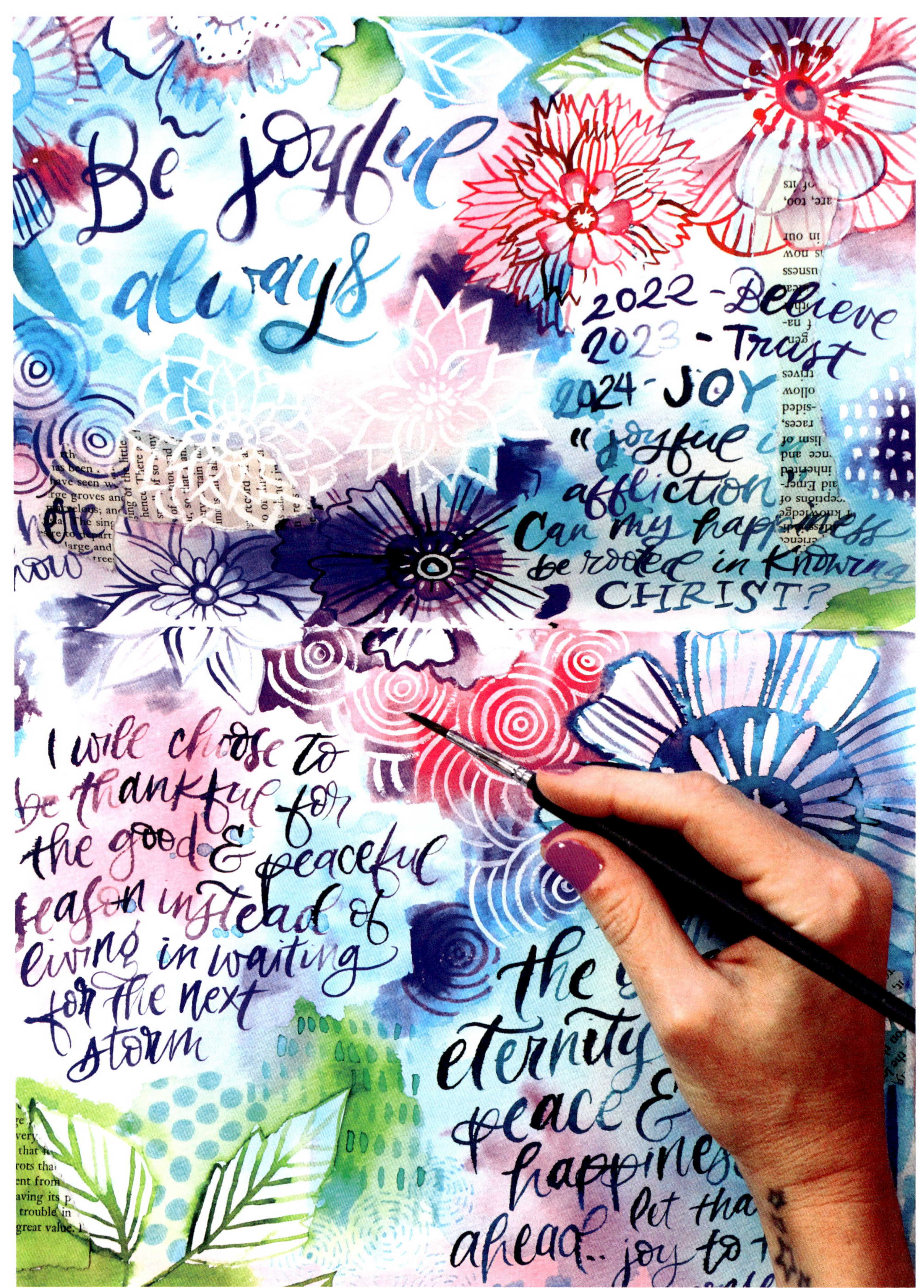

Be joyful always
2022 - Believe
2023 - Trust
2024 - JOY
"joyful in affliction"
Can my happiness be rooted in knowing CHRIST?
I will choose to be thankful for the good & peaceful season instead of living in waiting for the next storm
the eternity peace & happiness let tha ahead.. joy to

Creative Mindset

Have you ever been so in the zone creating that you forgot to eat? I hope so. But if not, this book will probably take you there. So make sure to eat a hearty breakfast before diving in!

Getting into a creative mindset can be difficult for new artists (and experienced ones too!). What stops you from creating? Is it fear? You can be honest—we'll keep it here in our inner circle of friends. If it's fear, ask yourself: What am I afraid of?

Are you afraid of messing up? Not being good at it? Ruining your shiny new supplies? Not knowing "how" to draw or paint a flower? Not liking your work or feeling proud enough to show it off?

As of the day this book hits shelves, I'll have been an art instructor for 18 years, and the one thing I've heard most from students of any age are the words "I'm afraid to mess up because I don't know how to (fill in the blank)."

"I don't know how to mix colors." "I don't know how to draw." "I don't know how to paint." That fear of not knowing how—which ultimately stems from the fear of messing up—is the easiest one to get past! Yet, if you don't tackle it head on, you can get stuck there for a long time. So let's address it right off the bat before we dive into this colorful mess of a book.

Did you know how to walk when you were born? Did you know how to read before someone taught you? Did you know how to ride a bike by watching someone else ride down the sidewalk? Of course not! You had to DO it to LEARN it. And you had to do it a lot to get the hang of it. But before you knew it, it became second nature.

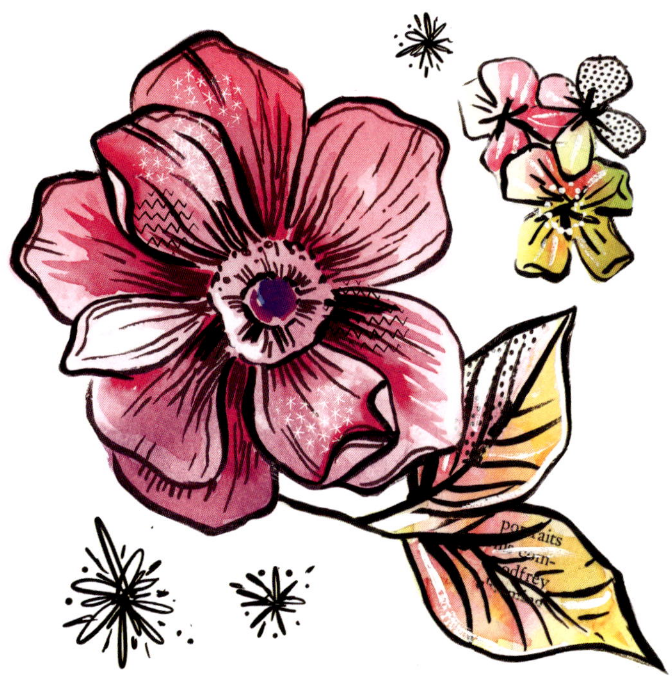

It's the same with making art. You must create it to learn it. Reading this book will only take you so far—at some point, you need to get out your supplies and make a mess.

My hope with this book is that creating will become like walking, reading, or riding a bike for you. I want creating beautiful art that you love to become an ingrained instinct in you, which will allow those fears of messing up, of not being good, or of ruining your supplies to disappear. That doesn't mean they'll never come back again, but you can at least learn to banish them temporarily and sit down and start making something!

One last thought I'd like to leave you with as you seek to enter into your creative mindset: You will make stuff you don't like. Accept it. Embrace it. You'll understand why as you turn the pages and work your way through this book.

I want creating beautiful art that you love to become an ingrained instinct in you, which will allow those fears of messing up, of not being good, or of ruining your supplies to disappear.

Finding Inspiration

"Finding Inspiration" is a somewhat misleading shorthand for what's actually two different things I want to recommend to you: training your brain to see inspiration everywhere, and taking some achievable steps for surrounding yourself with what inspires you.

Inspiration is a state of mind. If your soul longs to create, your eyes will seek out beauty and curiosity everywhere you look. You may have a delicious garden of blooms in your backyard, or you may be on the 12th floor of a downtown apartment with views of a factory, but either way, inspiration is already everywhere you look.

You may not think this way right now. But, just like with any habit, consciously pushing yourself to shift your thinking can lead you to naturally view the world in a different way.

I find inspiration everywhere I look: in patterns on clothing at the store, on packaging for products, and looking at nature (especially in the ocean— I spend a lot of time there). The key is to look deeper at the colors and shapes you are around each and every day. Don't just look at things, but instead, really SEE them.

When you make it a practice to seek out inspiration like this, over time it will become second nature to view the world in this way!

You can also encourage inspiration by taking steps to incorporate what inspires you into your life. Now, for someone who loves to paint florals, it is still quite tricky for me to have beautiful bouquets around me all the time. (Let's face it—that would also be quite expensive!) Full transparency: the flowers I would have loved to photograph for this book were impossible to find while I was writing it due to my location and the time of year.

But I have a large collection of realistic faux florals on hand to inspire the shapes and colors in my work. I also use photographs of flowers as references and inspiration and keep some of my favorites on my moodboard. While being surrounded by real flowers seems romantic and ideal, it's not necessary. It's a want, but not a need. Some days, I'll focus on loose studies of flowers to find new ways to work. I can work from real flowers if those are around, or I can simply lay out some of the faux blooms I've collected.

Think about ways in which you can bring what inspires you into your life (and your desk) without breaking the bank or adding too much clutter. If you're practicing seeing inspiration naturally, maybe you can take an "inspiration walk" before each creative session or visit a store you love to snap some pics (that's both free and clutter-free!).

Our brains are amazing, but it's easier to create when you're inspired than when sitting in a void!

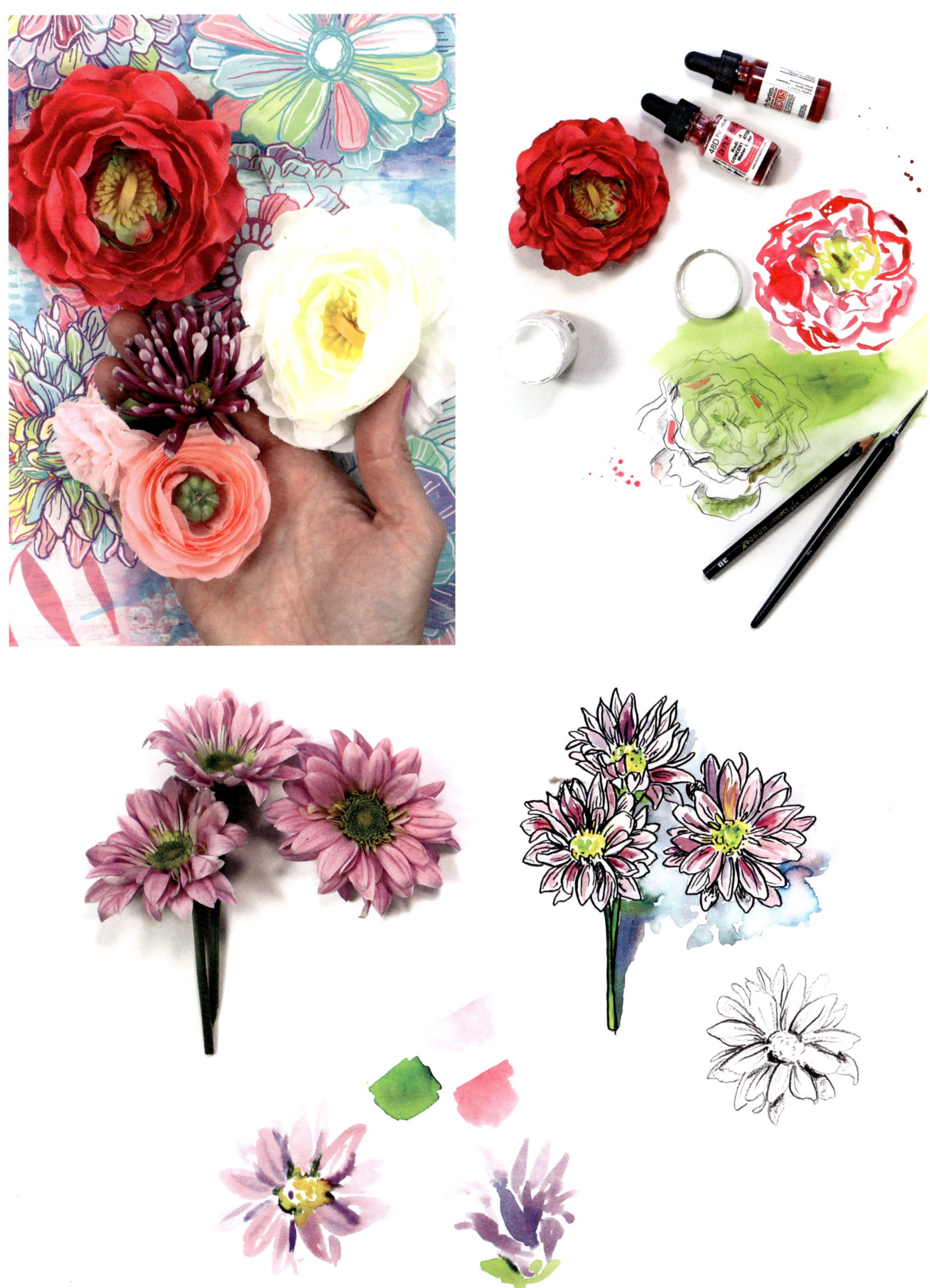

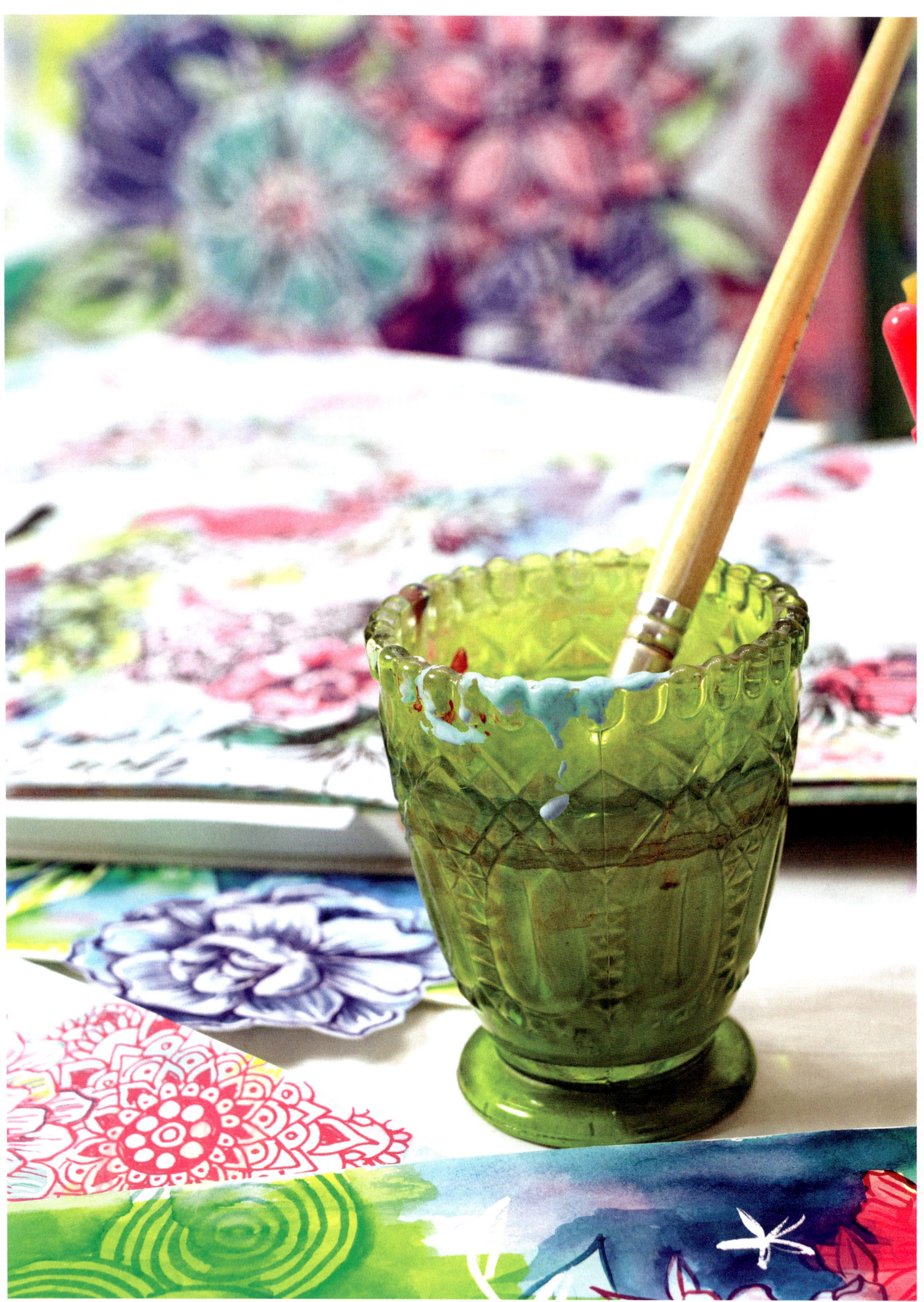

Tools and Supplies

My motto with supplies is "The more the better"—but, yes, "more" also means more room in the budget. So, while I will list all the supplies I recommend and use below, do not run out and purchase everything at once! I suggest working with what you have and adding new things to experiment with as you go. If you follow along with the projects in this book, you can likely start with just a couple of purchases and slowly build your collection with each new project.

The main supplies you will need for the projects in this book are:
- an art journal or pad of watercolor paper or mixed-media paper
- acrylic paints
- watercolors
- water-based markers
- round paintbrushes
- an adhesive (such as glue sticks or matte medium)

Let's go over each of these categories in more detail over the next few pages. You can also find my specific product recommendations under "Supply Favorites" on page 173 at the end of the book.

Surfaces

I most often prefer to work in an art journal as opposed to on loose sheets of paper. Look for art journals that indicate watercolor paper or mixed-media paper of heavier weight (somewhere between 98 lb. and 140 lb.). I prefer larger journals with pages that are around 8.5" x 11" (22 x 28 cm).

Whether it's in an art journal or as loose sheets, paper specifically labeled for use with watercolors is more expensive but will withstand watercolors, acrylics, and water-based markers with no problems. Mixed-media paper may not hold up to heavy watercolors as well but is a great lower-cost option for projects that don't use watercolor. Bristol board is another good option. As a general rule, the

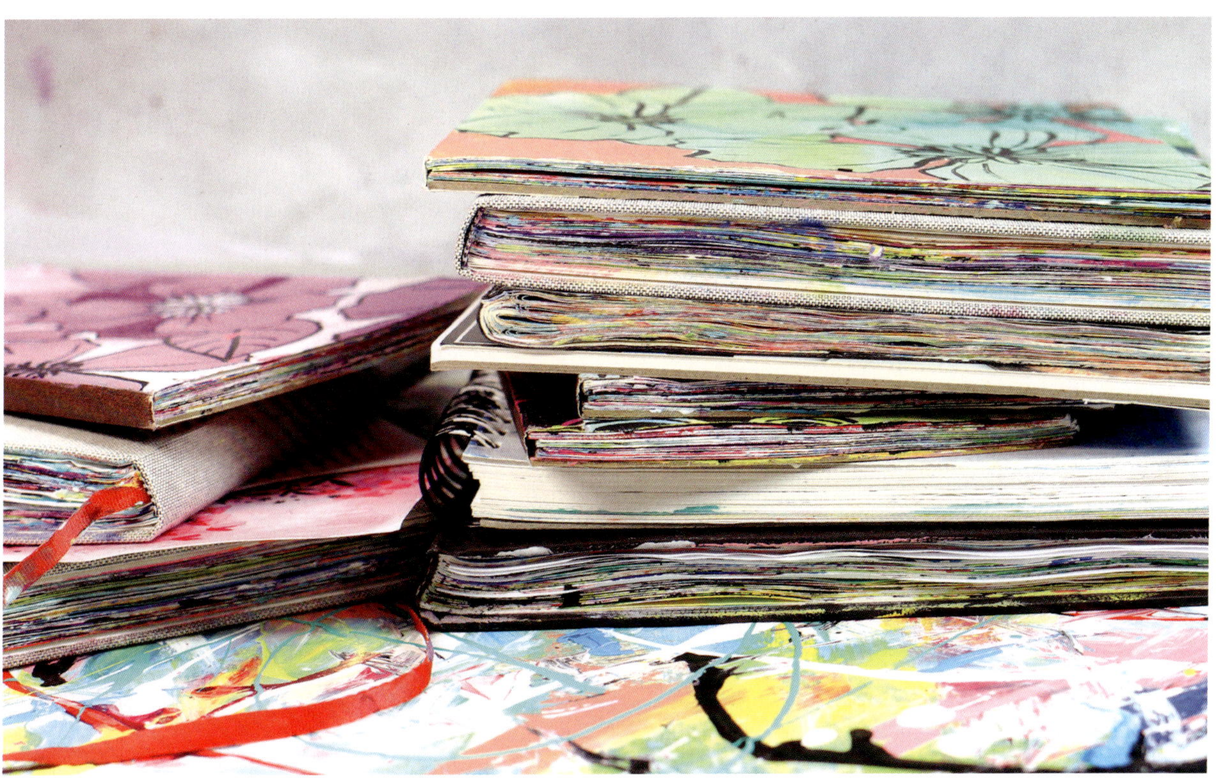

thicker the weight, the better for wetter media!
I often purchase whatever watercolor paper
I can find a good deal on at the time I'm buying.

Note that some watercolor and mixed-media
papers work better than others with the water-
based markers that we use many times in this
book. If you choose to use a product that isn't
listed in my "Supply Favorites" at the end of the
book, you may want to experiment with a small
quantity or single sheet of a new kind of paper
before buying a ton of it.

If you want to work in just one art journal but
want to experiment on several different types
of paper, here's an idea: tear out the pages from
other books or pads and tape them securely
into your master art journal.

Paintbrushes

I tend to stick to mostly round brushes, which
in various sizes give you pretty good control,
but having a couple flat brushes in large sizes
on hand is also a good idea for painting large
background layers, especially in acrylic. Brushes
are one of the supplies that I tend NOT to splurge
on, but other artists have a different outlook.
See what works for you!

To start off, get your hands on four round brushes
so that you have a large, medium, small, and
extra-small option to work with. Brush sizes are
indicated by numbers: the smaller the number,
the smaller the brush. For your starting set of four
brushes, I recommend choosing a large round
brush between sizes 8–12, a medium round brush
between sizes 4–7, a small round brush between
sizes 1–3, and an extra-small round brush between
sizes 000–0. As you invest in your supplies more,
you can add other sizes as well as flat brushes.

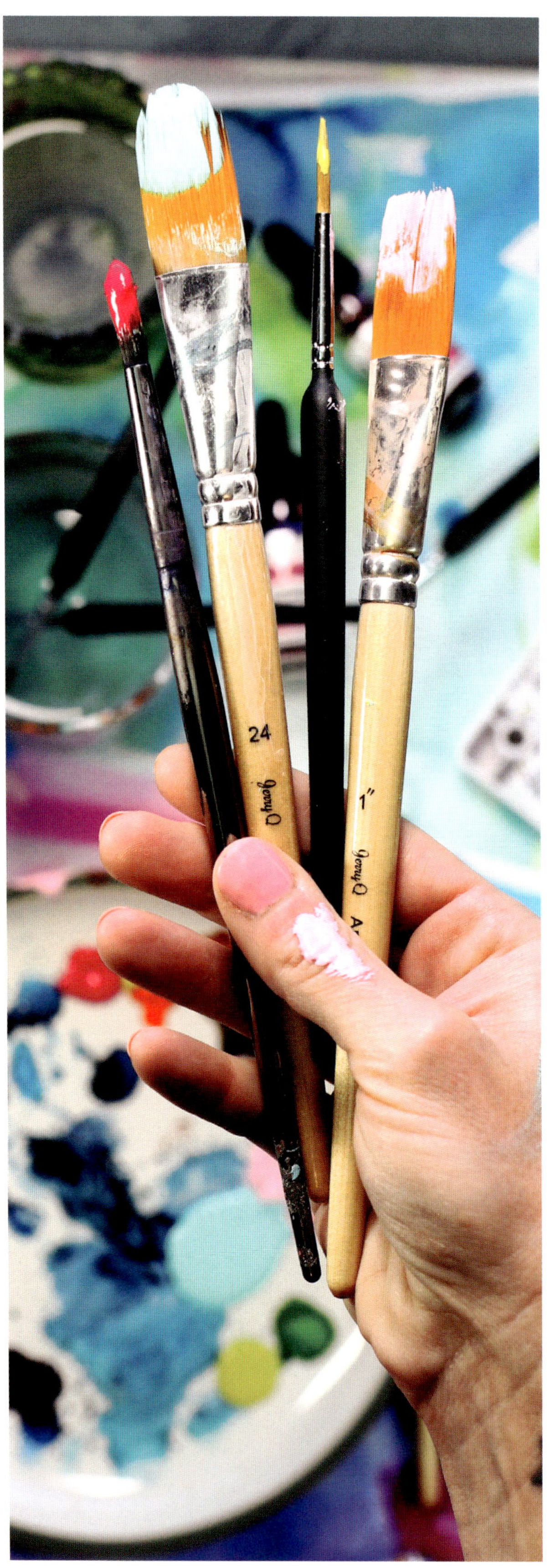

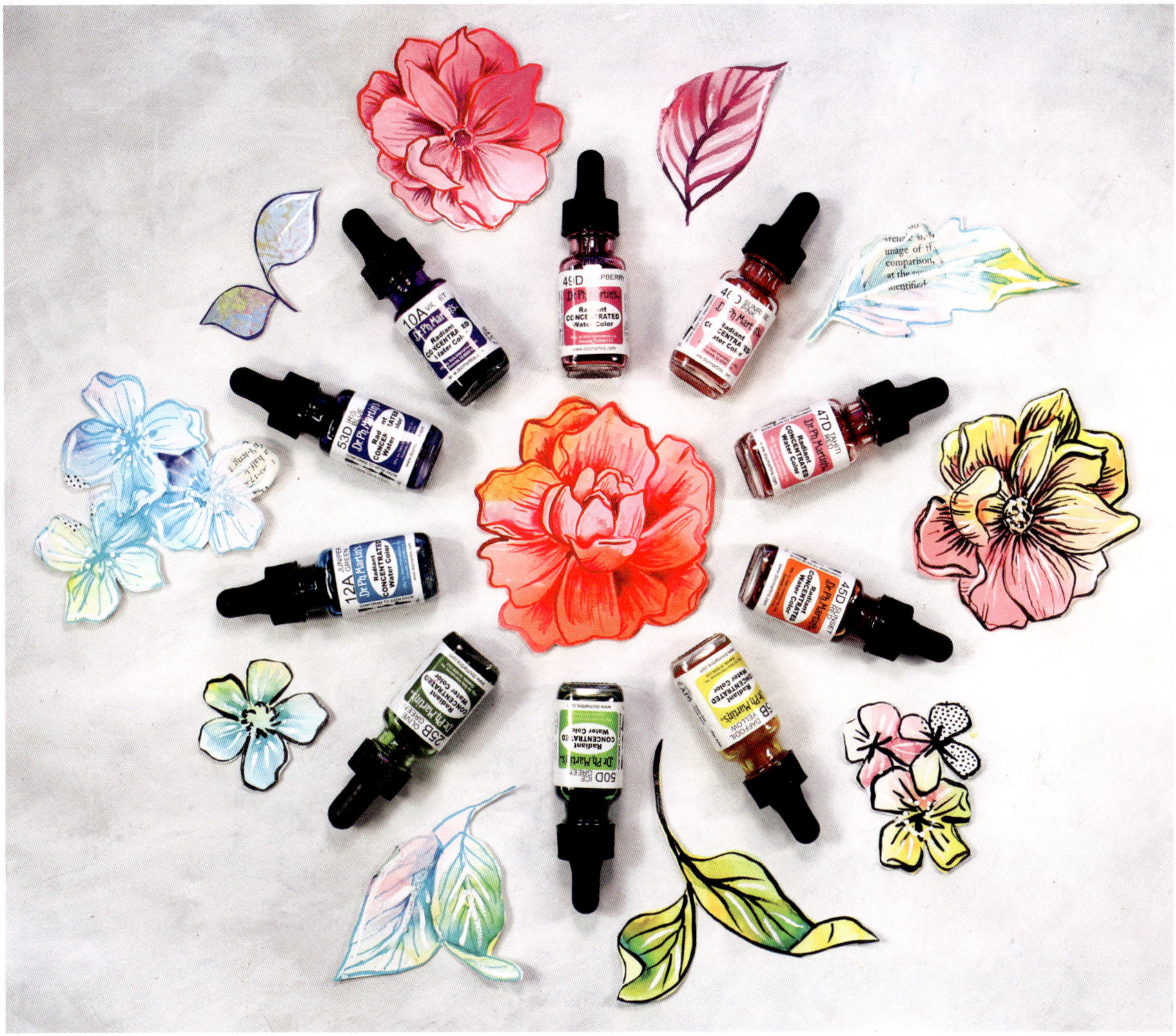

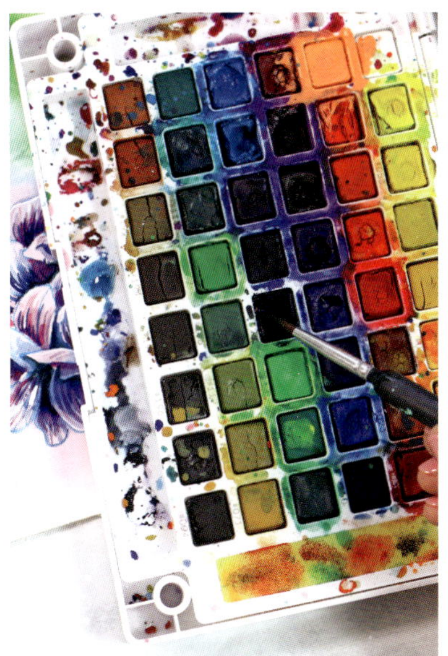

Watercolors

I tend to splurge on watercolors, but you can start with whatever you already have or can afford. The most common and affordable watercolors tend to come in multicolor pans; this is a good place for a beginner to start. Personally, I like pan sets for when I'm traveling. You can also buy individual bottles of liquid watercolor. These can be pricier than pan sets, but you can purchase them individually and slowly build up a nice collection of hues. I use these most of the time.

Although not technically watercolor, I also love to use Dr. Ph. Martin's bleed-proof white paint when working with watercolors and water-based markers. This is a super-opaque white paint that is, as the bottle claims, bleed-proof. You can achieve a very bright, opaque white on top of the most vibrant of colors without it simply sinking and blending into your watercolor layer below. This comes in a tiny 1 oz. bottle, and I only use it for small details and thin linework.

Water-Based Markers, Gel Pens, and Pens

Water-based markers are so fun to work with, as you can add water to them to create a watercolor effect. If you are trying to stick to a tighter budget, I recommend reading reviews and experimenting to find a favorite brand that blends well. Dual-brush pens, which have a thicker tip on one end and a finer tip on the other, are a great versatile option for both art journaling and lettering.

Gel pens will also pop up in several projects in this book. These are great for laying fine, opaque color detail on top of existing layers of (dried) paint or marker. Read reviews to find a super-opaque white gel pen for layering on top of black (or check my recommendation on page 173).

It's great to have some all-purpose permanent (that is, alcohol-based) markers on hand as well—you probably already have some of these in your house!

Lastly, for linework and hand lettering, I recommend a calligraphy brush pen—they are especially wonderful for creating line variation. You can also use any of the other pens or markers you have instead, though.

Acrylic Paints

When working in my art journal, I lean toward using affordable craft paints. I do splurge more on a few colors, however—mostly black and white, as these are what I tend to do my linework with.

The more colors you can buy individually, the less you need to worry about mixing your own shades. That said, you can really learn a lot about color by trying to mix your own shades, so don't shy away from it even if you have the budget to buy lots of colors.

Adhesives

We will work with collage elements in some of the projects in this book, so a good adhesive will be necessary. I typically use a matte medium, but glue sticks and decoupage medium (like Mod Podge) will work as well. I use a matte medium not only to coat on the back of papers that I want to stick down, but also as a clear coat on top of pages and papers.

Miscellaneous

We will use stencils, collage papers, bubble wrap, and washi tape in our work. Collage papers can be anything from old book pages and notebook paper to patterned scrapbook papers and graph paper. I love collecting scraps to use in my art journaling and recommend that you collect interesting papers to keep on hand. Stick them in a folder in a filing cabinet and they won't even take up much space!

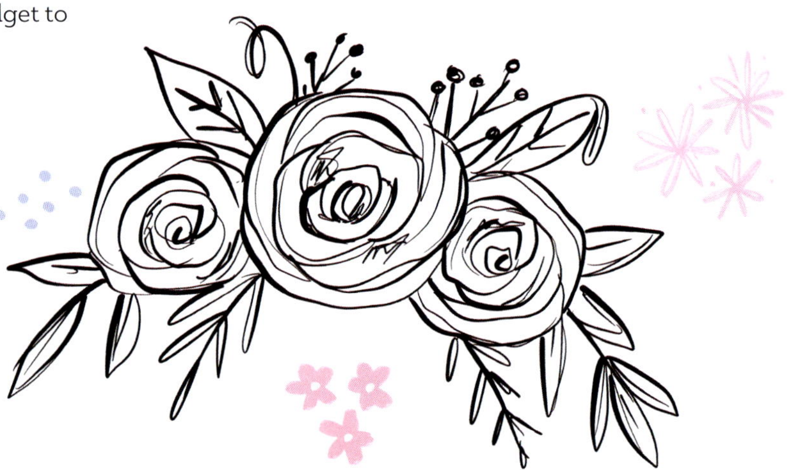

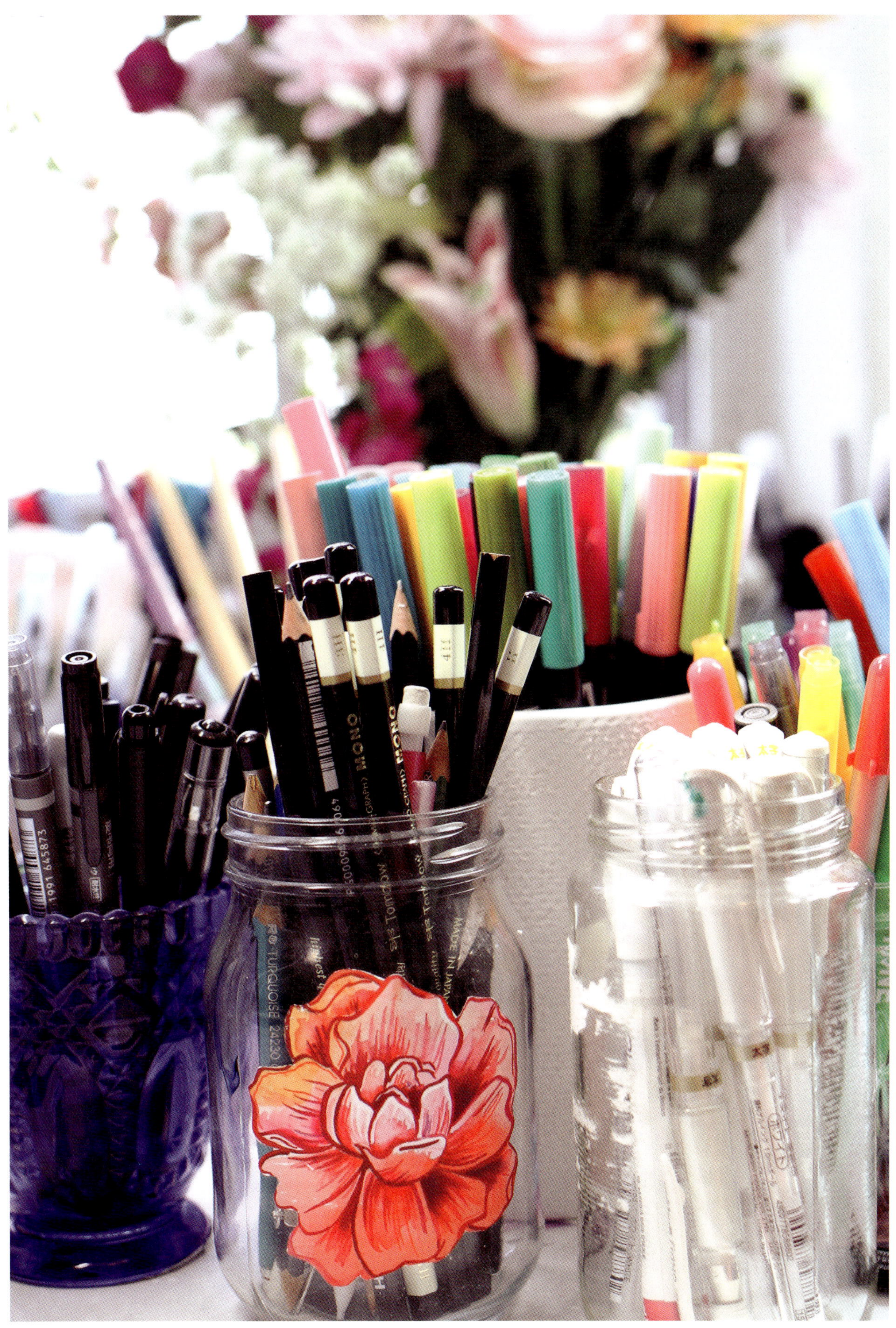

Color Theory

Let's talk color! If you couldn't tell, I'm a bright, happy color maximalist. The more colors, the merrier. And while I'll continue to push you to be fancy and free with color while you create, it's also helpful to know some "rules." That way you know when you are breaking them and can do so intentionally.

Shown here is a basic color wheel. It's broken down into primary, secondary, and tertiary colors. This is elementary stuff, but you may have forgotten a lot since third grade, or you may have just had a terrible art teacher! Either way, it's good to get a refresher.

Primary colors are pure hues that cannot be created by mixing other colors. These are red, blue, and yellow.

Secondary colors are created by mixing two primary colors. These are orange (red + yellow), green (yellow + blue), and purple (blue + red).

Tertiary colors are created by mixing a primary color with a secondary color. These are red-orange, red-violet, yellow-orange, yellow-green, blue-green, and blue-violet.

In between all these colors, of course, are infinitely more—and don't forget white and black, which, while they don't appear on the color wheel, are decidedly part of your color repertoire.

Choosing colors may be a struggle for you, so knowing some basic color theory can guide you. There are also some terms I'll use in the book that you'll want to be familiar with. Let's go over those now.

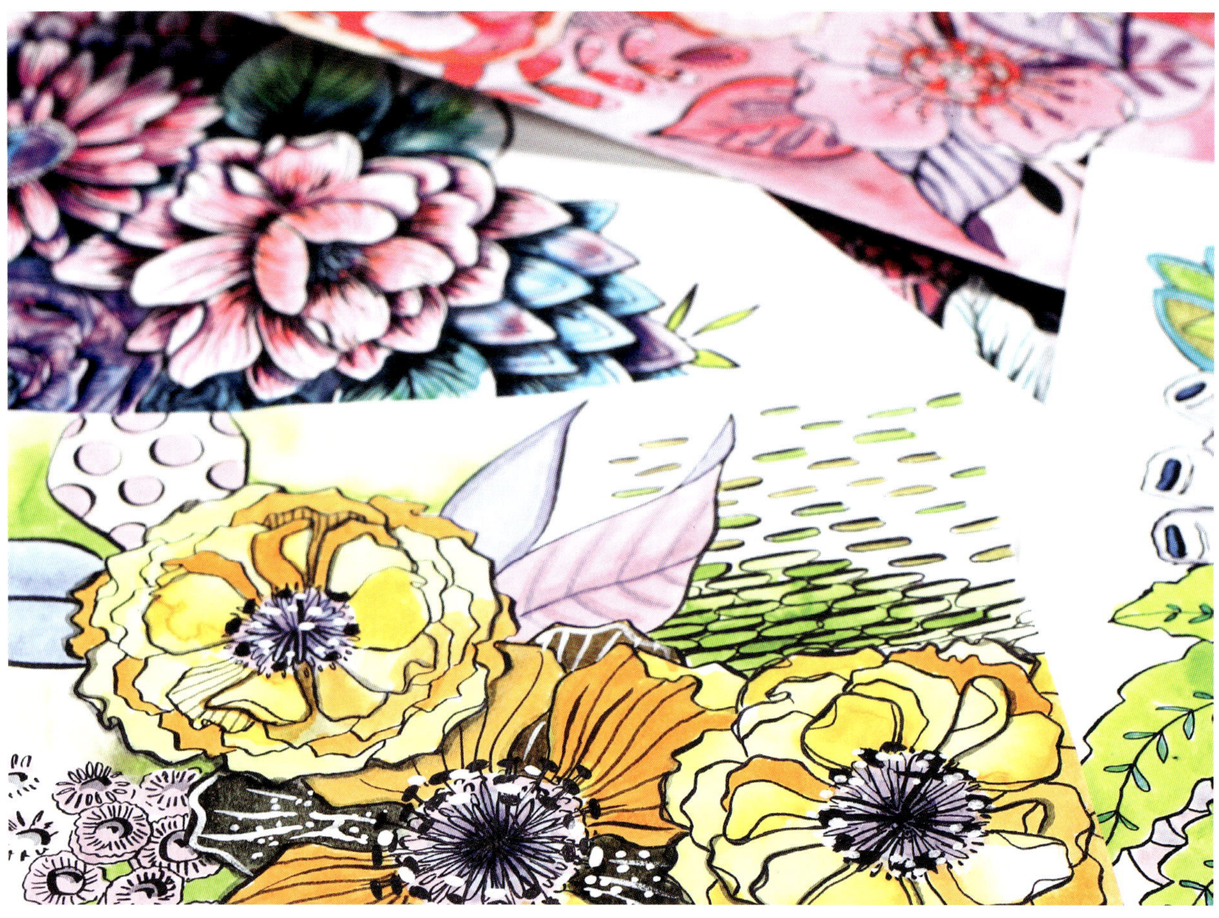

The Color Wheel

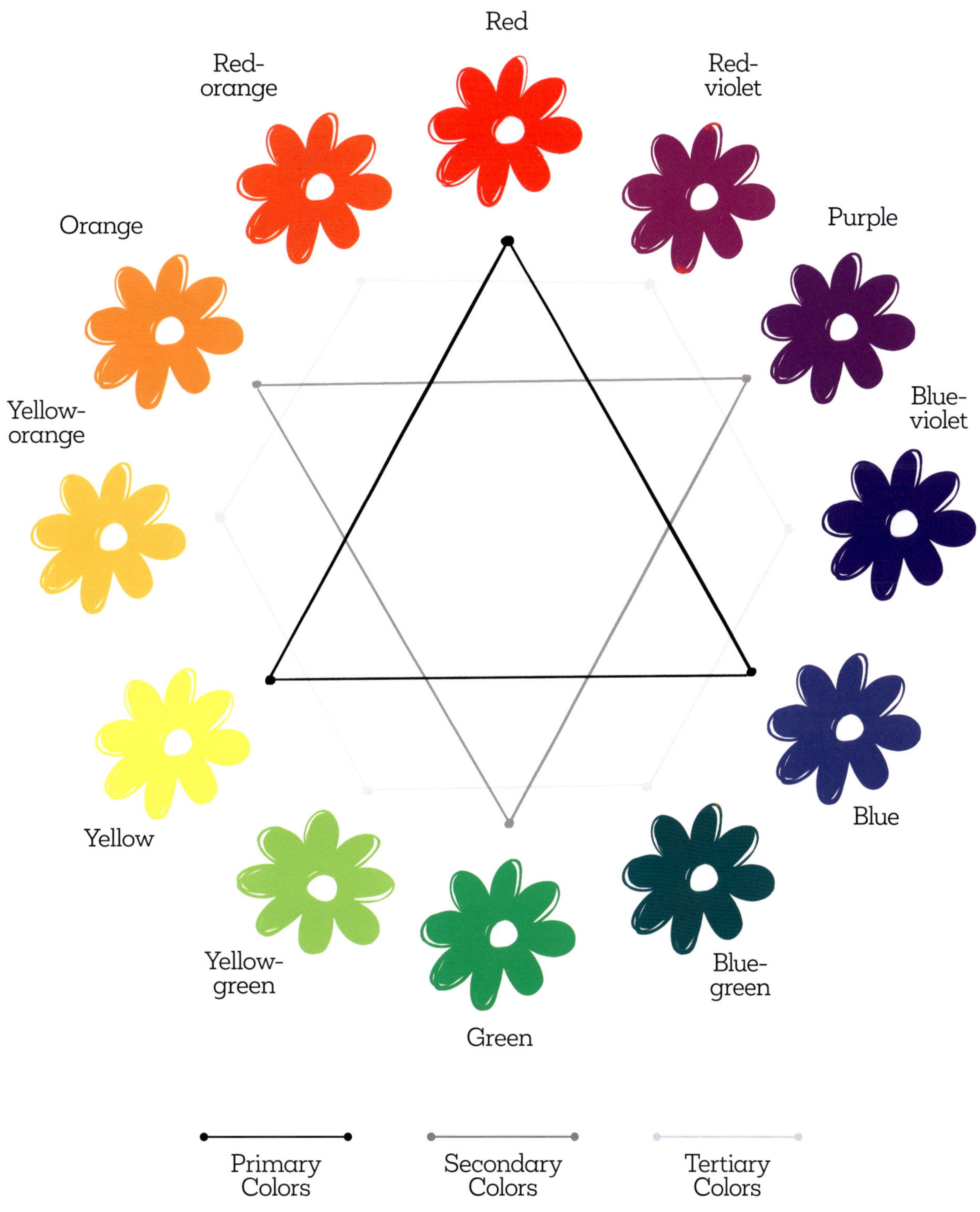

First, let's talk **value**. This is how light or dark a color is. Using blue as an example, a blue that is dark in value could be a navy blue, and a blue that is light in value could be a sky blue. The simplest way to change the value of a color is to add black or white: black will make the value darker, whereas white will make the value lighter. See a visual example of possible values of red below.

Next let's discuss **intensity**. This refers to how bright or dull a color is. A bright color is going to be pure and saturated—it's either straight off the color wheel or was mixed with similar colors. A dull color is going to be less intense and not as bright. We can create dull colors by mixing colors that are opposite one another on the color wheel. Let's look back at our wheel again. Green is the opposite of red on the wheel, so, if we want a dull green, we can add a little red to it. The more red we add, the duller the green will become, until somewhere in the middle they will meet, essentially cancel each other out, and turn into a neutral brown color. See a visual example below of possible intensities of red (left) and green (right), with the neutral brown in the middle.

From here, you can change the value of any given intensity! That is, for example, you can add white to a dull green or add black to a bright red, or any combination of colors and white/black that you want. Check out the variety you can achieve in the visual below.

Value Scale

Intensity Scale

Values + Intensities

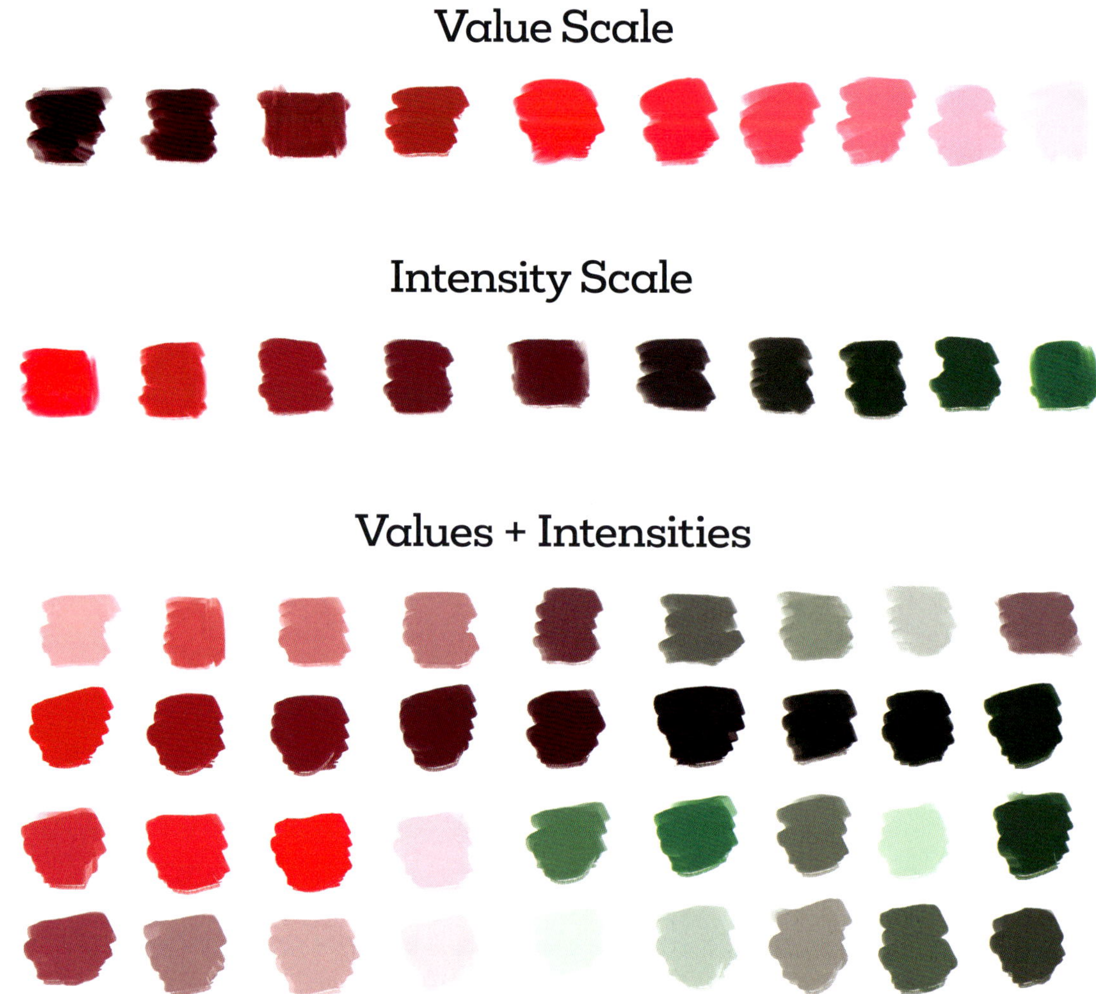

Color Schemes

Now we can talk color schemes! We'll explore some of these in the projects ahead, so let's look briefly at five basic color schemes. For any of you indecisive color choosers out there, you can always refer back to these basic color schemes to help you decide what combinations to use. Or you can be the way I am 99% of the time and just wing it!

Monochromatic: This color scheme consists of just one color, including different values and intensities of that color. If I'm doing a monochromatic piece in red, for example, I can create interest by using a full range of red values and intensities.

Analogous: This combination consists of colors that are next to one another on the color wheel. For instance, red, orange, and yellow can form an analogous scheme, or purple, blue, and green. Again, you can use any values and intensities you'd like.

Complementary: This color scheme consists of colors that are opposite one another on the color wheel. Think classic combinations like blue and orange or red and green. And—you guessed it—any values and intensities of those colors.

Split Complementary: This color scheme consists of one color and then the colors on either side of its complement. So, for instance, one split complementary scheme would include red, yellow-green, and blue-green (those last two colors being on either side of red's opposite/complement, green).

Bright Happy Rainbow: Another name for this scheme could be "whatever goes"! I hang out here a lot. Bright and happy colors always complement each other, so this is my comfort zone.

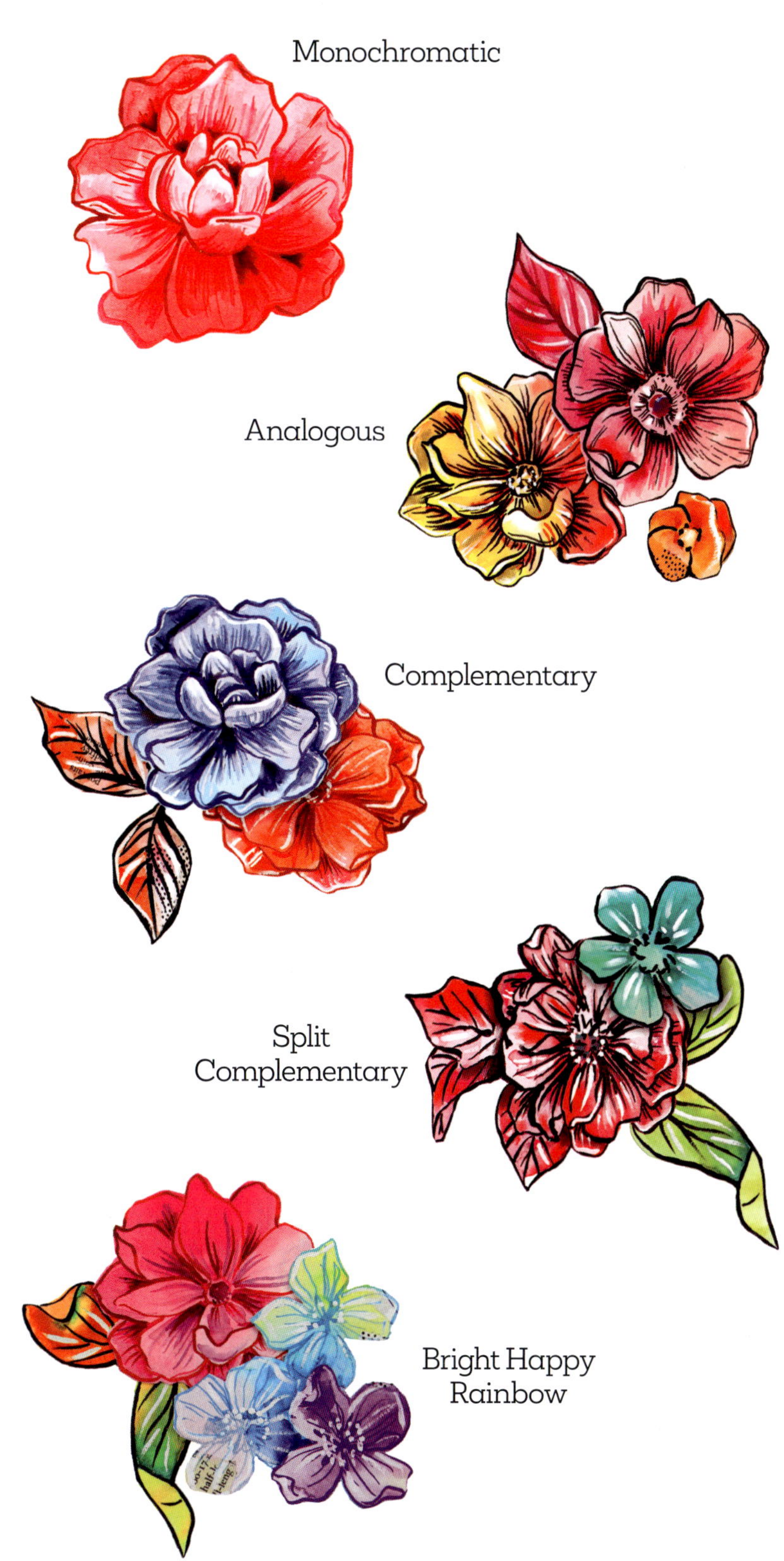

Composition

The last thing I want to address before we dive in to actually making stuff is composition. Merriam-Webster defines the word as "the act or process of composing, specifically: arrangement into specific proportion or relation and especially into artistic form." What that means is: where to put the stuff.

I want to approach composition in the same way as color theory: let's get to know a few rules or, better yet, suggestions and tuck them away in our subconscious while we create. As a high school art instructor, the very first thing we did in Art 101 was talk about the principles of design. Because I drilled these into my students' heads, they became drilled into mine, and I rarely create a piece without thinking about the following six principles.

Contrast: Contrast in art is simply using two things that are different to draw attention to an area in the piece. We can contrast values (lights and darks), colors (such as complementary colors), sizes, etc.

Emphasis: Having a focal point in a piece adds hierarchy and structure. Your focal point could be the brightest, most detailed, or largest area or stand out for some other reason. Your eye will be drawn to an area that shines in some special way.

Movement: We don't want to get so stuck on our focal point that we don't look around and take in the rest of the piece. Once our eye checks out the focal point, we want other elements to move us around the piece, eventually leading us back to the focal point. We can create movement in a variety of ways, but the next principle, repetition, is a go-to for creating movement.

Repetition: This refers to repeating a color, a shape, or any other element in the piece (but not necessarily identically). Repetition helps move the eye around. If my eye first sees orange in the focal point, it is naturally going to look for something

similar. If I have orange as the contrasting element that draws me to the focal point, but no touches of orange anywhere else, my eye might get stuck.

Variety: Repetition and variety do not compete but instead can help each other out. We can vary shapes, colors, sizes, etc. while repeating characteristics in our focal point as well.

Balance: Balance does not need to be symmetrical and exact, but we should strive to avoid all the emphasis being in just one area and none in another. That imbalance can create an awkwardness when the composition is viewed as a whole.

Let's apply these principles to the piece of art shown at right. See if your eye moves in the same way as mine. While there is a lot going on in the piece, because of the thoughtfulness in my composition, there is order within the chaos.

My **focal point** is A, the large black-and-white flower in the top right. I've established this focal point through **contrast** in value, color, and size. Once my eye takes in this flower, there is **movement** to flowers B and C. These are the supporting elements that have caused my eye to move because of **repetition**: I have repeated the same black-and-white treatment as A in some areas of C and repeated a similar size and shape as my focal point in B. These flowers also have high **contrast** in value. Once my eye takes in B and C, I'm drawn back to my **focal point**, A. It's at this point that I take in the rest of the piece. There is a lot to look at, and I've used **variety** in floral shapes and colors. It is **balanced** because there is not too much emphasis in one area heavily outweighing another. I have other areas that show **repetition**, such as the areas of pink, the white dots on top of black, the washier blue florals, and additional areas with the black-and-white treatment.

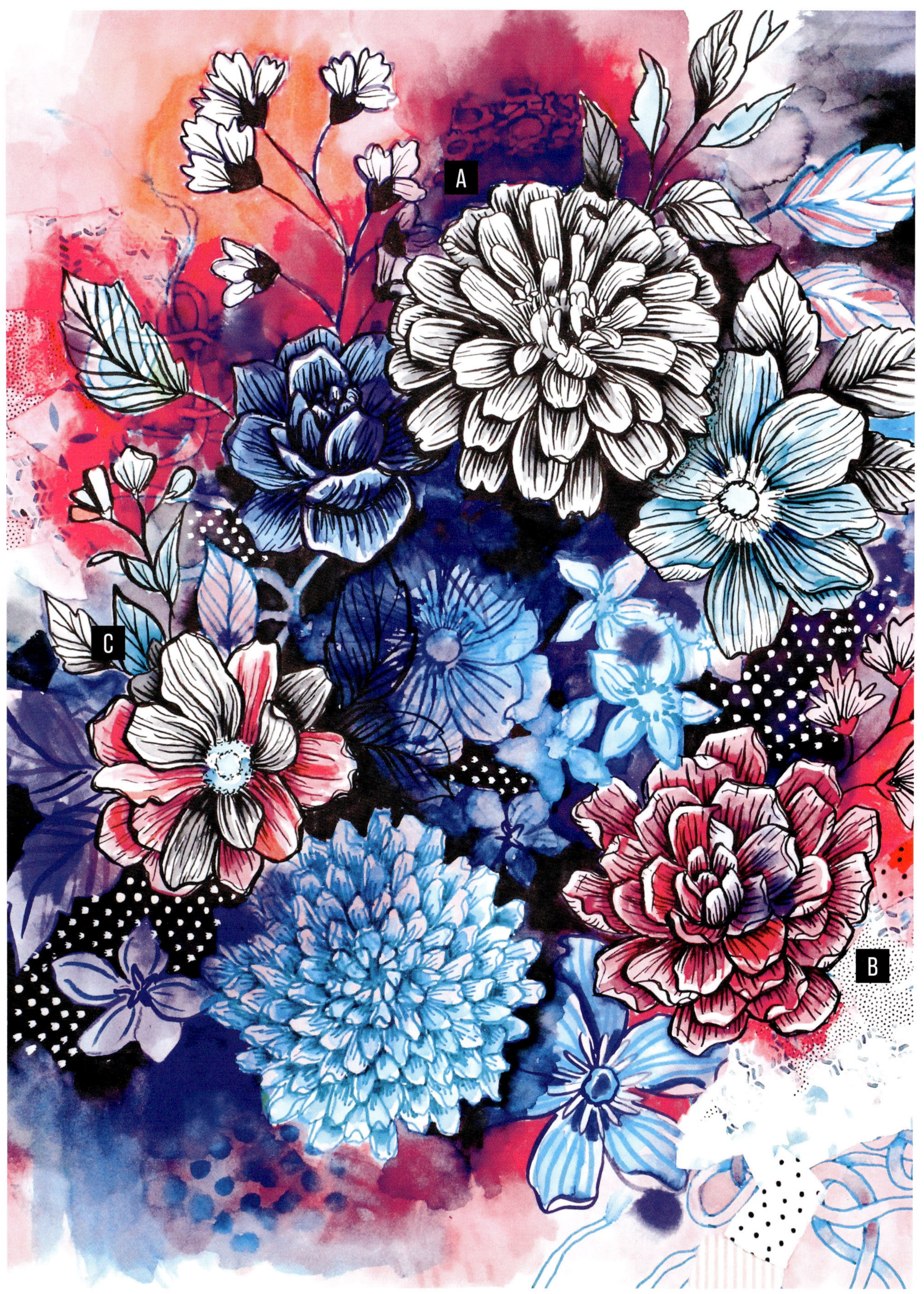
A
B
C

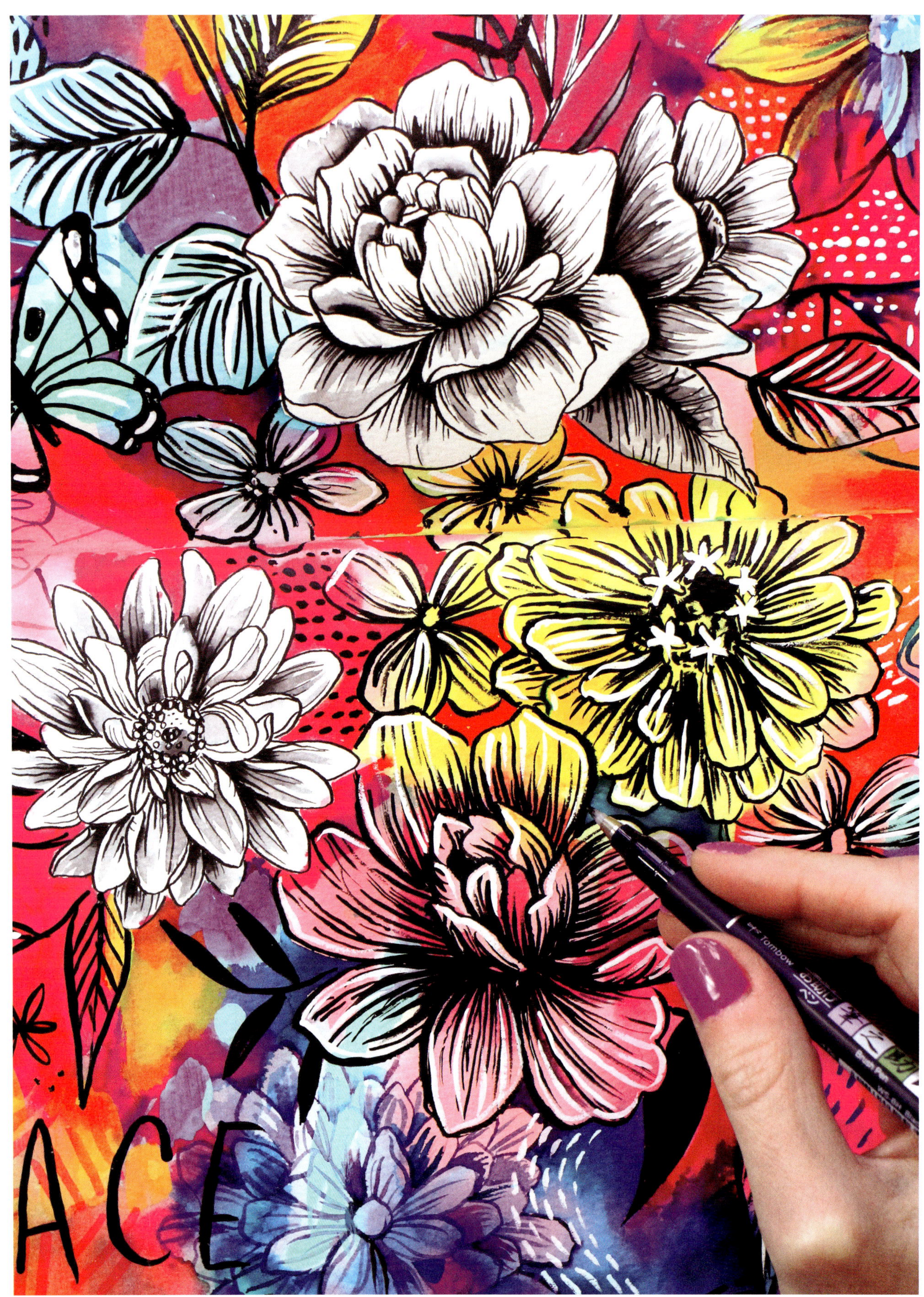

Drawing Flowers

I often use my imagination to draw my florals. With so many different shapes of pistils, petals, and leaves, it is fun and freeing to create flowers without references. The easiest and clearest step-by-step approach when it comes to making up your own flowers is this:

- Draw the flower center (pistils/stamen)
- Draw the petals
- Add leaves (optional)
- Add details

A great exercise that will lead you to many creative ways to draw imaginary flowers is to challenge yourself to draw 10–20 different variations of the elements (flower centers, petals with and without details, leaves, etc.). Then you can mix and match the centers, petals, and leaves to create a vast pool of florals to pick from.

Florals typically look better if they include many layers of petals and line details to enhance them. Check out the exercise at right. In it, you can see that each of the three concepts starts with just a simple center and single corona of petals; then you add a second layer of petals underneath the first, and, finally, you add detail lines.

From here, you can add more detail to the center, or add leaves, or do whatever works for your composition!

On the following four pages, you will take a tour through **a smorgasbord of floral elements** that you can practice sketching and refer to whenever you want to build an imaginary flower.

Then, on pages 40–51, you will learn how to draw **12 real flowers step by step**. This will get you on your way to being able to draw more-realistic floral shapes when you feel so inclined. These are only meant to give you a foundation and general understanding of the shapes of these flowers and how their petals lie. Once you have that understanding, you'll be more able to draw them without a reference. And, of course, I encourage you to customize them however you want and turn them into your own imaginary flowers!

Start with a center and some petals	Add a second layer of petals	Add details

CENTERS AND PISTILS

In my view, anything goes when drawing the center of a flower—
even just a simple circle! Once you start simple, you can build on different shapes
to make them more expressive, detailed, and interesting.

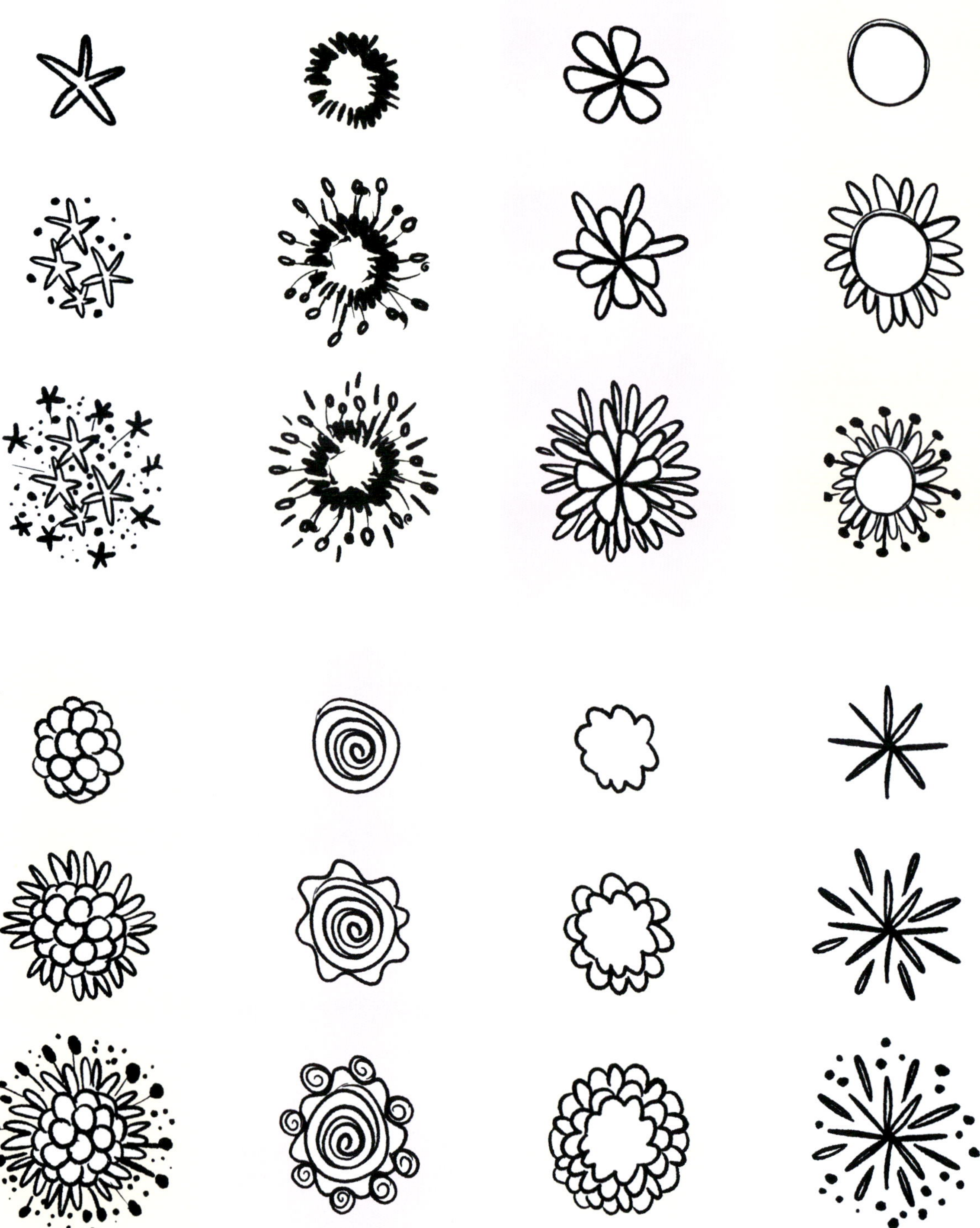

There are so many ways to draw petals. These shapes can get you started—
see how many more you can come up with on your own! Petal shapes can easily be modified
by changing the height or width, folding them over, and varying the edges.

Start simple	Add details & modify	Start simple	Add details & modify	Start simple	Add details & modify

LEAVES

Approach leaves in the same way as petals—start simple,
then modify! Here are 12 leaf ideas to get you started.

Start simple	Add details & modify	Start simple	Add details & modify	Start simple	Add details & modify

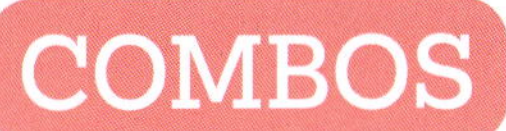

COMBOS

Now for the fun part! Mix and match the centers, petals,
and leaves that you've created. I'm not a math whiz, but it
seems like there are a ton of combinations you can come up with!
Here are just four examples.

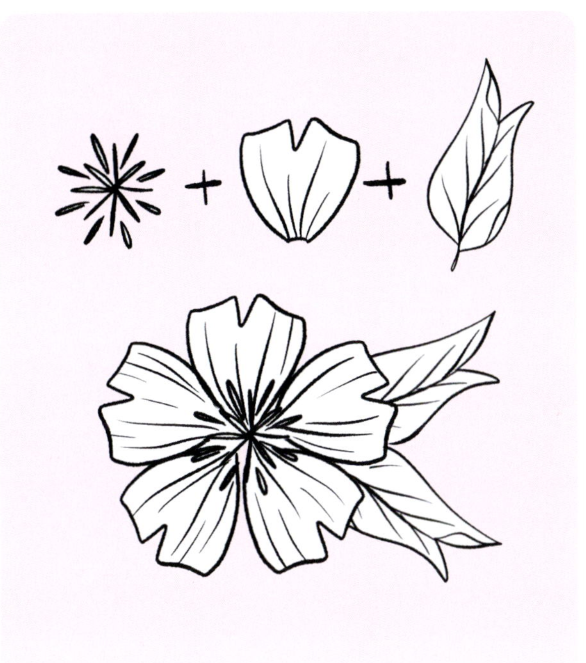

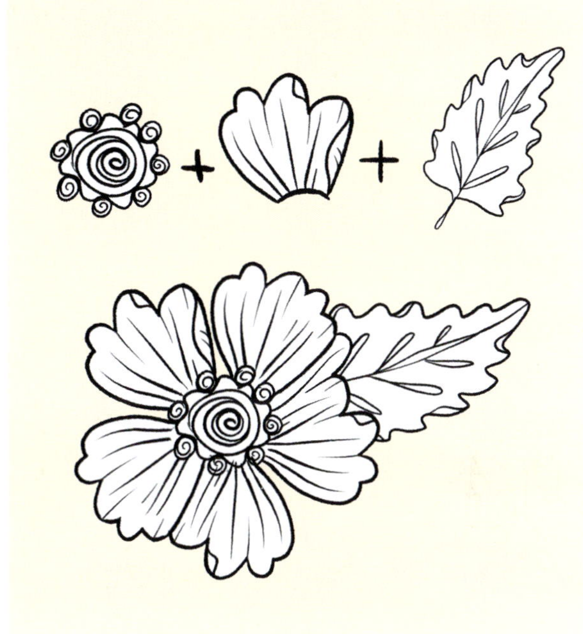

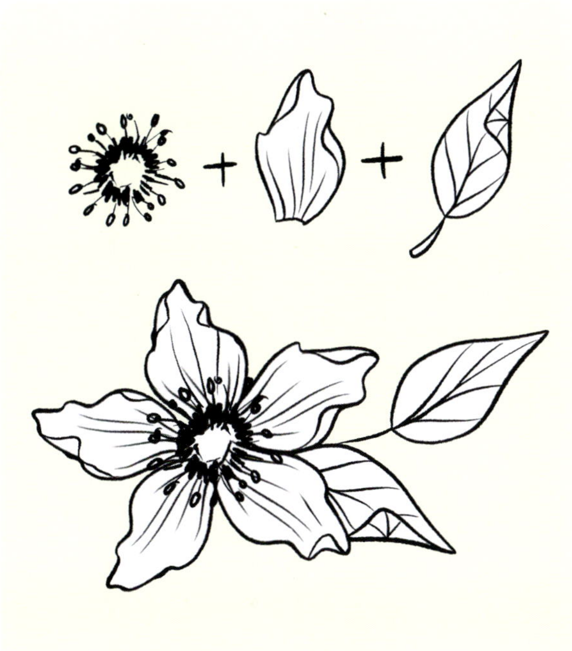

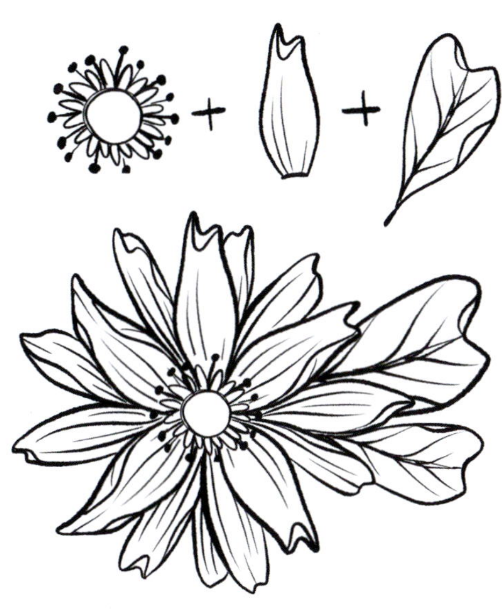

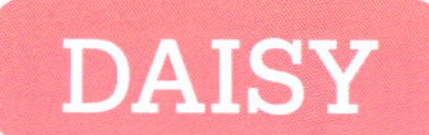

DAISY

The trick to drawing a daisy is really focusing on the layering of the petals. Beyond that, they are one of the simplest flowers you can draw. So here are two possible views to choose from!

Top view

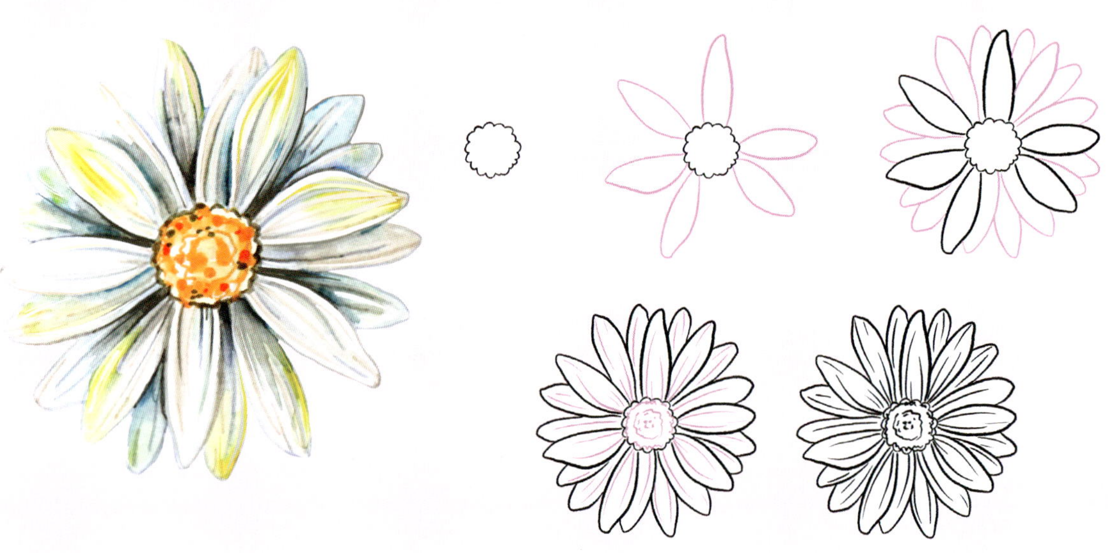

Side view

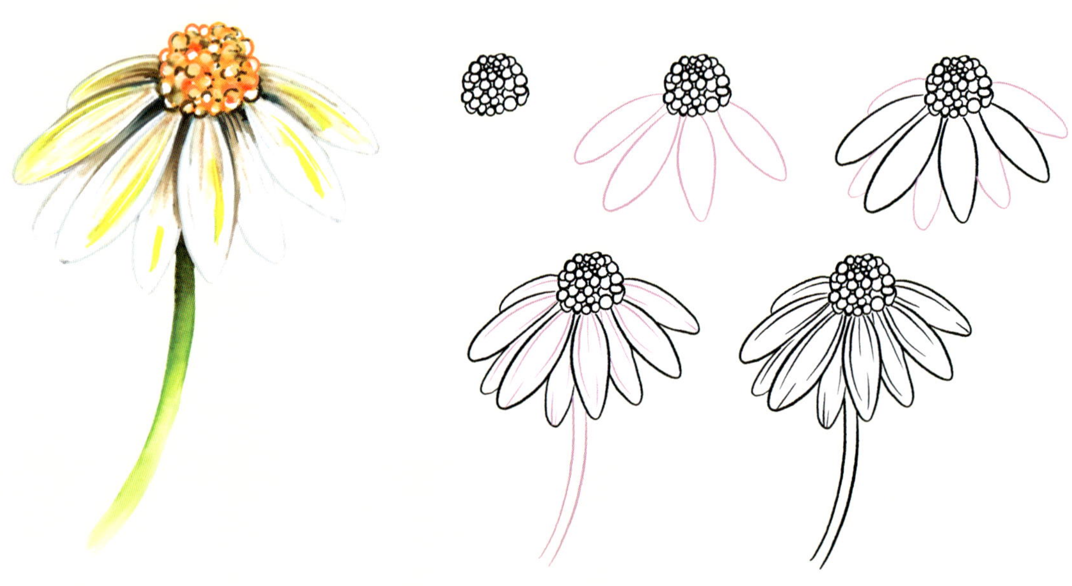

HELENIUM

Heleniums are quite similar to daisies, but the petals have a bit of a dip or notches at the end, and the center has lots of tiny protuberances all over it. Here are two views to work with.

Side view

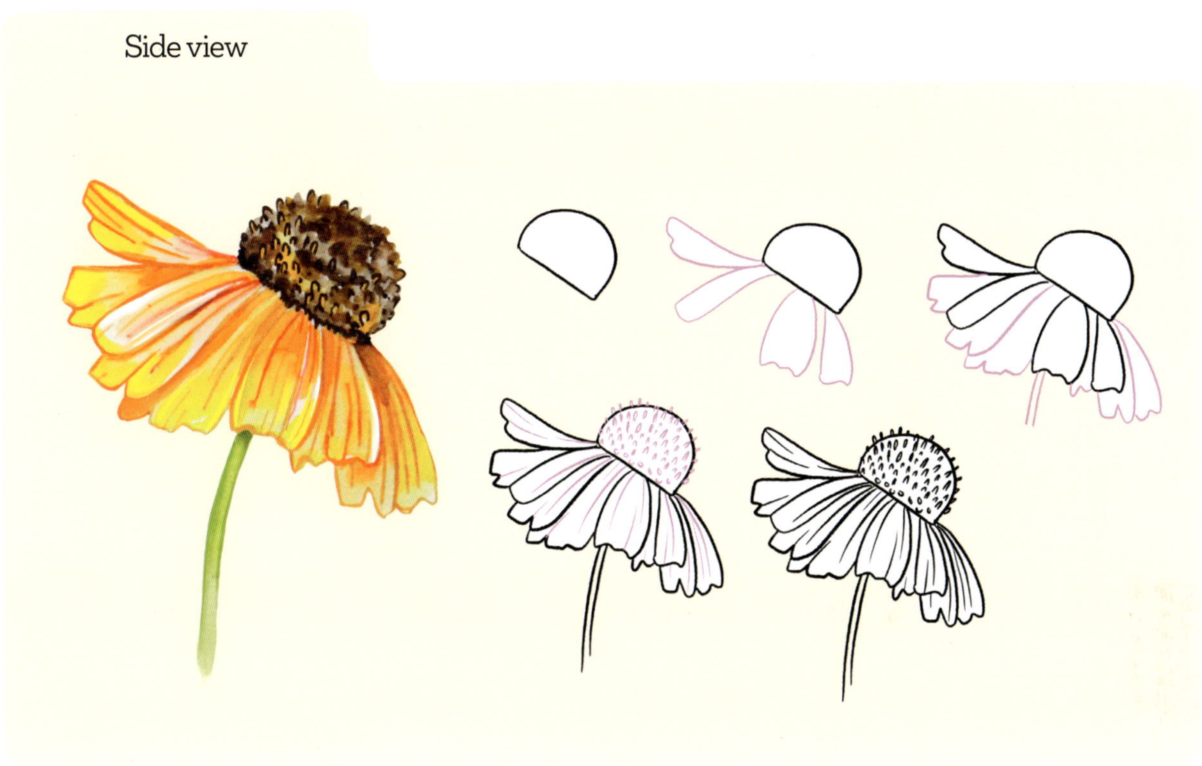

Three-quarter view

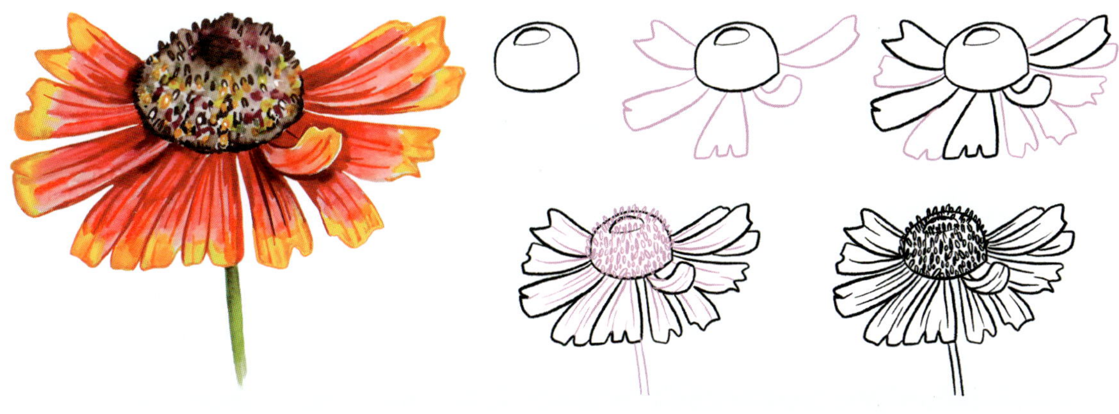

MAGNOLIA

To create dimension in your magnolia petals, first draw the basic shape of the petals, then add a short line along one or two edges to indicate where the petal curls up. (These curls don't apply to the side view, though!)

Top view

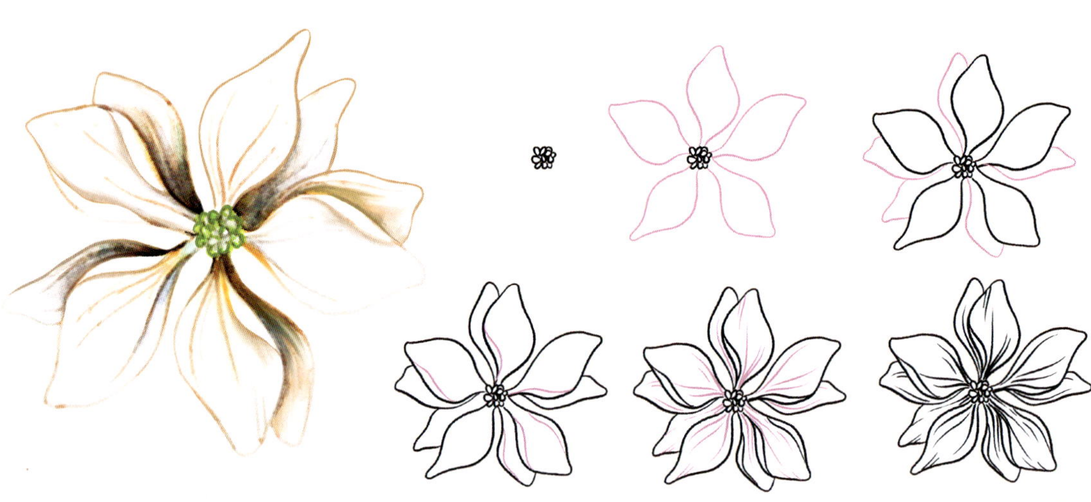

Side view

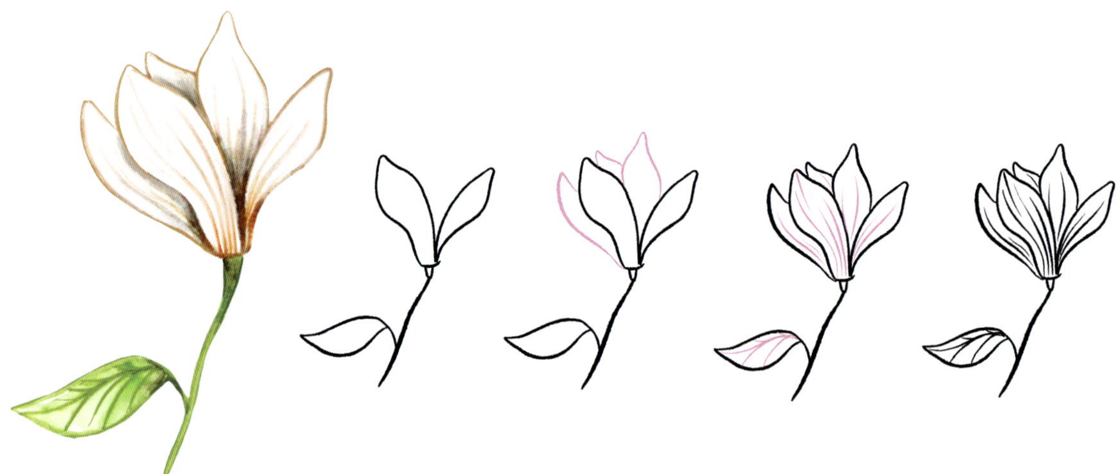

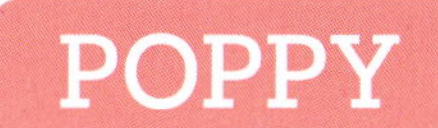

POPPY

The poppy is a pretty, dish-like shape where the curved detail lines
really create the impression that the base petals are gently curving downward.
And try mixing in some side, closed views for variety!

Open view

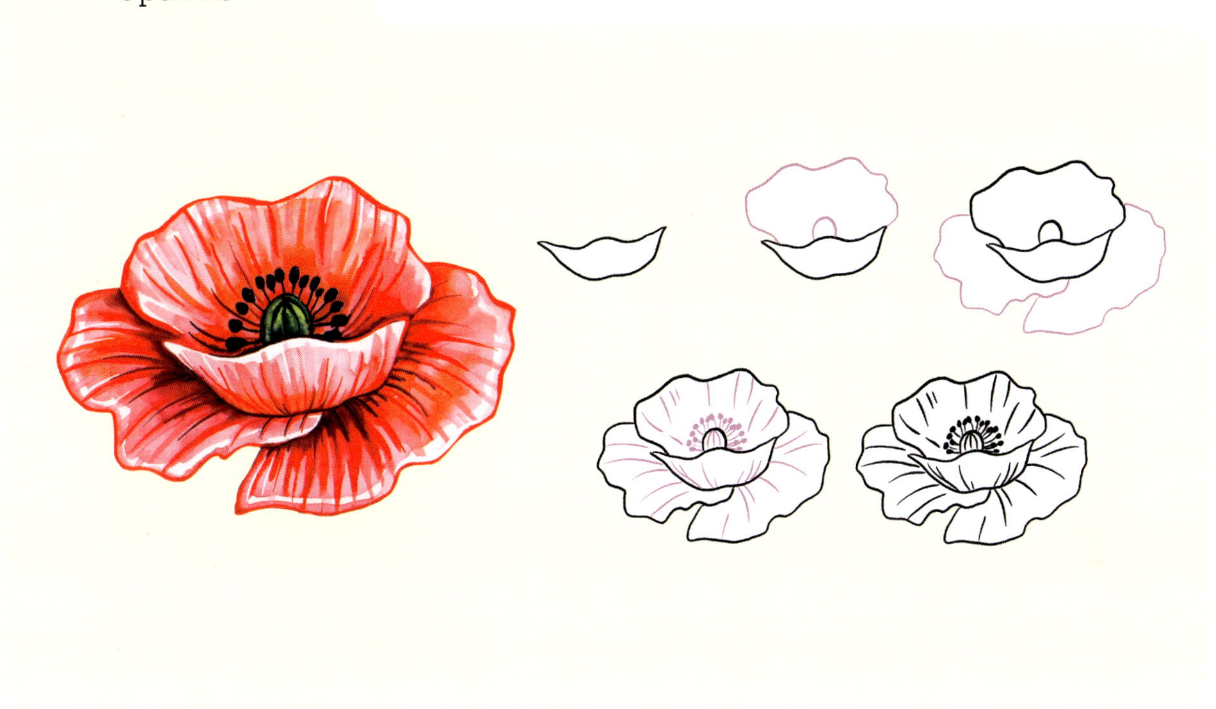

Closed view

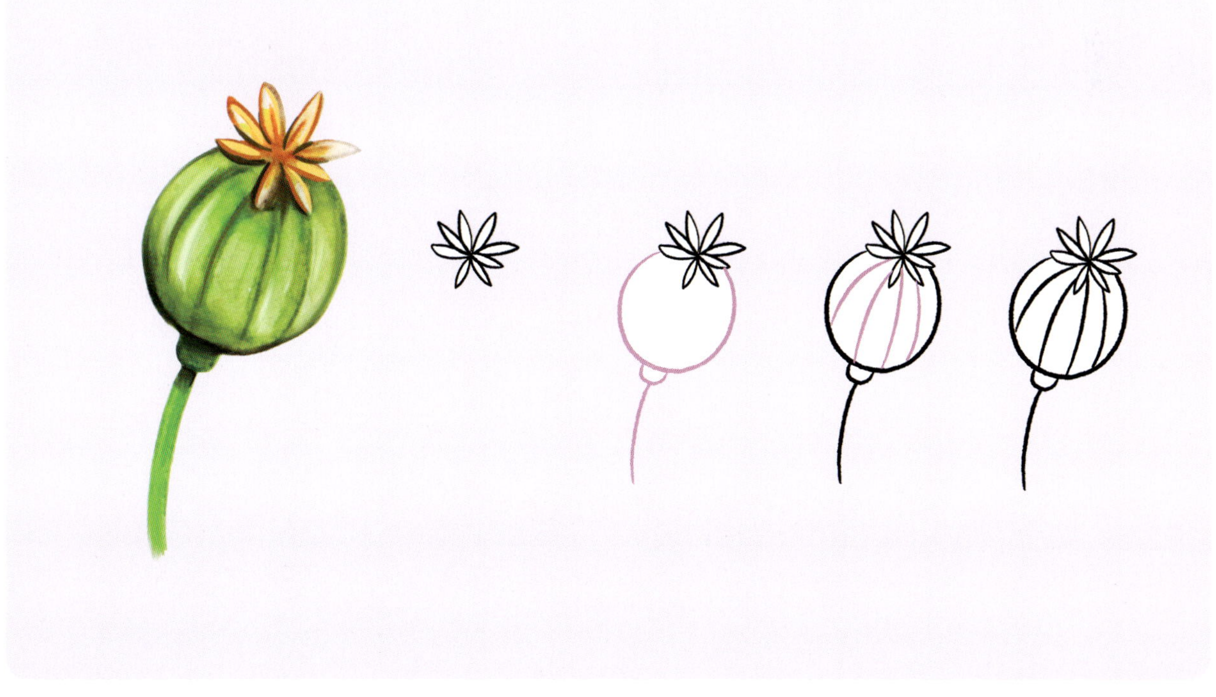

ANEMONE

Don't be afraid to make petals different shapes and sizes—you don't want your flower to look too perfect. And you don't need perfectly matched numbers of petals in each layer either—real flowers aren't necessarily "perfect"!

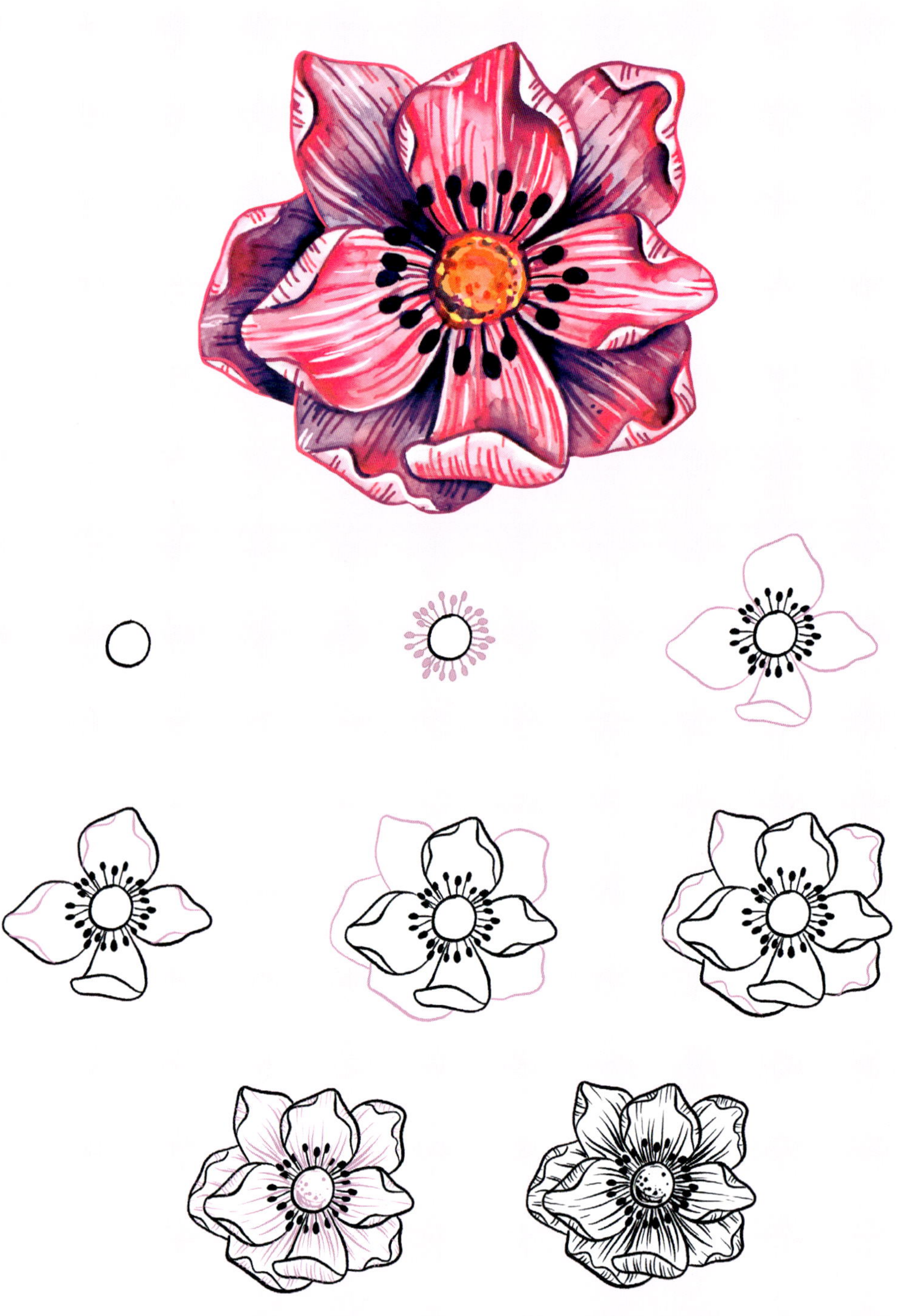

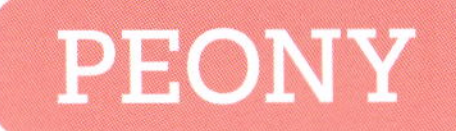

The trick to a peony is to start with a dense core and then gradually add petals that open out wider and wider. If you start too wide, your peony might end up too wide overall or lacking vitality without enough layers.

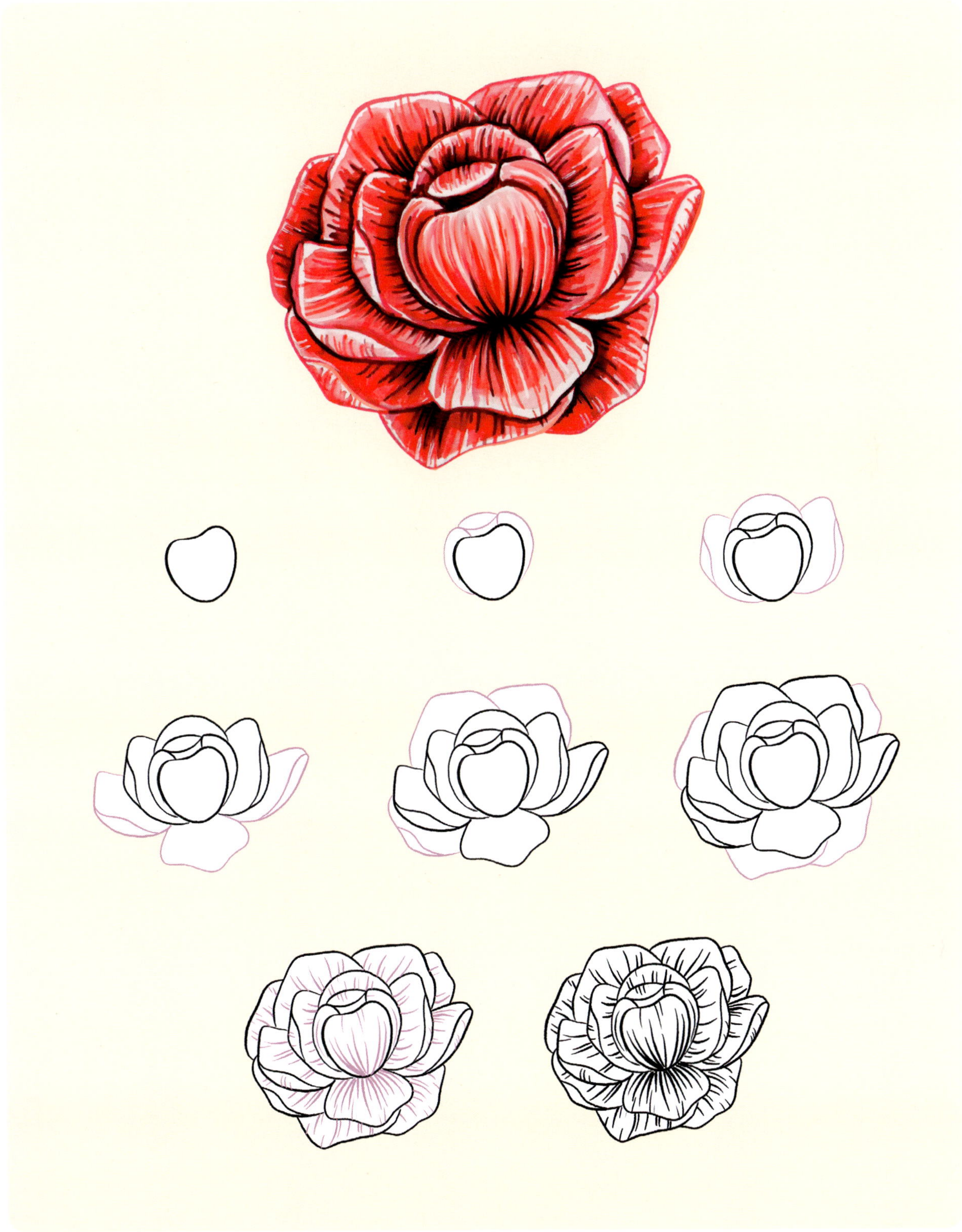

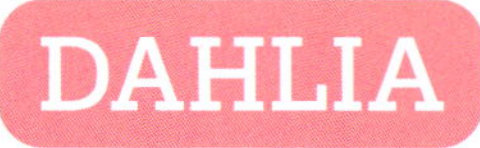

A dahlia is like a daisy to the max! Each of the many petals should start simple and short and be packed together with other petals in dense, close layers. The lines indicating the curls of the petals add serious dimension.

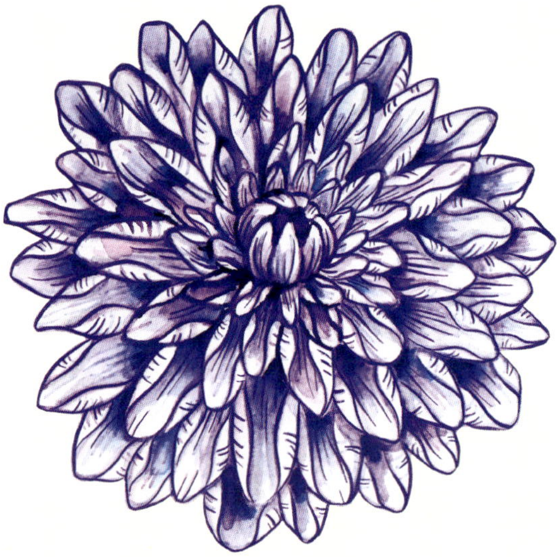

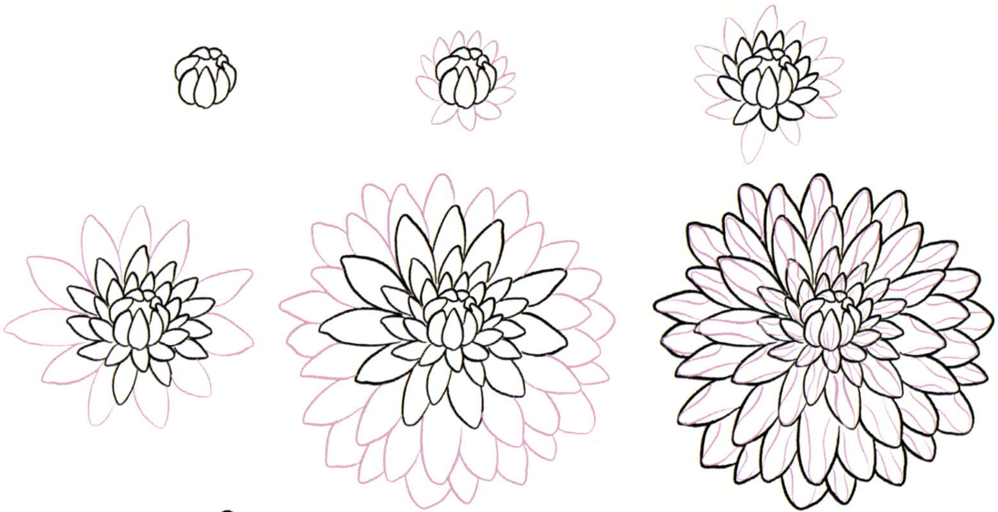

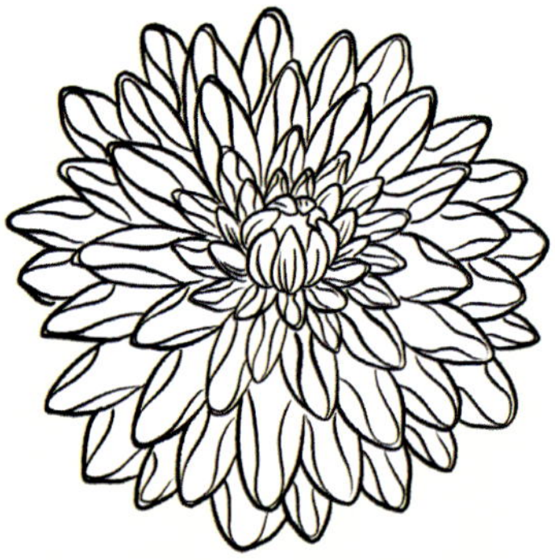

Up-close petal

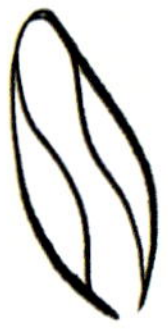

ZINNIA

A zinnia is a bit like a dahlia, but with squared-off,
short petals instead of pointed ones. Don't be afraid to pack in
the detail lines in the last stage.

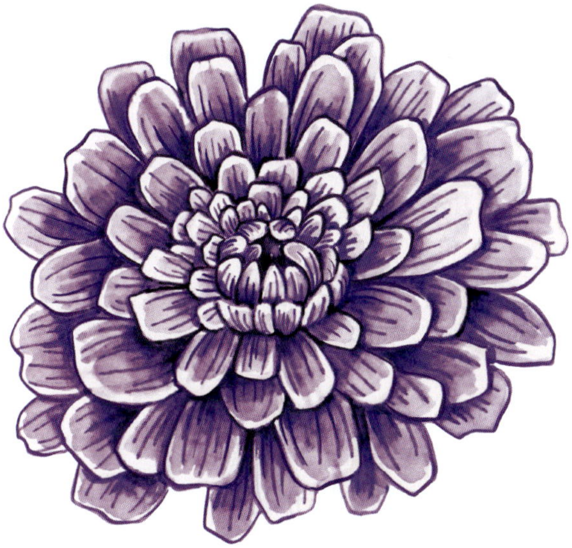

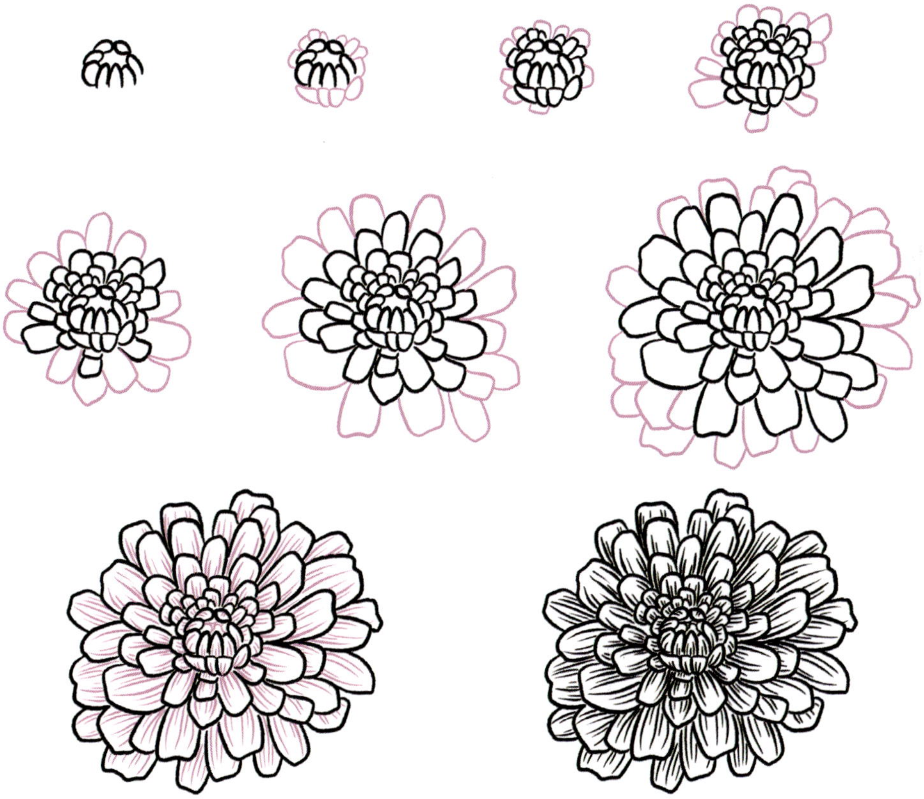

When drawing a daffodil, start with one of the petals in the foreground so that the center of the daffodil can be tucked easily behind it. Concentrate the detail lines on the petals toward the center of the flower.

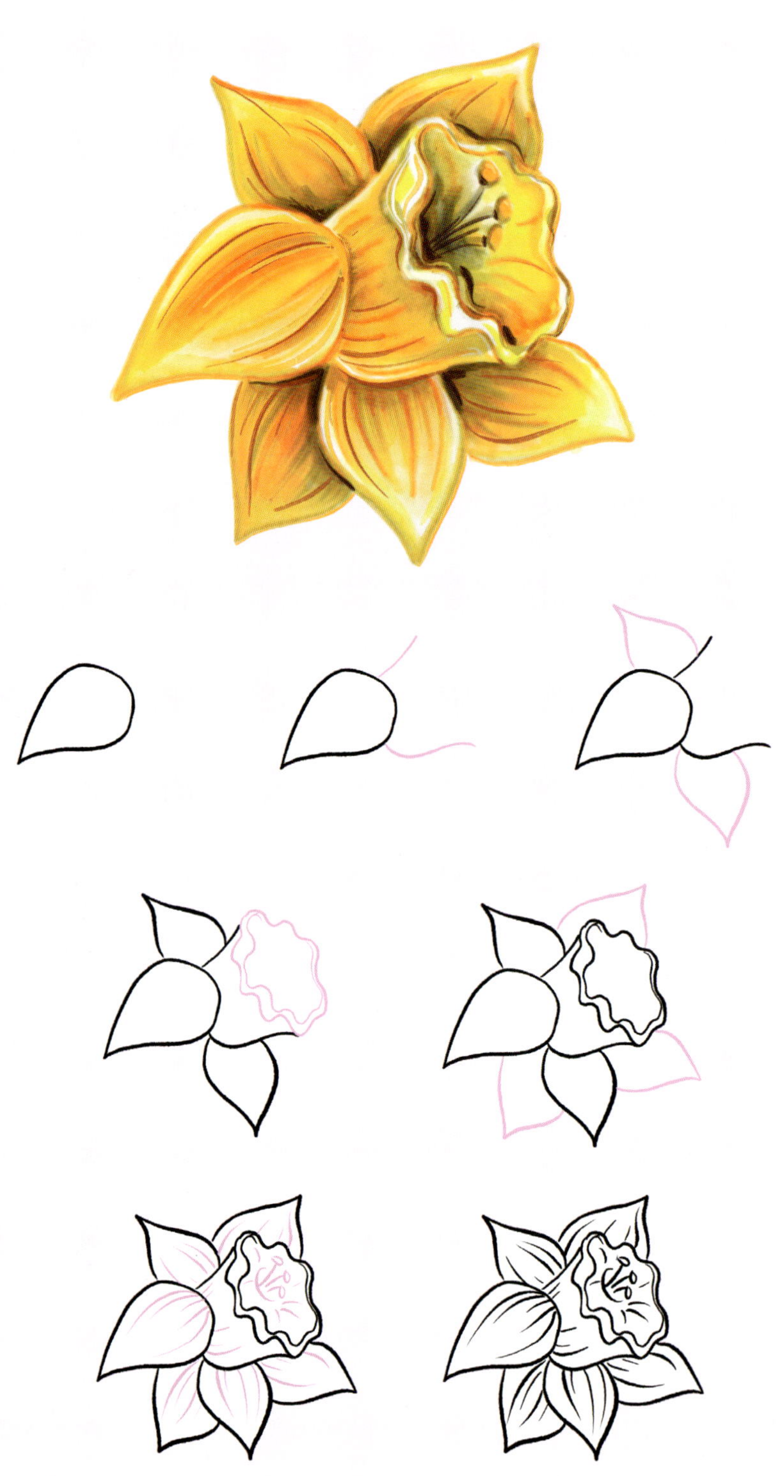

DOGWOOD

Here's another flowering tree! Dogwoods have distinctive notches in their petals that aren't difficult to draw. Including a short sprig of stem and leaves will give your dogwood an anchoring point.

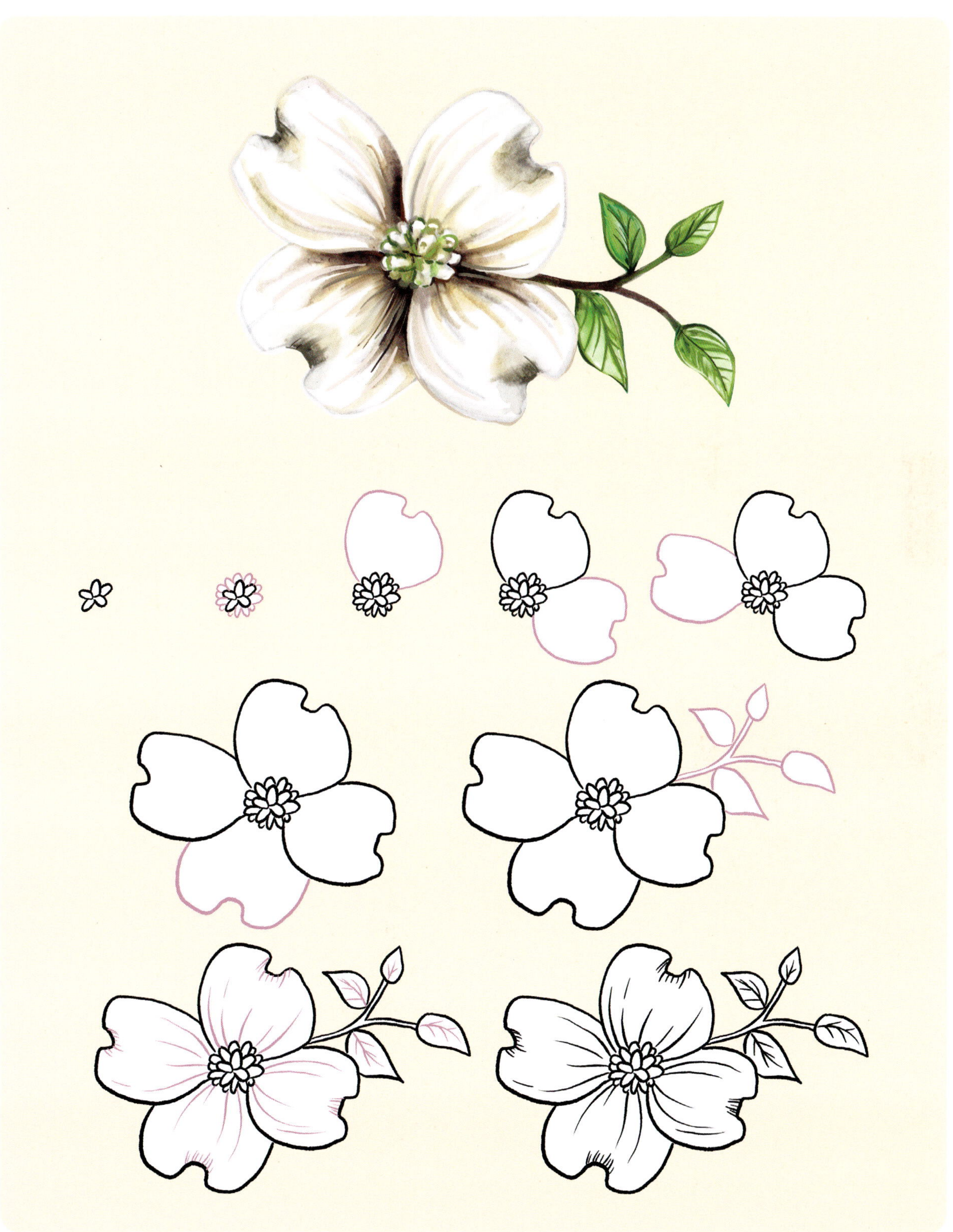

Don't be intimidated by this challenging-looking flower—the steps are here to break it down for you! The gardenia is characterized by its irregularly edged, semi-swirling petals. Be sure to give it lots of dimension through the detail lines and folded petal tips.

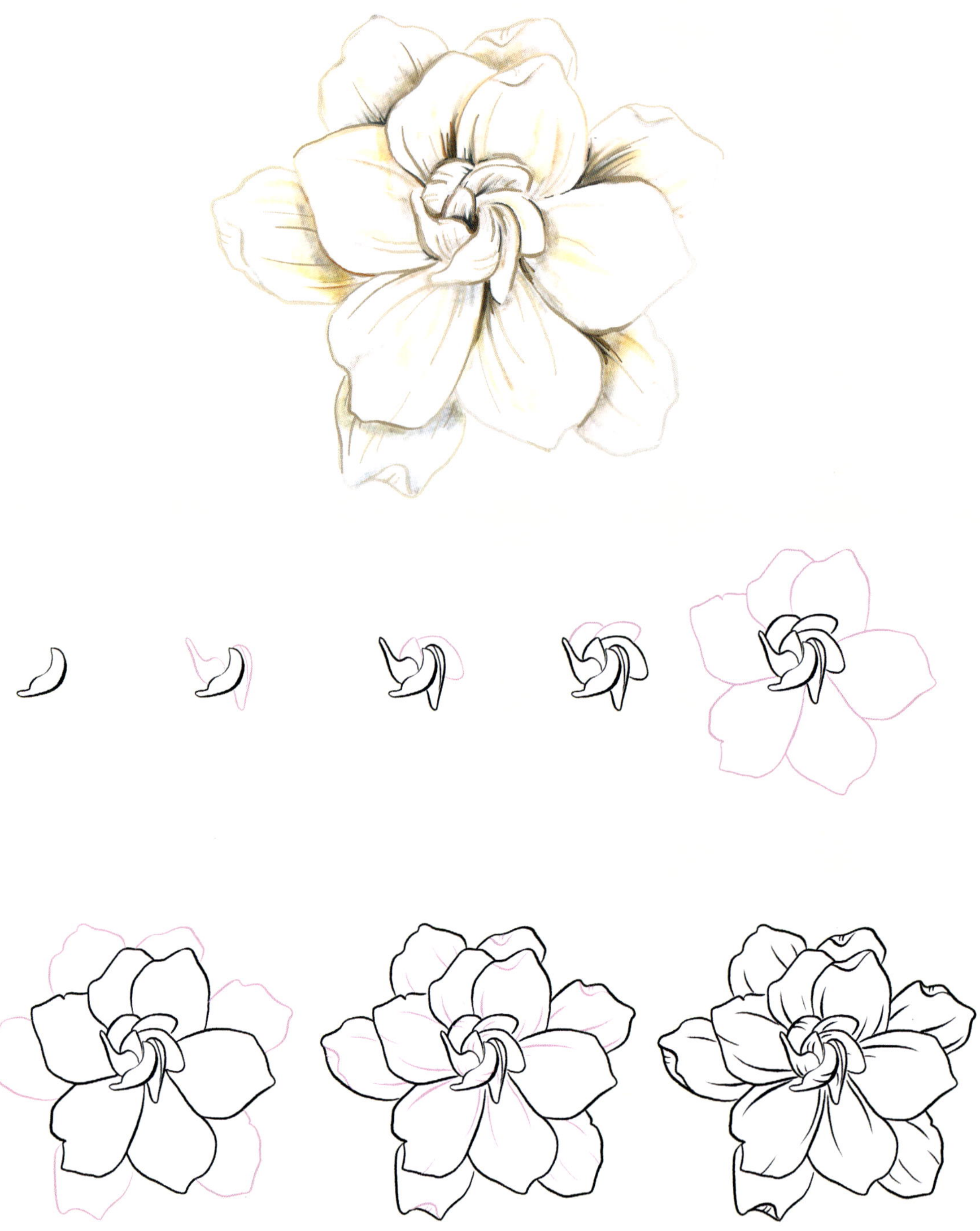

Though it's not technically a flower, I had to include this! Like the gardenia, this succulent has a semi-swirling structure, but its petals are more even and neat.

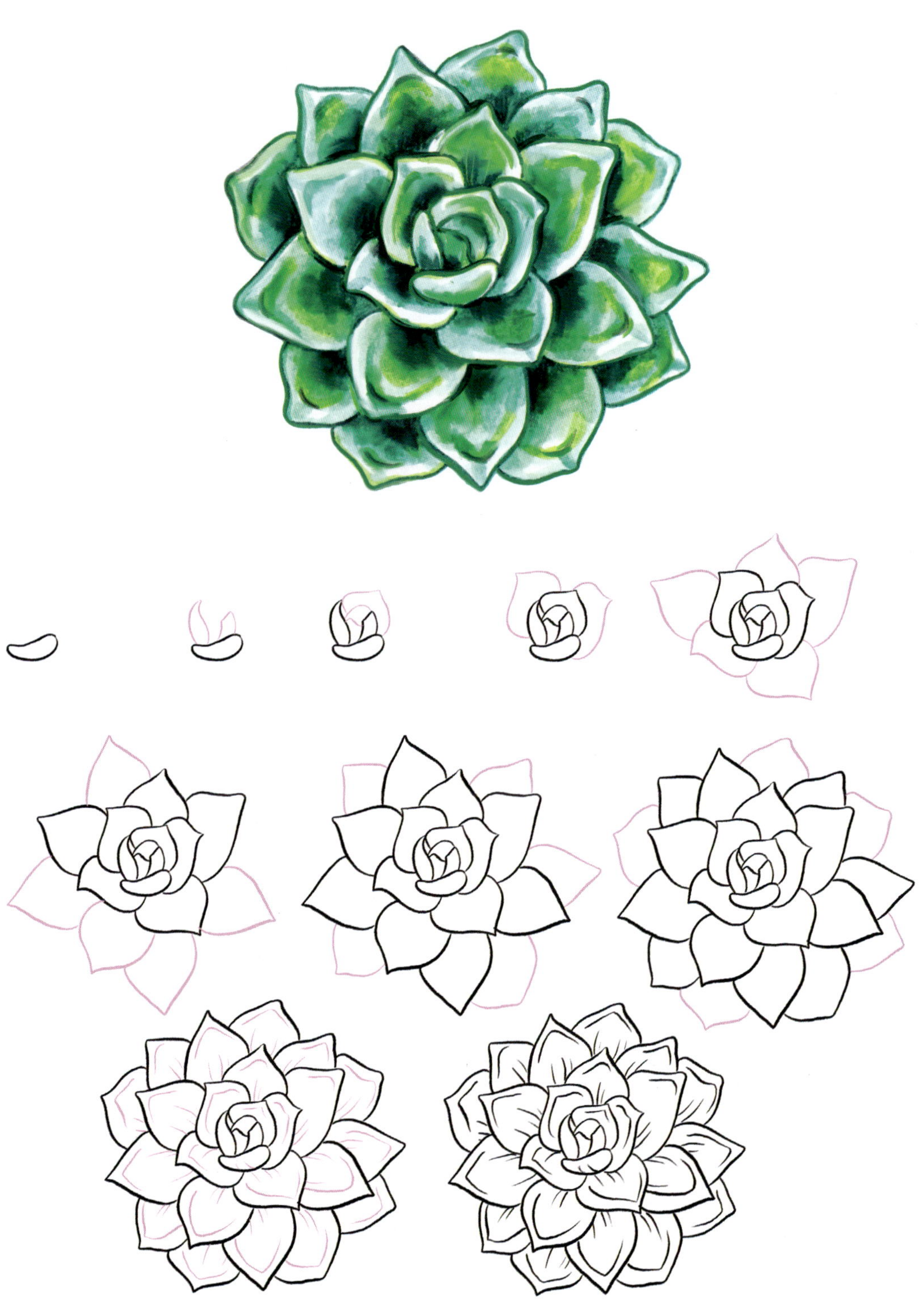

Lettering

We are going to dip our toes into incorporating lettering and writing in two projects, "Letter It Out" and "Watercolor Words," so I want to take a moment to introduce some basic techniques as well as offer tips and encouragement.

I can't even count the number of times my students have told me they can't be good at hand lettering because they don't like their handwriting. Well, guess what? Neither do I! Here's the good news: **hand lettering is not the same as handwriting, it's drawing**, and you only need a very simple mindset switcheroo to cross over from writing letters to drawing them. My first book and online courses are centered around approaching hand lettering from a drawing perspective, so I've spent a lot of time thinking about this!

As you improve with your lettering, it will become meshed together with your writing—this has happened to me over time. But if you are just starting out with lettering or are afraid to try, let's look at a few ways to letter and get over those fears, shall we?

My top three tips for crossing over from writing to lettering are:

- slow down and draw
- embrace line variation
- stick to three main styles

Let's go over each of these in more detail!

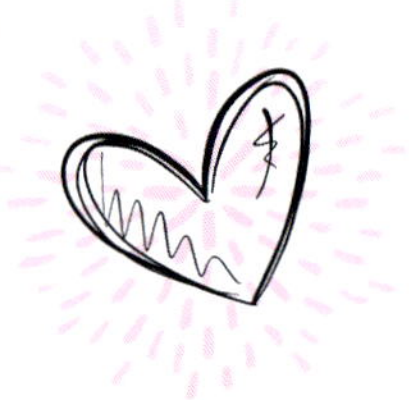

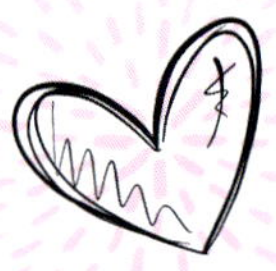

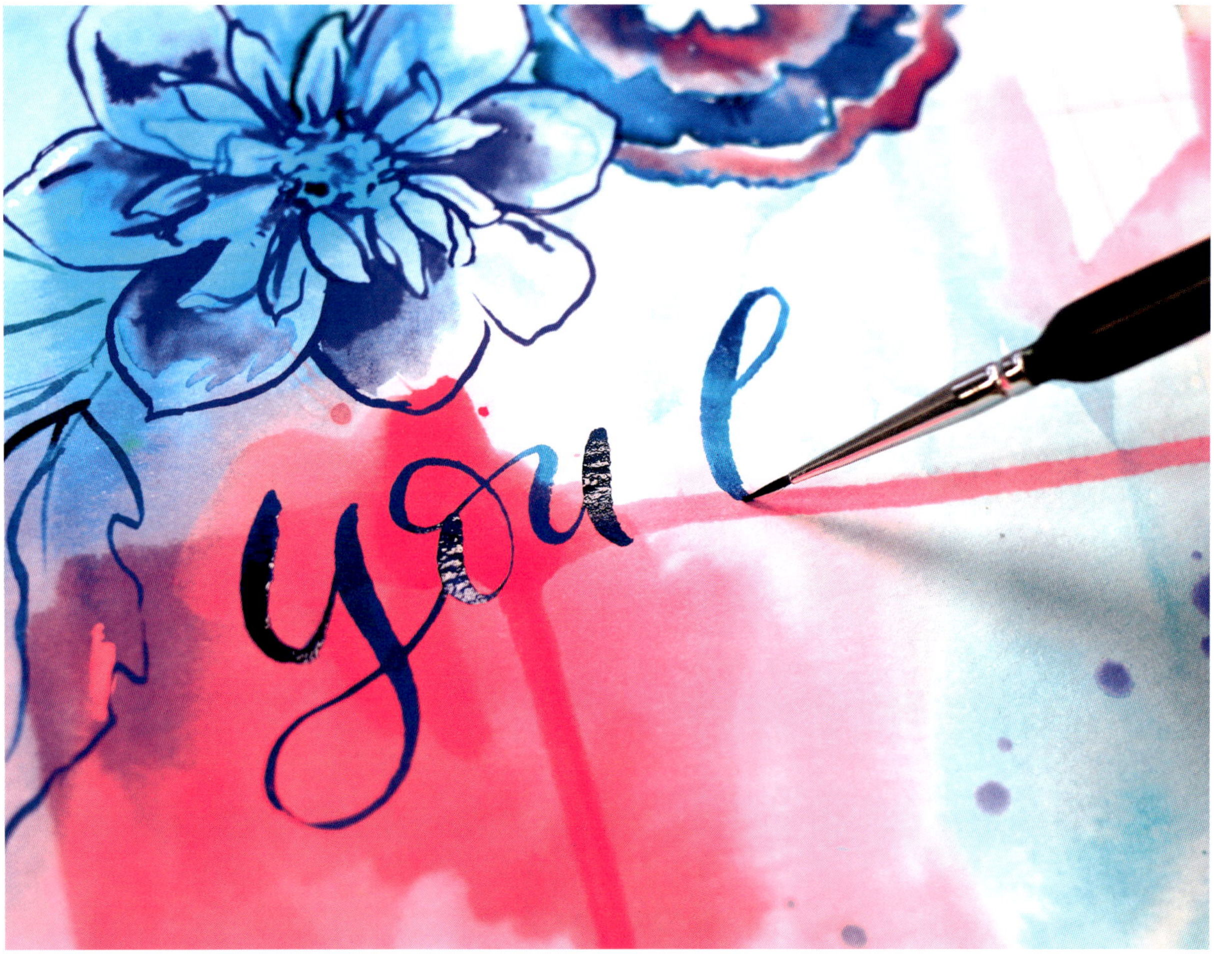

Slow Down and Draw

Sketch with a pencil lightly when getting started and get yourself into drawing mode. Think of each letter as a shape as opposed to a symbol, and draw your letters with the same mindset with which you draw or paint your flowers.

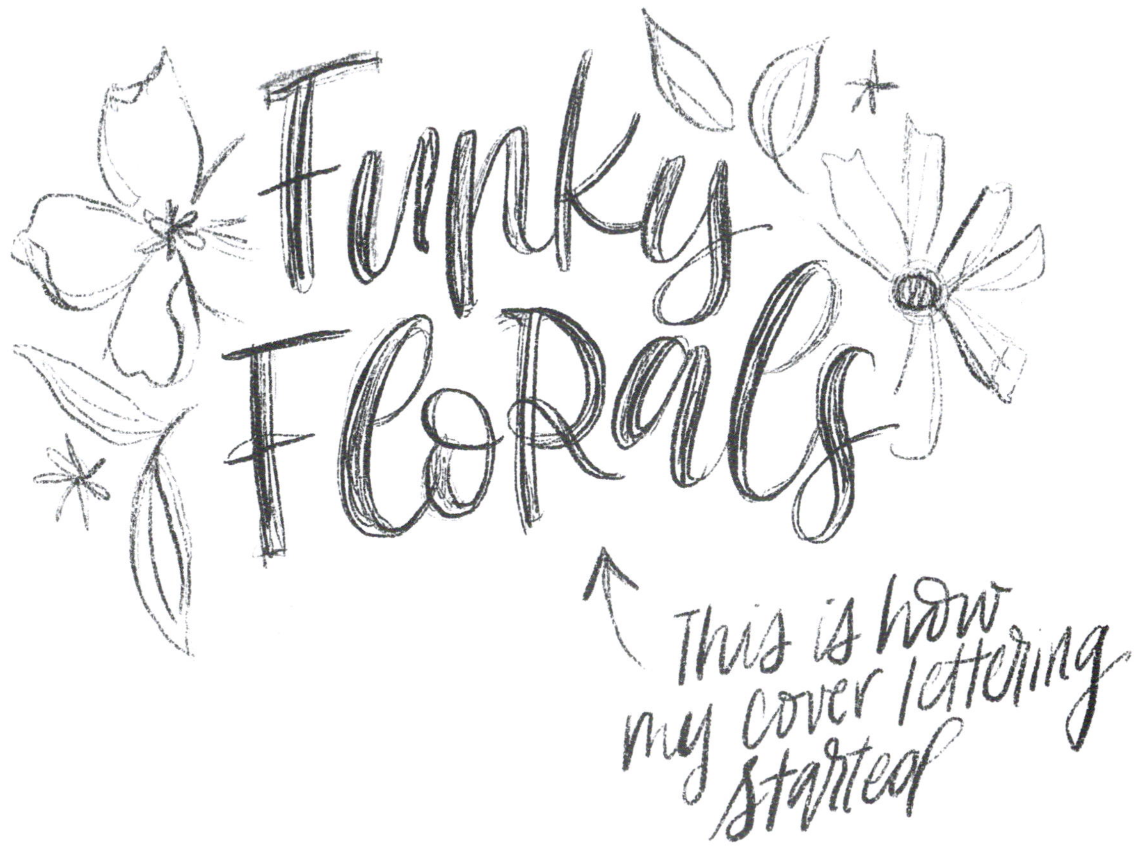

Embrace Line Variation

By adding thicker downstrokes to your letters, you can easily create more visually interesting letters. First sketch the "skeleton," or basic shape, of the letter, then add thicker downstrokes. The downstrokes are the lines and curves in the letter that you naturally draw (write) in a downward motion.

Let's analyze the capital letter B below. My natural first stroke is a downstroke when drawing the stem of the letter from top to bottom. Next, my downstrokes happen as I curve around and down from the stem for the two curves.

So, I add weight to the initial stem downstroke, then I leave the horizontal parts of the curved strokes thin while adding weight to the more vertical parts of the curved strokes.

When using a brush pen, you can add these thicker strokes by pushing down harder as you draw the letters. When you're just getting started with hand lettering, though, I recommend sticking with sketching the skeletons first and returning to add the thicker strokes after the skeletons are established.

Stick to Three Main Styles

The three main styles of letters are serif, sans serif, and script letters. From these three categories, there are endless ways to draw letters!

A **serif** letter is a printed letter with clothes on. Serifs can be simple lines added to the endstrokes of letters, most often on the "feet." Here you can see a simple serif alphabet with weight added to the downstrokes. You can get very creative with serifs, making them thick, wavy, round—anything goes! In the bottom row you can see some creative serif ideas.

A **sans serif** letter is the simplest of printed letters. Sans means "without," so a sans serif letter is a letter without clothes, or, you could say, a naked letter. Sans serifs may be simple, but they can be drawn in tons of different ways. The easiest ways to modify sans serif letters are by changing the height, width, and weight of the letters—see some examples in the last row of the image.

Lastly, let's take a look at **script** letters, which are my personal favorites. Script lettering is essentially cursive lettering, which, sadly, is not widely taught these days. Script letters are packed full of possibilities when you add flourishes (fancy tails added to endstrokes, cross-strokes, etc.). We can draw these letters in so many ways, but even using simple cursive alphabet styles and simply adding weight to the downstrokes will enhance your lettering tremendously.

A fun exercise to get you warmed up with lettering is to take one letter and see how many variations of it you can make! Here are just a few ideas for the letter M (on the facing page).

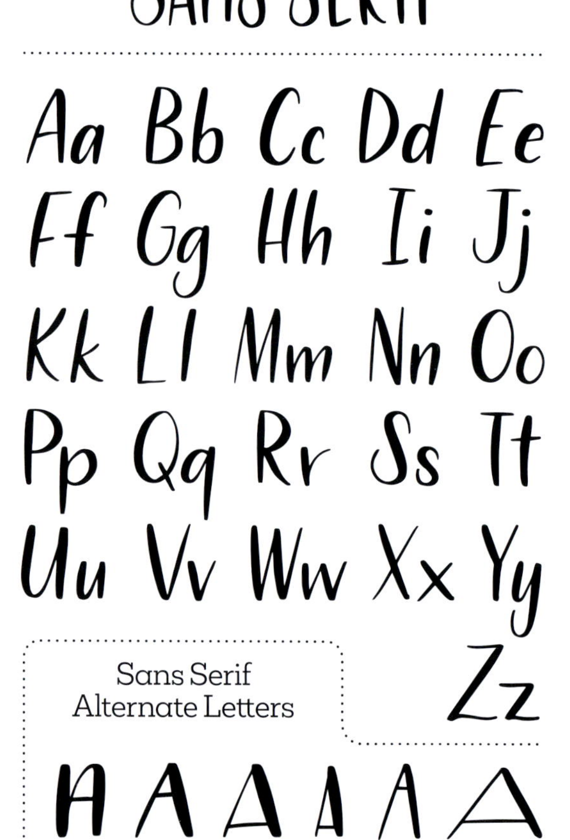

Aa Bb Cc Dd Ee Ff
Gg Hh Ii Jj Kk Ll
Mm Nn Oo Pp Qq Rr
Ss Tt Uu Vv Ww Xx
Yy Zz

Handwriting When and How

Let's talk a little about handwriting. When I'm journaling, I usually don't want to take the time to approach my letters as drawing the way you need to for hand lettering. I want to get my thoughts out quickly and rely on my natural handwriting to do so. If you don't like your natural handwriting, here's my big tip: Make it messier! Write quickly and expressively. Your writing only needs to be legible to you. Allow your thoughts to spill out, and try to keep the writing pace up with how fast you think. I like my handwriting better when I write freely and messily. It's the in-between that messes with my brain—the space between carefully lettering and freely writing is my no-go zone.

You can also try different pens and experiment with writing with a paintbrush and paint. Your handwriting can become a messy pattern in the negative space of a piece and be visually beautiful and interesting when added to your work, so embrace it!

This is my Lettering

This is my handwriting

Doodling

We are going to explore doodling in the first project soon, but before we get there, I want to give you some ideas to get your creative juices flowing. We will be adding doodles and patterns to other projects as well, and I encourage you to explore your own ideas and do what comes naturally. To get you on your way, here are some of my favorite doodles to add in my work.

Doodads

Any little shape can spice up your artwork. These don't need to be complex, and they look great in small groupings.

Straight repeats

Take any simple shape and turn it into a pattern by repeating it in a straight line in neat rows. It's that easy!

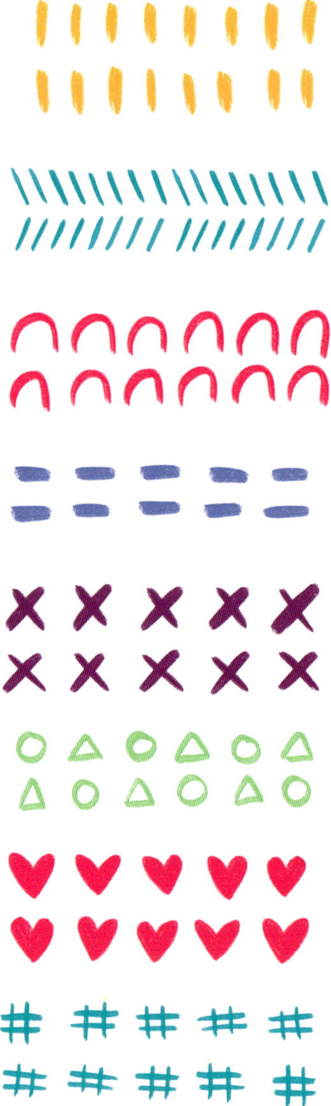

Half-drop repeats

Just like straight repeats, create an interesting pattern by repeating a shape, but this time do it in a half-drop (or checkerboard) pattern. These are great for areas of negative space!

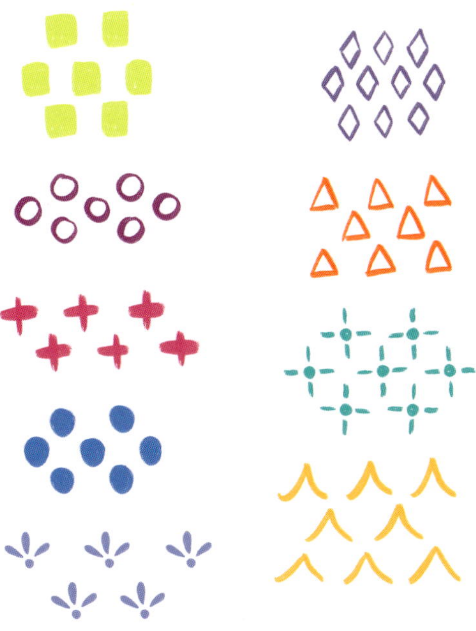

Shake it up

For this approach, repeat the same shapes, but in an organic, haphazard way with no specific structure.

Mix and match

It's fun to explore putting different shapes and colors together to create your own unique doodle patterns. There are infinite things you can do!

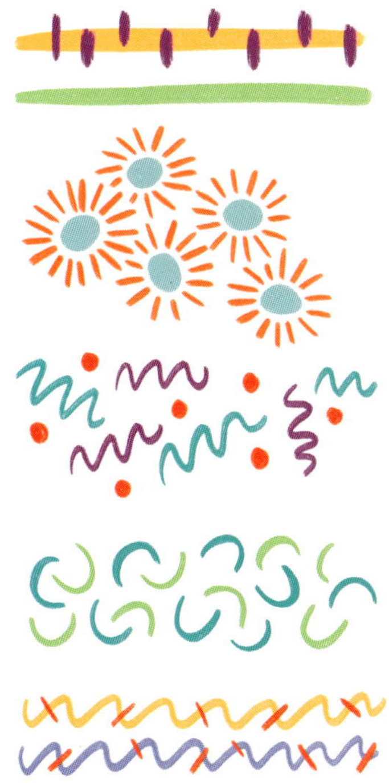

Borders

Doodling borders and adding them to your work can give things an extra-special finish. Borders can be as simple or complex as you want.

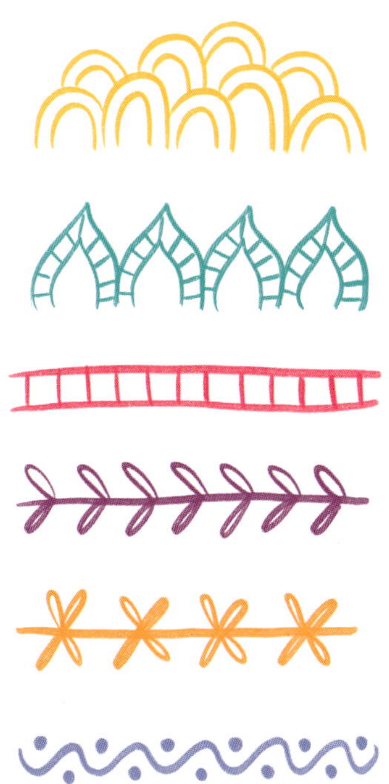

Warm-Up Exercise

Before we turn the page and kick off the first project, let's take a moment to warm up by doodling! This exercise can be done right here in the book on the facing page. Use a black permanent pen or marker; be careful to allow the lines to dry for a moment as you go if you're using a water-based marker.

Now, doodle all over the page! Approach this like a piece of scrap of paper you doodle on while talking on the phone, just stepping it up a few funky notches. Think about the floral shapes (both real and imaginary) that you learned earlier in this book, the elements of design you read about, and the fun doodles you just saw in the previous pages, and give yourself time to play. Allow the washy, colorful background to inspire your shapes, working until you fill up the page! You can see an example of how I did this exercise below.

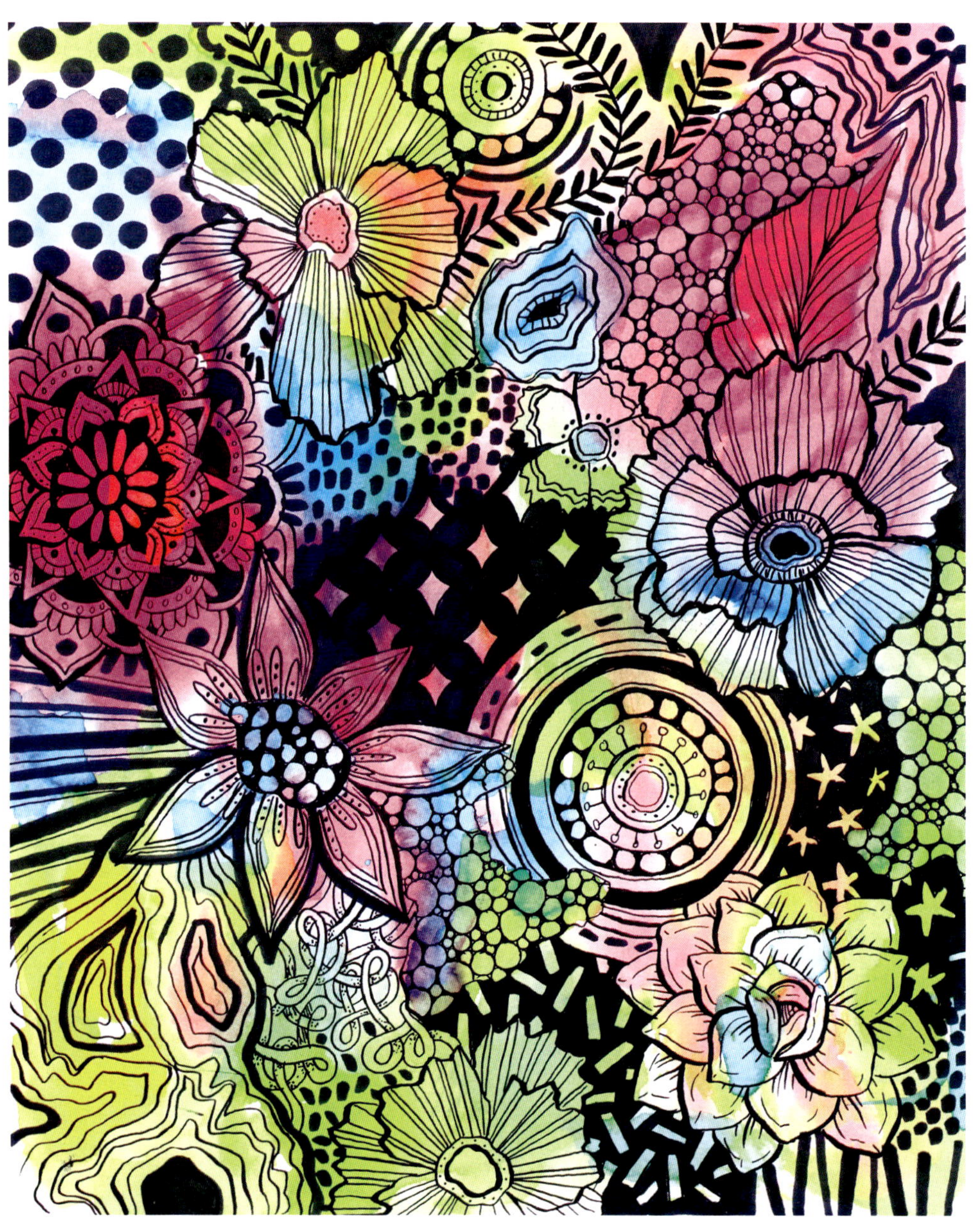

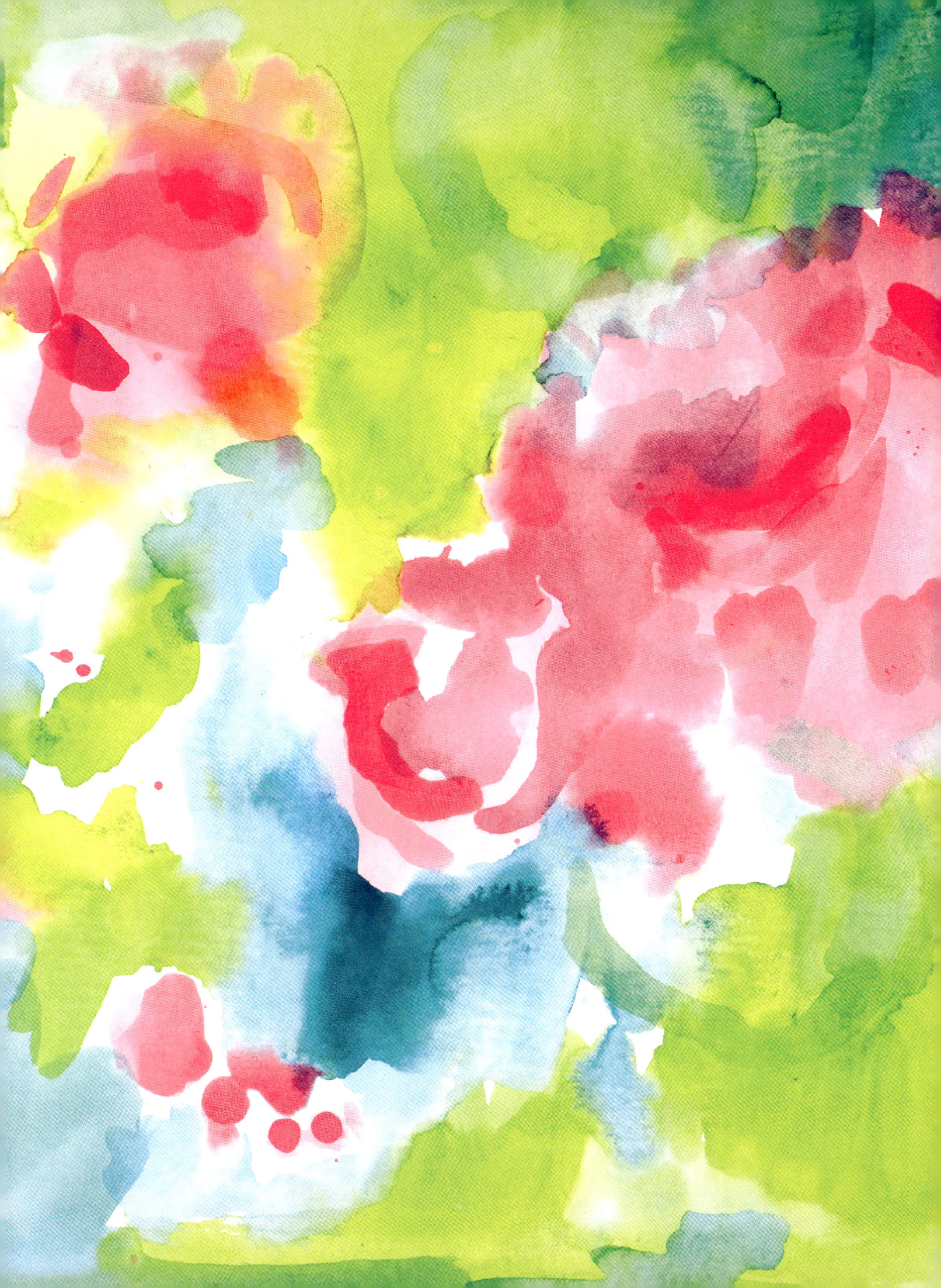

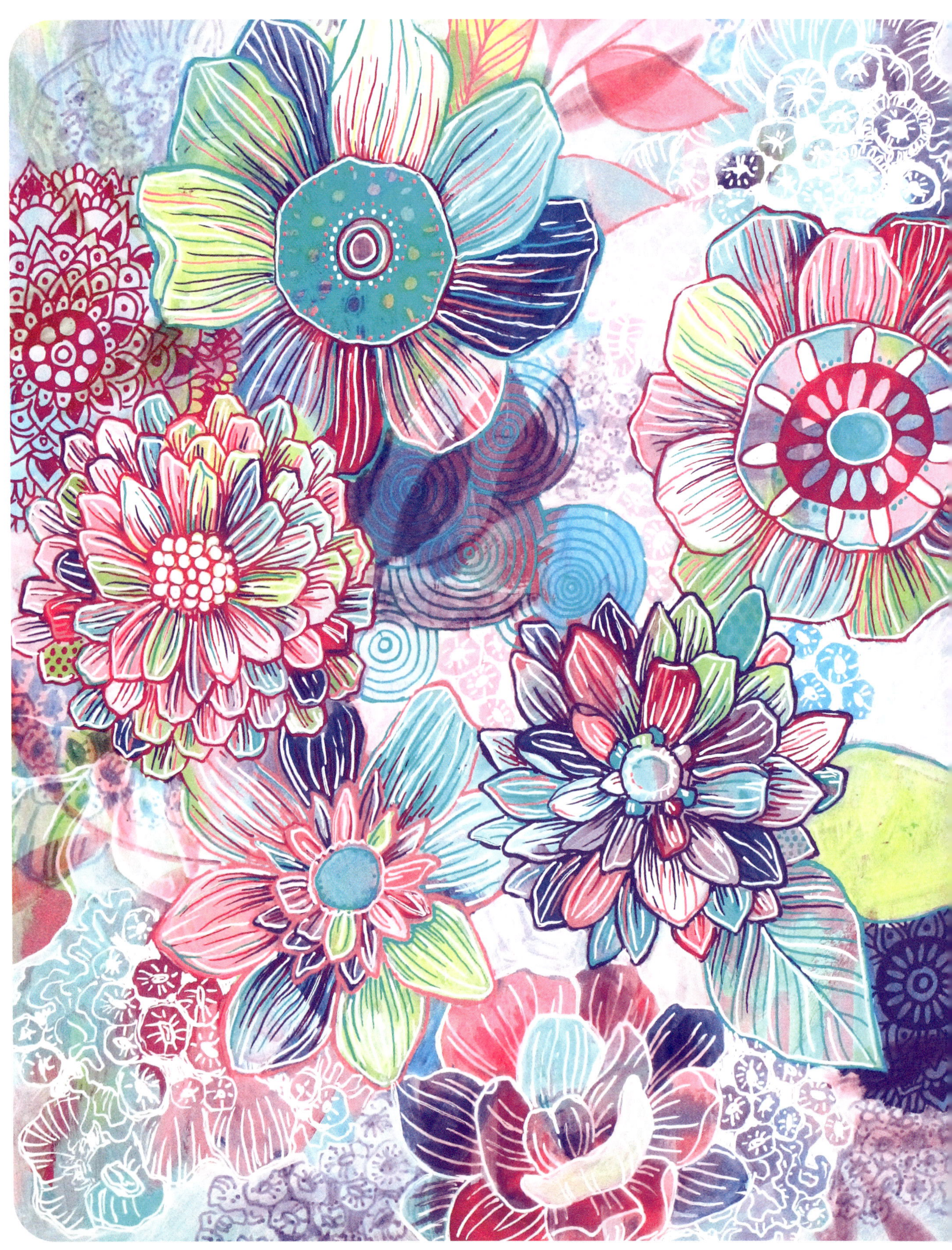

PART 2
Creative Projects

It's finally time to crack open those paints and sit down to create! In this chapter, you'll find 12 projects that progress in terms of the tools used and skills learned. The truth is, you can start with any project that calls to you, but I do recommend working your way through the projects sequentially so you can build up a solid foundation. Each project offers something special and unique, and the pieces you create inspired by them are guaranteed to be special and unique as well.

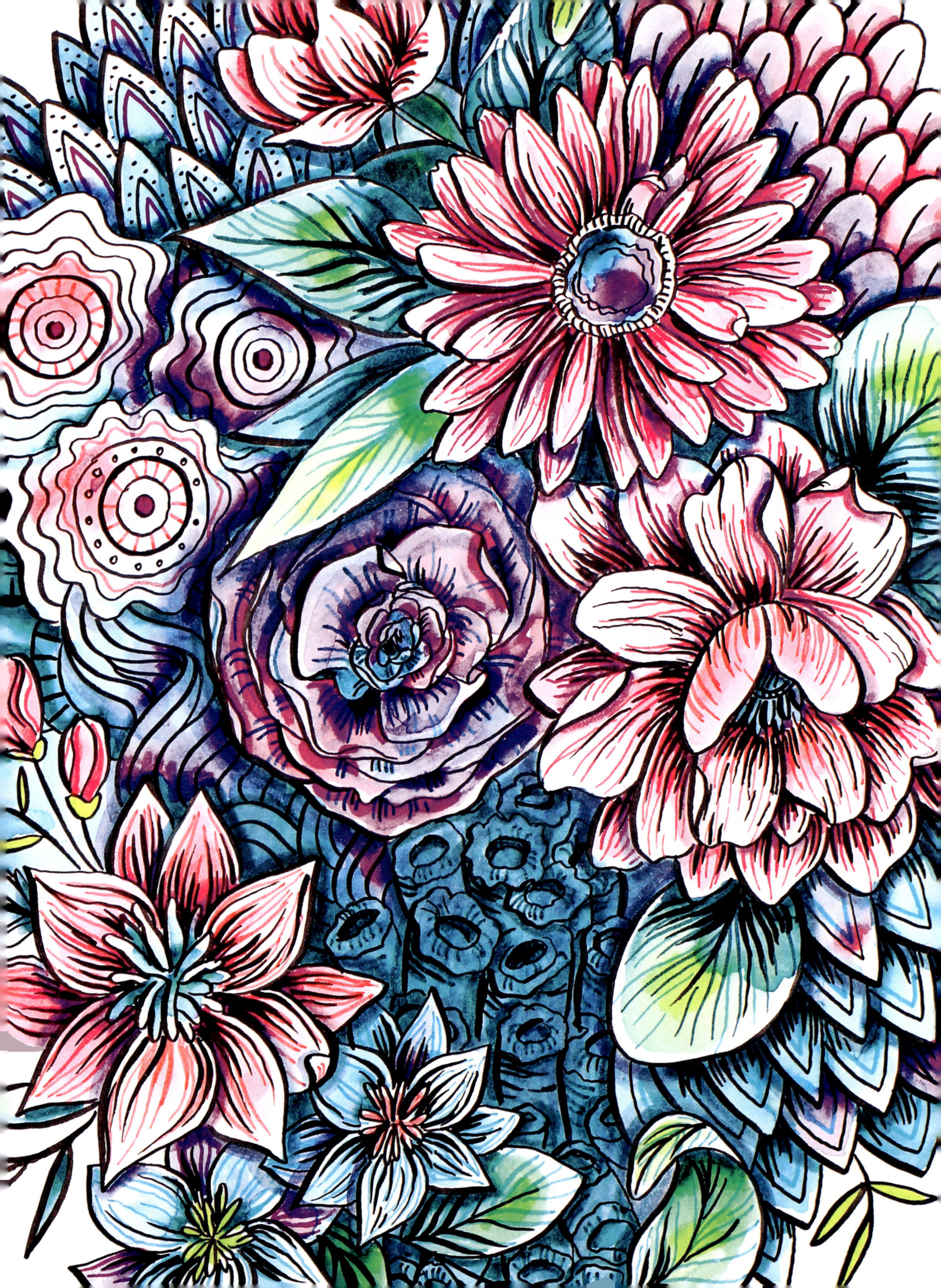

Freestyle Floral Doodling

Learn to doodle florals using a black marker and add color using water-based markers

Before we start dripping, splattering, and layering supplies on top of supplies, we will start things off by just sitting down together and doodling. Doodling is drawing, but it sounds less intimidating! It's casual and free and needs no purpose other than to amuse you while you do it. That's why we are here, isn't it—to enjoy the process of making (pretty) art. By enjoying the process of creating, we are simply amusing ourselves with tools that make marks on a surface. It's as simple as that.

You'll have to occasionally remind yourself to stay in doodle land, because when you leave that place, pressure likes to sneak in. We are starting out with a no-pressure mindset to train ourselves for the projects ahead.

Even though we are going to start with a simple set of supplies and approach, we will still be creating something exciting, fresh, and vibrant. We will take floral doodles to a new level with just a few tricks that you will keep with you through all the projects ahead

Tools & Supplies

- ▶ Water-based markers (try to choose at least two with dark values, two with medium values, and two with light values, plus gray)
- ▶ Black pen/marker that is NOT water-based
- ▶ Size 1 round paintbrush (or your choice of a small brush)
- ▶ Water
- ▶ Watercolor paper, mixed-media paper, or Bristol board

What You'll Learn

MINDFULNESS: Although going into your little happy place while creating may be more difficult as you are first learning something new, try to sink in and get lost in each step as you get used to the process.

LINE VARIATION: The contrast between thick and thin lines is a simple but effective way to add interest to your work.

SHADOWS AND DIMENSION: By recognizing that dark and dull colors recede (get pushed back) and light and bright colors advance (come forward), you will be able to add gorgeous dimension to your piece.

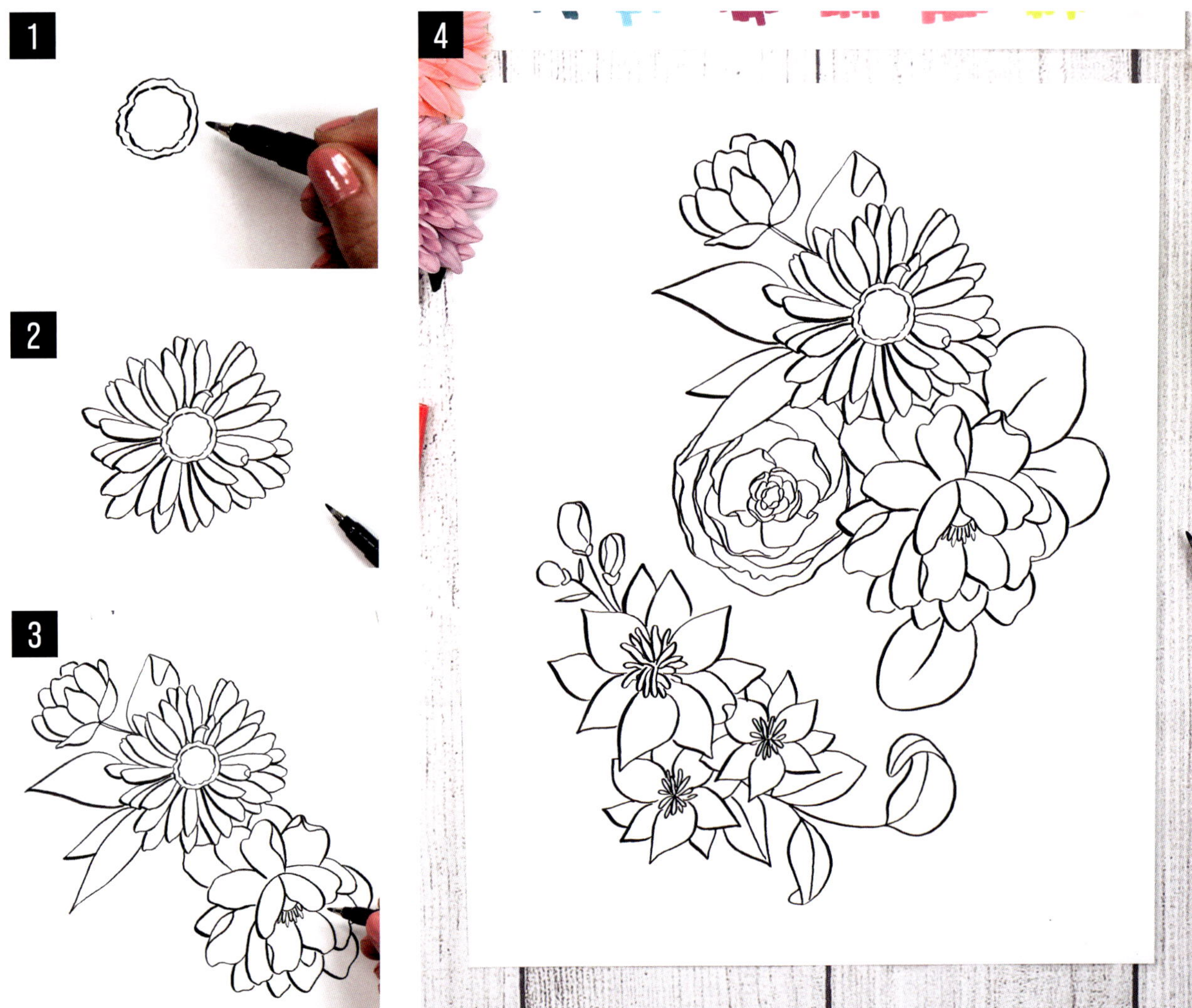

1 Start doodling. Here's a great way to begin a new page of doodles: simply pick a spot and draw the center of a flower in pen! Once you've done this, that blank white page staring at you is gone. Don't overthink it—just start drawing, and everything else will flow from this first move.

2 Flesh out your first flower. Add petals to this first flower. Try incorporating line variation by including thicker and thinner lines, as I've done here. You can begin with a basic flower from your imagination or try your hand at something more realistic or complex. I chose a daisy as my inspiration and layered my petals in a somewhat realistic approach.

3 Add a few more flowers and leaves. From here, it's time to simply get lost in what you are doing, creatively. My first flower led me to leaves and another small flower coming out from it at top left. Next, I drew a second, and different, flower below. We will be adding detailed linework later in the piece, so focus on doodling in just the main shapes for now.

4 Continue doodling. To build up dimension in your work, draw some flowers in front of others and some behind others. Let the flowers overlap instead of having them all float around by themselves. As you doodle, vary the shapes and sizes of both the flowers and the leaves. Some can be more whimsical and imaginative while others are more realistic.

Remember, there is no wrong way to draw a flower!
But if you want some guidance, check out pages 35–51.

5 **Complete the main floral shapes and start adding details in the remaining space.** Fill up as much space as you'd like. You may want your composition to extend off the edges of the page, but I'll be keeping mine confined within it. Now it's time to really let loose and get creative. Begin incorporating more-abstract doodles.

6 **Finish the drawing work.** Many of the detailed doodles you drew in the space between the main flowers will become pushed back later, becoming part of the background, once color is added. Continue adding details within your composition until you are happy with it. It's time to move on to color!

7 **Begin adding shadows.** Select your darker and midtoned colors to begin adding shadows. Any petal, leaf, flower, or doodle that is behind another should get a bit of these darker colors to begin building up dimension. You do not need to add a lot of color in each shape—just a bit in the corners and edges. Do this across the entire piece.

8 **Layer some colors.** Experiment with overlapping colors to create new ones. I limited myself to just eight markers total, but when I layered my dark teal on top of my magenta, it created a deep violet. (You'll soon see this effect better when we begin to blend with water.) You don't need a lot of markers to create a ton of hues!

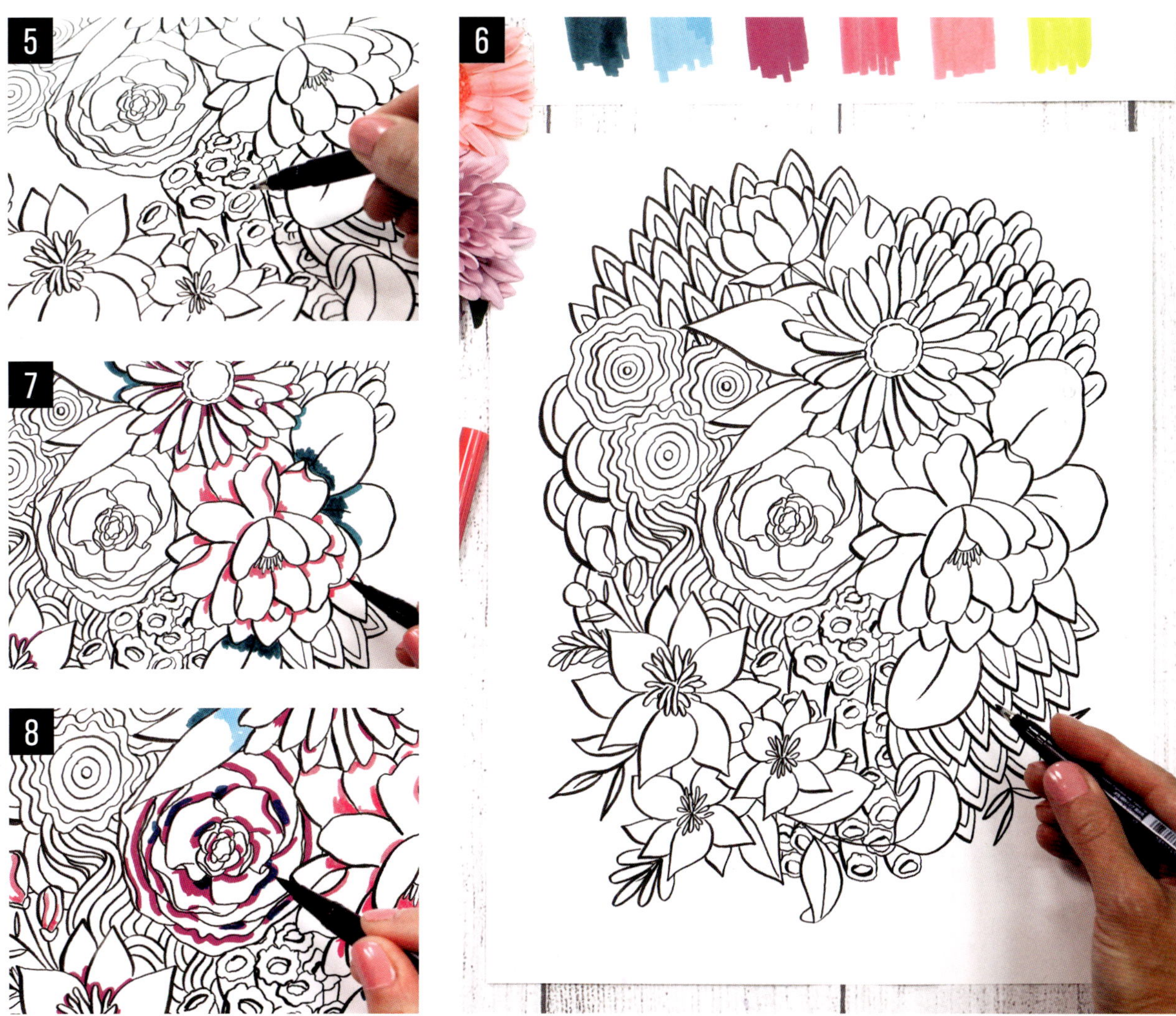

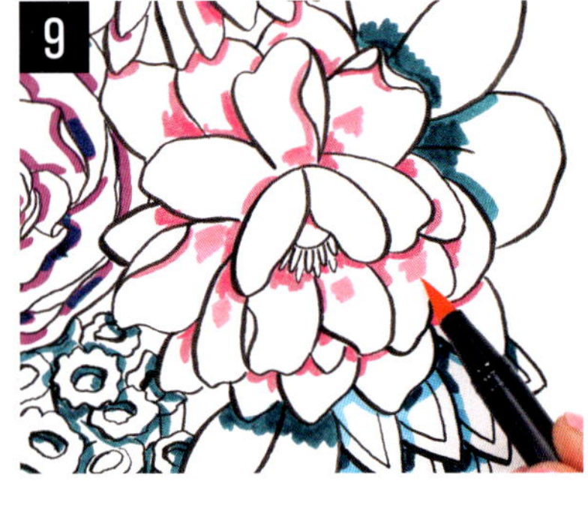

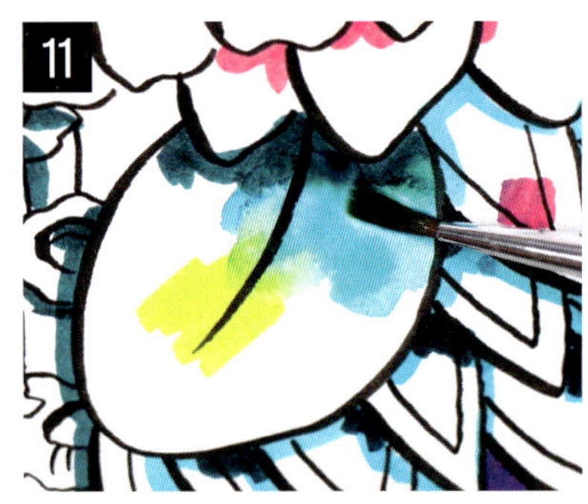

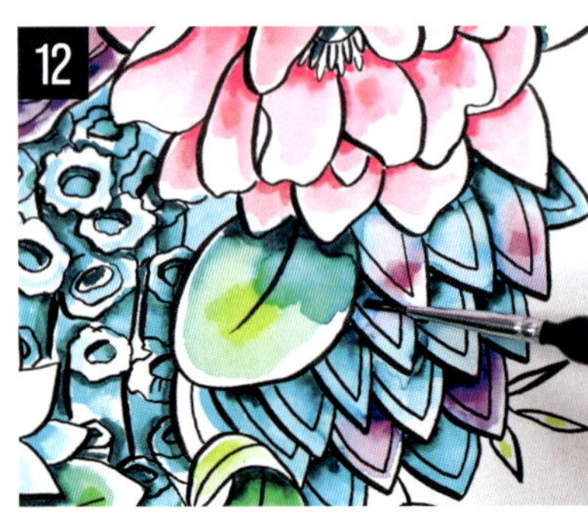

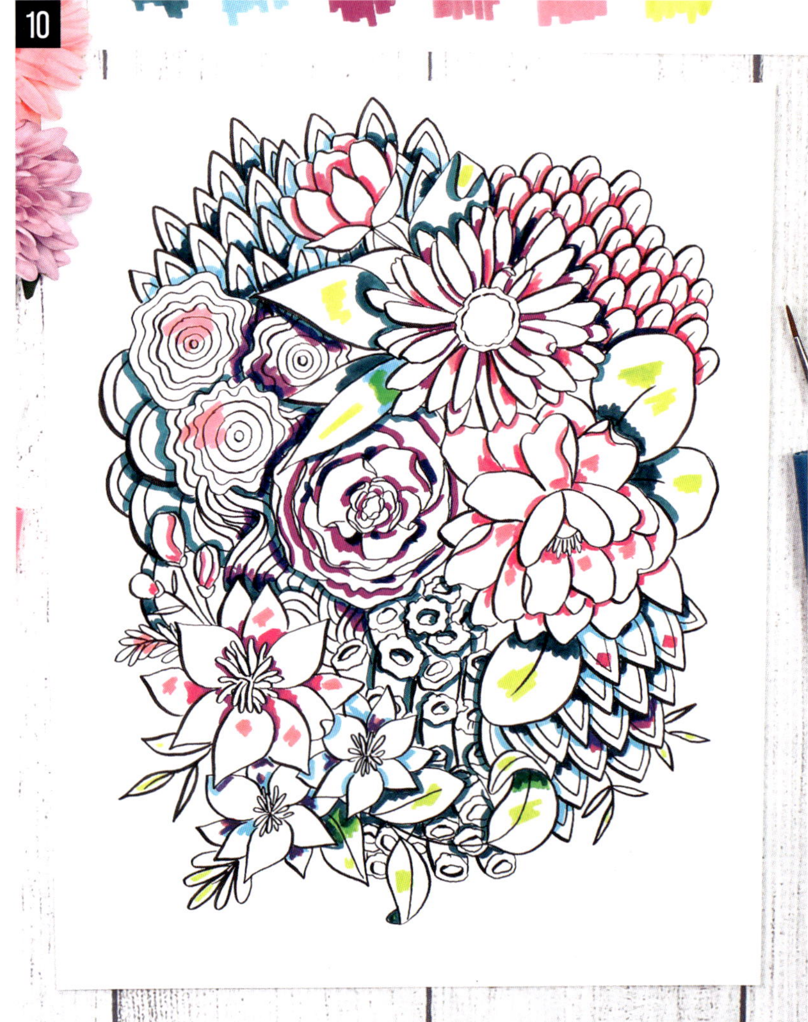

9   Switch to your lighter markers. Once your darker shadows are in, switch to your colors that are lighter to medium in value. Put some small patches of color in most of the leaves, flowers, and doodles, but don't color in the whole shapes or add color to every space.

10   Get ready to blend. Check to make sure you haven't left any areas completely neglected. Here is where I am at this phase. We are now at the moment of the project where you might be asking yourself, "How am I going to pull this off?" But have no fear—we are about to bring this baby to life.

11   Start blending. Switch to your paintbrush and water. To blend, dip the brush in water, brush it on top of the color, and gently pull away as you blend outward. The water-based markers will begin to act like watercolor paints when touched with water. It's so fun to watch beautiful marks appear from the colors bleeding together!

12   Leave some white areas. Continue blending your patches of color throughout the piece. However, don't cover every single area in color— leave some white highlights to maximize the amount of value variation in the piece. You can always go back and add more color in later.

When you start blending, it is your first chance in your journey
to truly let go of control and allow your supplies to take the lead. We will be doing this
all throughout the book, so get yourself warmed up to it right at the start!

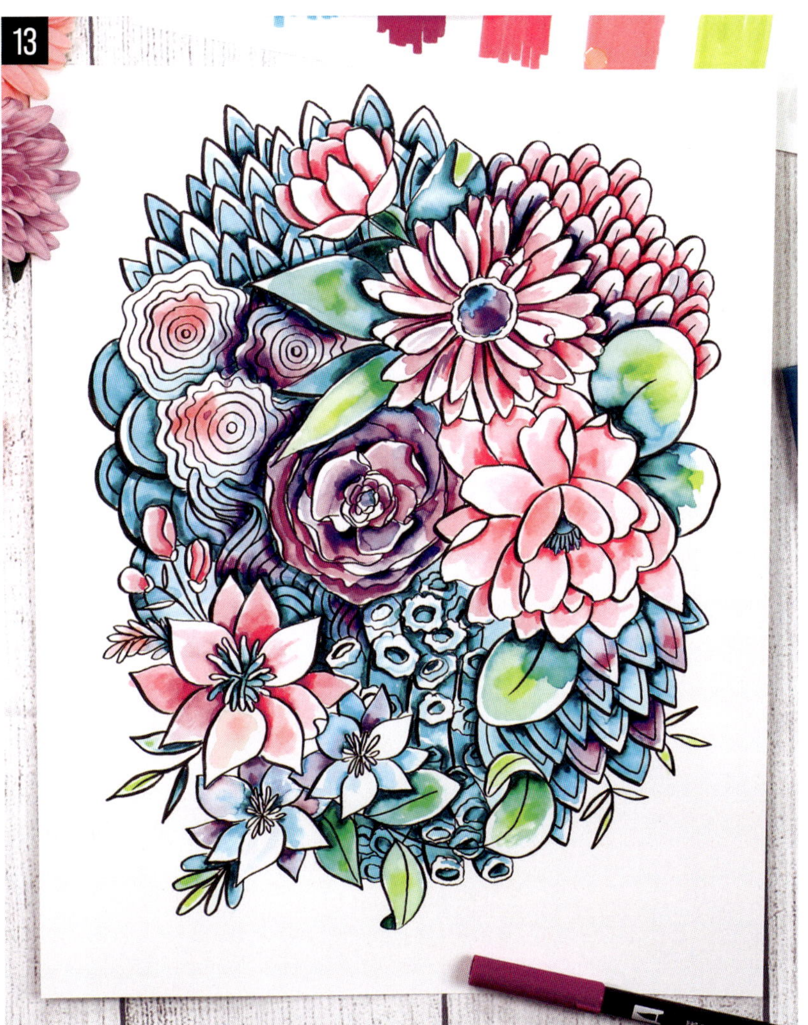

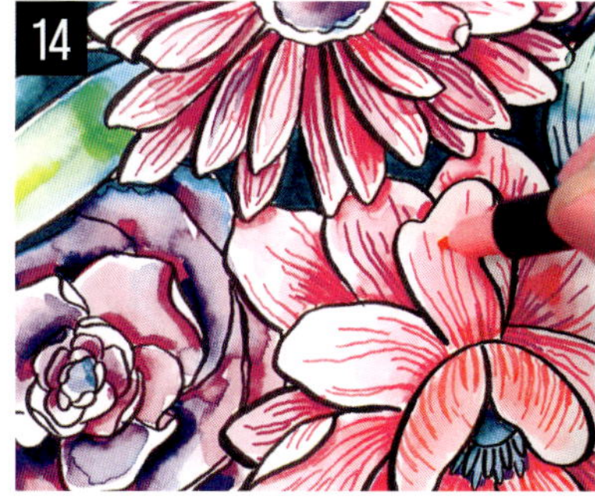

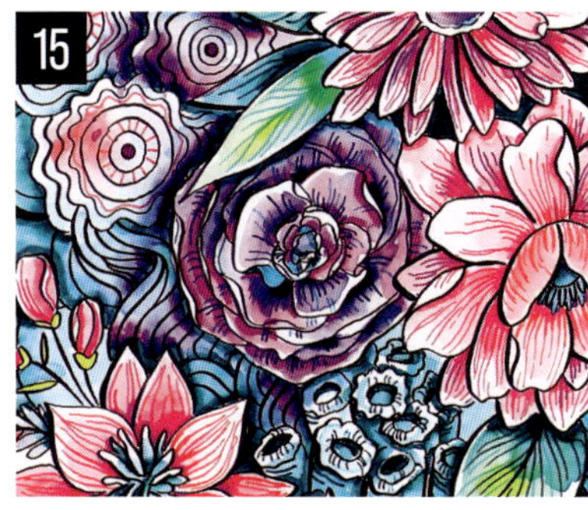

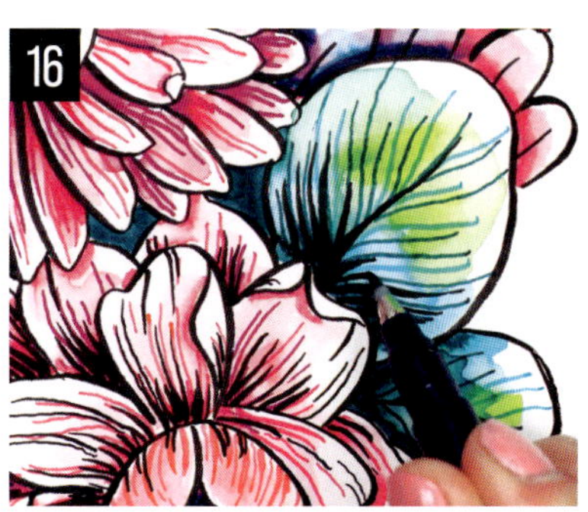

13 **Finish blending.** Check that you are satisfied with your blending work and that you haven't missed any rough color patches that need to be blended out. In areas that I knew I wanted pushed back farthest to the background, I didn't leave much white or any at all, such as in the swirly doodles in the middle left.

14 **Add color line detail.** It's time for the first phase of drawing your detailed linework! Use the fine tip of your markers to add detail lines to your petals and leaves. As a general rule, make the lines thicker toward the inside of the petals and taper them out toward the edges of the petals.

15 **Enjoy the process.** Visit each flower and leaf throughout the piece. Try to get lost in the process. Once you are happy with the color linework, it's time to move on to the final step: black linework.

16 **Add black linework.** Switch to your black marker or pen, preferably one that is not water-based and therefore won't bleed. Once again, try to push yourself with line variation to continue to develop depth. Remember that the thicker and more numerous the lines are in an area, the more they will push that area into the background.

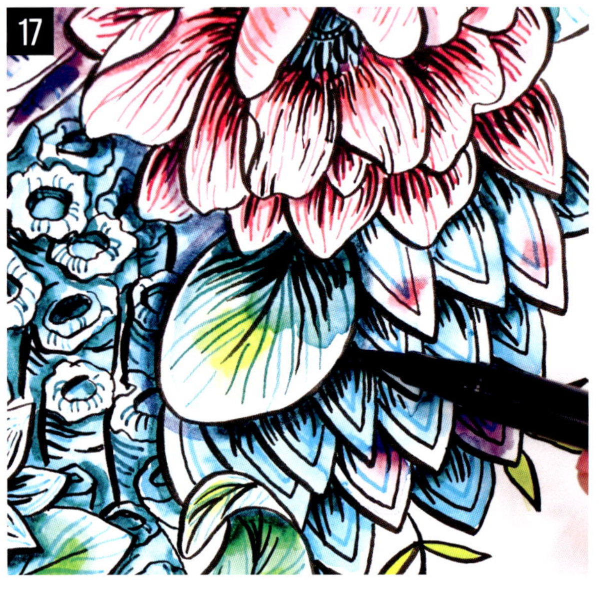

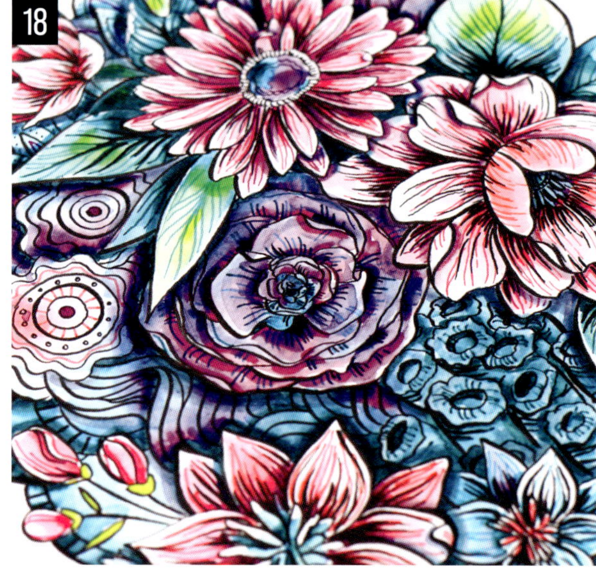

17 **Add dark shadows.** Let's push just a little more to get the florals, leaves, and abstract shapes in the background even deeper so that the lighter and brighter elements really stand out. Choose a color that isn't too dark, such as a medium-toned gray. Anywhere something is behind another thing, add a soft but thick outline along the edge of the thing on top. (If it's a petal on top of another petal, perhaps make these shadows a little thinner.)

18 **Finish creating dimension.** Look everywhere around the piece and make sure to find and shadow all the areas where things overlap. You will see the dimension and excitement in your work continue to build. Keep in mind that as you color over the other colors, your water-based marker will pick some of those colors up—but that's a good thing!

19 **Take a final look.** Step away from your piece and decide if there is anything else your heart is telling you to do. Mine usually tells me to keep going, but this time it's telling me that I'm done. Once your instincts tell you it's time to stop, congratulations! You've created your first funky floral work of art!

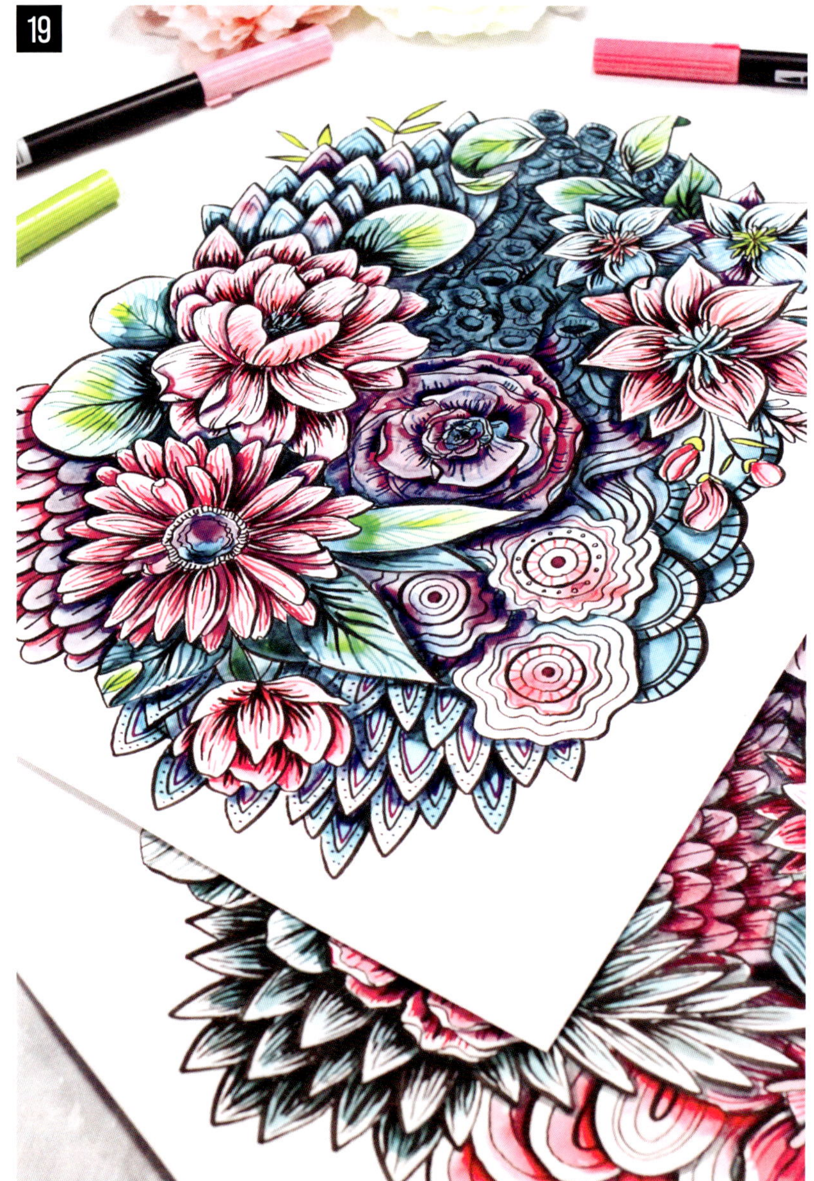

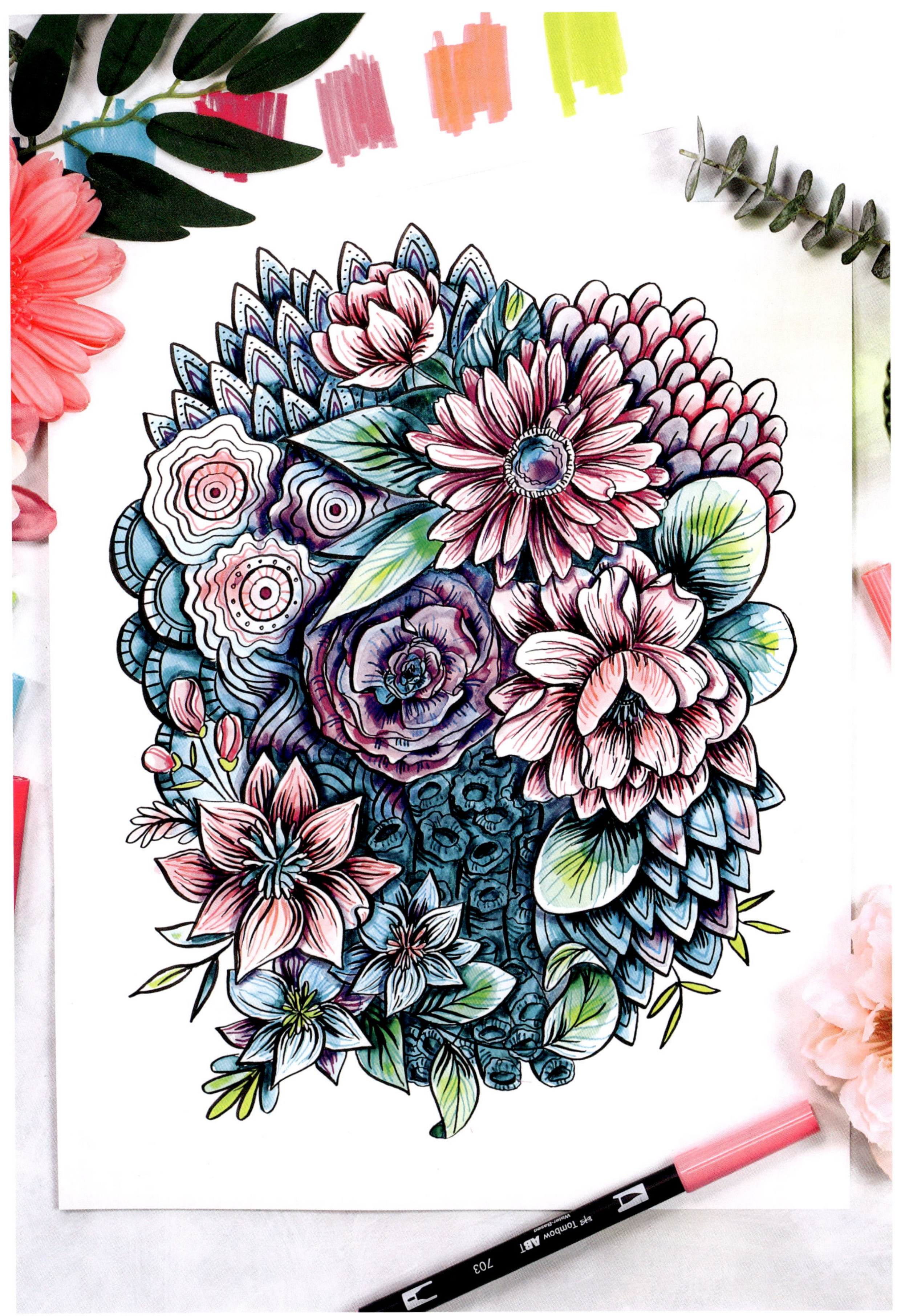

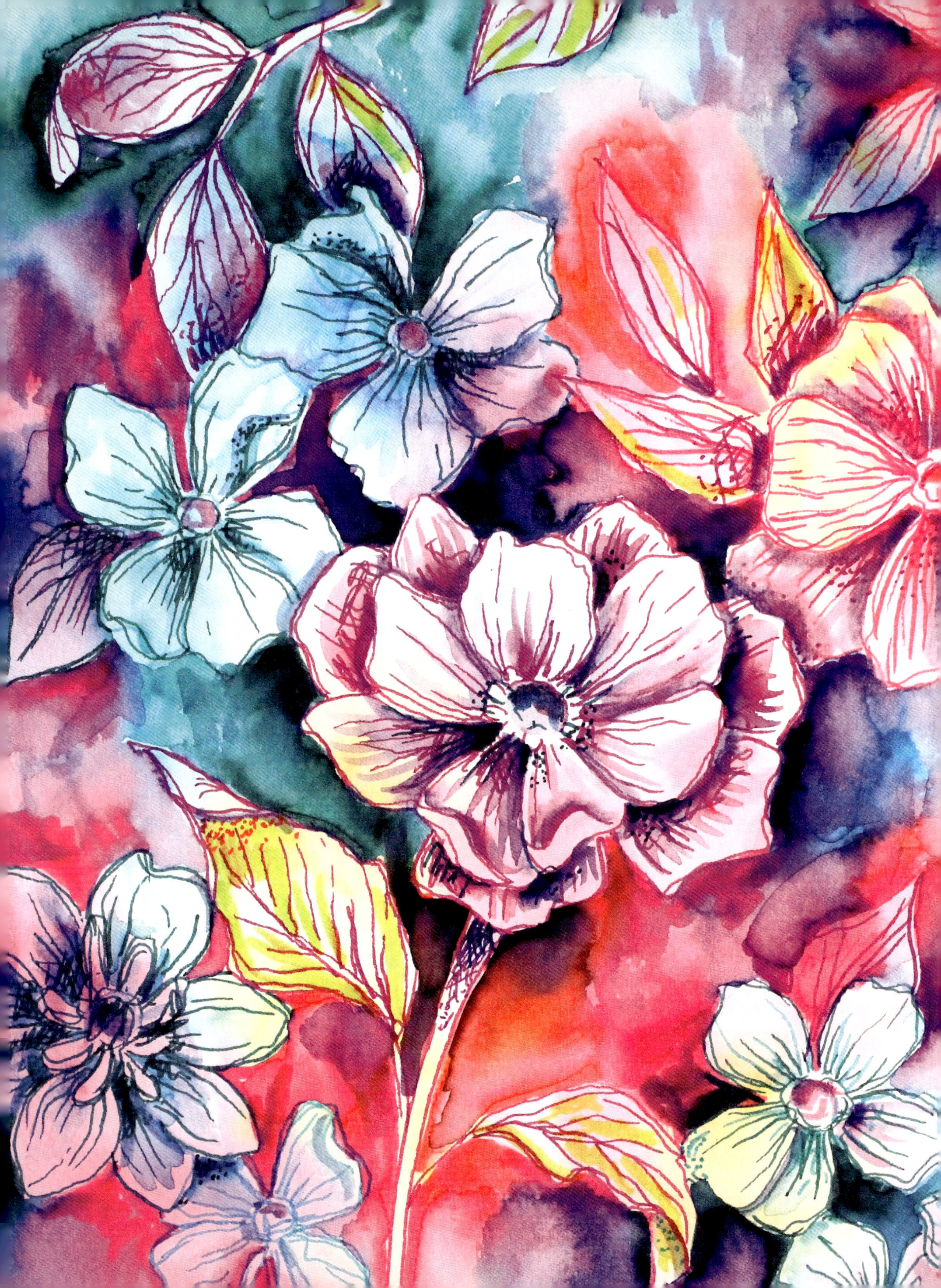

Washy Negative Space

*Learn to fill negative space with washes of color
and draw with water-based markers*

That white paper just stares you down, doesn't it? The hardest part for you in the first project was most likely that first flower placed on a daunting, blank, white page. Now it's time to flip the process and get started with a wash of messy color instead! In this piece, we are going to cover up the white quickly and then use negative space to bring our florals to life. We will build off what you learned about drawing florals and shading in "Freestyle Floral Doodling" and use the same supplies (minus the black pen), but the results will be astoundingly different.

Negative space is a fancy word for the background between elements in two-dimensional art. It can be easy to ignore the background and think that the foreground is most important, but I'm here to tell you that's not the case. Negative space needs your attention as well because what's happening in the negative space will make your subject matter come to life. You can be intentional and creative in the negative space while keeping the emphasis on the foreground.

Tools & Supplies

- ▶ Water-based markers
  (about eight different colors)
- ▶ Sizes 2 and 5 round paintbrushes
  (or your choice of a small and a medium brush)
- ▶ Water
- ▶ Watercolor paper, mixed-media paper,
  or Bristol board

What You'll Learn

LETTING GO: By scribbling color on the paper right at the start, you'll learn that letting go of control is the first step toward unexpected happy accidents.

NEGATIVE SPACE: It's your friend. Don't ignore it and think it's unimportant. Negative space is the supportive music backing up the lead vocalist in the band.

EXPRESSIVE LINEWORK: We'll explore a new kind of expressive linework in this project, using cross-hatching, stippling, and scribbling to add detail and shading.

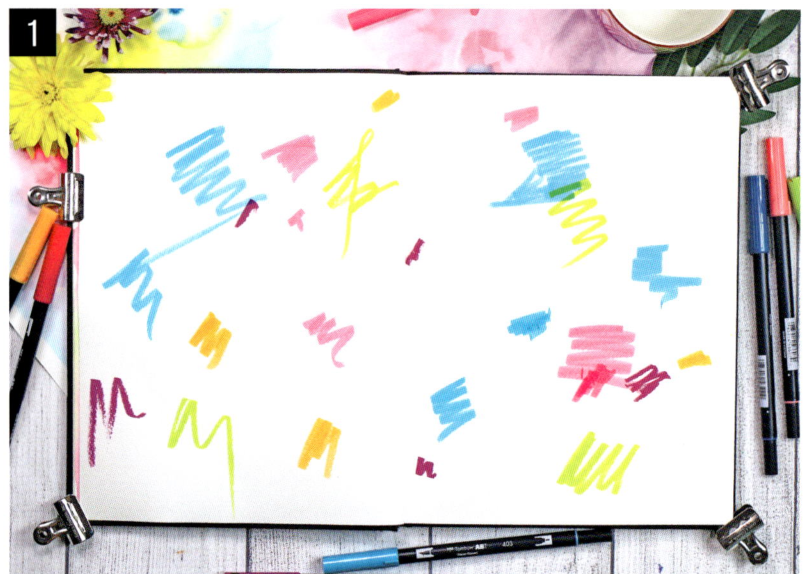

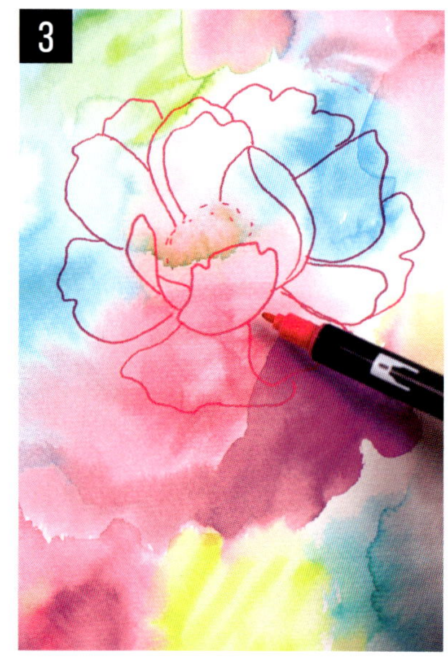

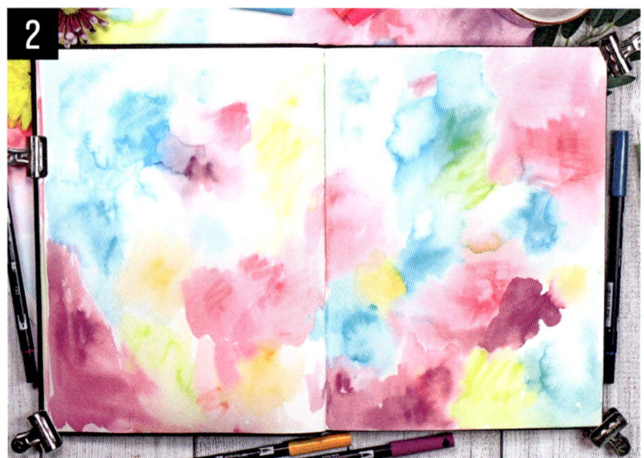

1 **Add colorful scribbles.** Start scribbling messy marks in various spots across your paper. Don't think—just do it. Hold on to some of that white space by spreading out these areas. Try not to use super-dark colors right off the bat. You don't want the background colors to be so faint that you can't see them, but you can't go back in time to lighten things up once the color is applied.

2 **Blend with water.** Saturate your size 5 (medium) round brush with water and begin to blend your colors. As in "Freestyle Floral Doodling," your water-based markers will magically transform into watercolors! Let these colors pool together and dry naturally, doing their thing. You'll be left with a page of colors and gorgeous marks that you couldn't create intentionally.

3 **Draw the first flower.** Use the fine tip of one of your markers to draw in the basic shapes of a single flower. Simply find a spot and go for it.

4 **Add several more basic flower shapes.** Continue drawing basic shapes of flowers and leaves throughout your piece. Be mindful of leaving plenty of negative space. Overlap some of your flowers and leave breathing room around others. Strive to fill about two-thirds of your composition with flowers at this point.

Don't let the "I can't draw" lies take up any space in your head. I am drawing more-realistic flowers here, but you can't go wrong with the simple formula of starting with a center and then adding petals and leaves.

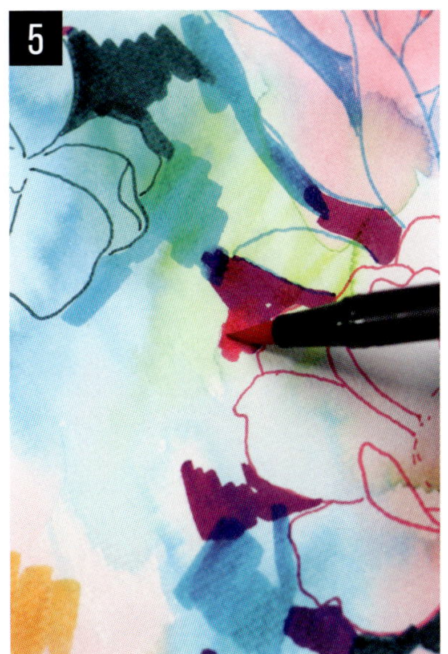

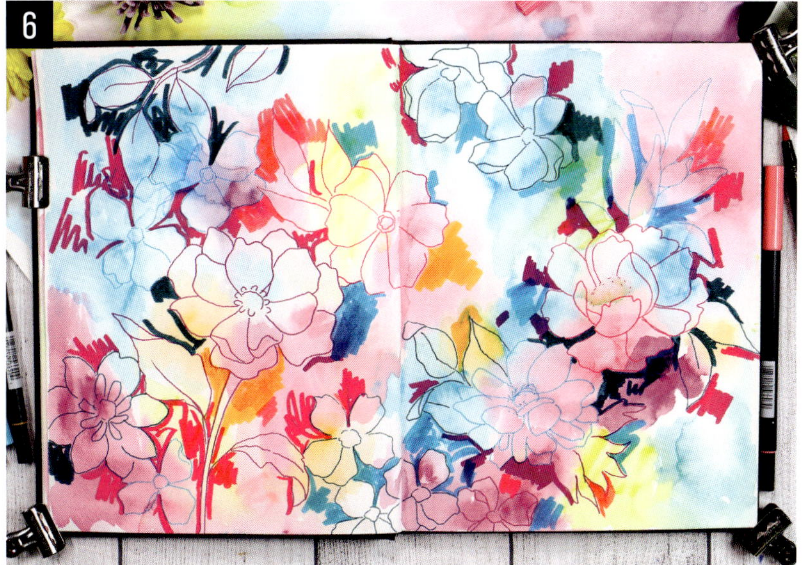

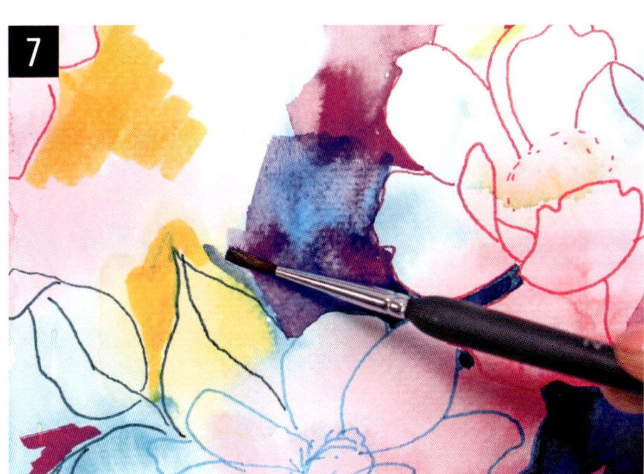

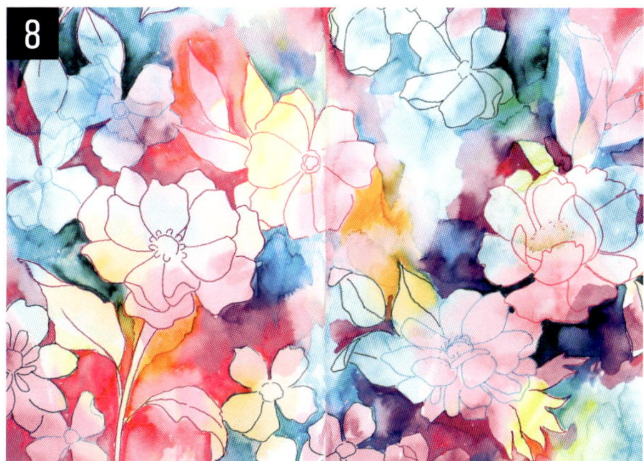

5 **Add patches of color in the background.** This piece is all about layers, and this second layer is going to be a transformative step. Start adding patches of color with your markers inside the negative space around the flowers and leaves. The goal is to start pushing the background back and bringing the foreground forward.

6 **Get ready to blend.** Continue adding patches of color around the flowers in the background until there is a good amount to work with, as shown. You do not need to add color everywhere.

7 **Blend the color patches.** Get out your size 2 paintbrush and water and begin to wash in the new colors. Be careful to keep your strokes inside the negative space and preserve the lines of your flowers.

8 **Finish blending the background.** Address each of your color patches. You can drag the color from some patches into areas that are far from any patches to create light values that still contribute to pushing the background back.

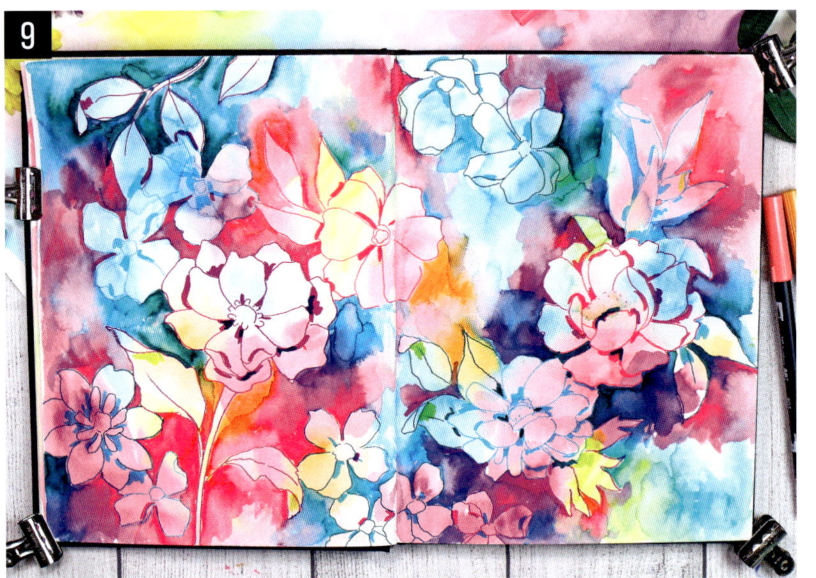

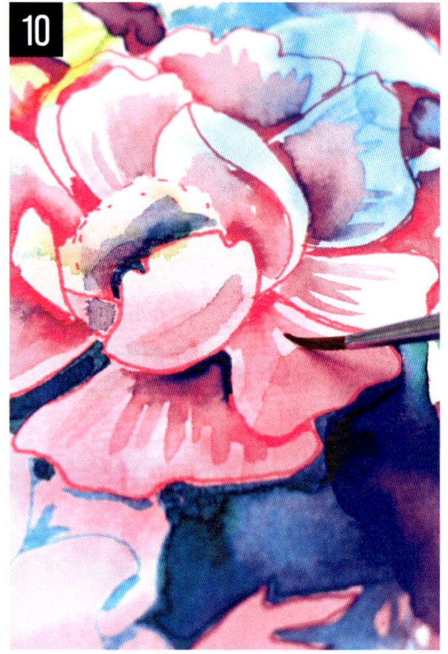

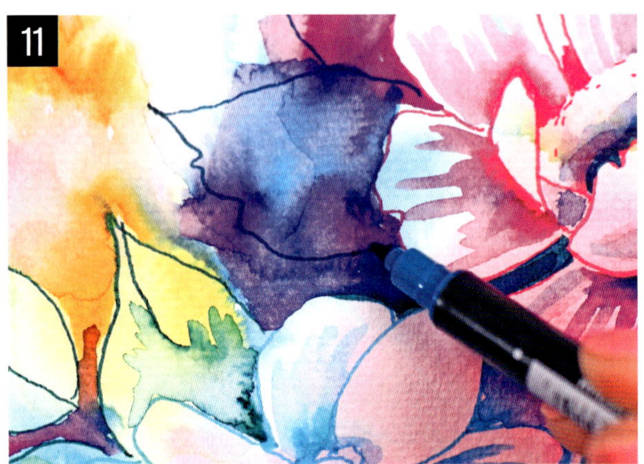

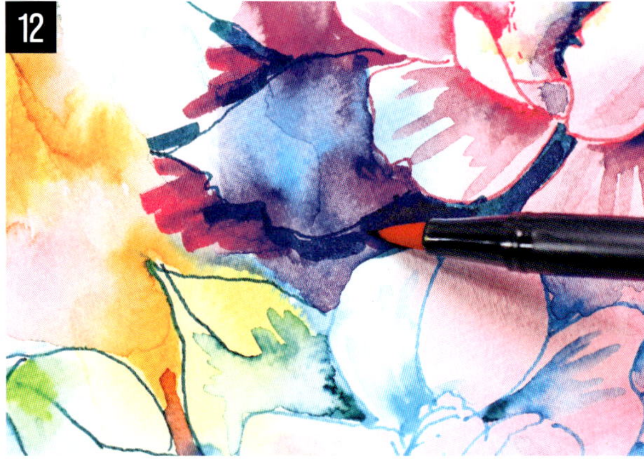

9 **Prepare color within the flowers.** While your negative space is drying, begin shading in the flowers. Just as you did in "Freestyle Floral Doodling," add only small amounts of color in areas that are underneath or behind the other flowers and leaves.

We are in the hot-mess stage of this piece right now, and things may seem a bit TOO out of your control, but stick with me — we are about to pull things together.

10 **Blend and wash out the colors in the flowers.** Begin washing out the shading in your flowers with your wet paintbrush. Be intentional with your brushstrokes by pulling the color away from the initial shading patch. Begin to hint at the detailed linework that you will be adding in later steps.

11 **Draw more flowers in the background.** After blending all your main flowers, while they are drying, let's move back to the negative space. Draw a few new leaves and flowers in the negative space on top of the areas you've already began to push back.

12 **Add more color.** Add color surrounding these new flowers and leaves and then wash over the color with water to fade it out. Now you've added another layer and are really building up the depth!

13 **Check your progress.** Make sure you've addressed any lingering patches of color before proceeding to the next step. Here is the piece with all the patches blended and ready to continue. See how different it already looks from step 9?

14 **Add loose, detailed linework.** It's time to make those flowers and leaves come alive! Using your markers, begin adding detailed linework to emphasize the shapes of the flowers. This is where I really want you to loosen up. Hold your pen loosely in your hand and allow your linework to wander and even become shaky as you bring back the edges of the flowers and leaves.

15 **Try cross-hatching.** Let's continue pushing the dimension in these flowers by using three new shading techniques. Instead of blending with water, we will blend with mark-making. First, try cross-hatching. This is when you use small crisscrossing lines to add shading. The more lines you use, the darker the shading will be. The fewer and more spread out the lines are, the lighter the shading will be.

16 **Try stippling.** Stippling is a technique that uses tiny dots to add shading. The more dots there are and the closer together they are, the darker the value. Fade out the shading by adding fewer and fewer dots.

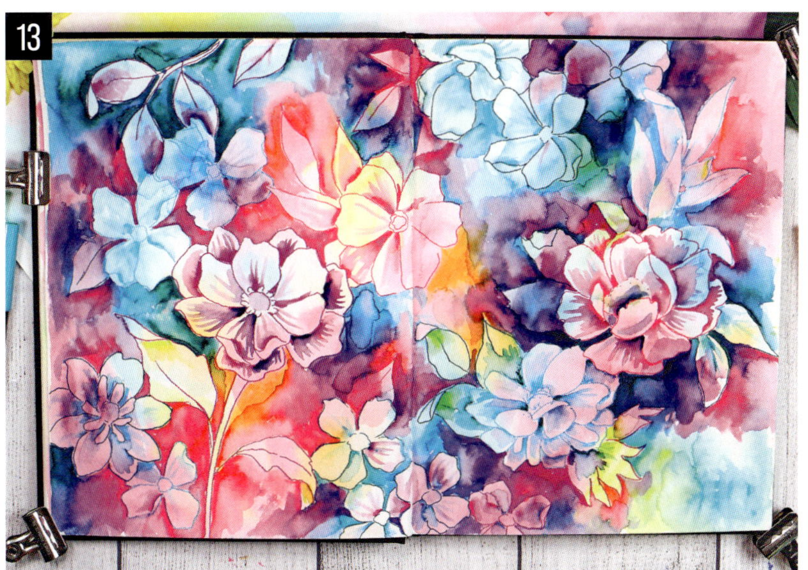

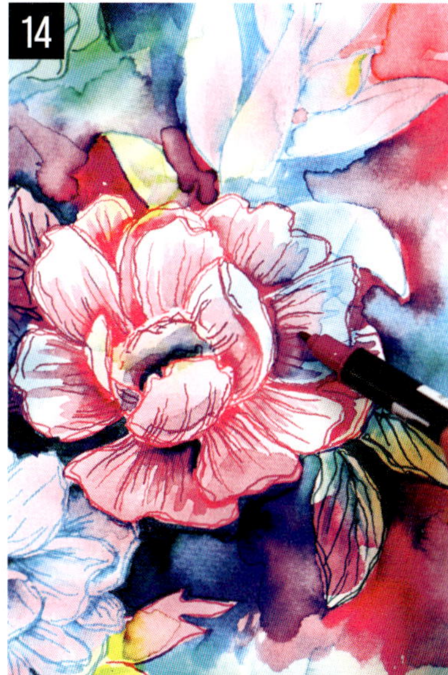

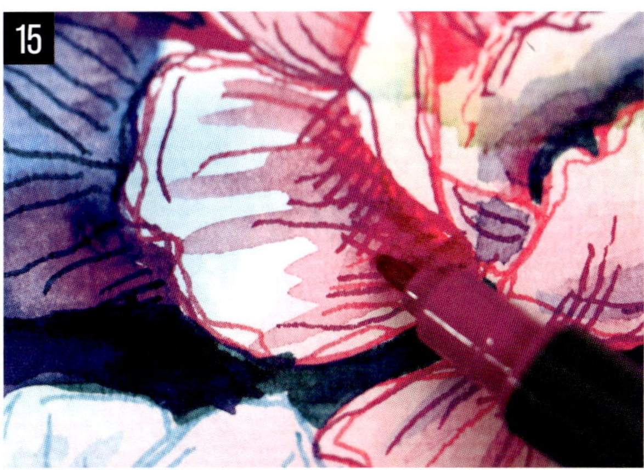

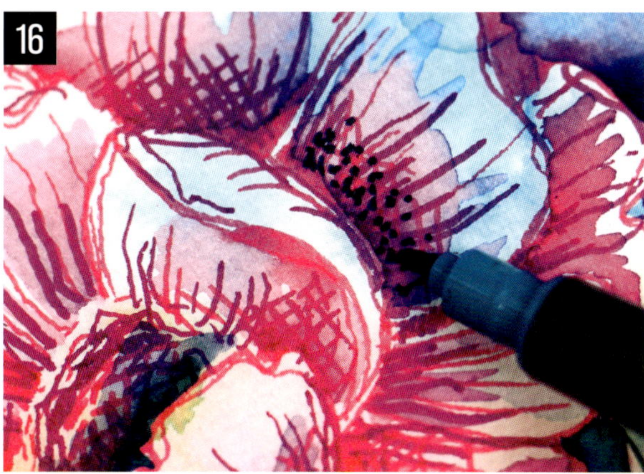

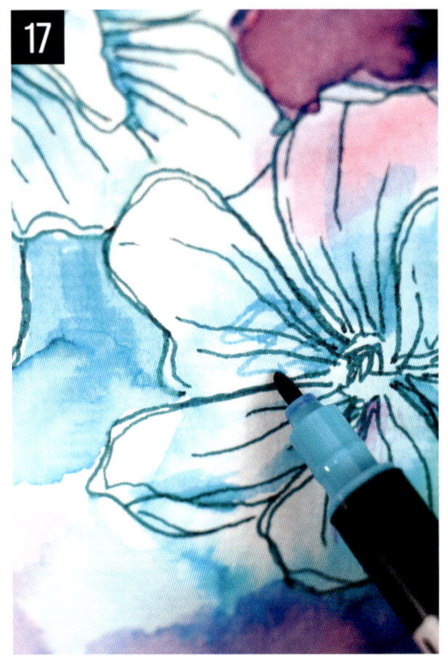

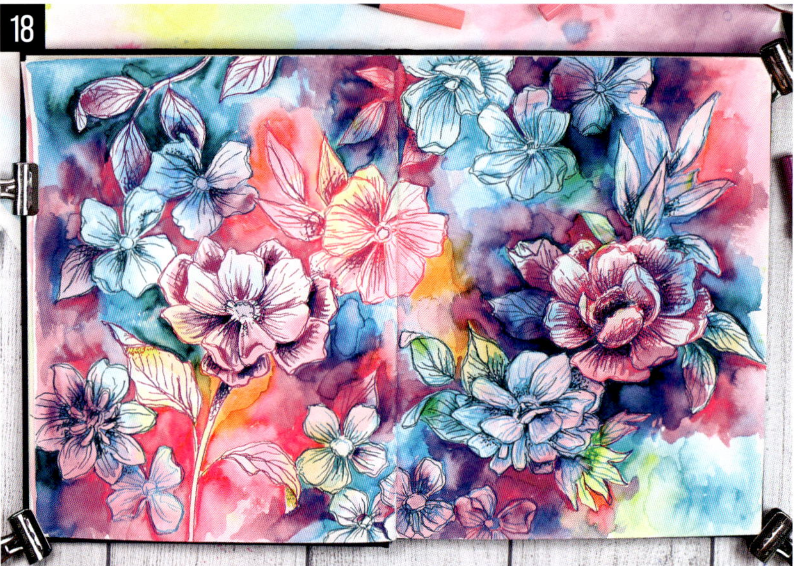

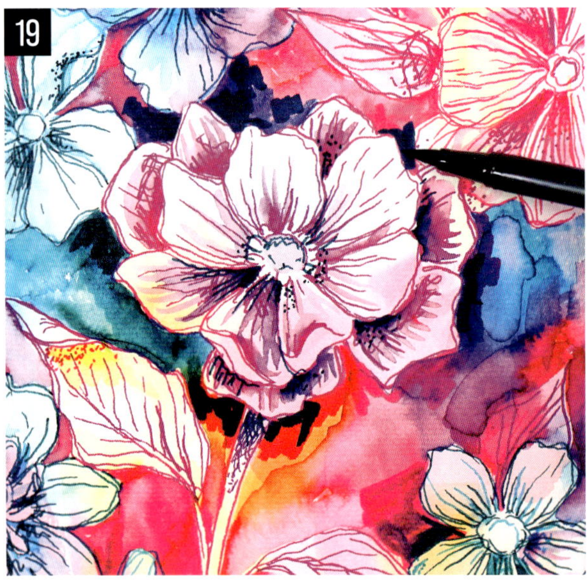

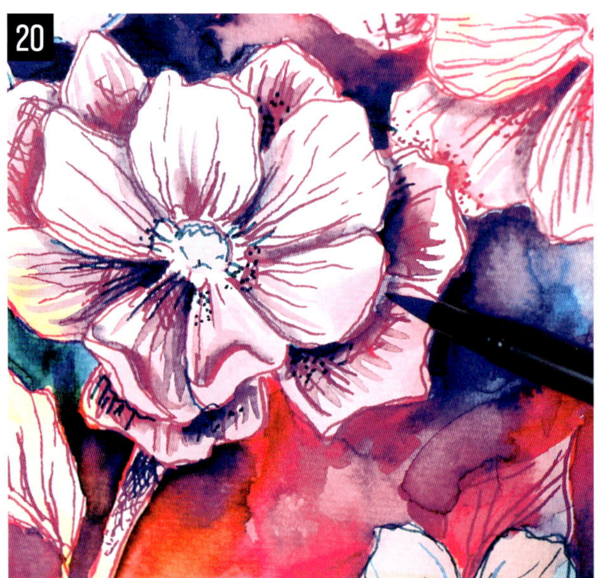

17 **Try scribbling.** This is my personal favorite! Just like with cross-hatching and stippling, scribble more and tighter marks for darker values and fade out by decreasing the amount of scribbling.

18 **Add this dimension throughout your flowers.** Find the areas in your flowers and leaves that could use the extra push of these three mark-making techniques.

19 **Assess the "pop."** Step back for a moment to assess your piece. Look for areas in the negative space that, if darkened further, could bring out your positive space even more. Add color in those areas and blend it using a paintbrush and water.

20 **Add edge shadows and final details.** Just as you did in "Freestyle Floral Doodling," choose a lighter, more neutral color and add shading around areas that need just a bit more dimension. I've chosen a very light violet for this purpose. At this point, also add a bit of darker color to the center of each main flower. And that's it! You've completed your second funky floral.

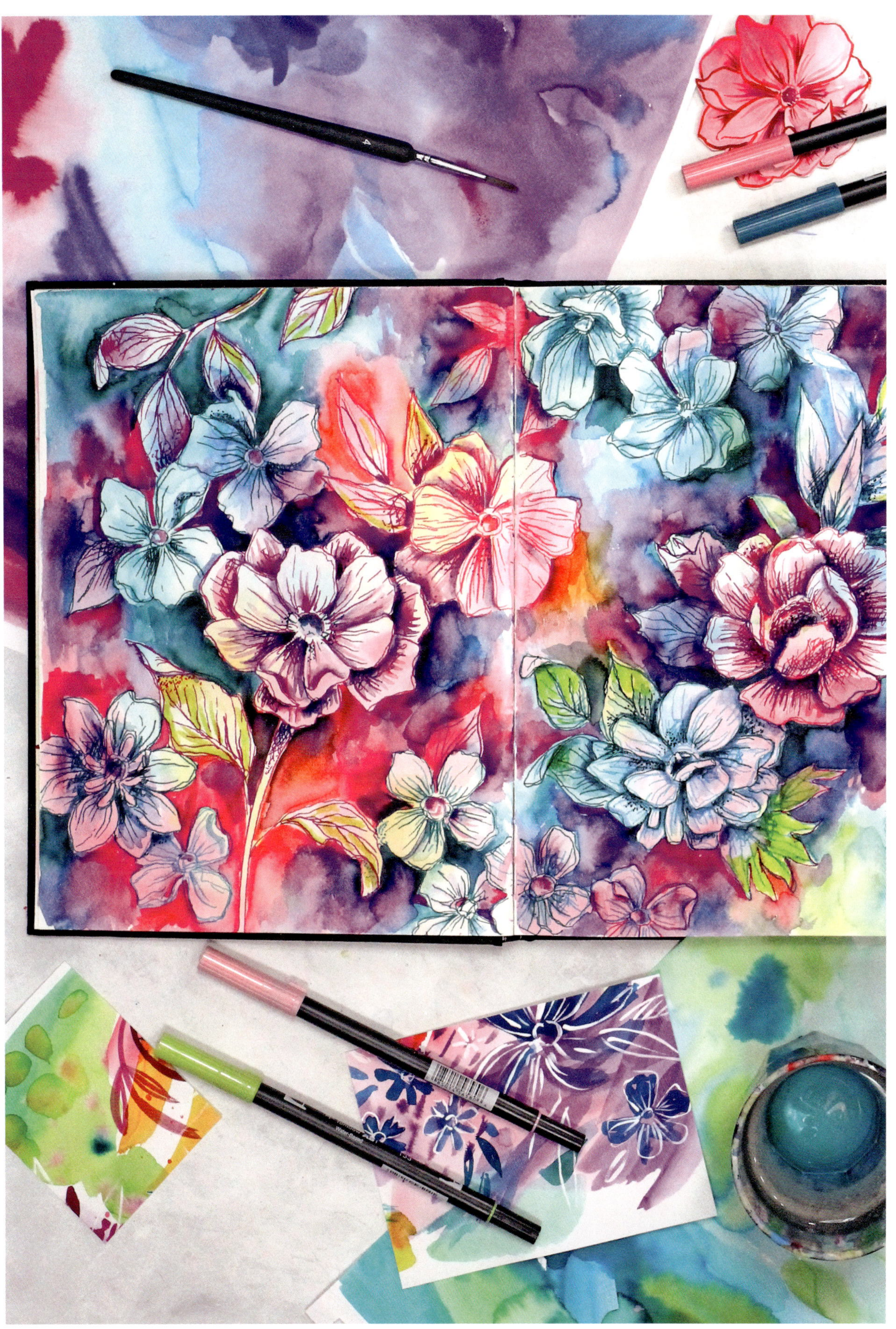

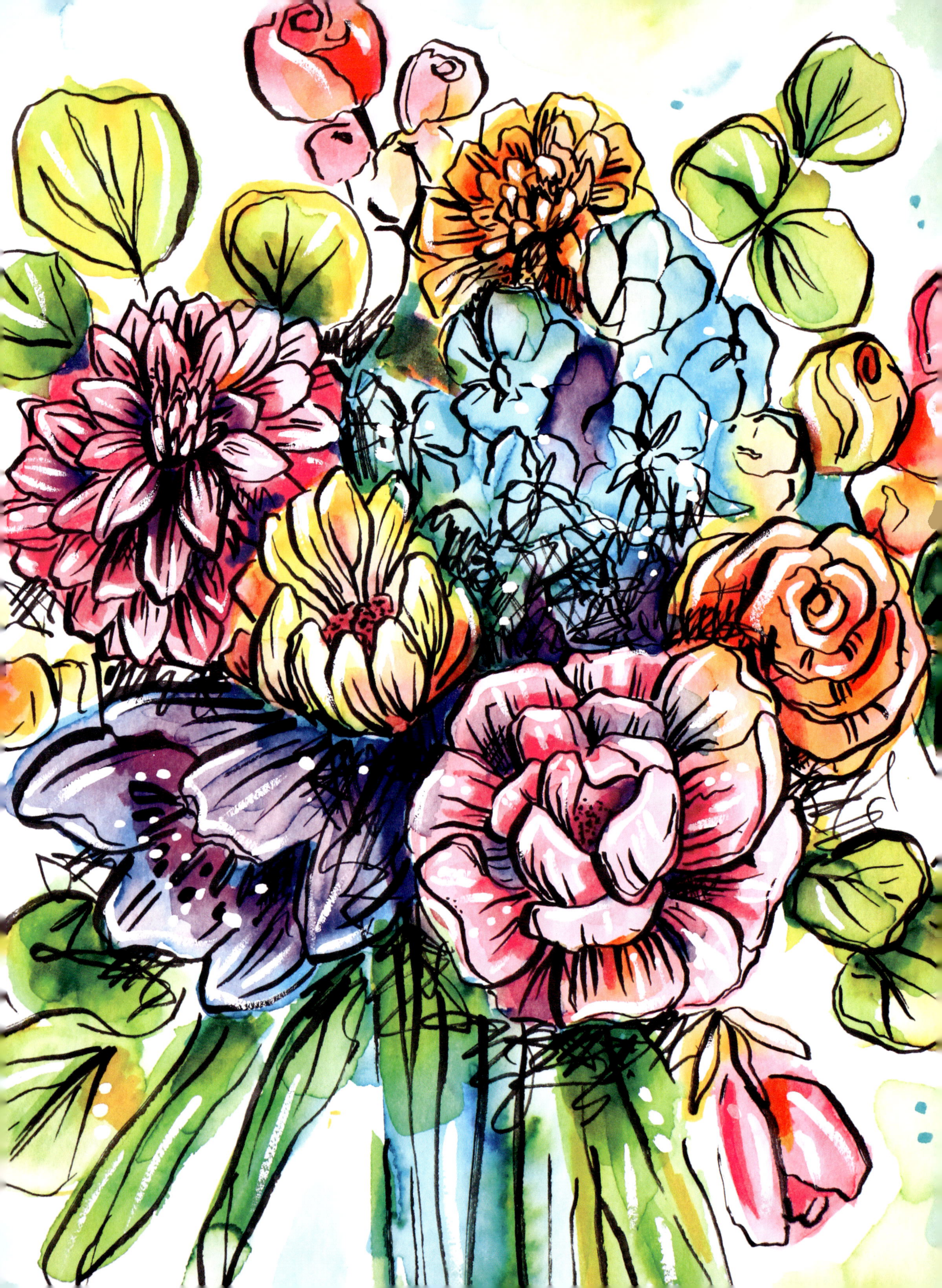

Joyful Bouquet with a Limited Palette

Learn to create a piece with a limited color palette of water-based markers and add white highlights

In my dream world, I would have beautiful, fresh bouquets of colorful flowers in every room of the house each and every day. Sigh. Wouldn't that be lovely and inspiring? I'm smiling just picturing it. But . . . I don't. So, painting beautiful bouquets will have to suffice on those days that my vases are empty. Thankfully, painting flowers is even more enjoyable for me than having real ones around the house! So, on that note, it's time to paint a happy bouquet with washy, gorgeous colors. In this piece, we are going to use a floral arrangement to inspire our composition. This can be a real bouquet or a photo of one (and the photo makes things even simpler).

Speaking of simple, it's time to challenge ourselves by simplifying our color palette! Although I have a no-rules approach to creating, it is still a good idea to push ourselves and get outside our comfort zone. This will always lead to growth and discoveries. My natural tendency is to use ALL. THE. COLORS—and while that is freeing, it also feels great to do the opposite sometimes. Therefore, for this project, I challenge you to choose just three markers. I have chosen three that I'm very familiar with—a pink, light turquoise, and yellow. Make your choices and let's go!

Tools & Supplies

- Three water-based markers (preferably dual-brush pens with both fine and medium tips)
- Black marker
- White acrylic paint
- Sizes 0, 3, and 5 round paintbrushes (or your choice of an extra-small, a small, and a medium brush)
- Water
- Bouquet of flowers or photo of a bouquet
- Watercolor paper, mixed-media paper, or Bristol board
- Tracing paper or plain white printer paper

What You'll Learn

CHALLENGE YOURSELF: Limiting your color palette is one good way to challenge yourself. It happens to be a big method for me, but as you'll see as we get further into the book, there are all sorts of ways to step out of your routine and see what happens.

SIMPLIFY: As a more-is-more artist, this could sound boring if I didn't view it as a challenge. But you will be surprised by what you can do with a simplified palette, simplified shapes, or a simplified composition.

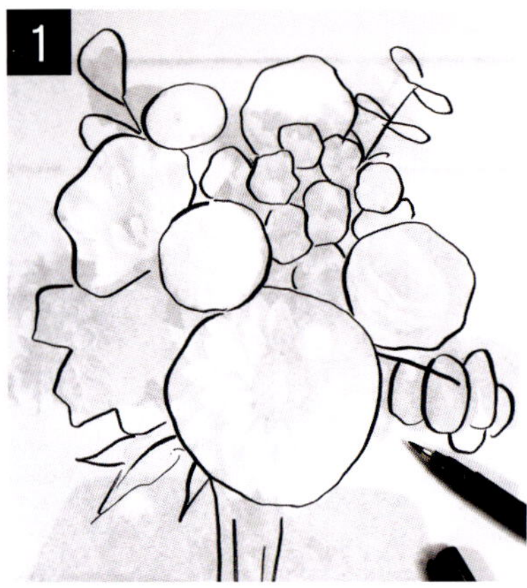

1 **Copy the shapes of the bouquet.** Print out a photo of a bouquet and trace it onto tracing paper, tracing just a very basic composition of simple shapes that are devoid of any detail. (If you have chosen a real bouquet as your reference, freehand draw the shapes instead). Once you have captured the main composition, put the image or bouquet aside. We'll be using our imagination to create the flowers in more detail.

2 **Create a color sketch.** Referencing your tracing sketch, roughly freehand outline the shapes of your sketch on your final paper in color, then scribble rough patches of color inside the shapes. You can layer some colors right on top of others.

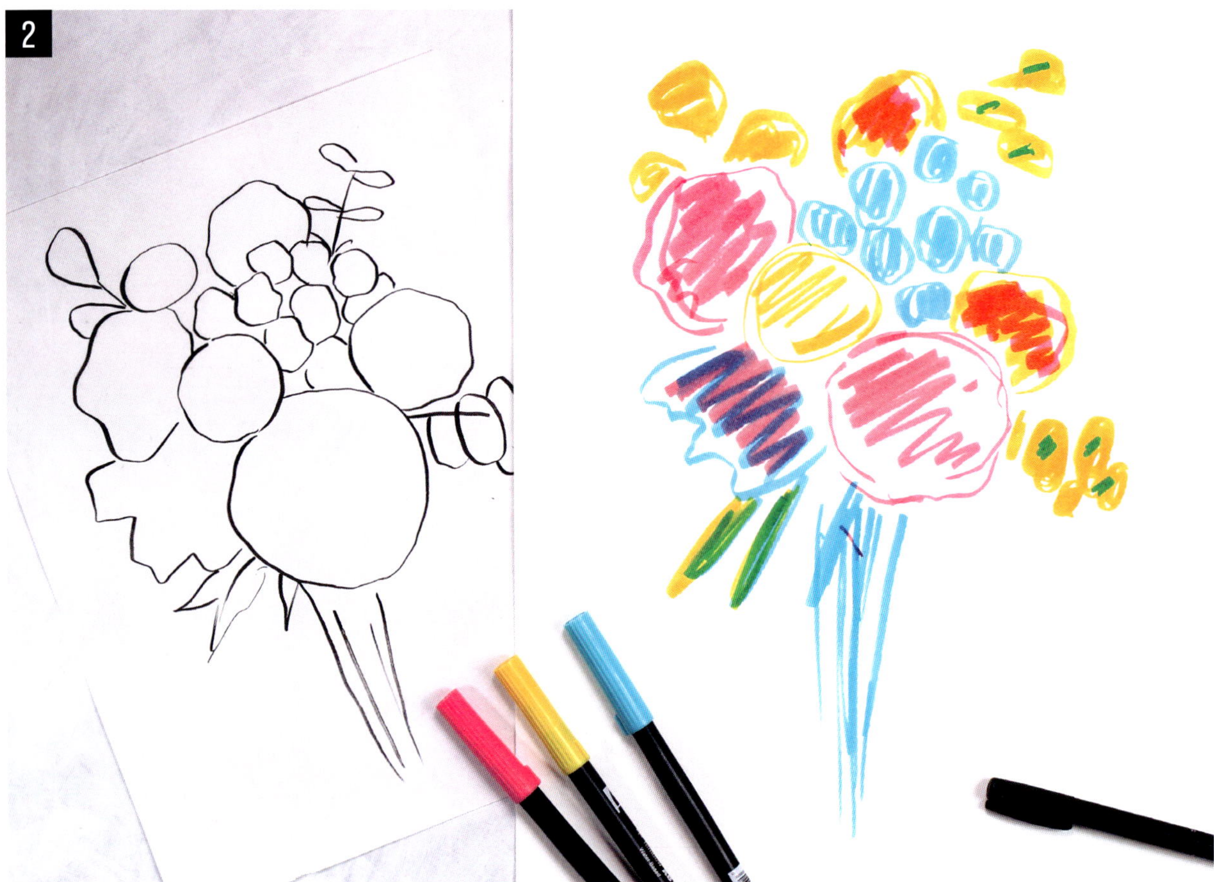

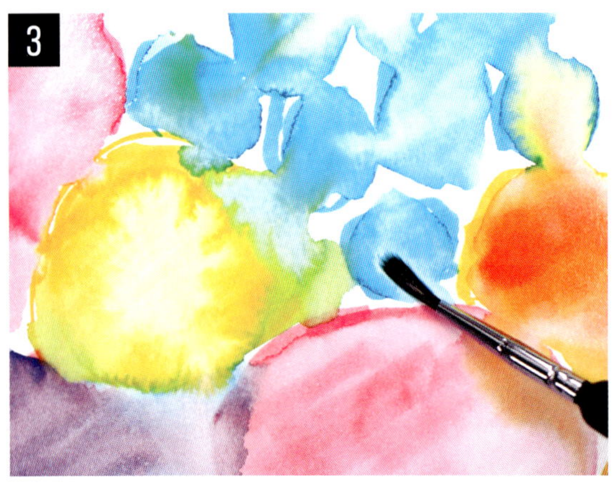

3 **Blend the colors.** Wash over your flowers with your larger paintbrush and water. As in previous projects, aim to create beautiful pools of color. If you do not want the colors to blend together in particular spots, keep the watery edges of each shape from touching. I, however, do not mind the occasional happy accident that comes with colors bleeding into one another, so I am not very careful!

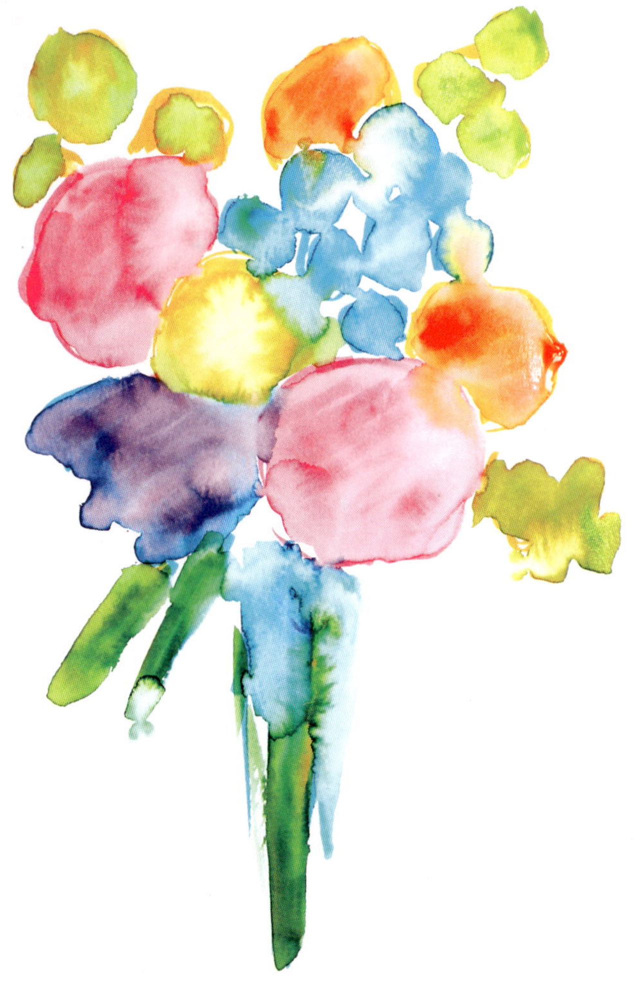

4 Allow to dry. Allow the colors to dry naturally. At this point you will have a lovely abstract representation of the bouquet. It's time to add detail!

5 Start drawing flowers. Use what you learned in "Freestyle Floral Doodling" and "Washy Negative Space" to direct your flower drawing, combining drawing black lines with variations in weight with using expressive mark-making. Try holding your pen in a relaxed manner to achieve loose, wandering lines that imitate the loose, flowy base colors.

6 Cover the entire bouquet with drawn flowers. You can draw your flowers from your imagination or reference your bouquet—it's up to you. Continue drawing until you've drawn on top of all the main shapes of your bouquet.

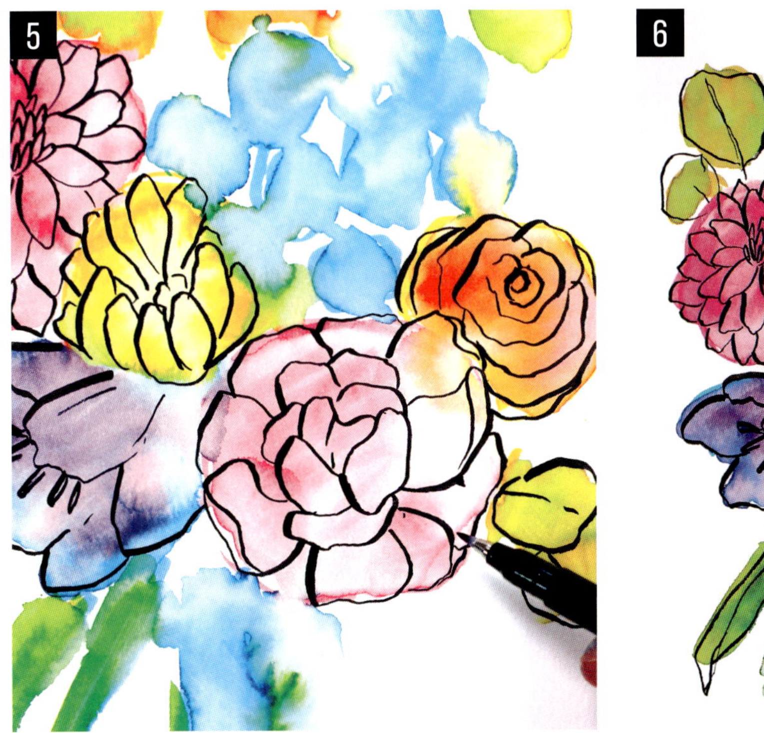

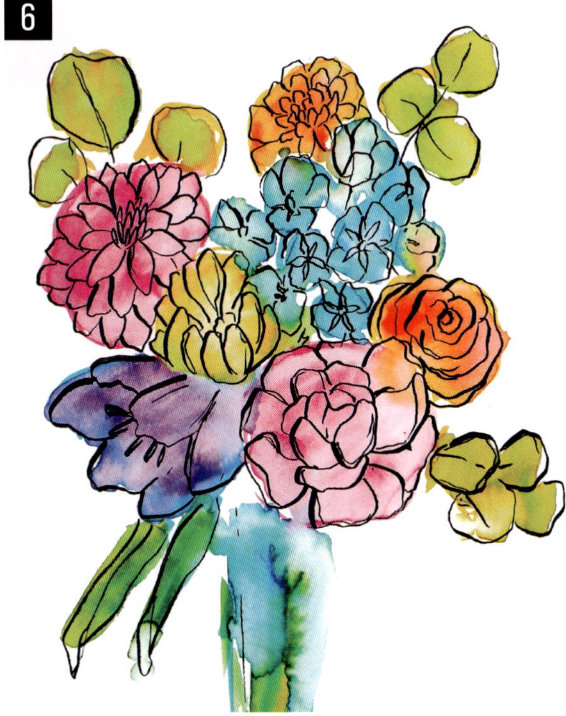

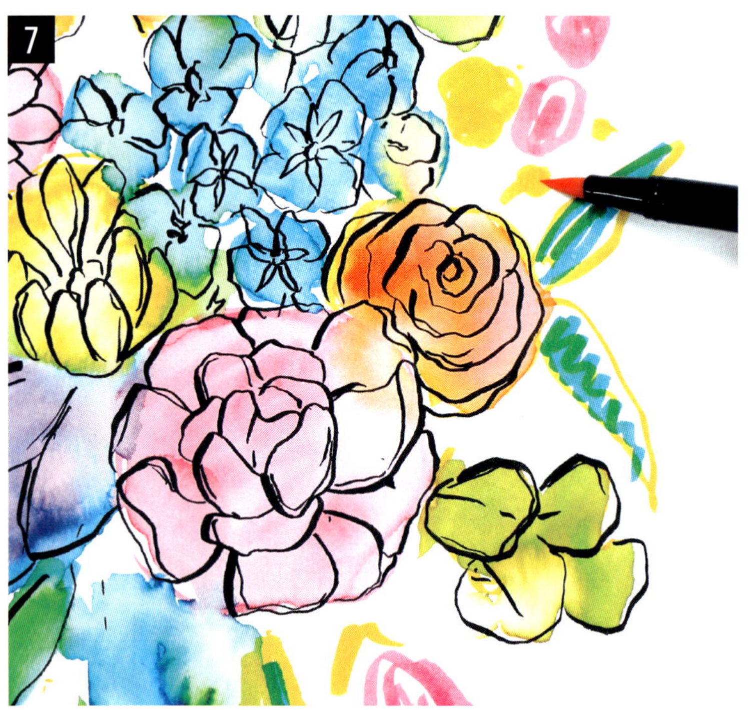

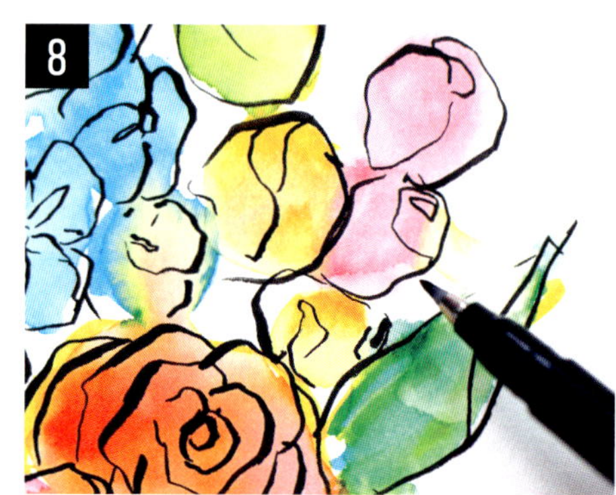

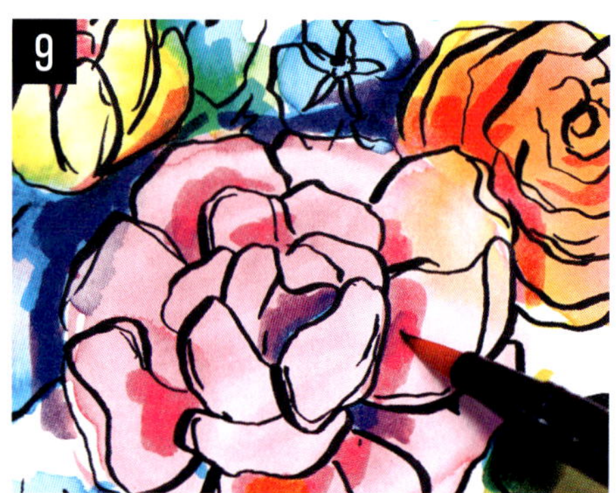

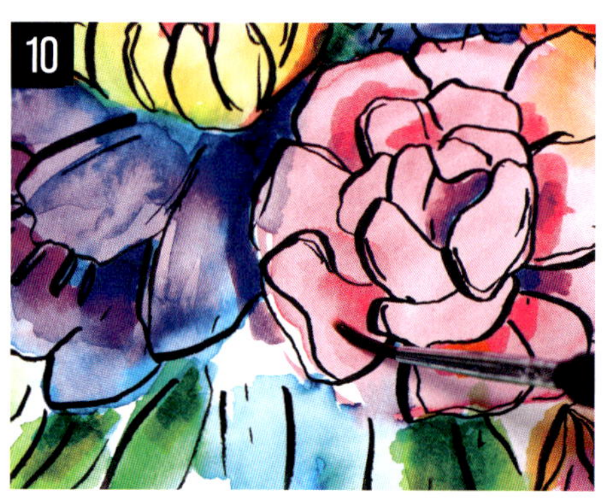

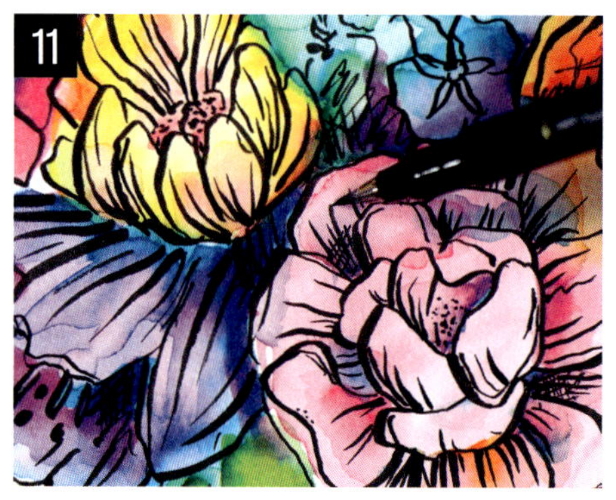

7 **Add more colored flowers.** Assess your bouquet and decide if you'd like to add more flowers or leaves. To do so, make some scribbly shapes that float right outside the existing flowers, then blend them with water.

8 **Draw in the added flowers and leaves.** Once the newly blended flowers have dried, go back in and add black linework as you did with the initial flowers.

9 **Add shading.** Now that the bouquet's shape is more defined, begin to add shading within and around flowers using your markers. I do not have a color in my limited palette that is very dark in value, but by adding layers of marker on top of the washy colors, I can still create deeper values that I will push back even further with my black pen in a following step.

10 **Blend the shading.** Use your smaller paintbrush and water to wash and blend these shaded areas. Add more color as you see fit in areas that are still dry, and blend those in as well.

11 **Add linework details.** Using your black marker, add linework details in the florals and leaves. Experiment with the stippling, scribbling, or cross-hatching techniques you learned in "Washy Negative Space," or simply rely on varying your line weights to continue building up dimension.

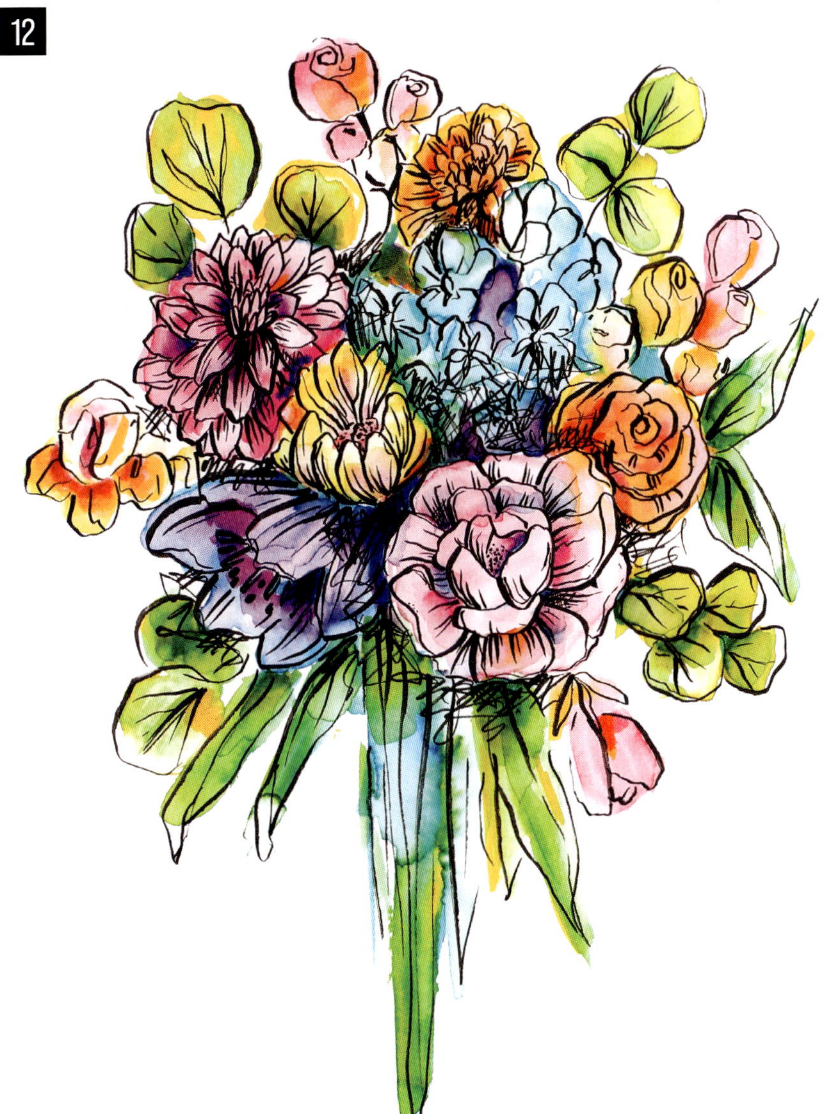

12 **Scribble in the areas you want to really shadow.** Use messy black scribbles to push certain areas really far into the background, such as I've done between the central flowers here.

13 **Add color patches to the background.** Select a color or two from your palette and scribble small patches throughout the background. When deciding what colors to use, think about which of the flowers in your composition you want to stand out the most. My pink, orange, and yellow flowers are most prominent, so I used blues and yellows (as well as blended blue-greens) in the background to contrast those further.

14 **Blend the background.** Using your larger paintbrush and water, blend the colors in your background. Leave a white halo uncolored between the blended background and the bouquet (foreground).

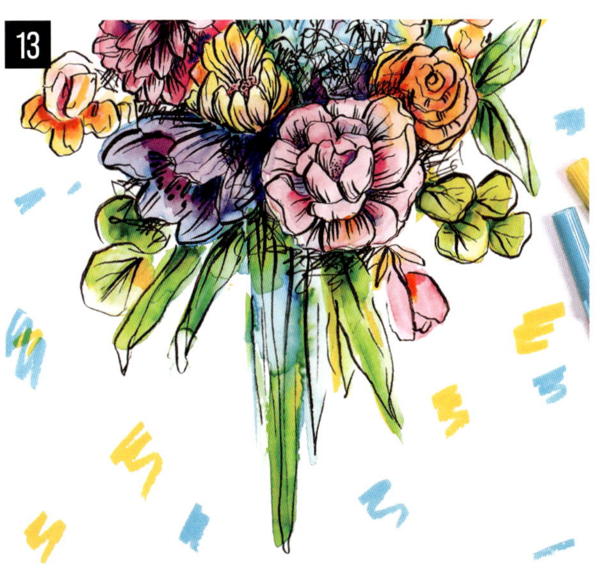

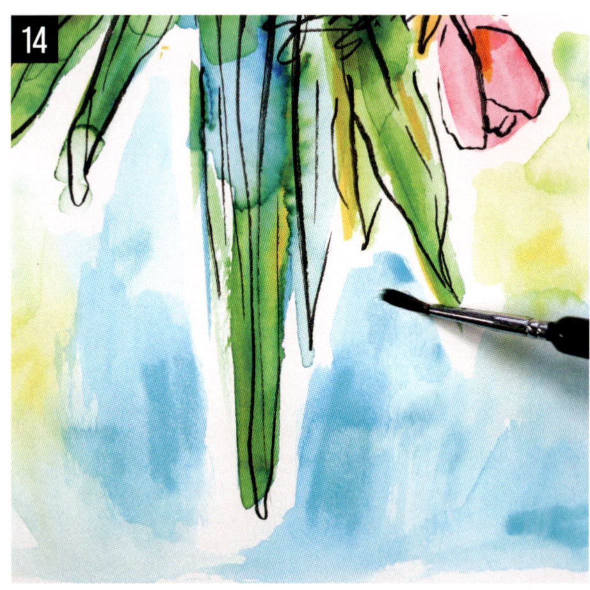

15 Add white details.

It's time to break out your white paint! Using your small paintbrush, add white highlights to your florals and leaves. Think about what areas you want to stand out, and add white highlights to these areas. If you are using a bleed-proof white, as I am, the white will remain completely opaque when you apply it; if you are using acrylic paint or a white gel pen, you may experience some bleeding that will decrease the opacity of the white. Both looks are perfectly nice!

16 Assess your work.

Step back from the piece to assess it. If possible, take an actual break and come back to the piece with fresh eyes. What do you feel? Do you sense the piece is complete, or do you see something it needs? I decided to add two things. First, using my pink markers, I added just a bit more color to my pink flowers to give them more of a saturated, bold look.

17 Add finishing touches.

Then, using my turquoise marker, I added a few messy dots outside the bouquet. This is something so small, but I instinctively felt it could help give the bouquet just a bit more energy and movement. Once I made these final adjustments, I was ready to call it complete!

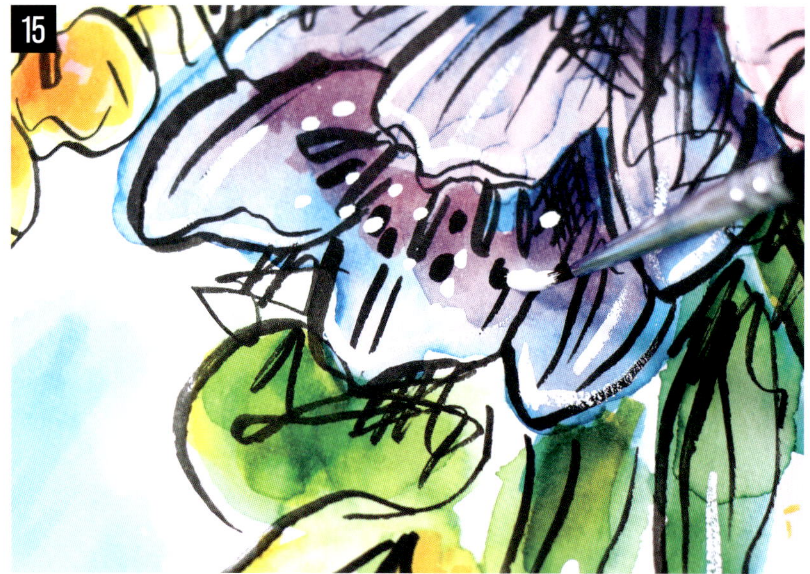

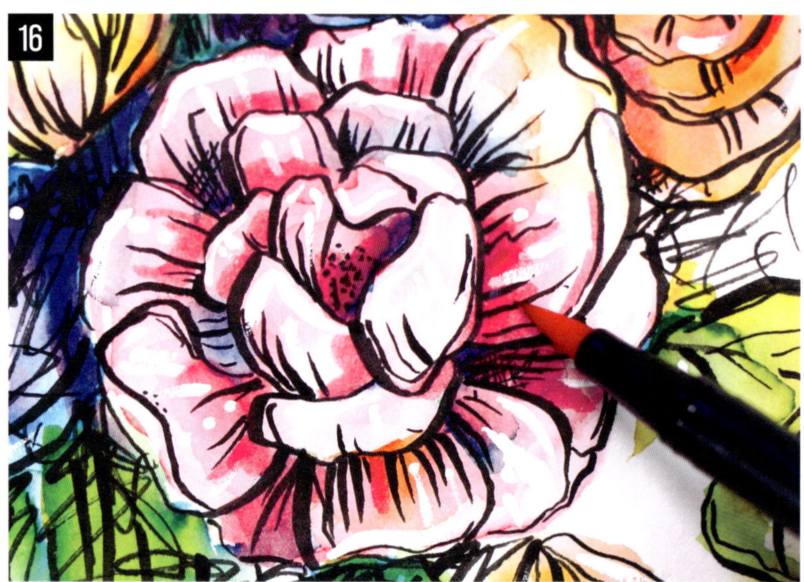

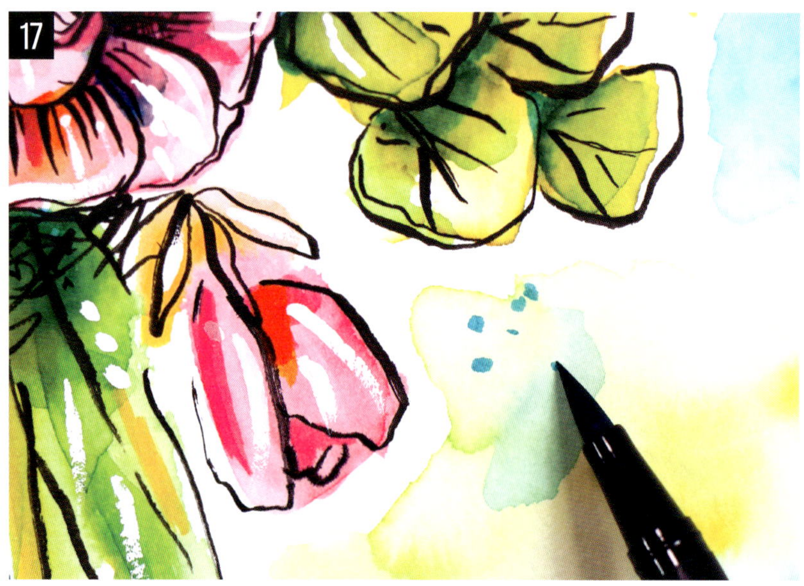

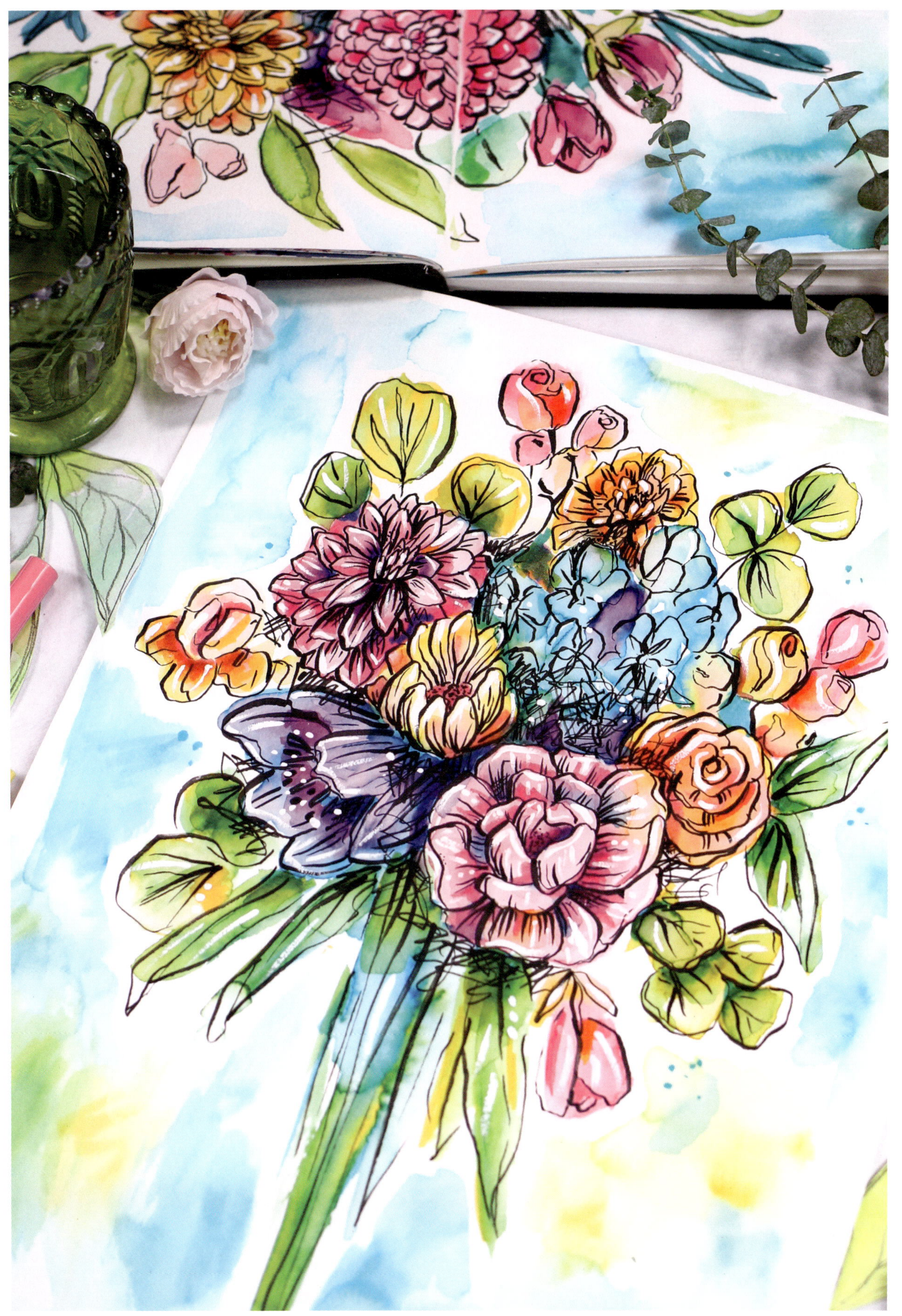

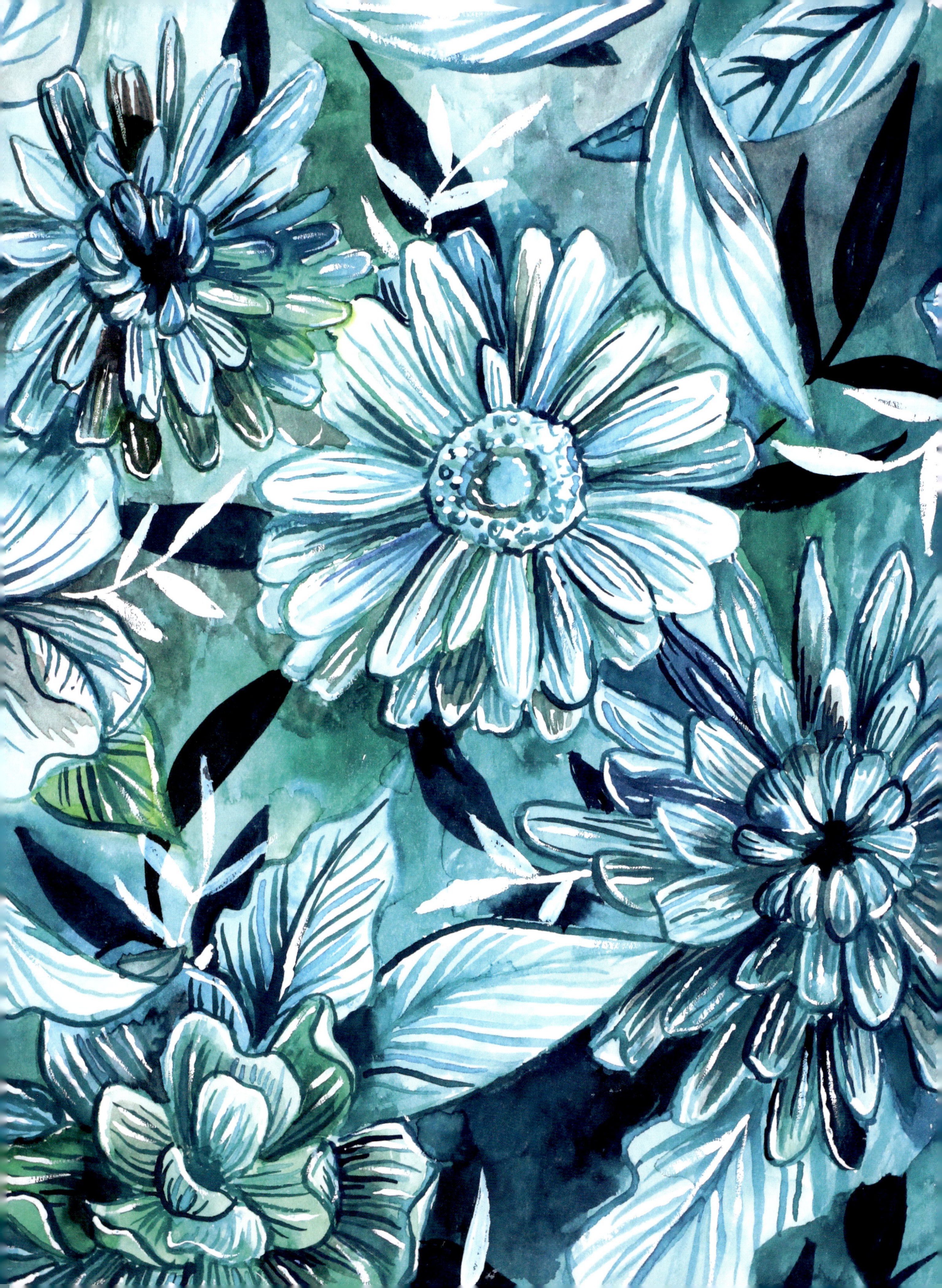

Monochromatic Wanderings

*Learn to create a monochromatic design
using exclusively watercolors*

It's time to set aside our markers and bring out the watercolors; I want us to shift and start leaning toward painting mode. But we are only going a few steps in that direction—we will use paint and a brush, but we'll keep a foot over in drawing mode. Drawing . . . with paint!

"But using paint and a brush means we are painting!" you may protest. It doesn't have to mean that! Drawing is simply making lines and marks with a tool. It can be pencil, pen, chalk, or even a stick dipped in ink . . . or it could be with paint and a brush. Drawing is a mindset. We will shift fully into painting mode soon enough, but for now, keep a piece of your brain over in drawing world.

For this project, we are going to continue challenging ourselves by simplifying our supplies even further, all the way down to just one color. I want you to see the endless possibilities in creating this way. We are also going to take a new path as we create by working from left to right (or right to left if you're a lefty). Why? Because the more we try, the more we discover. This may help you dig deeper into mindfulness as you create.

Tools & Supplies

- ▶ Watercolors in one main hue plus its opposite/complement (for example, blues and blue-greens plus orange or red-orange)
- ▶ White acrylic paint
- ▶ Size 00, 1, and 4 round paintbrushes (or your choice of an extra-small, a small, and a medium brush)
- ▶ Water
- ▶ Watercolor paper, mixed-media paper, or Bristol board

What You'll Learn

CONTRAST: As we discussed earlier in the "Composition" section, contrast uses differences to draw attention and excitement to a piece. We will be pushing the contrast in value to achieve this by using just one hue.

PUSHING COLOR TO ITS LIMITS: While we will be using just one hue, that hue holds practically limitless possibilities. Using a main hue of blue-green, you can create so many varieties of color by slightly changing the value and intensity. Blue-green can become just a tiny bit greener or a tiny bit bluer with a subtle change in the mix. It can also become duller and less intense by adding its complement. We will push our one hue as far as possible, giving us as many options as possible within the confines of a monochromatic color scheme.

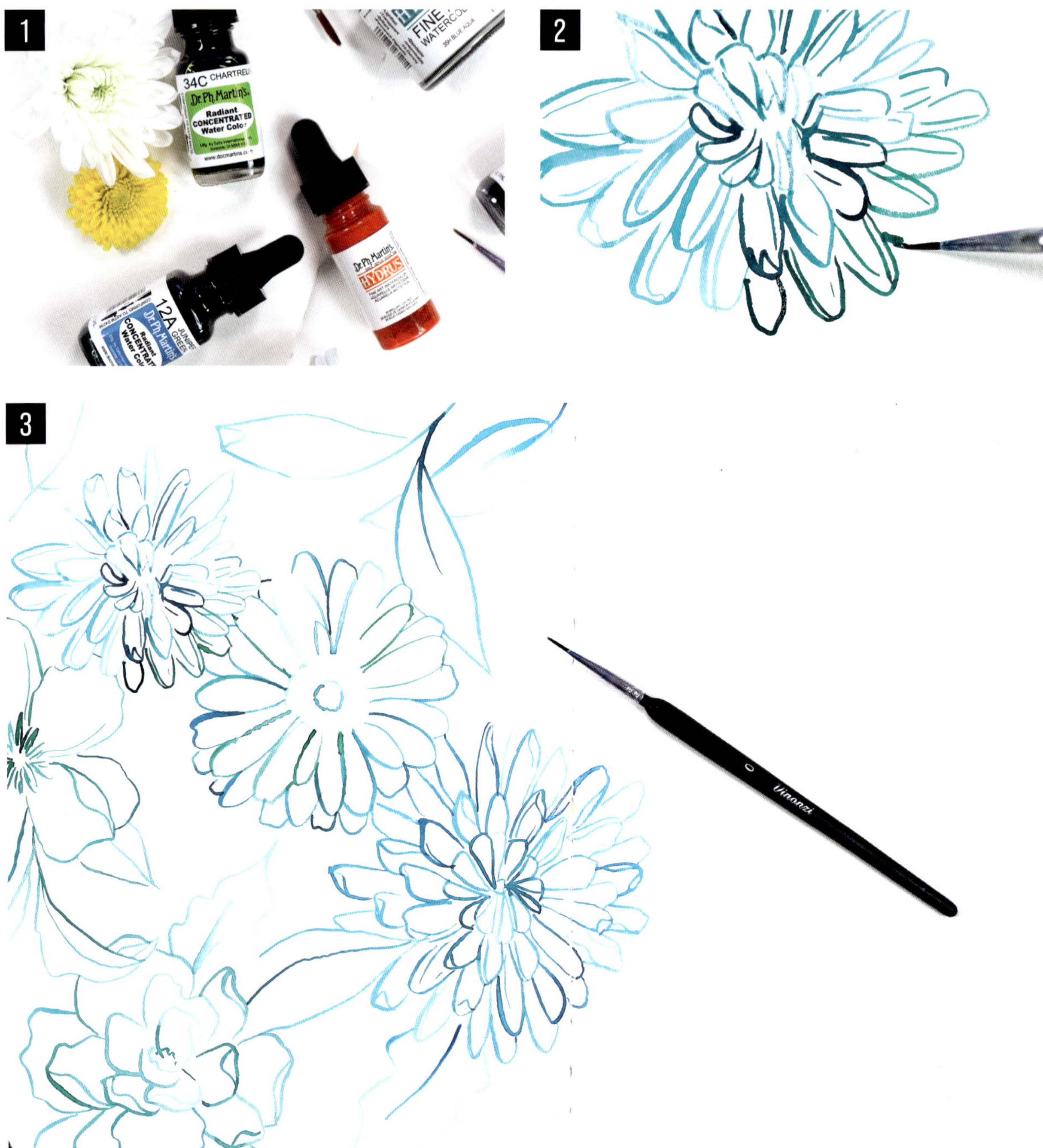

1 **Choose your raw colors.** Choose your hue and correlating watercolors. While we are only using one hue as our main color, that still leaves you with many possibilities in terms of color, value, and intensity. I am using turquoise (or blue-green) as my main hue, so I am including a blue and a green to mix in and stretch my color. Then, I'll also have my hue's opposite, which is a red-orange. When you select your colors, refer to the color wheel. For another example, if you choose red as your main hue, you can lean toward orange for a red-orange or toward blue for a red-violet and then include the opposite of red, which is green.

2 **Start "drawing."** Mix your watercolors. Begin on the left-hand side of your paper (or right-hand side if you're a lefty) and start doodling in your flowers with your paintbrush and watercolors. Just as you've done in the previous projects, create a mix of shapes and sizes. Dip into the different variations of your chosen hue within single flowers.

3 **Keep moving across the page.** Leave room between your florals for negative space in some places and overlap your flowers and leaves in other places.

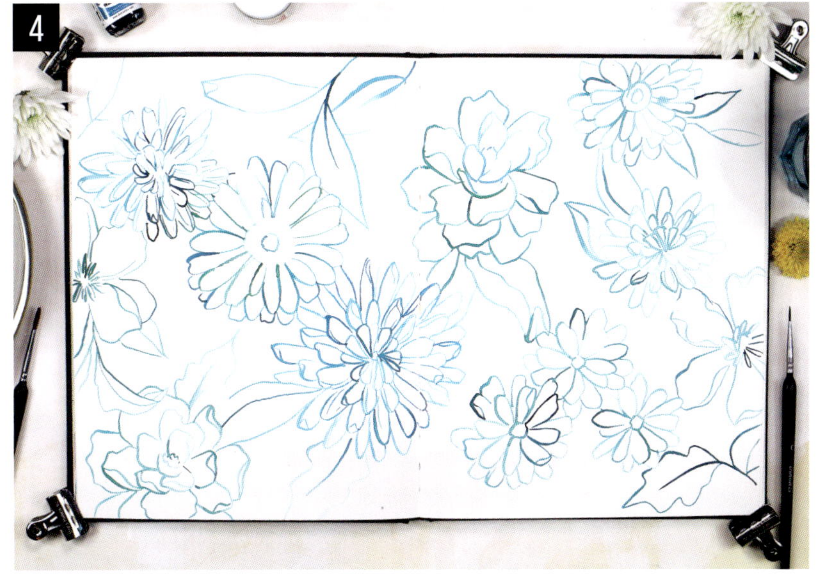

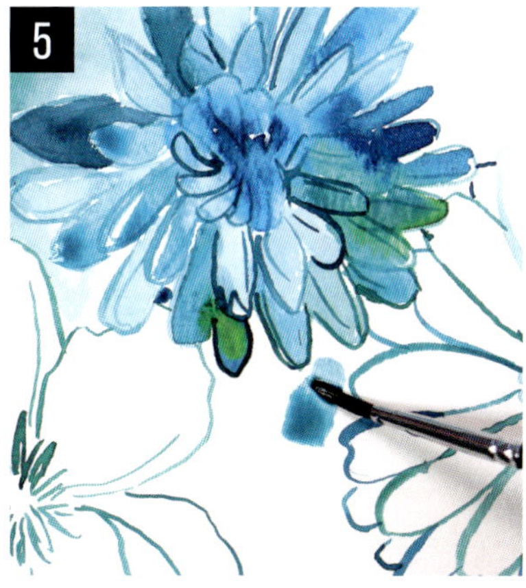

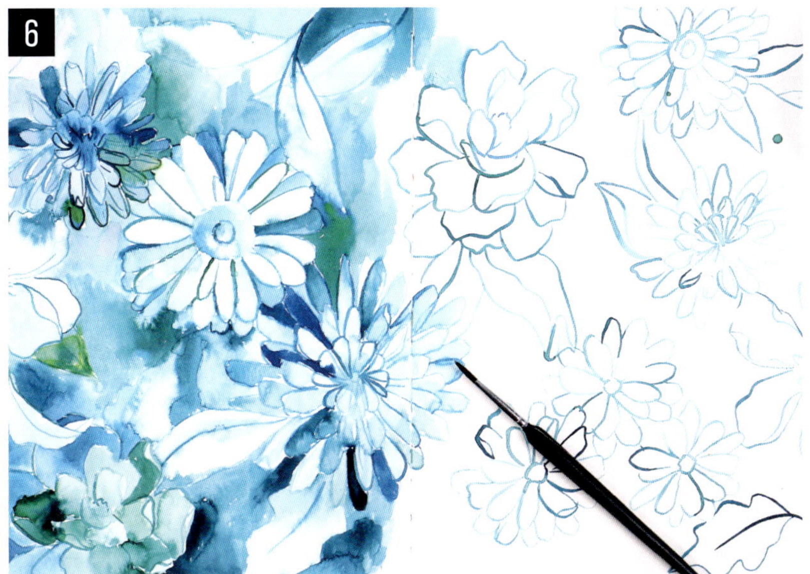

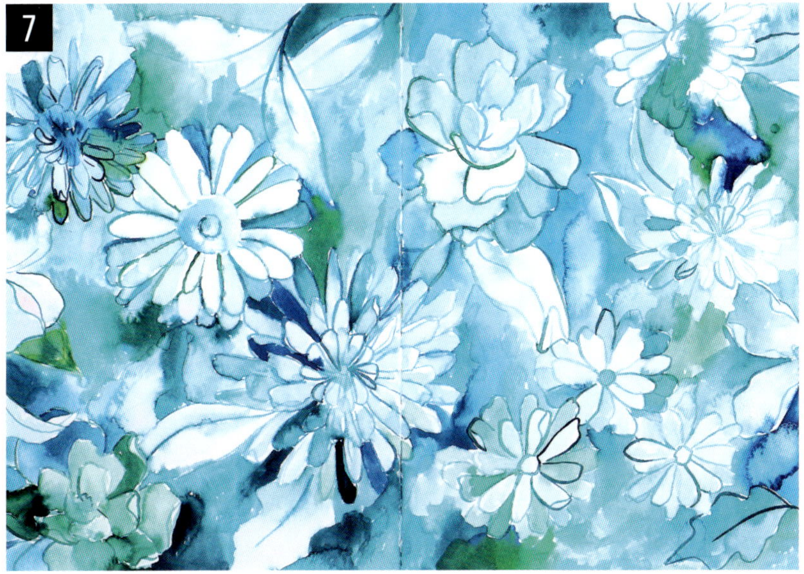

4 Finish filling the page.
Continue moving across until
the paper is full of flowers and
leaves, as shown. As you draw
from left to right, you don't have
to be strict about not going back
in the direction you came; you
can go back and add in petals
or small flowers as you go. Just
be sure to keep the general
movement going in one direction
rather than hopping all around.

**5 Start filling in the flowers
and background.** Once the
page is filled with line drawings,
move back to the starting side
and begin filling in every spot
with color.

6 Leave no white spaces. The
goal for this piece is to leave
no white paper showing, but
that means you can have very
light values of color in some
places. With watercolors, the
more water and the less pigment
you use, the lighter your values
will be. The more pigment and
less water you use, the deeper
your values will be. Layering color
on top of color will also deepen
your values.

**7 Continue filling in the
composition.** Keep going until
you've filled all the spaces.
Embrace the mess—you will
have bleeding and begin to lose
some definition in your linework,
but not only will we be bringing
back the definition in a future
step, but the gorgeous washes
that happen by their own only
add to the beauty.

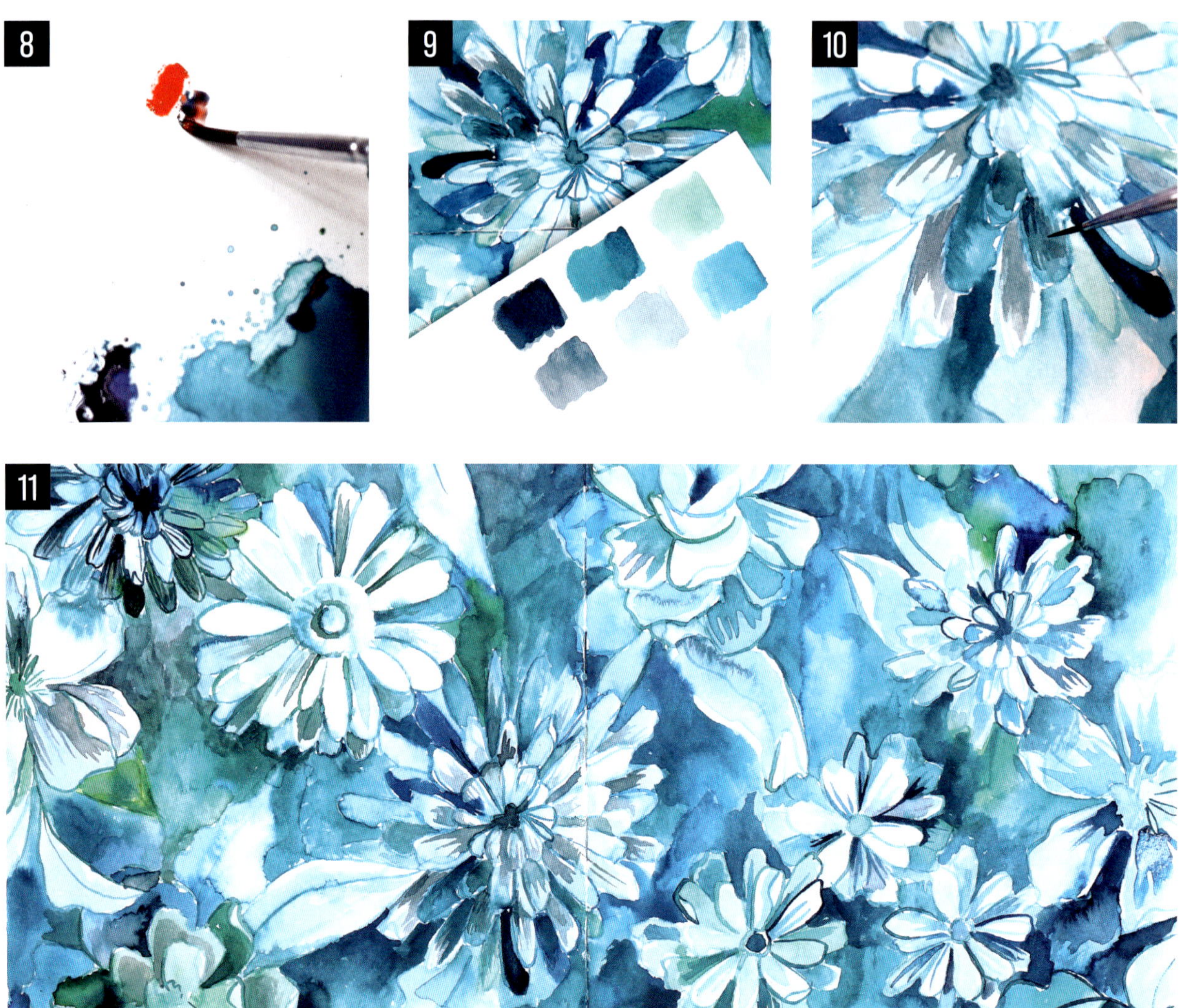

Don't be afraid of "ugly" colors. Maybe you personally don't find any colors ugly, but even so,
you probably know what I mean. Muddy browns and dull colors can be a bright color's biggest helpmate!
We'll explore this further in "Transformative Contrast."

8 **Prepare to mix duller shades.** It's time to start building up the dimension in this piece. This is when we will begin using the complementary color to create some duller intensities of our dominant hue. Since we are not using black, the complementary color will also help us create deeper, darker values—we can achieve values that are one step shy of black by mixing complementary colors together. My main hue is a blue-green, so I will use red-orange for my complement.

9 **Practice and compare mixes.** On a separate piece of paper, practice mixing opposite colors together to get the hang of mixing colors of less intensity and darker value.

10 **Use the duller shades to build dimension.** With your duller shades, add shading to petals that are behind others. This will begin to enhance the dimension in the flowers by pushing those petals back. To fade these shadows, try using soft lines instead of blending as you pull away from these areas of deeper color. Add duller and deeper shades to the negative space to push those areas further back as well.

11 **Continue using duller shades across the piece.** Continue building up dimension as you move across the page, creating duller hues to push back both the petals and leaves beneath others, as well as the negative space.

12 **Go back in to add detail.** It's time to clean this thing up! Use your brightest color to add linework and definition to your petals and leaves. Add darker and/or thicker lines in some areas where you'd like more contrast.

13 **Keep adding detail.** Continue moving across the page, adding linework to all your flowers and leaves.

14 **Add dark leaves and vines.** Let's revisit the negative space. Use your darkest values to create simple silhouettes of leaves and vines behind the flowers. This adds to the beautiful, washy layers you've already created and gives the piece even more dimension.

15 **Build in layers if needed.** Depending on your watercolors, it may require two or more layers to create values as deep as what you're seeing here. This is one reason I adore concentrated watercolors—I can achieve these deep values much more quickly.

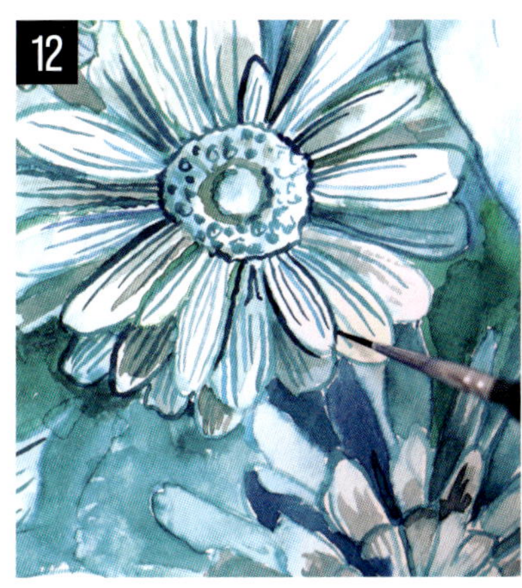

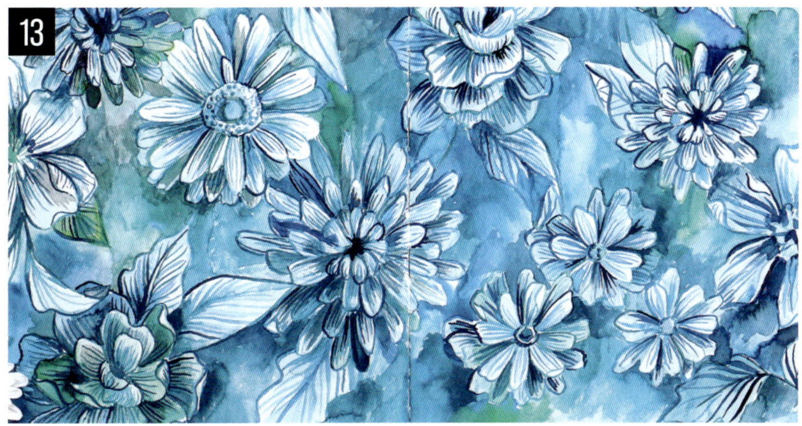

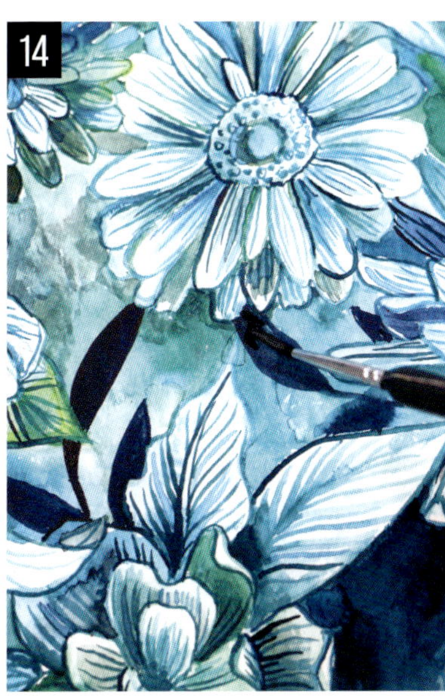

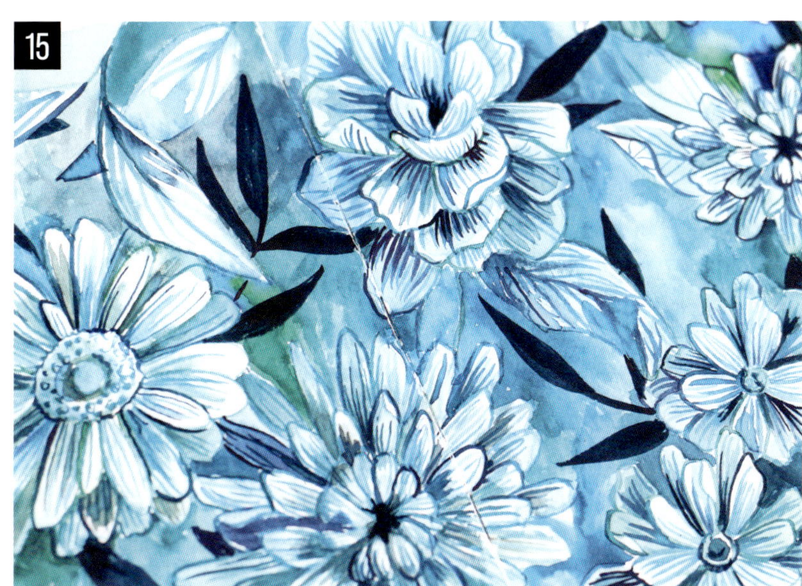

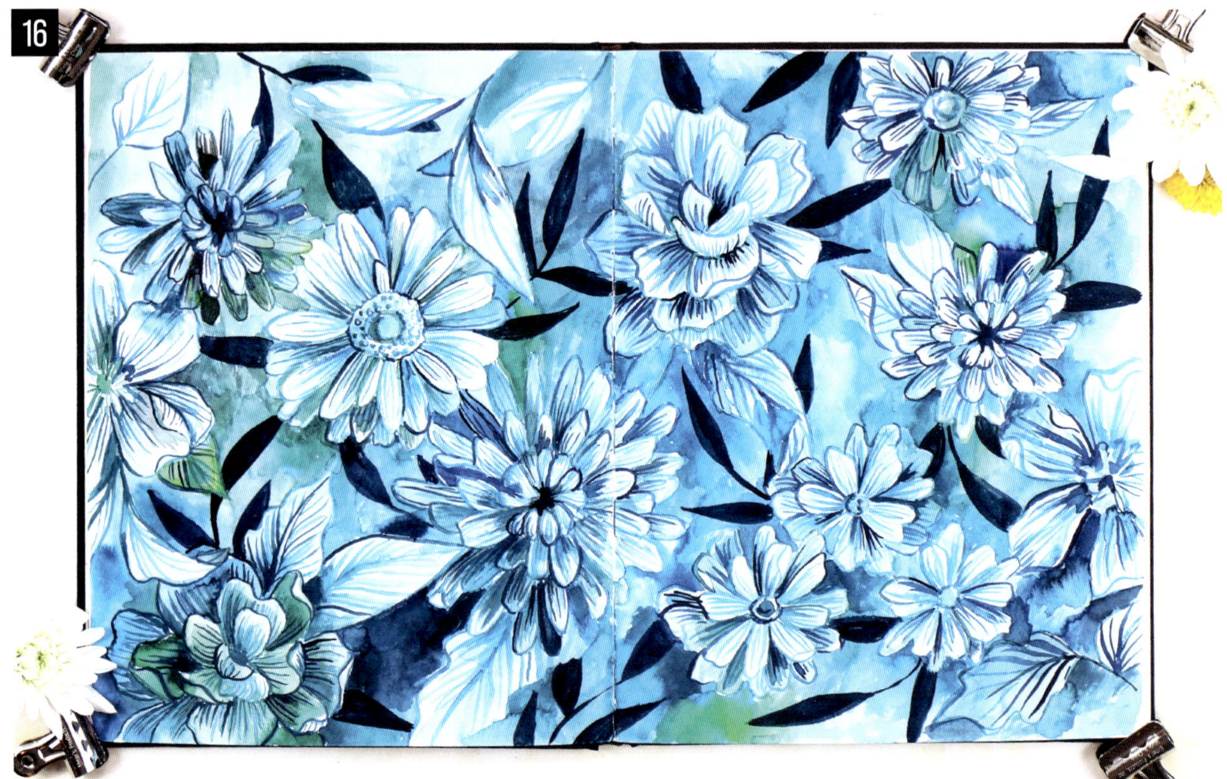

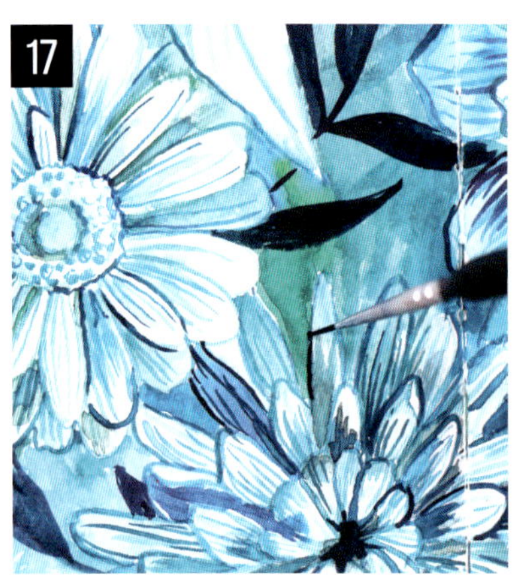

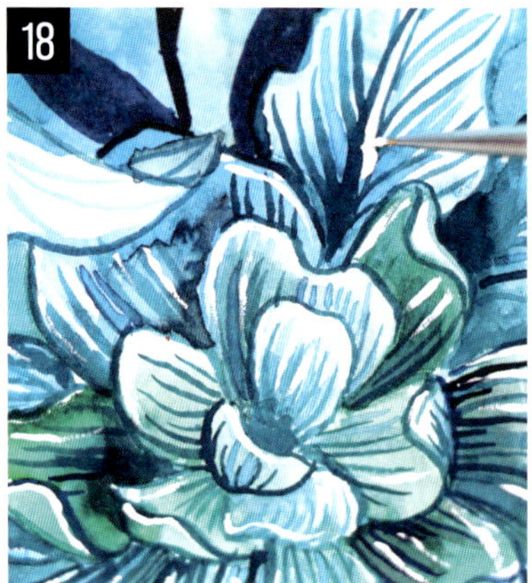

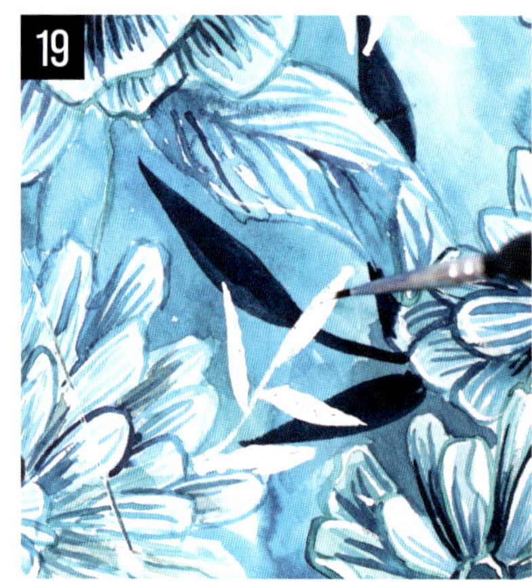

16 **Finish adding dark shapes.** Continue incorporating these silhouettes across the entire piece, allowing them to peek out from behind flowers and pass beneath leaves.

17 **Assess and add final dark details.** Take one more stroll through the piece to add additional linework. Step away, leave the room for a few minutes, and come back with fresh eyes. I see just a few petals and leaves I'd like to sharpen up.

18 **Add white highlights.** Let's get out that white now! This piece is about to burst with life. Using the best white you have, revisit all your flowers and leaves to add white linework and highlights. I like to address the outside tips of the petals, especially those that are similar in value to the negative space around them, to bring them forward a bit.

19 **Add white leaves.** More is more! Revisit your negative space to add small silhouettes of leaves and vines in white. After this step, I'm done with my piece, but you may want to add more linework, push areas of negative space even further back, or bring out more white highlights. This is your piece, so it's up to you to decide if my last step is your last step as well.

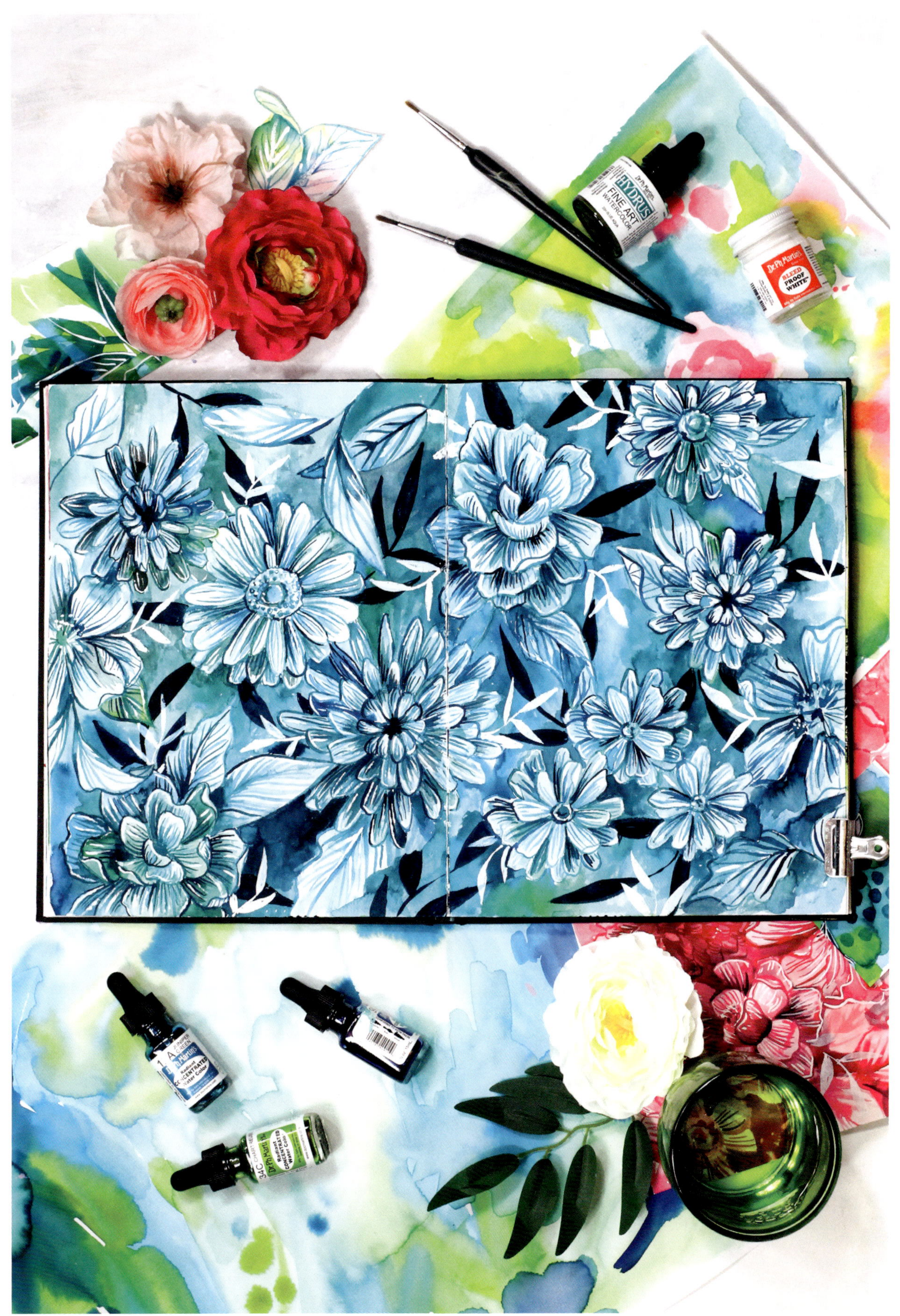

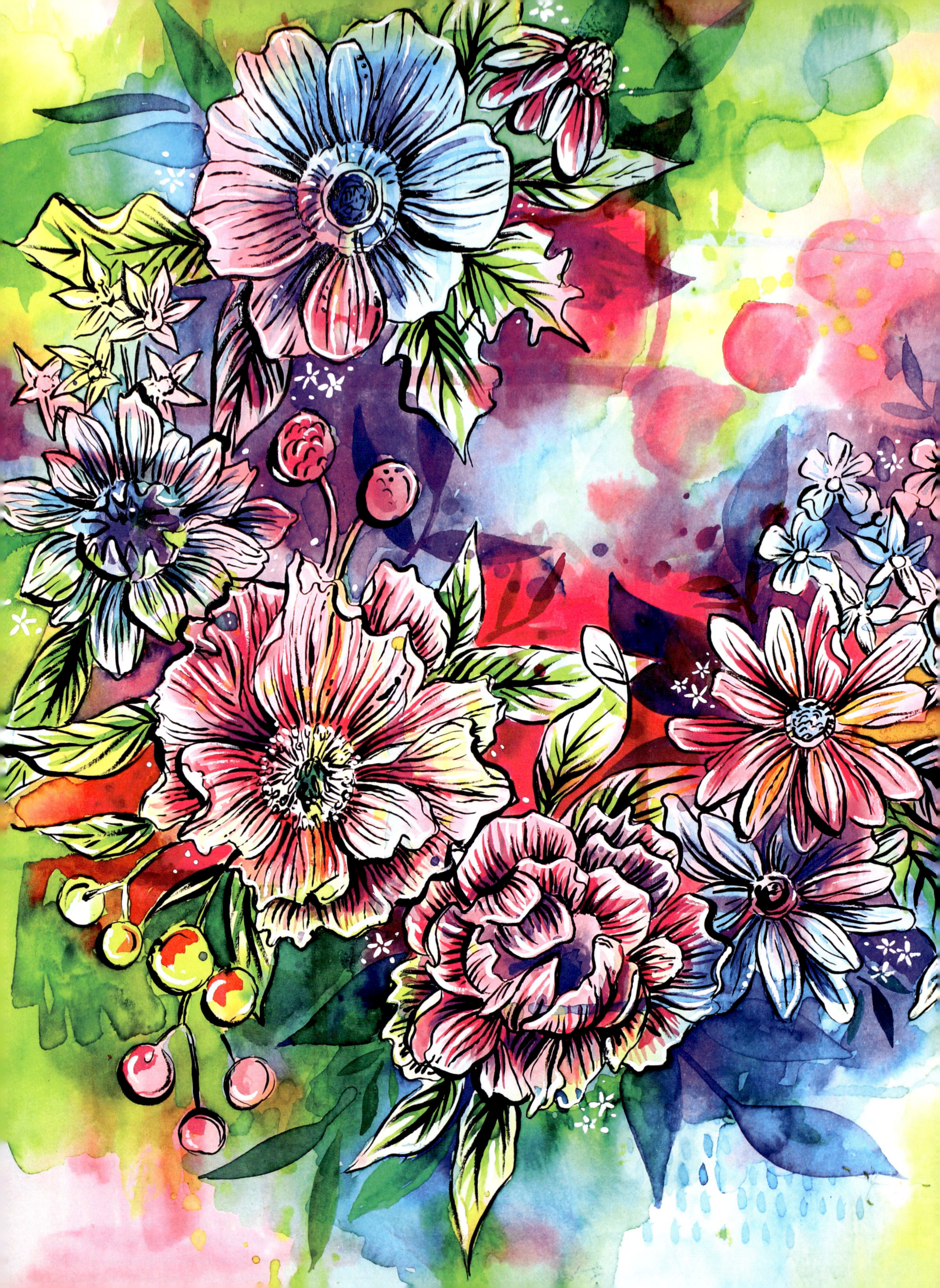

Party in the Background

*Learn to create an elaborate watercolor background
for your piece and draw florals with black acrylic*

It's time to get funky! You may already feel like we've gotten there, but we are just getting started. We started working past the fear of the white space in "Washy Negative Space" and "Joyful Bouquet with a Limited Palette," but now it's time to take a flying leap over it!

Spending time playing in the first layer of a piece is my favorite way to start. I often sit down and have no idea what I'm about to create. The first layers are where I sink into my happy place, allowing the colors to be the boss and take the lead. It's one big happy accident that sets the tone for what's to come.

In this project, we are going to have a party on paper, spending a good chunk of time building up our background with gorgeous layers of watercolors. This process is where my "funky florals" style was born. Eliminating the white space with abandon sets me on a path that always leads to pure enjoyment in what I'm doing. Make sure to eat a snack and hydrate before getting in your creative space, because once you start, you will not be able to walk away!

Tools & Supplies

- Watercolors
- Black acrylic paint (high-flow if possible)
- White acrylic paint
- Black permanent marker
- Sizes 00, 1, 5, and 8 round paintbrushes (or your choice of an extra-small, a small, a medium, and a large brush)
- Water
- Watercolor paper, mixed-media paper, or Bristol board

What You'll Learn

WORKING THE BACKGROUND: This is the second project where we eliminate the white space right from the start, but now we are leveling up and will truly learn to have a little party while we paint on the first layers of washes, splatters, drips, and patterns.

LAYERING WATERCOLORS: As we work through each step, we will see the beautiful results that layering gives us when working with watercolors.

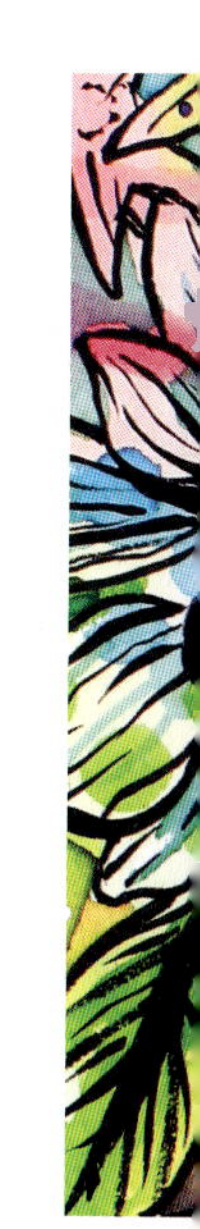

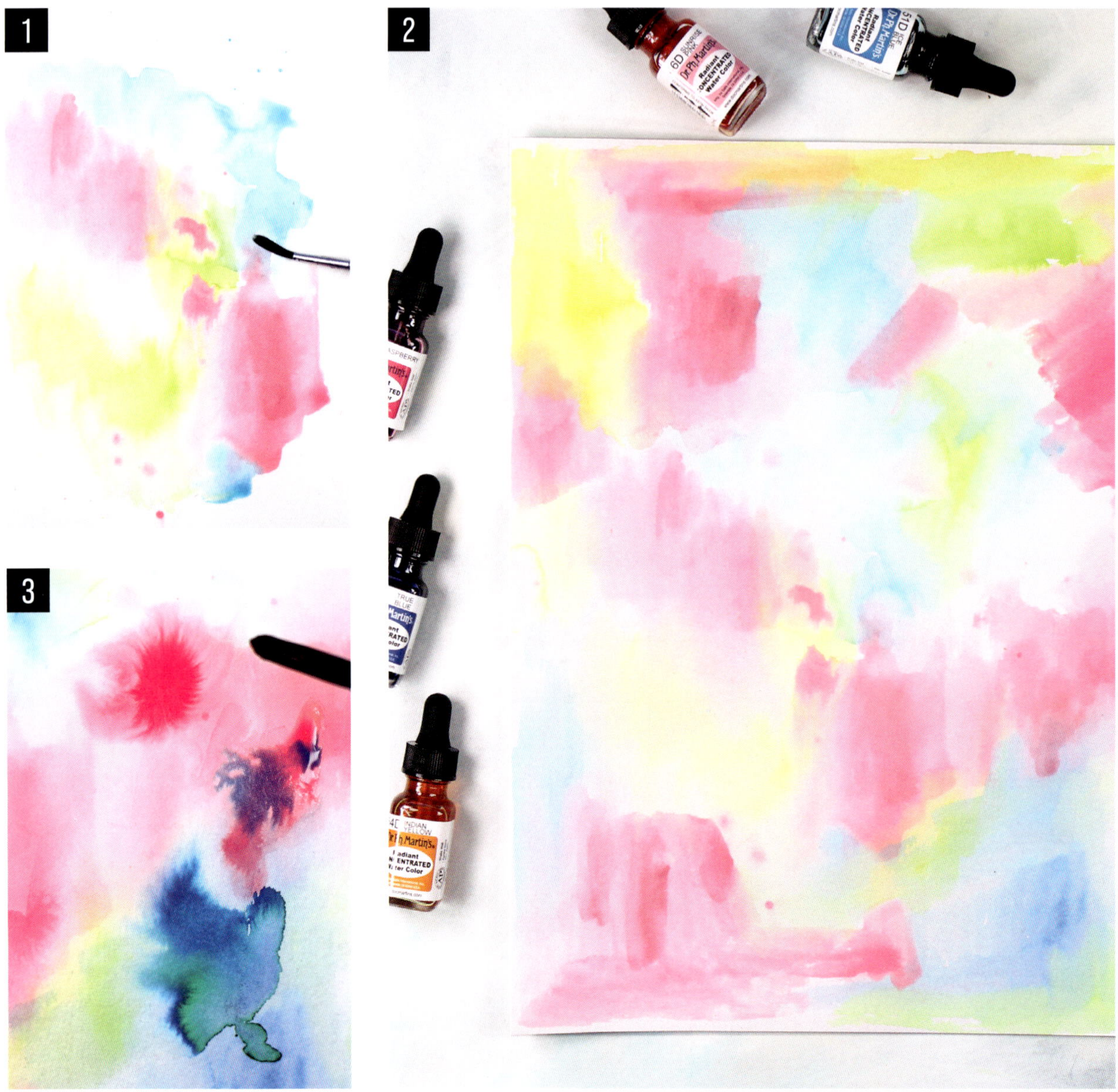

1 Start painting a washy background. Choose a few bright watercolor colors, water them down considerably, and begin to apply a wash of different colors all over the page. This first layer is a time to brush off the cobwebs, dust off the insecurities, and sink into that special little creative happy space.

2 Fill the entire background. As you fill the page, keep your values mostly light, with some midrange values mixed in, and continue until you've filled up the entire sheet.

3 Pool on new colors. Now it's time to learn a new technique: pooling. This is a great method that strips you of control and allows the watercolors to take the lead, creating marks you could never create intentionally. Begin by coating the entire paper with a thin layer of water. Then dip your brush into a pure color and lightly touch the water with that color in one spot. Voilà—magic! Watch as the color gets sucked down into the water and spreads.

4 Add pools of color across the page. Each little area you dab color onto will react differently. Depending on how much your paper is buckling with the water, some areas will spread out, bleeding in all directions, while others will pool together. Allow each area to dry naturally.

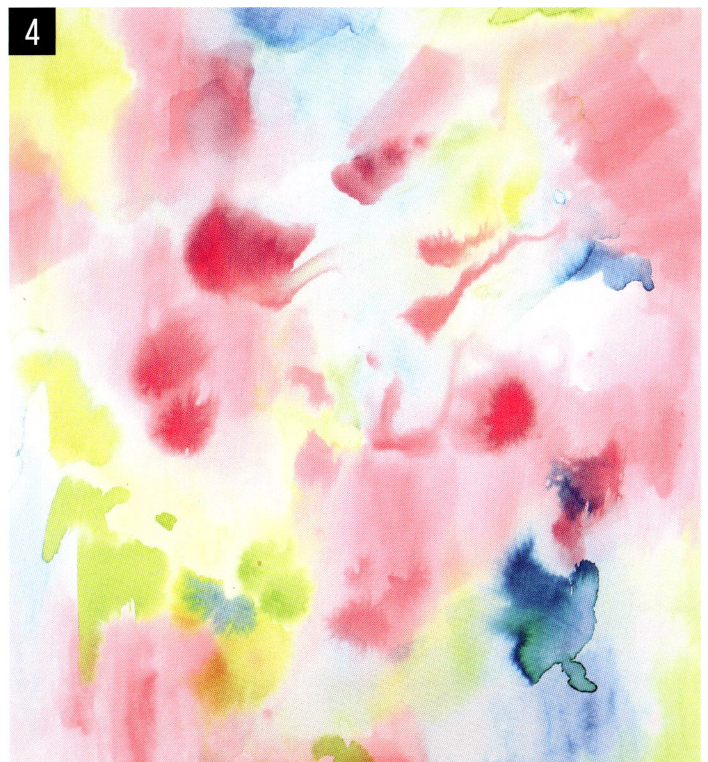

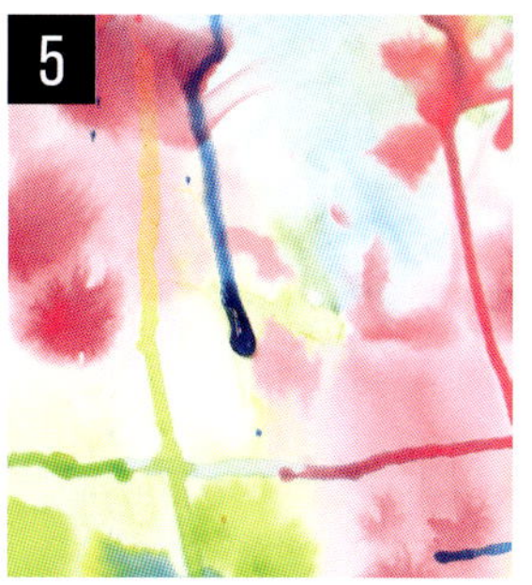

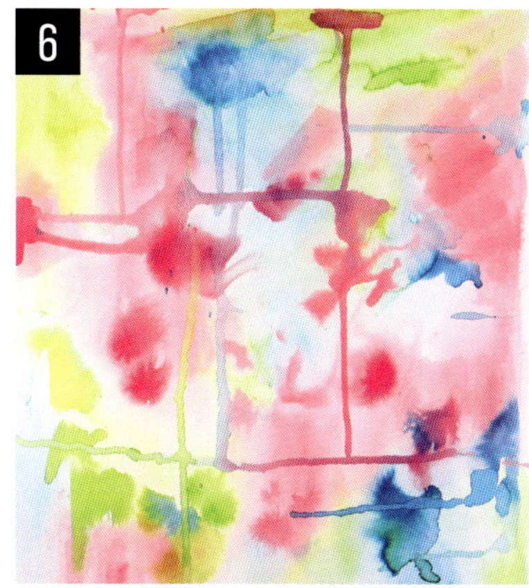

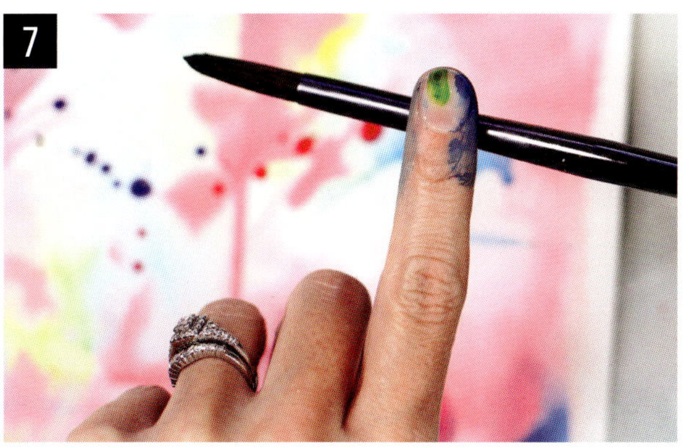

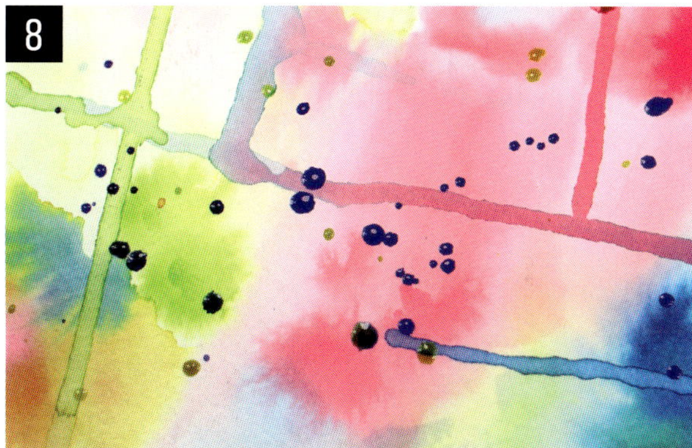

5 **Add drips of color.** Let's keep the magic going. Continue to dab color spots onto the water, but this time encourage your colors to drip this way and that by picking up and tilting the paper. If the color needs some nudging, gently tap the paper to get the dripping started.

6 **Continue tilting the paper to create color drips.** Add these color drips from all sides of the paper, creating crisscrossing lines of color throughout the piece. Allow everything to dry before proceeding.

7 **Try splattering color.** If we are dripping and pooling colors, we might as well splatter them too, right? To do this, saturate your brush in water and dip it in color. Then hold your brush above your piece and gently tap it, allowing color to splatter down this way and that.

8 **Allow the splatters to dry.** Splatter in as many or as few spots as you'd like. You can also try dripping color into areas with pooled water. You will get the bleeding effect that comes from intentional pooling, as we did earlier, but will relinquish even more control this way. Once you're done splattering, allow the splattered layer to dry.

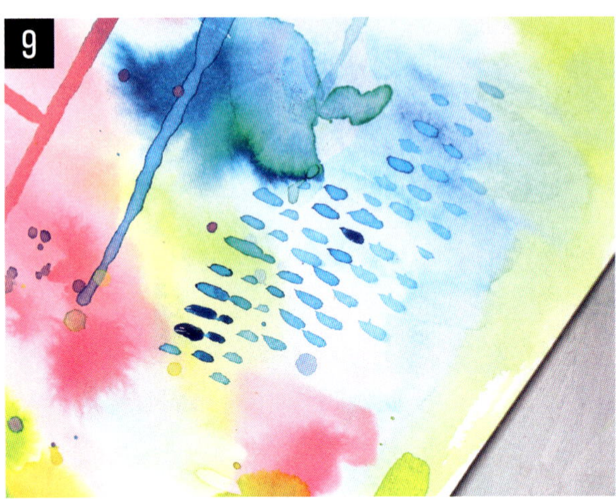

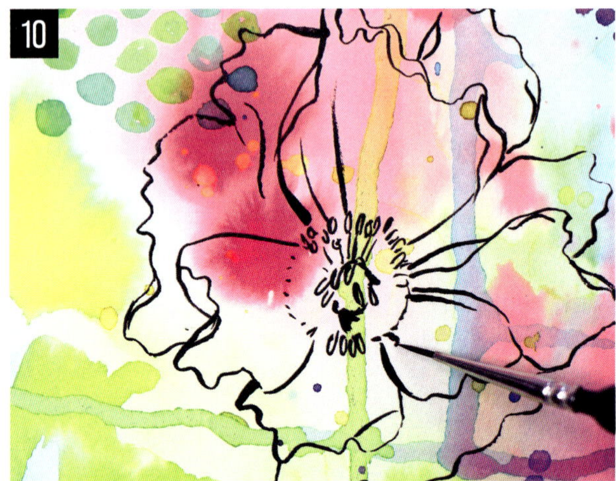

9 Add intentional patterning. Let's take the background one step further by painting in a few areas of simple, subtle patterns like dashes and dots. Work until you are happy and then let the piece dry. Next up is flowers!

10 Start drawing flowers. It's time to "draw" some flowers (with paint and a brush)! Let's try a new composition. In "Freestyle Floral Doodling" and "Joyful Bouquet with a Limited Palette," we had compositions right in the center of the page, while in "Washy Negative Space" and "Monochromatic Wanderings," we had pieces that took up the entire space. This time, let's aim for a sweeping composition that leaves more negative space in the top right and bottom. Use your smallest round brush and black acrylic paint to draw your florals, making thin and delicate lines. You can still use line variation to your advantage, but to start, avoid thick lines.

11 Complete the general composition. Continue painting in the main shapes of your florals. I mixed up the kinds of flowers as well as the sizes, trying to capture large and medium blooms as well as groupings of small flowers.

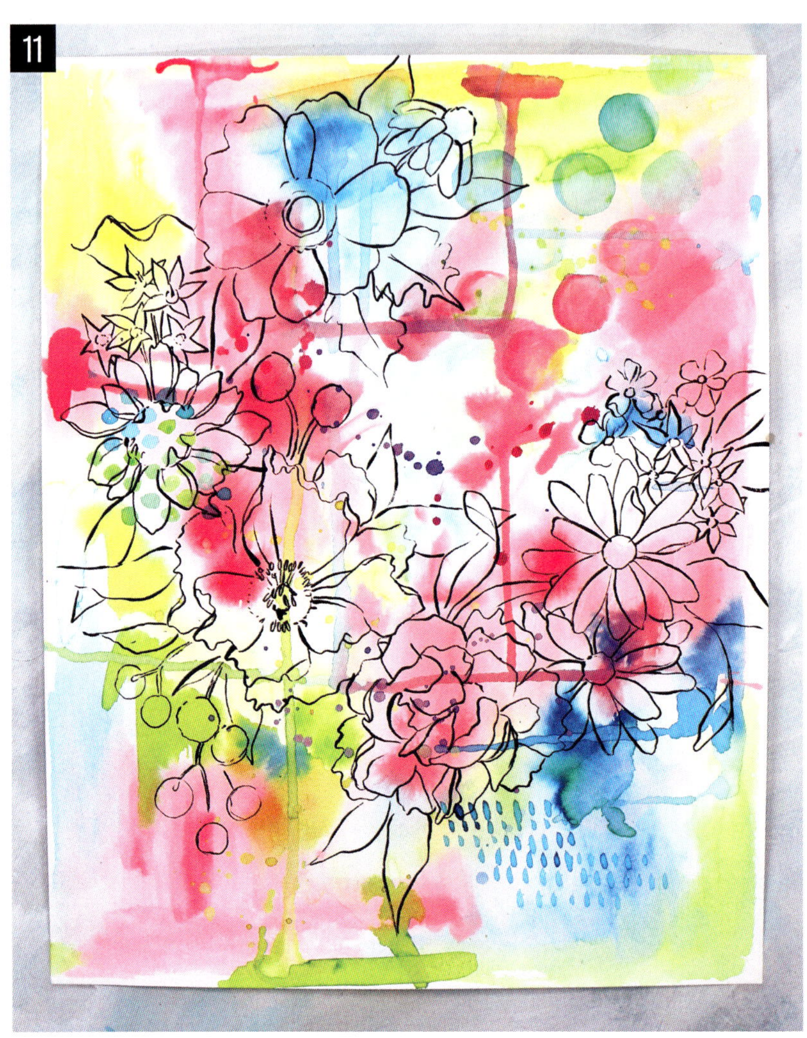

Remember what we've been saying about drawing flowers:
there is no way to mess up. Just because we are now using a bolder outline
(black) doesn't mean you need to change your mindset. Let yourself
pretend you are just using a pencil and drawing.

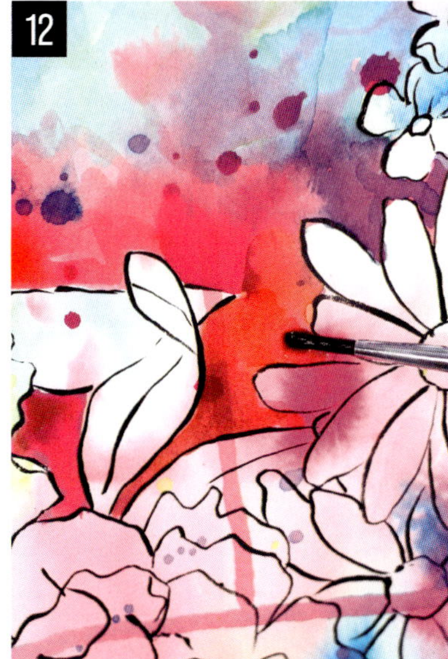

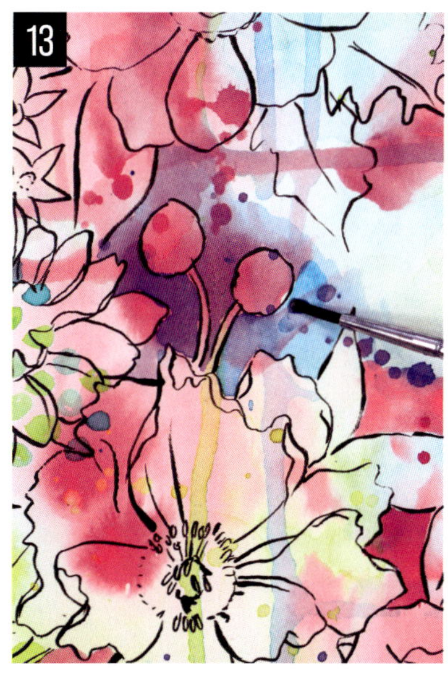

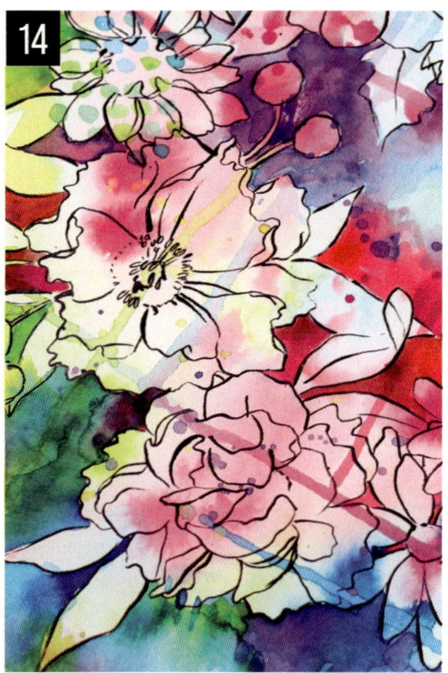

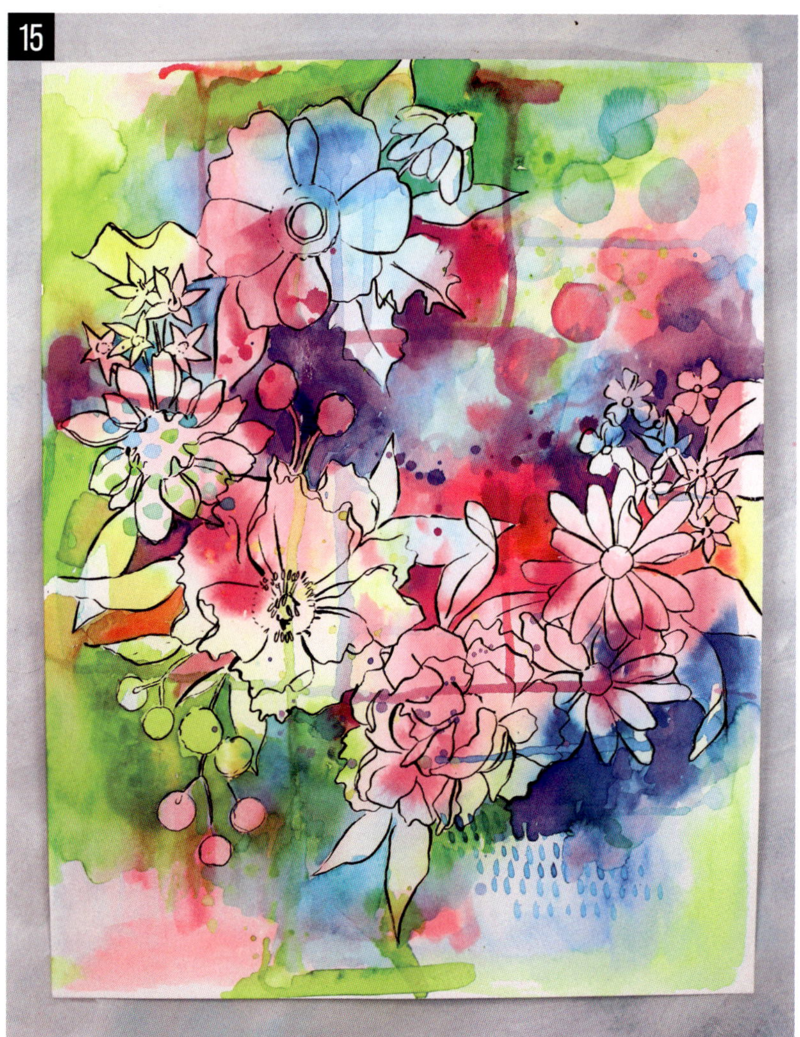

12 **Start darkening the background.** Let's now direct our attention to the negative space. As in the previous projects, use the negative space as a means to pull the florals toward the viewer by pushing the background back. Start with middle values rather than very dark ones.

13 **Layer colors.** Have fun layering colors as you work on the background. I did not choose a violet watercolor for my palette, but by layering pink on top of blue, or vice versa, I can achieve some gorgeous purple hues. At this point, do not fill in all the negative space but, rather, let your dark additions fade away to nothing as you move away from the edges of the flowers and leaves.

14 **Go back in with darker shades.** After working with midtones, go back in for another layer to push some areas further back by using darker tones. Note that you do not have to depend solely on value to bring the foreground forward—strong contrast between two colors can have the same effect.

15 **Check your progress.** At this point, your flowers and leaves should mostly pop nicely out from your darker background. You're ready to start adding dimension to the flowers themselves!

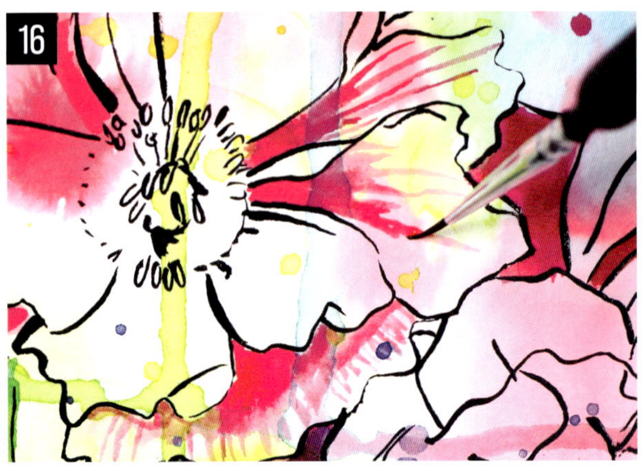

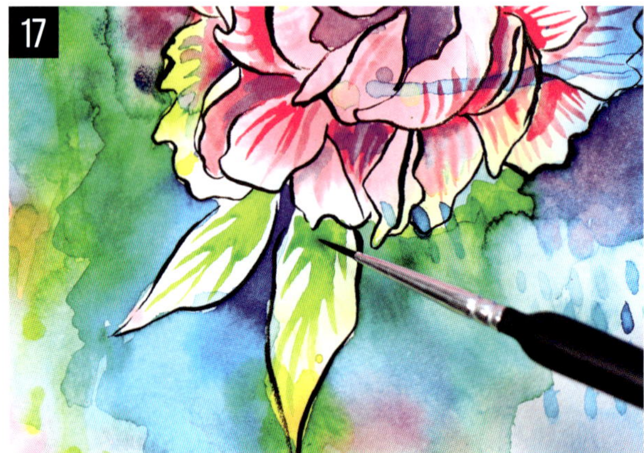

16 **Start adding details.** The details will consist of a first layer of color followed by a second layer of black. Focusing on the color first, begin adding lines to your flowers using watercolors and your smallest brush. Try including dense color where petals come out from the centers of the flowers.

17 **Don't forget the leaves.** Focusing on greens and yellows for the leaves will help them contrast the flowers.

18 **Check your progress.** Compare this photo to the photo for step 15. See how the flowers and leaves still pop out even though they contain a lot of color? If your piece doesn't have this contrast, you may want to try to darken your negative space further, especially around the edges of any flowers that aren't popping.

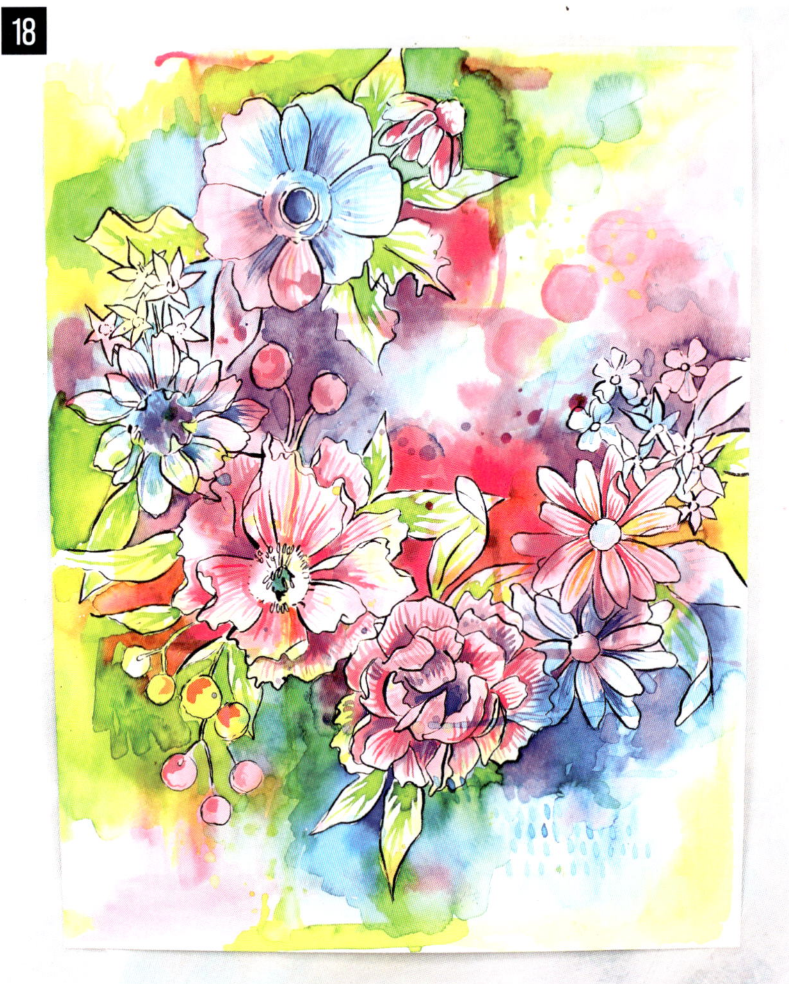

Just as we've said that there is no way to mess up drawing a flower, there isn't a way to mess up shading either. Perhaps you added shadows to a petal out front by accident. So what? You can go back later and add white or push the petal behind it further back. For everything that you think you've "messed up," there's always a creative way to "fix" it. Instead of approaching an "oops" with a negative attitude, see it as an opportunity to take on a challenge and discover something new.

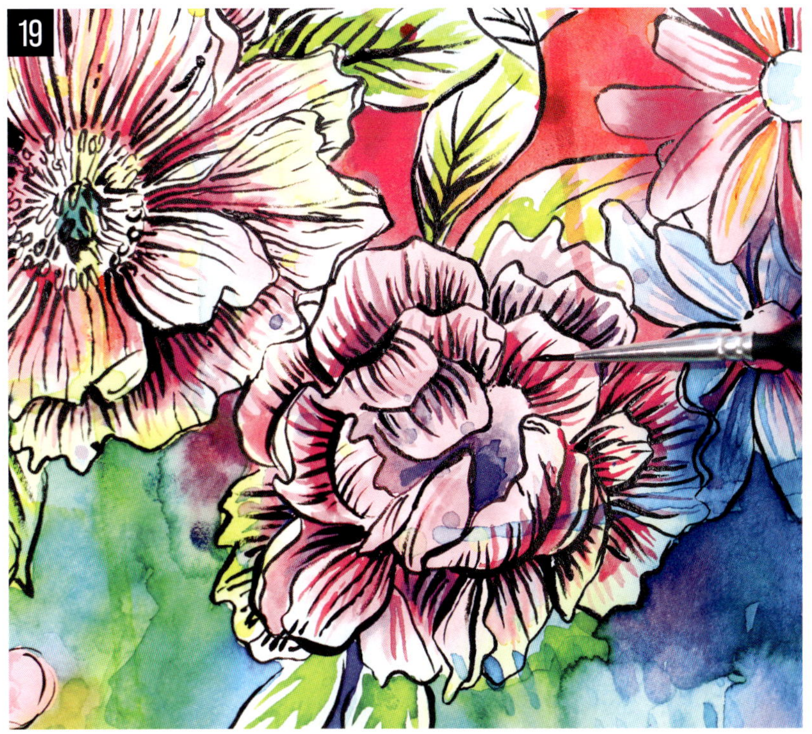

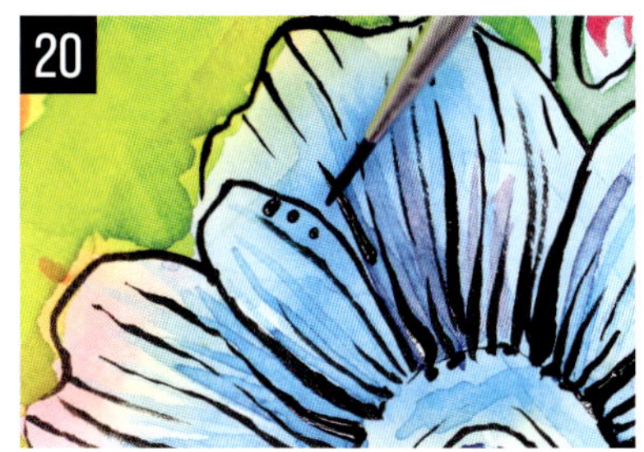

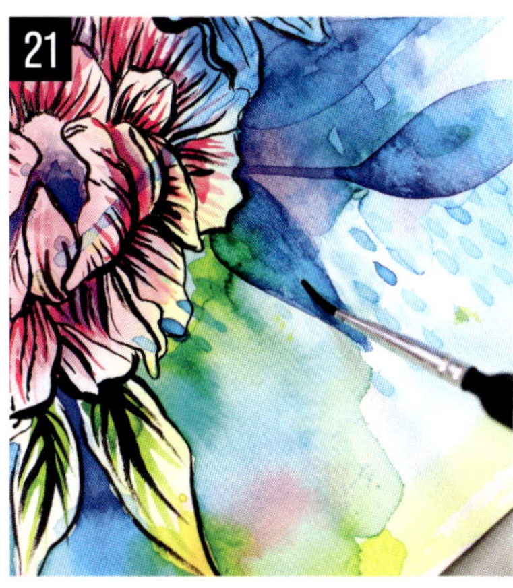

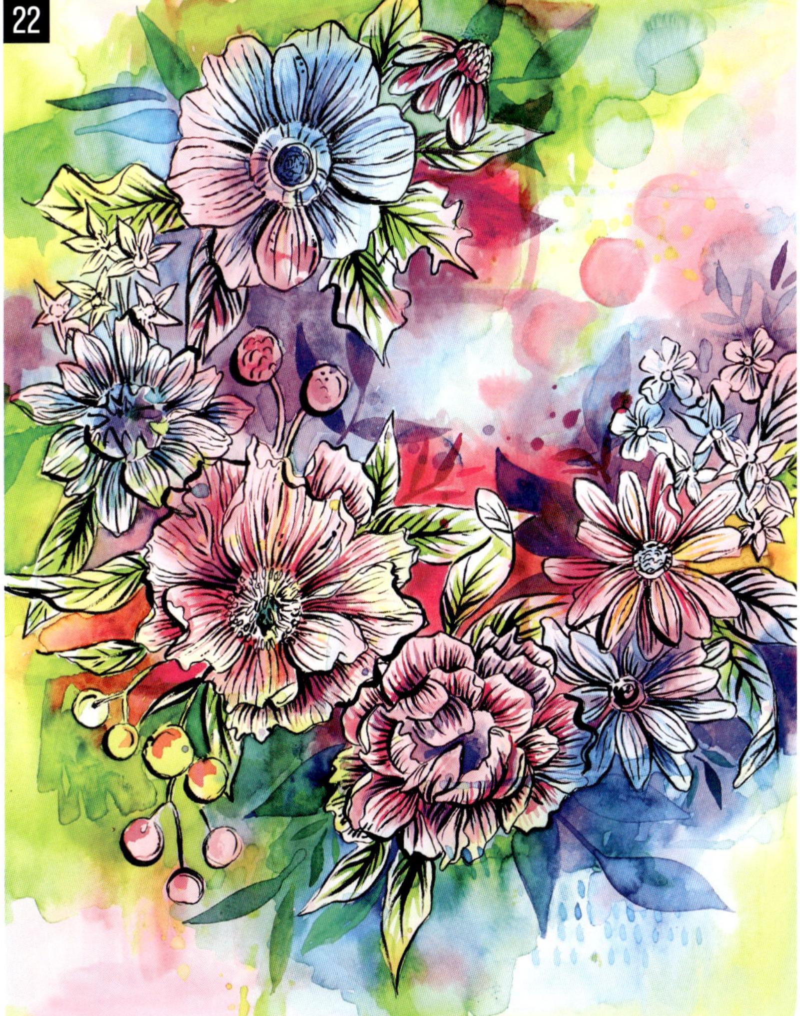

19 **Add black details.** Switch back to your black acrylic with your smallest round brush and begin to add very detailed linework to the flowers and leaves.

20 **Try adding dots.** Don't just add lines—try dotting on some dots in places as well.

21 **Add dark leaves in the background.** It's time for one more layer in the negative space. This time, use a deep, saturated color to add silhouettes of leaves and vines, similarly to how you did this in "Monochromatic Wanderings." Mix up the sizes and shapes of the leaves and vines and allow the colors to pool in some areas to add even more gorgeous diversity.

22 **Take a look at your progress.** Here you can see the full scope of the black details added to the flowers as well as all the silhouettes of leaves and vines added to the background. If you're happy with how these aspects look, it's time to move on to the last phase: white highlights!

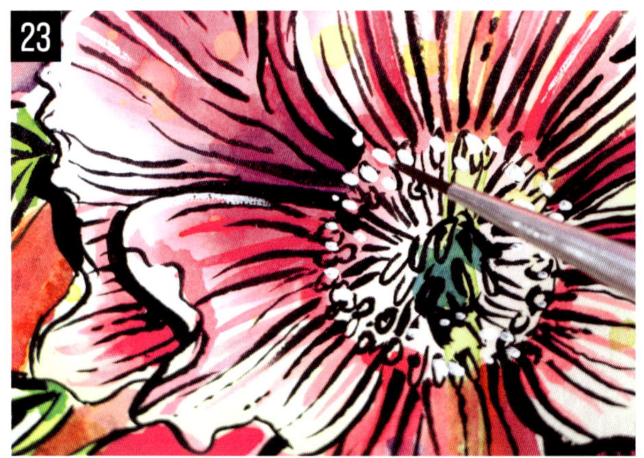

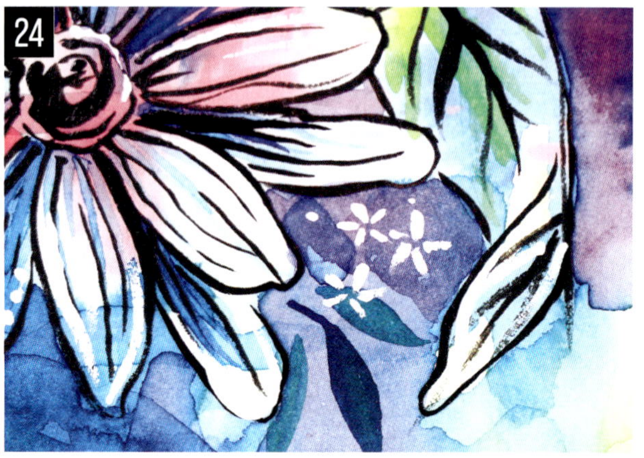

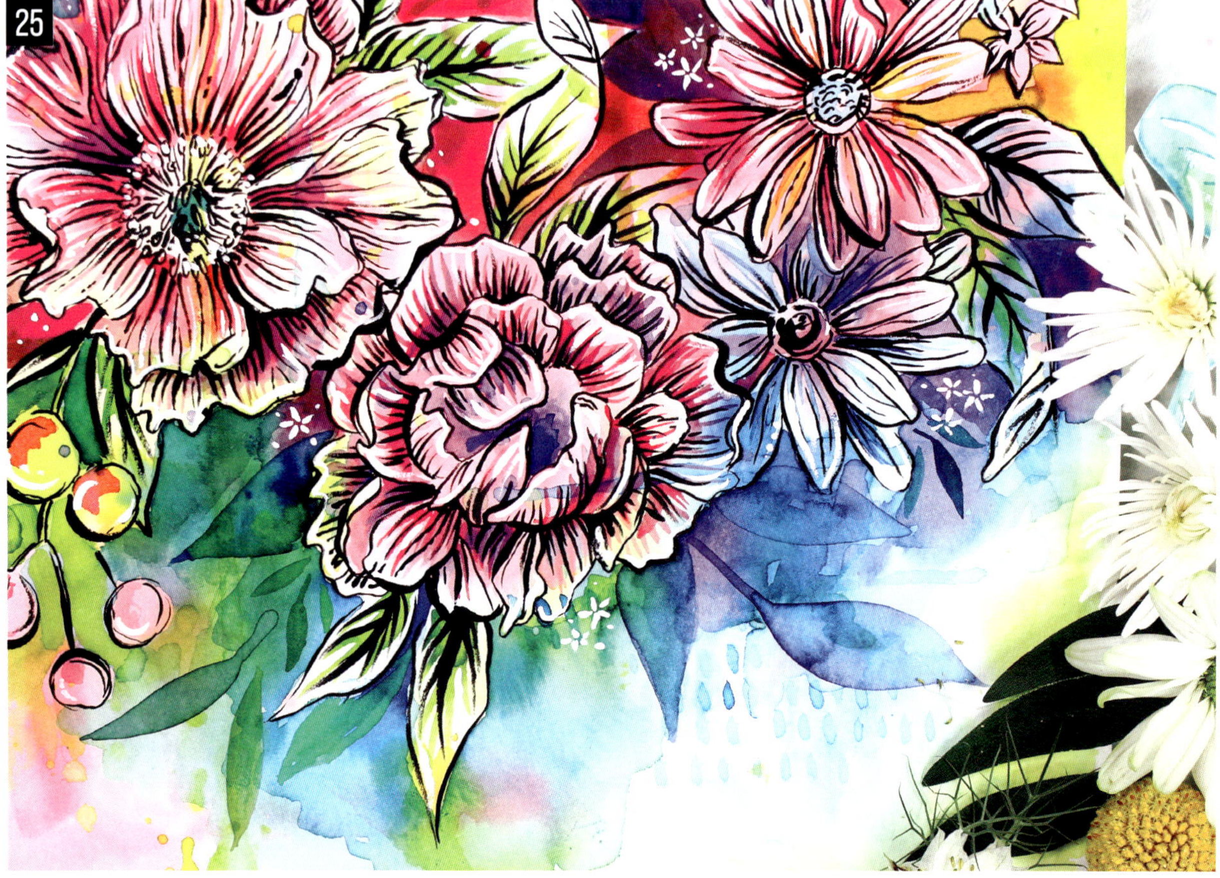

23 Add white highlights.
Using a very small brush, add white highlights to the areas in the flowers that need to come forward some, such as the centers and the tips of the petals, plus maybe a few streaks along the lengths of the petals here and there.

24 Add white sparkles. You know by now that for me, more is more, so if you're on board, go back into your negative space one last time to add small groupings of very simple white flowers. These teeny tiny dots will give the piece a light and airy feel, as if it's twinkling. These are an extra-special sprinkle on top. I like to keep these little touches close to the flowers rather than having them float lonely in the negative space.

25 Enjoy your work. Take a moment to journey through your finished piece. There are so many things to discover! I see polka dots peeking through flowers, beautiful areas where colors have pooled and bled, and layer upon layer of detail. There are so many little surprises when you take the time to search for them. A piece like this is a delight to see from afar and equally as special to examine up close.

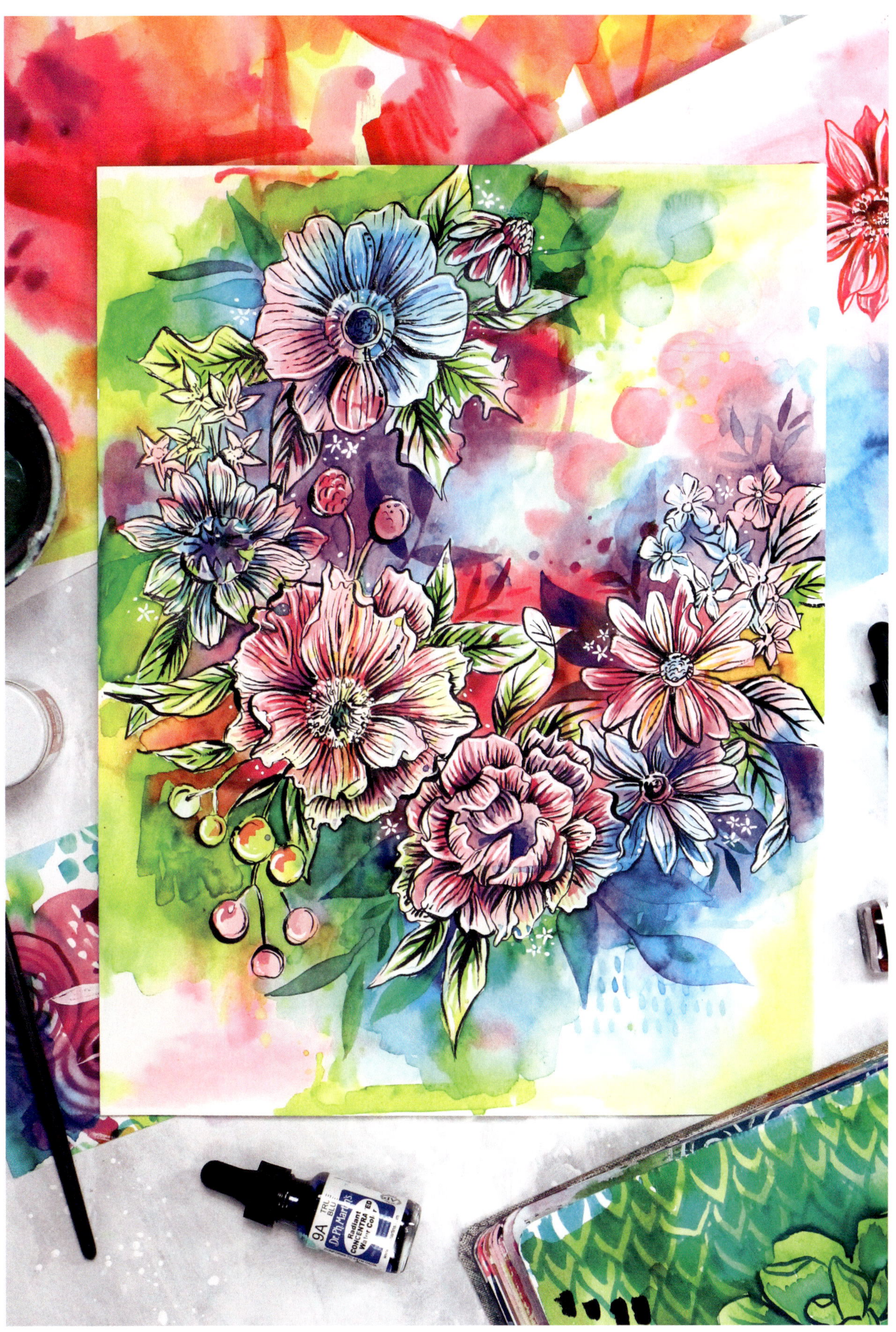

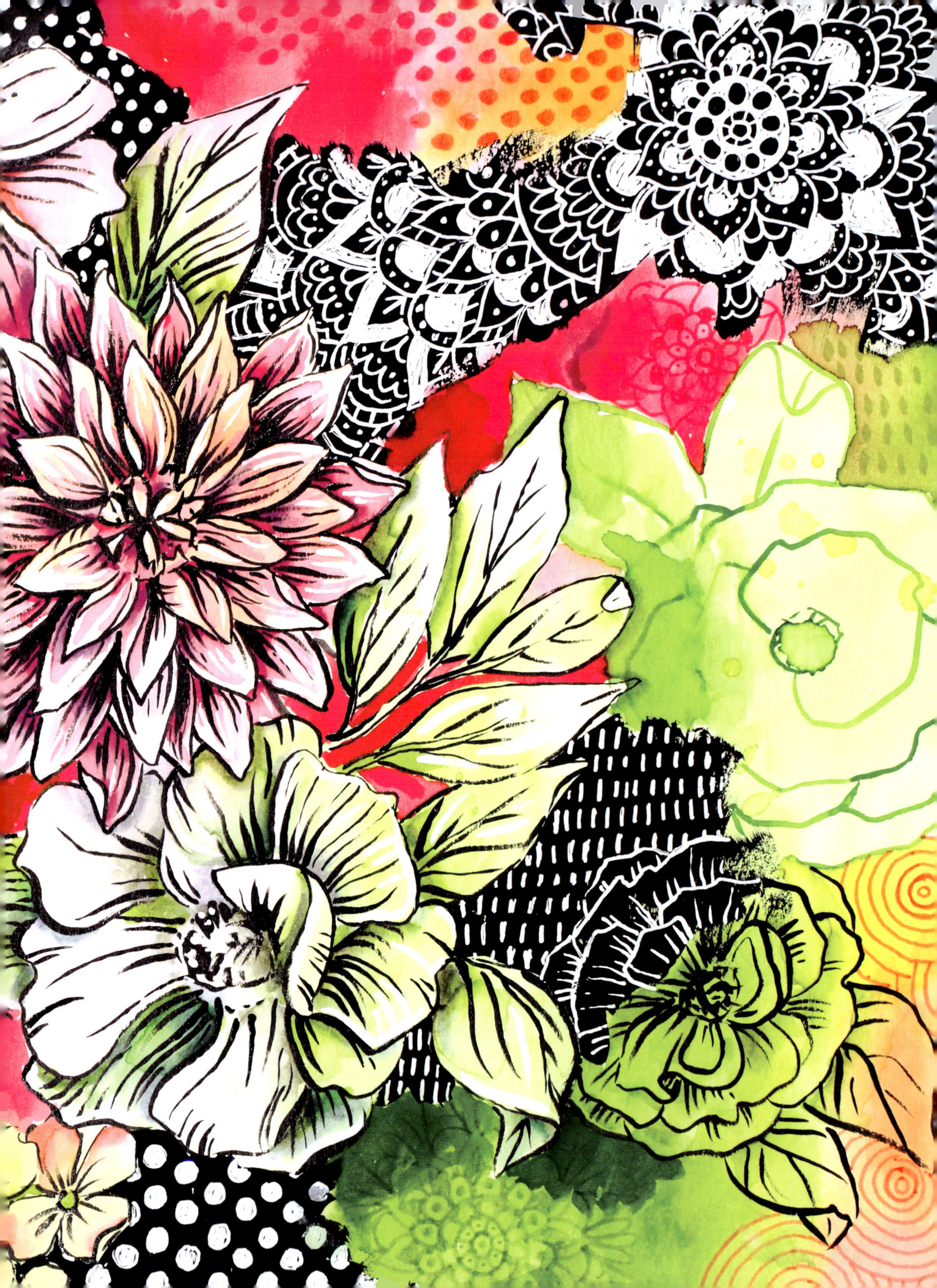

Risky Black

*Learn to mix watercolors and black acrylic to
create ample space for doodling in both white and colors*

Have you noticed yet that I'm all about filling the negative space? There are times when a simple background is what your project needs—but more often than not, I enjoy utilizing this space to the max. So, in this piece, we are going to keep moving in the layers direction, and we are going to combine markers, watercolors, pens, and acrylics—the more supplies, the merrier!

Many of my students get stuck in terms of which supplies to use. "Should I use watercolors to create this? Markers? Acrylics?" Well, I'm here to give you permission to use them ALL. I like to say, "You control the supplies; don't let the supplies control you." (I stole this phrase from my dad when he coached me in softball. He'd say, "Play the ball; don't let the ball play you." This phrase can be adapted to so many situations in life—who knew I'd be using it in a book about painting flowers 20 years later? Thanks, Daddy!)

One of my favorite things about this project is the "Oh dear, what have I done" phase. We will be taking a big step (step 5) that you will probably hesitate to do and may even dislike. But we must step into the uncomfortable to bring about something good in the end. Let's get started!

Tools & Supplies

- ▶ Watercolors
- ▶ Black acrylic paint (high-flow if possible)
- ▶ White gel pen (optional)
- ▶ White acrylic paint
- ▶ Water-based markers (optional)
- ▶ Sizes 00, 1, and 6 round paintbrushes (or your choice of an extra-small, a small, and a medium brush)
- ▶ Water
- ▶ Watercolor paper, mixed-media paper, or Bristol board

What You'll Learn

TAKING RISKS: This piece has a point where you will probably not like it. You'll cover up some areas you like, and, quite possibly, you will look at what we've done with disdain. You may even panic. But stay the course. Art involves taking risks. Sometimes diving into the unknown will bring about your most beautiful and unexpected work.

EMBRACING MIXED MEDIA: Allow yourself the freedom of using whatever you have at your fingertips. I often say, "When in doubt, use all the colors," but I'll rephrase that now to say, "When in doubt, use all the supplies."

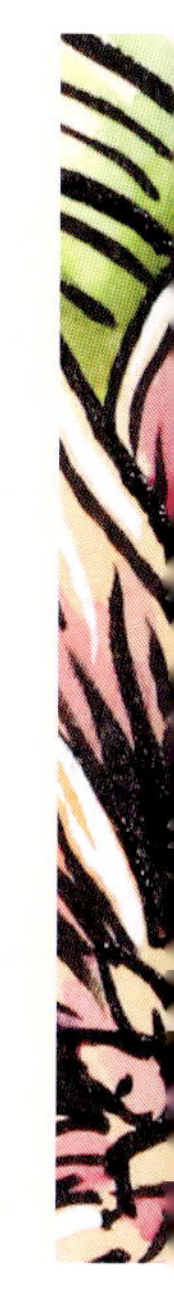

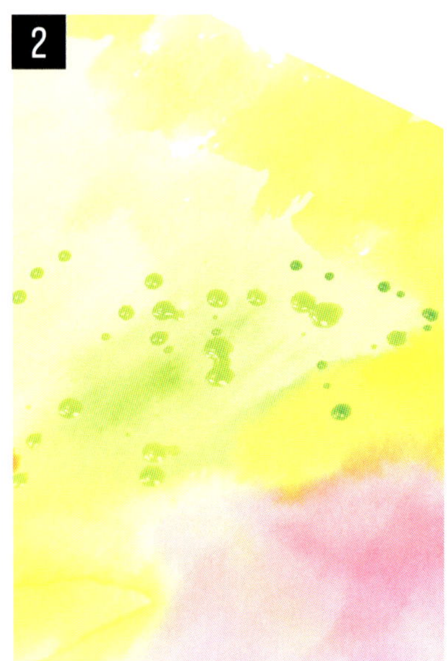

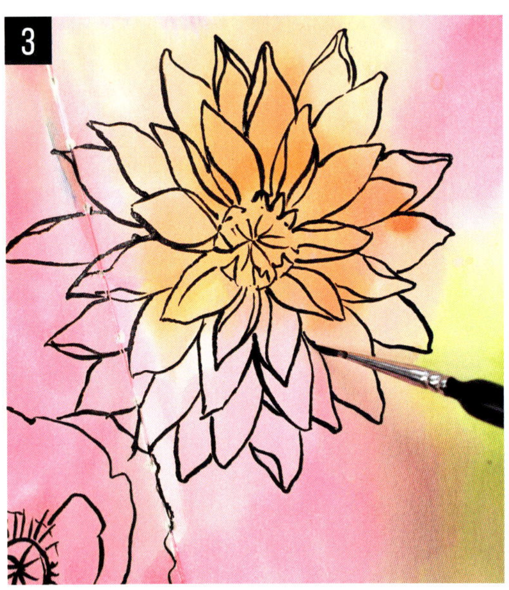

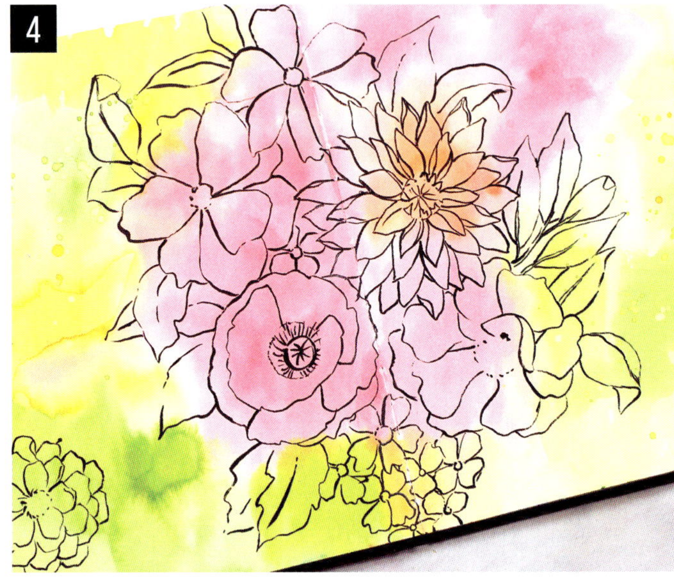

1 **Fill the background.** Let's get started with my favorite icebreaker: filling the background and eliminating all white space with a very light wash of watercolors using your largest brush. My color scheme is going to be bright, warm, and summery, so I have chosen pinks, lime greens, oranges, and yellows.

2 **Add splatters and drips.** If you'd like, incorporate some of the background techniques we played with in "Party in the Background": pool colors, splatter them, or drip them on. However, avoid going too dark with your values. I added some faint splatters and left the rest of the background as it was.

3 **Start drawing flowers with paint.** Use black acrylic paint and a small or extra-small paintbrush to start drawing in flowers. Keep them mainly in the center of the piece with the leaves spreading away from the florals. Use a variety of flower types and sizes.

4 **Finish drawing in your florals.** As you wrap up, make sure to leave a good amount of negative space. Aim for a ratio of positive to negative space of around one-half to two-thirds. I've also added one flower peeking out from the left-hand side.

5 **Paint some areas black.** Are you ready to get uncomfortable? Using black acrylic, paint in several splotches around your florals. It may appear jarring

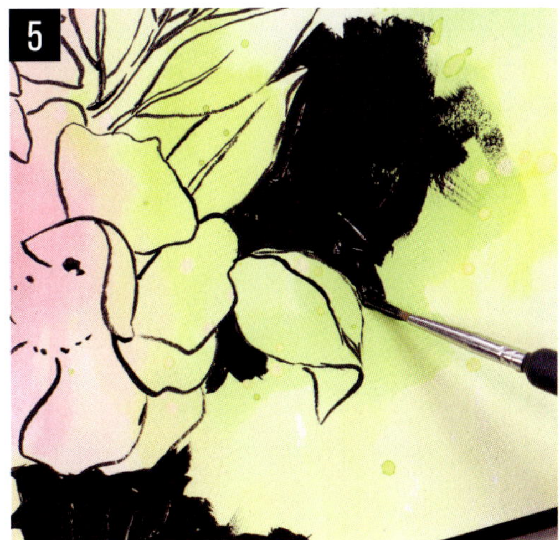

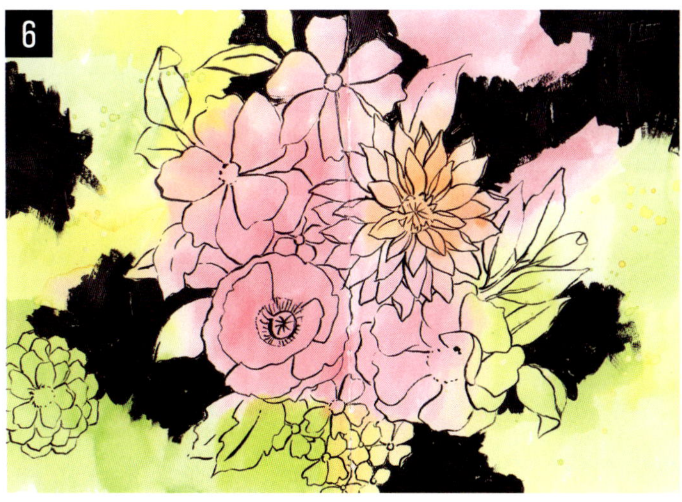

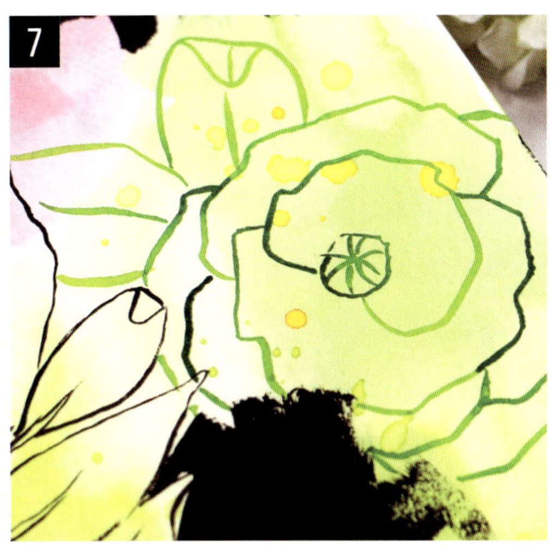

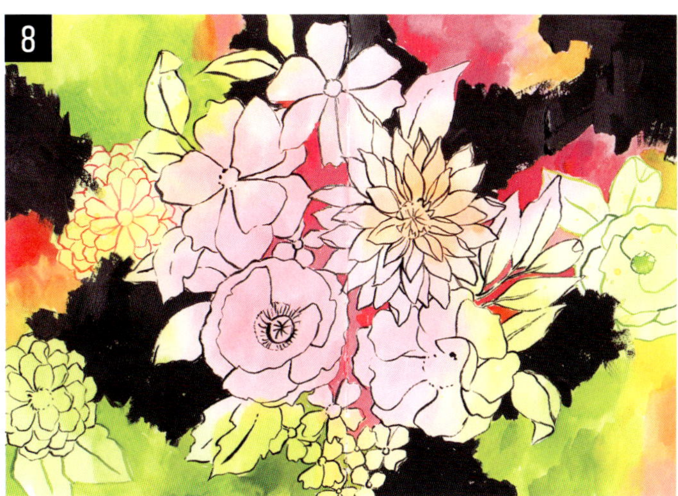

at first, and you may not enjoy covering up some of the beautiful areas in your first layer of background color, but we will be using these areas to create some exciting and unexpected details. Trust me here and allow yourself to take the risk!

6 **Finish adding black areas.** If there is an area in your flowers and leaves that you are unhappy with, you can cover it with black or paint it in as a silhouette. I was unhappy with a leaf to the upper right of my orange-toned central flower (you can see it in step 4), so I simply painted one of my black patches right over it!

7 **Paint some new flowers in color.** While the black areas dry, paint two or three new flowers in your negative space using watercolors. Allow some of them (or all of them) to butt up against the black areas and the already-drawn black flowers.

8 **Add deeper color to the background.** Continuing to use your watercolors, fill in a lot of the negative space around the black florals, black splotches, and watercolor florals. Strive for midtones, venturing into some deeper colors as well. Compare how the piece looks now to how it looked in step 6.

Would you rather draw your flowers with markers? Go for it! Would you like to add shading to your flowers first, or detailed linework? Do it! These steps are meant to guide you in the right direction, but there is room to swap steps and supplies. The more you create these funky florals, the more you will make the process your own.

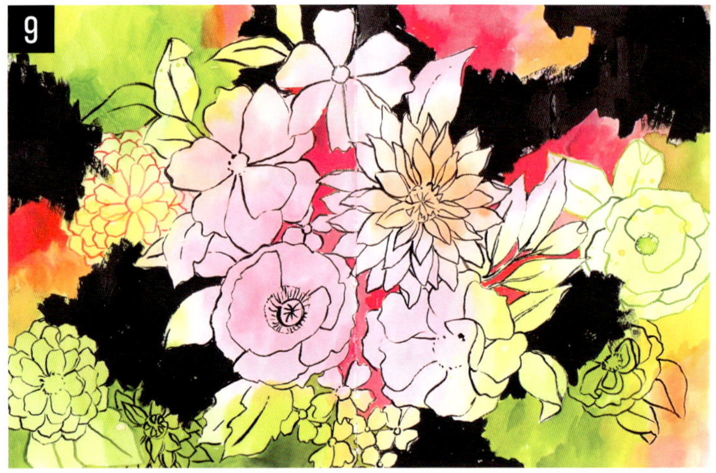

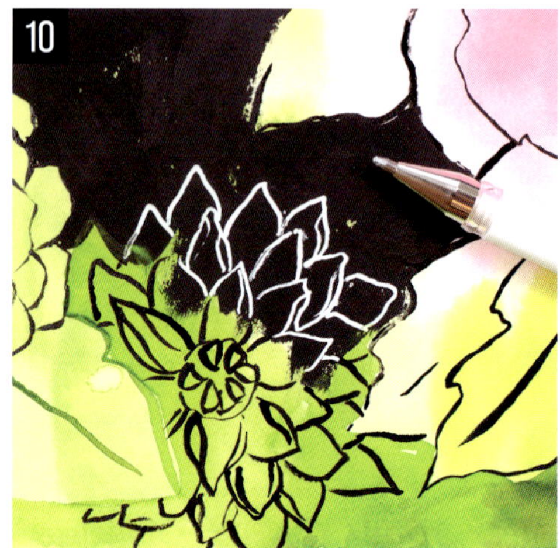

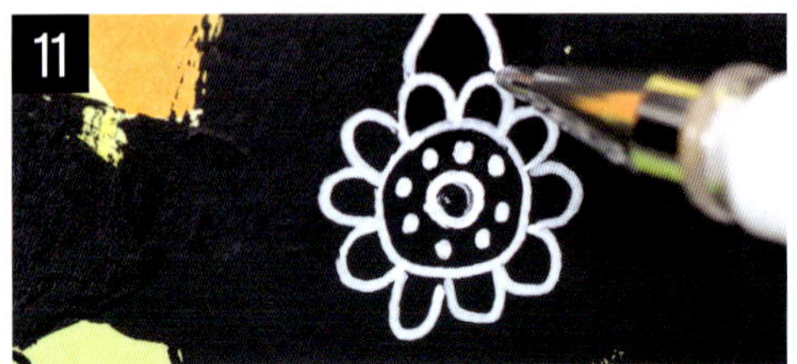

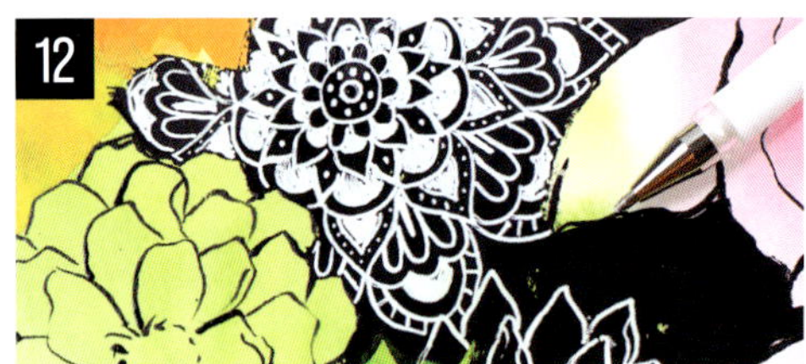

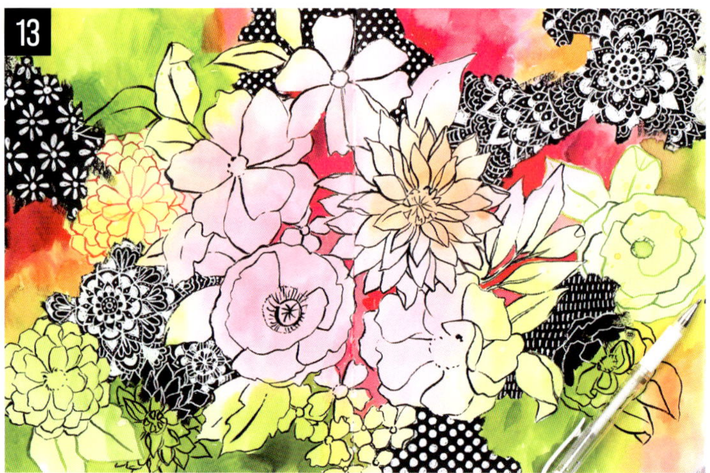

9 **Add some more black flowers.** Next, revisit the negative space you just filled in with color by drawing in two or three more florals and/or leaves in black acrylic. Allow these to butt up against the black splotches and other subject matter. I added one floral to the bottom right, one to the bottom left, and a leaf near the top left.

10 **Draw back in white flower petals.** It's time to address those glaring black splotches! Using a white gel pen, draw in petals of the flowers that disappear under splotches of black. You can use white paint instead of a gel pen if you prefer.

11 **Draw in some mandalas.** Continuing with the white gel pen, draw mandala-inspired circular designs in your two largest areas of black. These shapes are simply symmetrical designs that start in the center and build their way out in a circular

pattern. I'm not concerned with perfection (you know that by now!), so my designs are not always fully symmetrical or even. Wherever the black stops, my design will stop.

12 **Don't be afraid of imperfection.** What I love about including mandalas like this is that when the mandala stops right at the rough edges and flower edges, it seems to peek out as if it's always been there in the background. It can get tricky to continue the design as the space decreases, but that's where you can remind yourself that perfection is absolutely not required.

13 **Add simple patterns in other black areas.** Mix it up by including simpler patterns in the remaining black areas. Think polka dots, dashes, lines, triangles— any simple design or repeat pattern that will fill up the space in an interesting but less labor-intensive way.

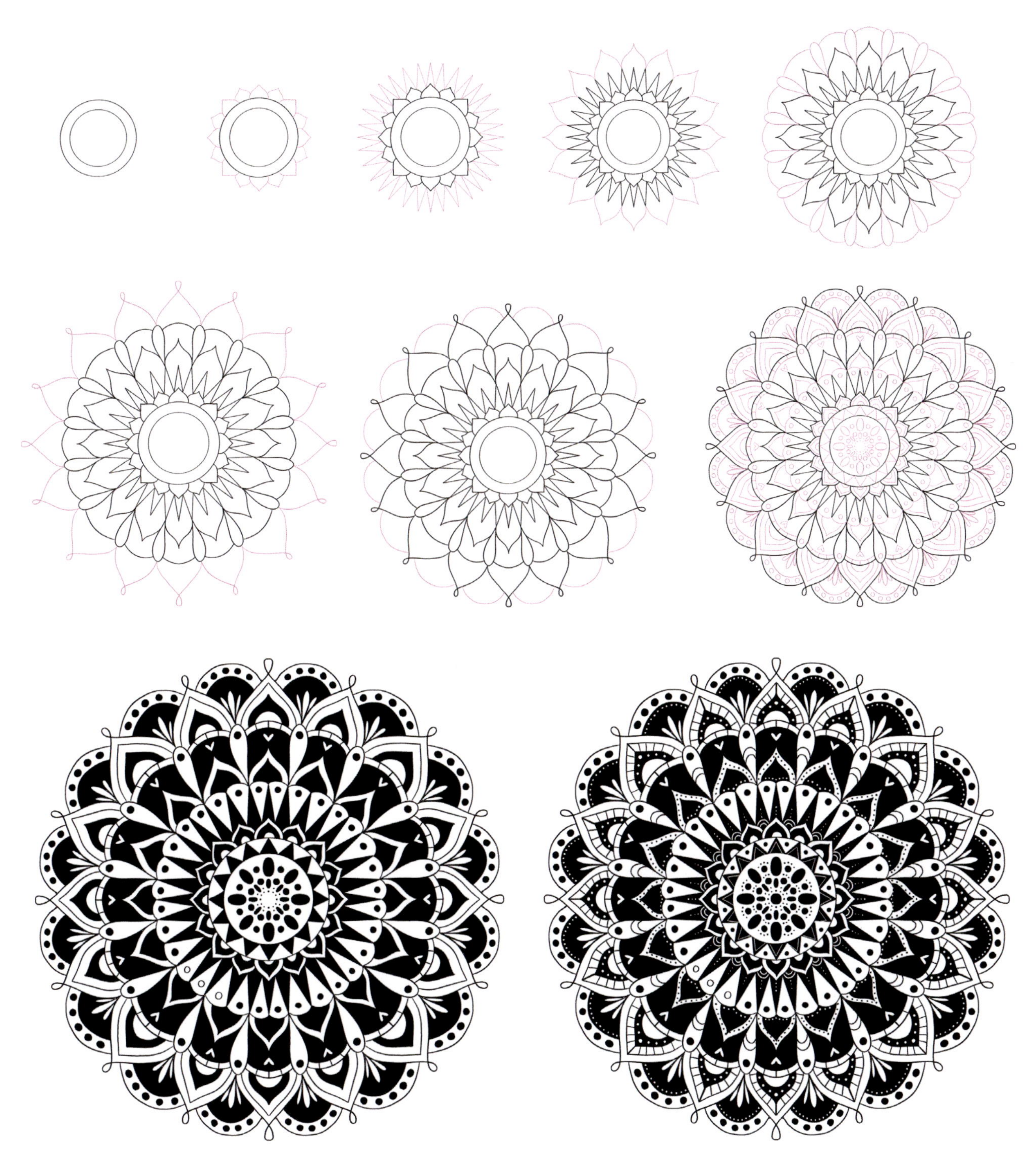

Mandalas are simple to draw yet complex visually. To create a mandala design, simply start
with a circle and expand upon it by adding symmetrical designs while working away from the center.
One you have completed the main shapes, return to each area and fill with color and/or fine details.
Here is an step-by-step breakdown of a mandala as an example to get you started!

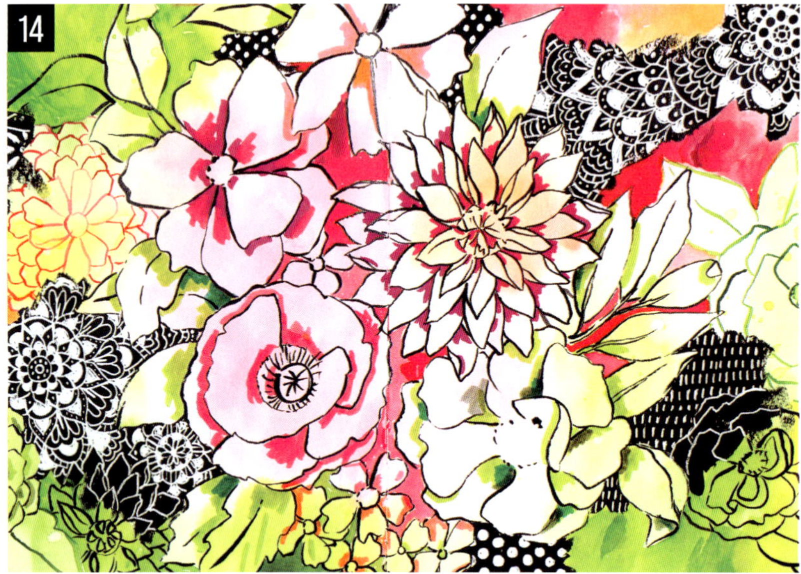

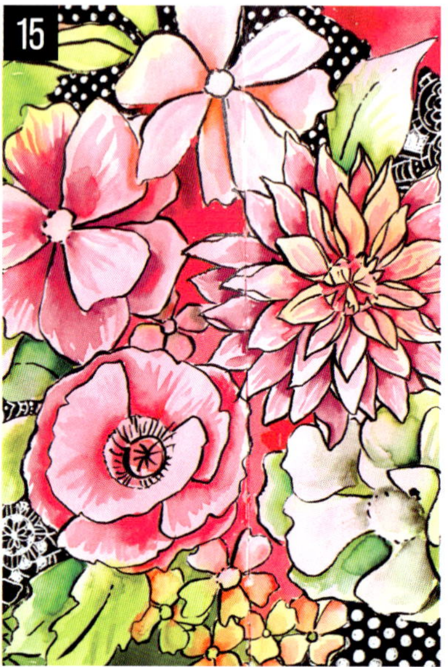

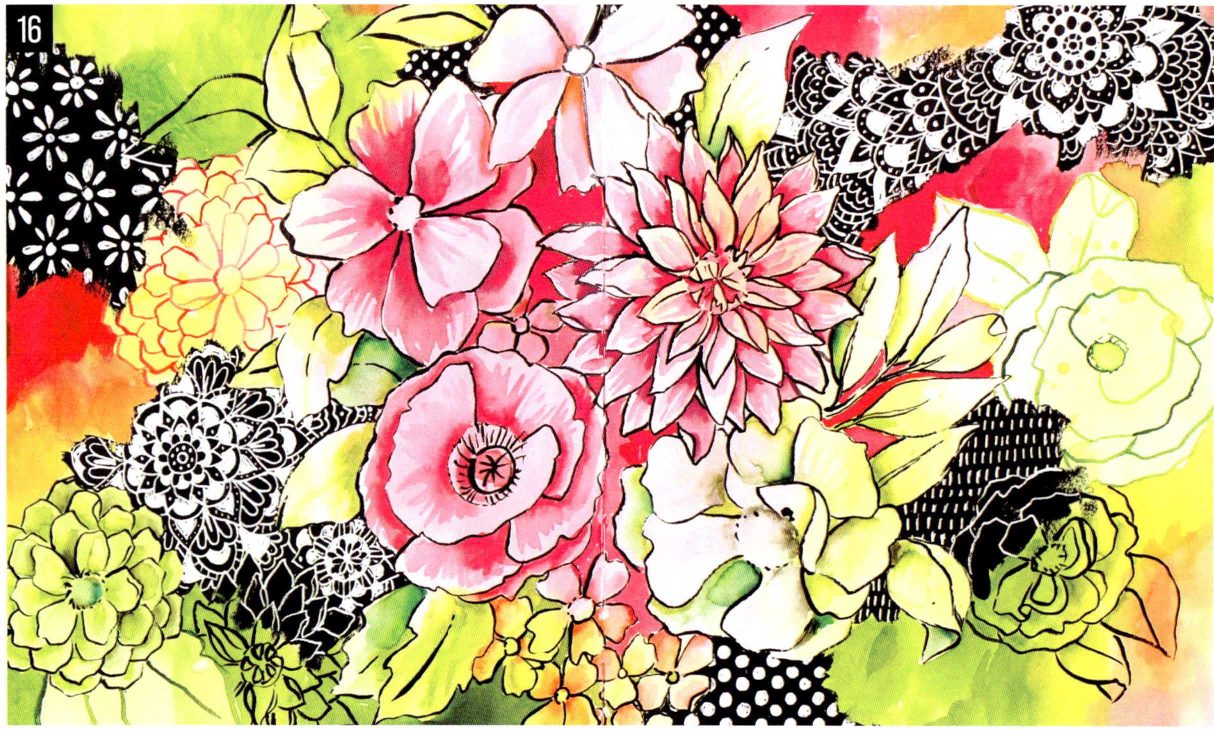

14 **Start adding shading.** Let's step back into familiar territory now and add shading to the flowers and leaves. I used water-based markers, but you can use watercolors if you prefer. Approach this in the same way you've learned to do in previous projects, by putting in areas of deeper color where you want the shadows to be.

15 **Blend the shading.** Use your paintbrush and water to blend out the areas you added shading to, pulling the color away from the areas where it was initially applied.

16 **Check your progress.** Once you've finished blending your shading, check to make sure you're happy with how much you've added. Next we are going to move back into the negative space by adding more doodles into the untouched colored background areas, such as the top left green patch, top right pink-and-orange patch, bottom right orange-and-green section, etc.

17 **Draw in a color mandala.** While the shading in the flowers and leaves is drying, use your markers to create subtle mandala designs and patterns in some of the remaining background spaces. This will give the piece yet another layer, adding to the magical feeling that is slowly building.

18 **Draw in other color designs.** Remember to experiment with simpler designs too, like concentric circles, polka dots, and the like.

19 **Add black detail.** Switch gears back to the main flowers again. Use black-paint linework to bring out the detail and emphasize the dimension.

20 **Add white detail.** Also add detail, in the form of white lines, in the flowers that spill onto the black splotches.

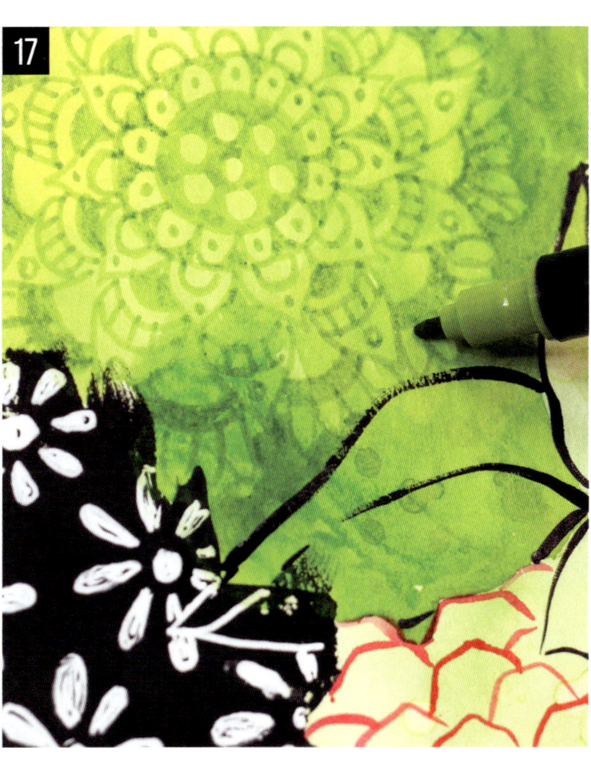

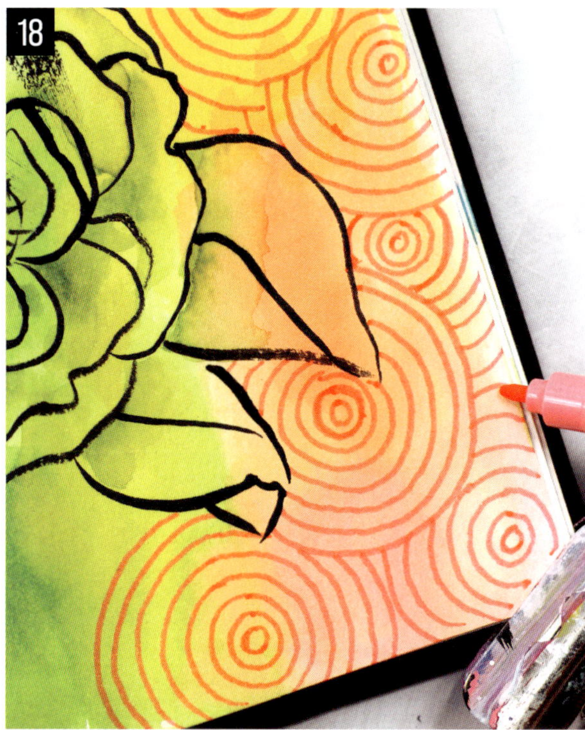

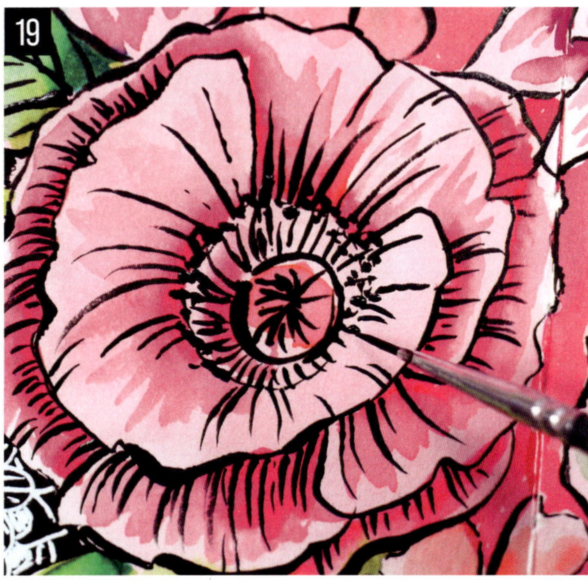

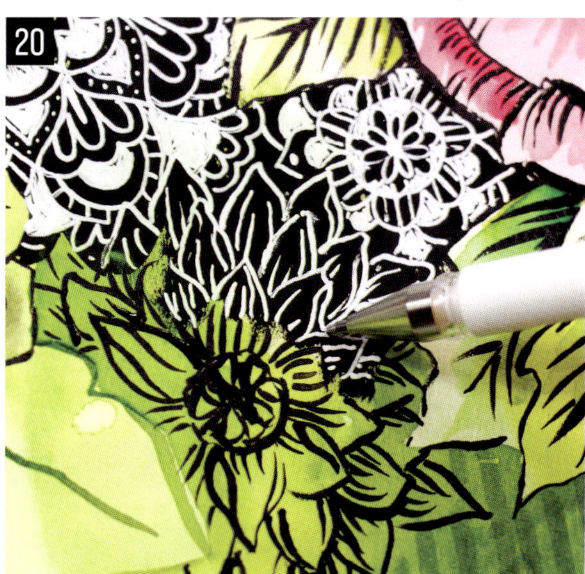

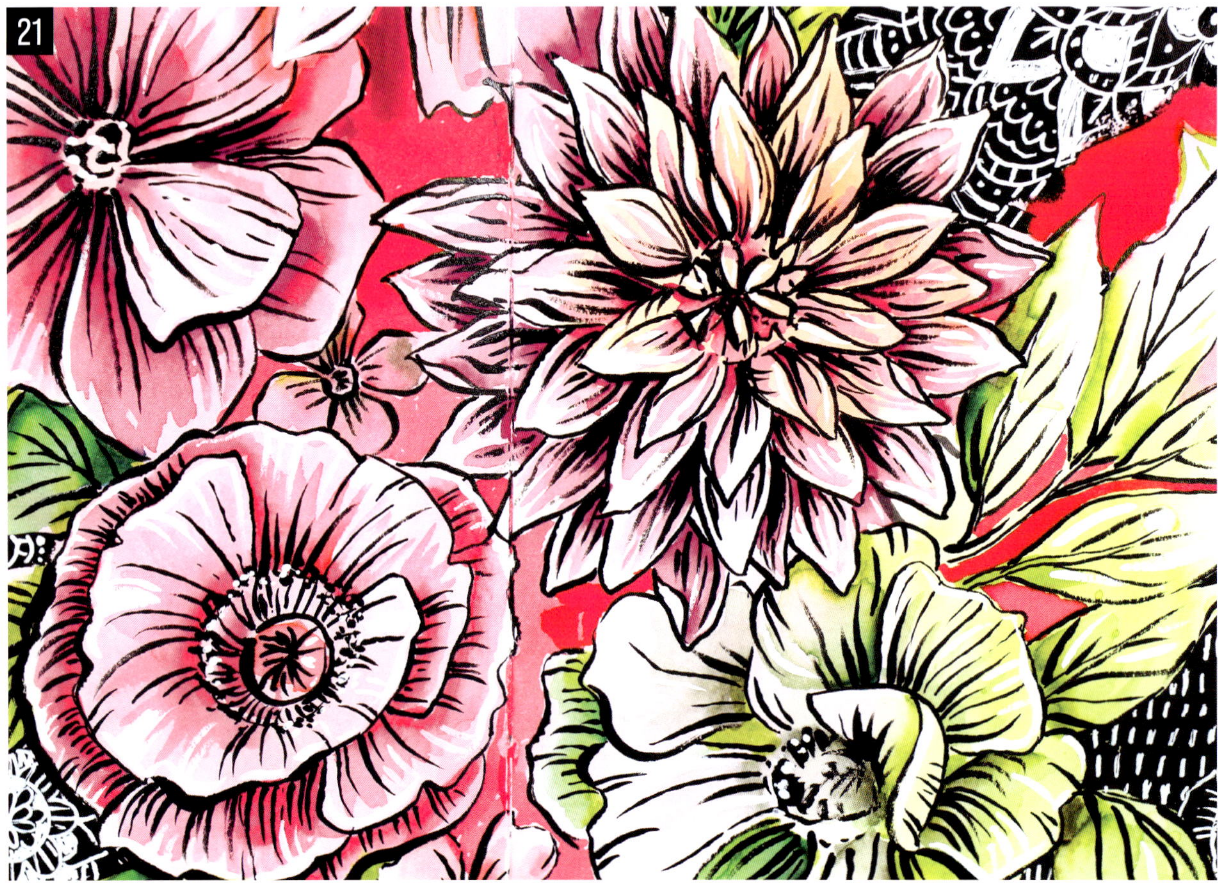

21 **Add white highlights.** Continue with the white to add highlights to the main florals and leaves, such as lines along the petals and dots in the centers. I switched to a bleed-proof white paint here, but you could also stick with the gel pen for a more subtle effect. These highlights will help pull the foreground florals forward even further.

22 **Appraise for final adjustments.** It's time for your quick stroll! Walk away from your piece and come back with fresh eyes. Are you done? I never am at this first fresh look—I always see something more to do. In this case, I decided to push my negative space back just a bit more around the main group of flowers in the center, so I used watercolors to wash in deeper tones.

23 **Make your finishing touches.** I also decided to take the dimension in my florals a step further by adding some more subtle shadows inside them with my markers. With that, I'm satisfied and ready to set down my tools. What more did you choose to tweak or add?

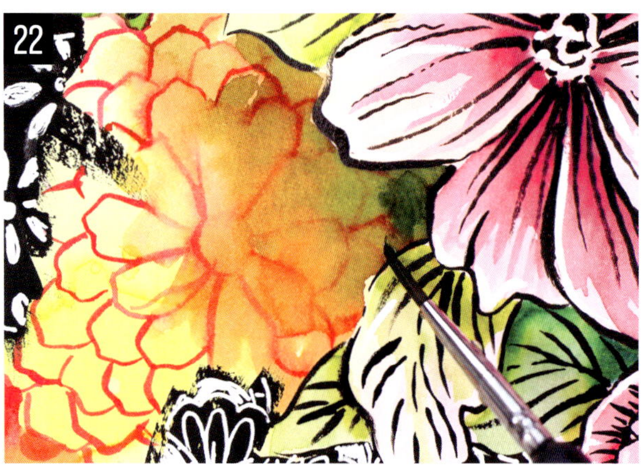

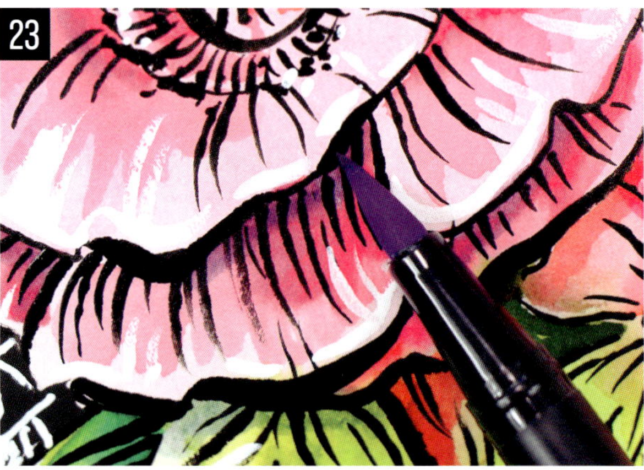

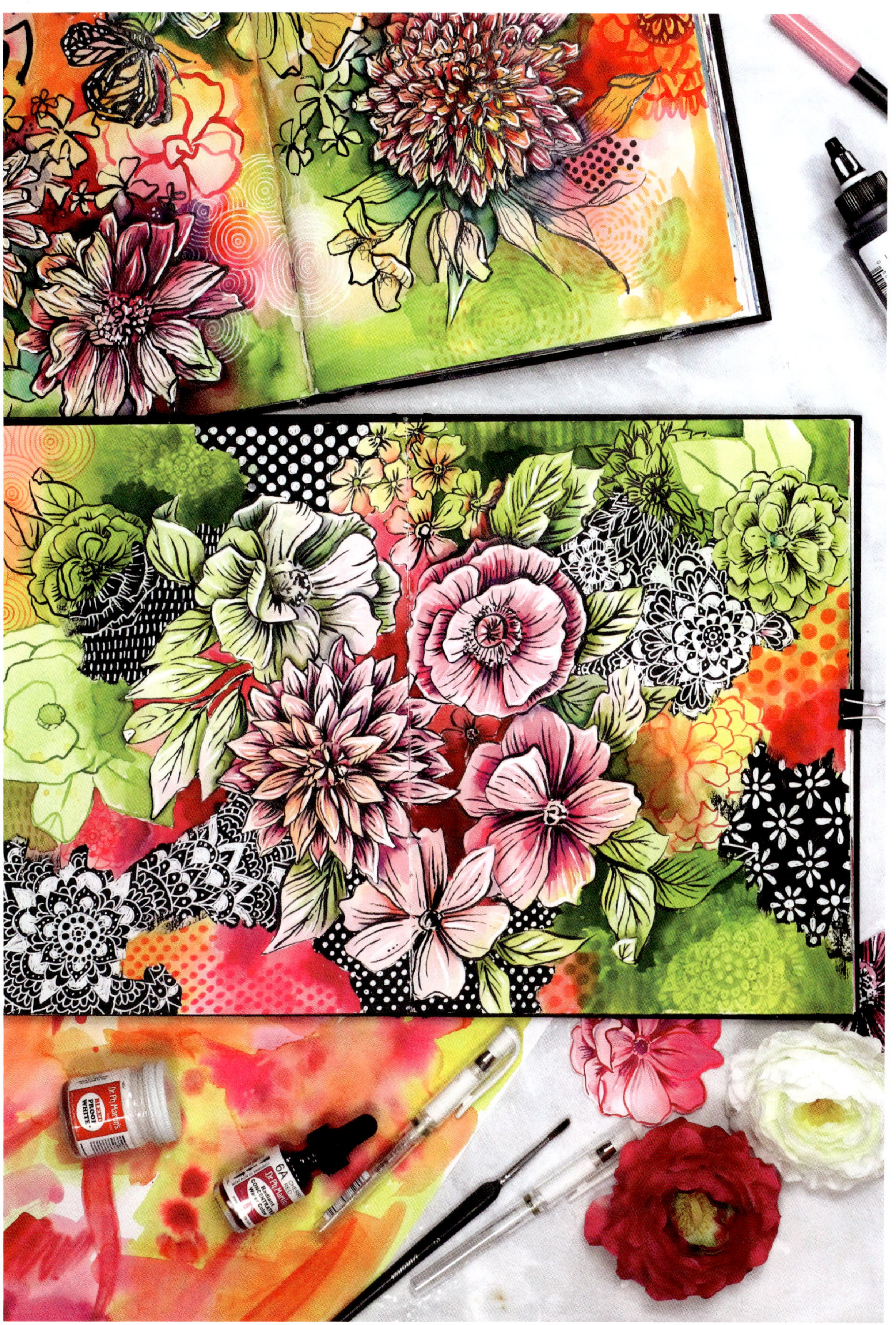

Transformative Contrast

*Learn to use "dull" acrylic colors to make brighter colors pop
and add texture using stencils and found items*

It's time for a big switch! Put those watercolors to the side and grab your acrylics. Acrylics are near and dear to my heart; since my first days painting in high school, I've leaned into acrylics hard.

As we've worked through the first half of this book, you've heard me say, "Start light," "Don't go too dark yet," and "Now add those midtones." Well, guess what? With acrylics, we can forget those instructions, because if you paint too dark, you can just cover it up. If you paint something purple and you want it green, let it dry and paint right over it. If you paint a daisy and you wish you'd painted a peony, slap some paint across it and start in again!

Acrylics are safe. There is no happy accident you can't reverse if it isn't that happy after all. And, because they are safe, we are going to take some major risks while we use them! We will give them a chance to swoop in and save us to embrace just how flexible we can be when we paint in this medium. In this piece, we will also get a little deeper into color theory and learn how to use dull colors to enhance bright ones.

Tools & Supplies

- Acrylic paints
- White gel pen or white acrylic paint
- Pencil (6B or other)
- A size 20 flat or size 8 round paintbrush (or your choice of a large brush), plus sizes 1 and 6 round paintbrushes (or your choice of a small and a medium brush)
- Stencils
- Makeup sponge
- Bubble wrap
- Glazing medium
- Watercolor paper, mixed-media paper, or Bristol board

What You'll Learn

SECOND CHANCES: When you paint something and you just don't like it, I always encourage you to problem-solve and use the experience to teach you something; every piece can be redeemed. But, when painting in acrylics, we have more of a choice in how we redeem our work. To discover this, we are going to make some purposeful things we don't like, to see how easy it is to cover up what we want gone.

COLOR INTENSITY: Because I most often use bright, vibrant colors, I often rely on value for contrast. However, for this piece, we are going to throw out the black paint and rely more heavily on dull versus bright colors to create eye-catching contrast. Duller colors can bring out even more beauty in a piece by allowing the bright, saturated colors to shine.

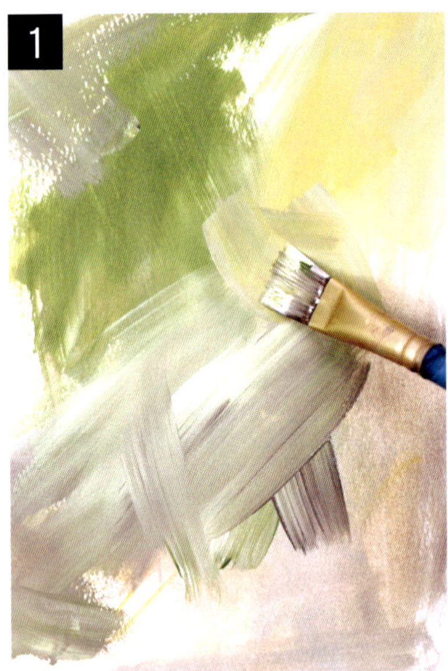

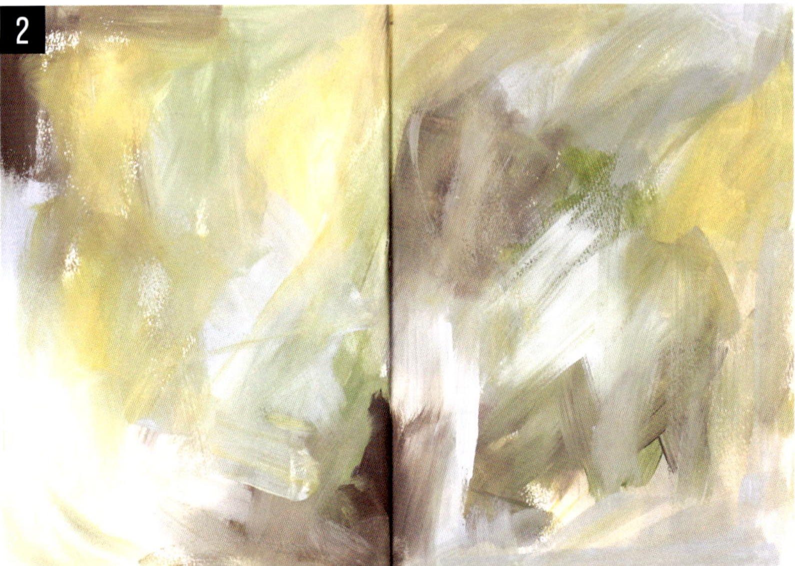

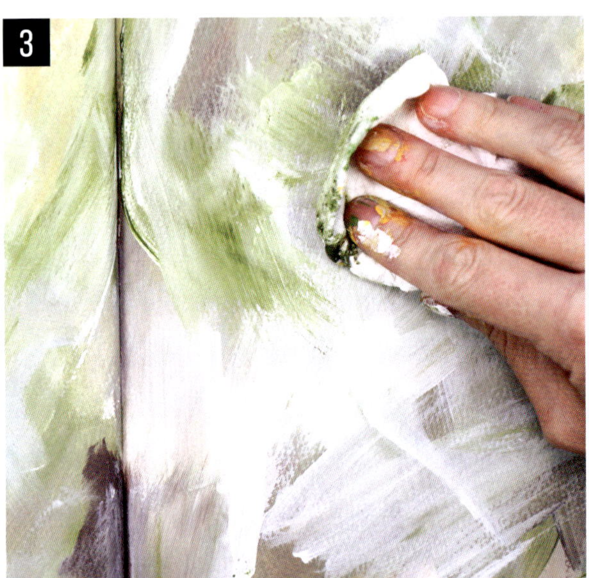

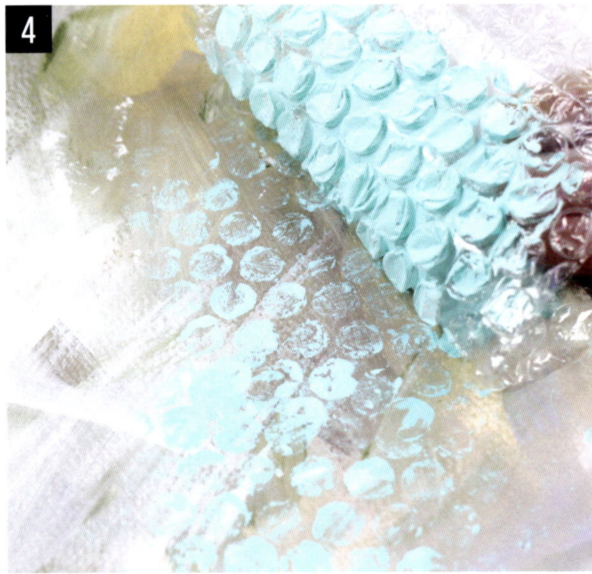

1 **Choose dull, muted tones for the background.**
We are starting off our venture into the world of
acrylics with dull, muted, earthy tones. This may
be your cup of tea, but by now you know that it's
not mine. Don't get me wrong—I appreciate these
colors in nature, and even in other works of art.
I just don't like to paint with them myself! But as
you'll see working through this piece, these colors
are going to play an important supporting role.

2 **Fill the background with abstract strokes
of mixed colors.** Keep slapping down strokes
of various dull colors until you've filled the entire
background of your paper. I often use a flat
brush as opposed to a round brush when adding
my background layers in acrylic.

3 **Add some messy texture.** It's time to get your
hands nice and messy! Take a paper towel or scrap
cloth, dip it in some paint, and rub it into your page.
I like this technique because I can create some
interesting texture while getting my hands dirty,
which always loosens me up for the artistic process
to come.

4 **Layer on bubble wrap texture.** I give you
permission now to switch to your favorite, brighter
colors. Bubble wrap is a cheap and easy way to
put interesting, grungy marks onto your paper to
continue building up layers. The marks can look a lot
like polka dots, which I love. Add several saturated
layers of different colors of bubble wrap texture
across your paper.

5 **Apply stencils.** Stencils are another fun way to add interesting textures and patterns to your work. I have a whole stash of stencils I've collected over time, and I find that using a makeup sponge to dab on the paint works best. Bring in more bright colors here; use as many colors as you'd like.

6 **Keep layering on stencils.** Layer on several different stencils on top of one another in a variety of colors until you are happy with the distribution and variety across your entire background.

7 **Paint outlines of flowers.** Grab a small paintbrush and some dark (but not black) acrylic paint; I chose blue-violet here. Although I love the contrast that black can give to a piece, sometimes I like to see what contrast I can achieve with colors alone. As you've done in previous projects, mix up the sizes and shapes of your flowers and leave plenty of negative space.

8 **Paint some leaf silhouettes.** Add some loose vines and leaves coming out this way and that from the flowers. Fill these shapes in with some rough brushstrokes, allowing the background to peek through in places.

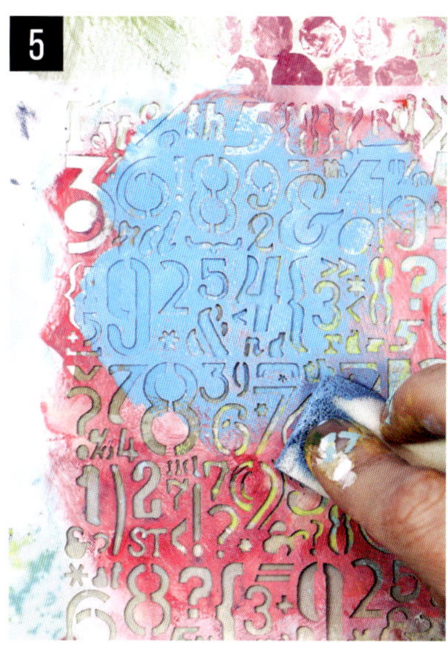

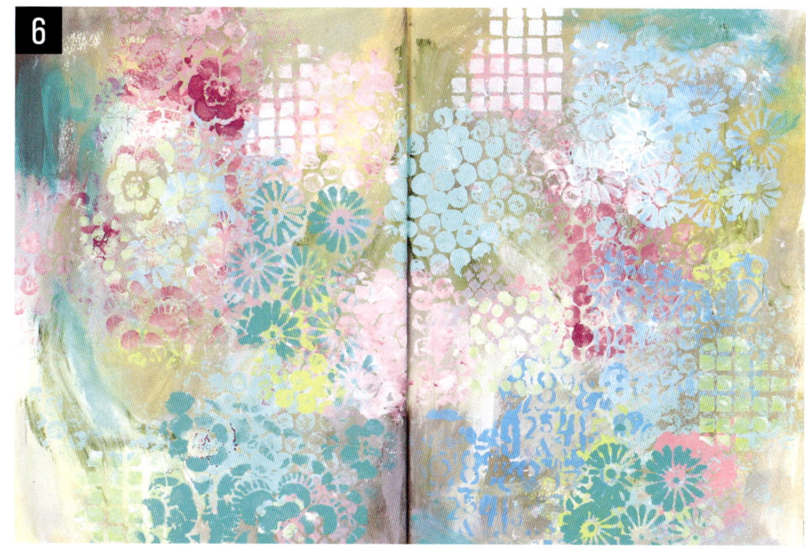

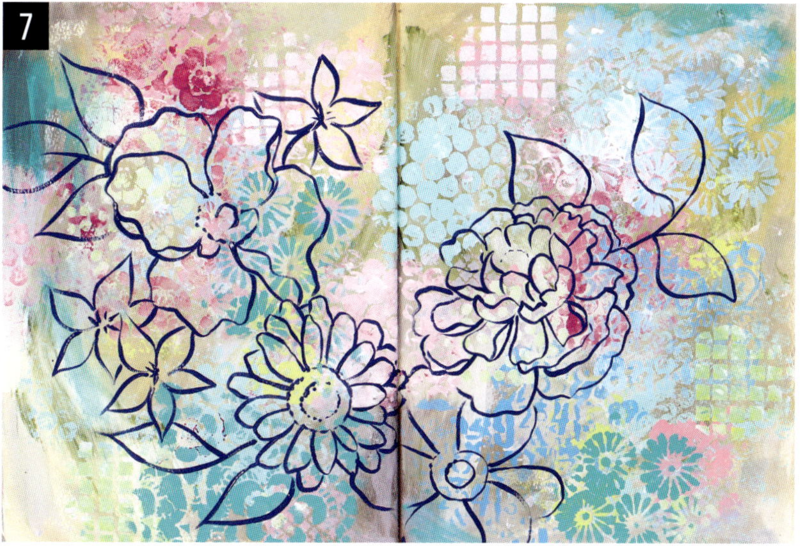

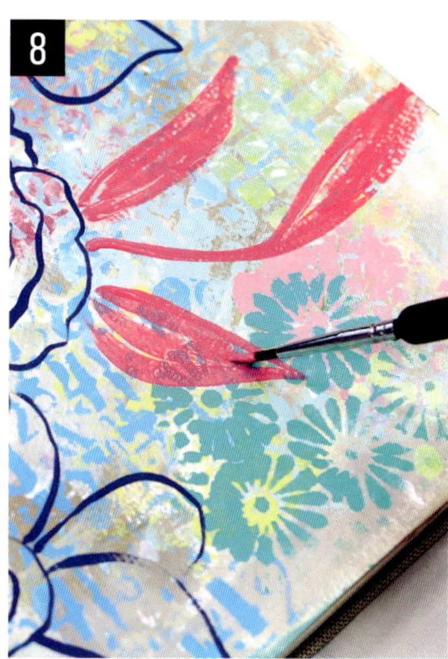

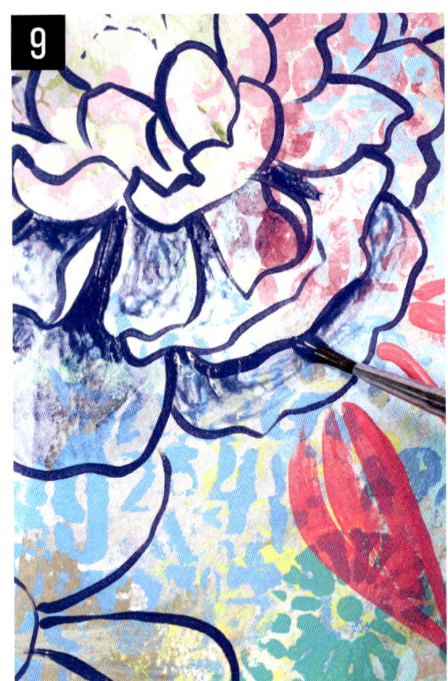

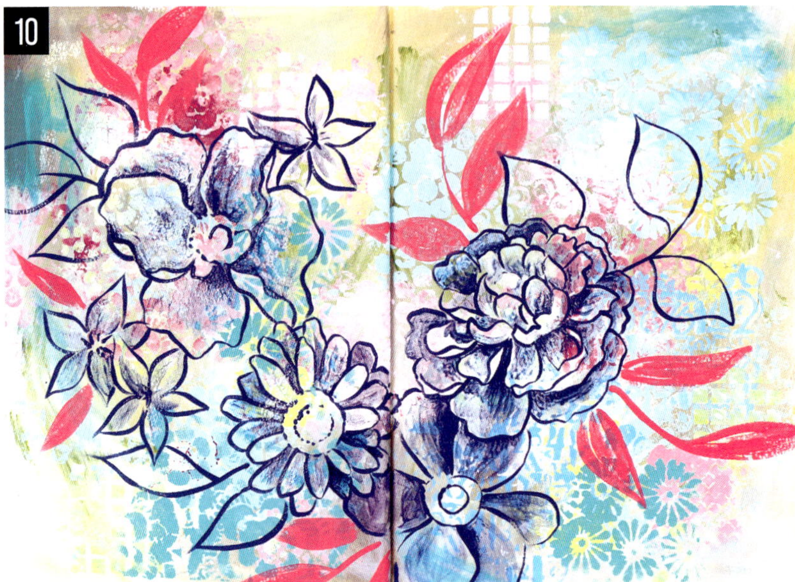

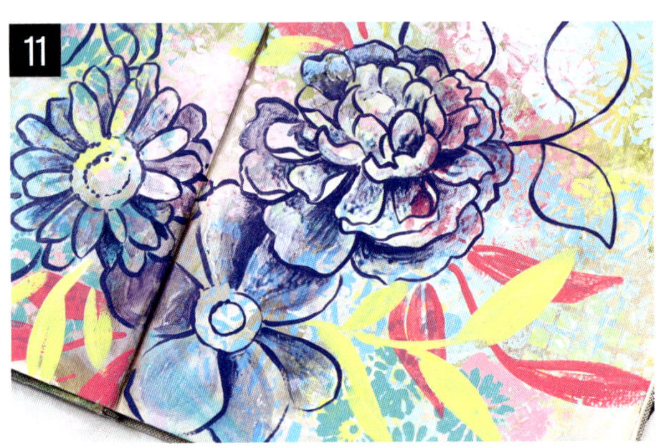

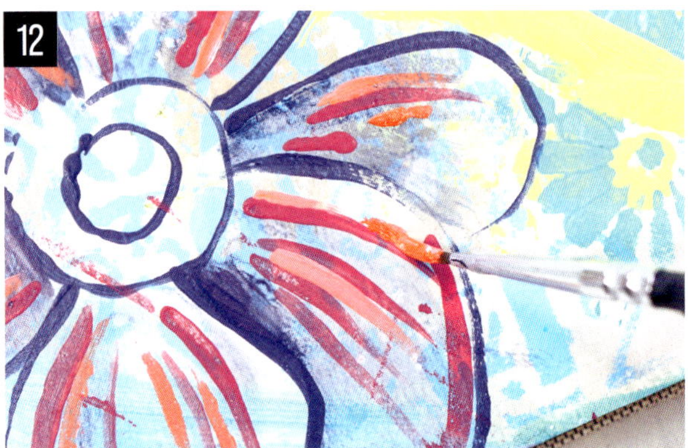

You don't need perfectly smooth blends. We will be adding plenty of linework
on top of this first bit of dimension, so do not worry about making seamless, neat blends.

9 **Mix paint with glazing medium.** To add shading to the flowers, first create a mix of glazing medium (or matte medium) and the same blue-violet used to outline them. (If you do not have either of these media, simply water down your paint a bit to help fade the color out.) The more glazing medium you add to the paint, the more transparent the color will become.

10 **Finish shading the flowers.** Add more-opaque shading in the areas you want to be darkest, and then add more glazing medium to the mix to add to the areas you want to be less dark. Using a mix like this will create a nice transparency that preserves some of the interesting mark-making and texture in the background while still adding a cohesive tint of color.

11 **Add another layer of leaves in the background.** Next, choose a vibrant yellow-green and add another layer of messy, silhouetted leaves that overlaps the first layer of pink leaves. At this point, a tiny miracle is beginning to take shape: those dull, muted colors are beginning to bring the brighter and more pure colors to life. The contrast between dull and bright is just as beautiful as a deep contrast in value.

12 **Add color details to the flowers.** Switching back to the foreground, begin to add linework to the florals using midtones that are neither too dark nor too light. You can use a different combination of colors in each flower, such as red-orange plus pink in one flower, lavender plus sky blue in another flower, etc. At this point, I am still ignoring the original leaves I created in my initial line drawing.

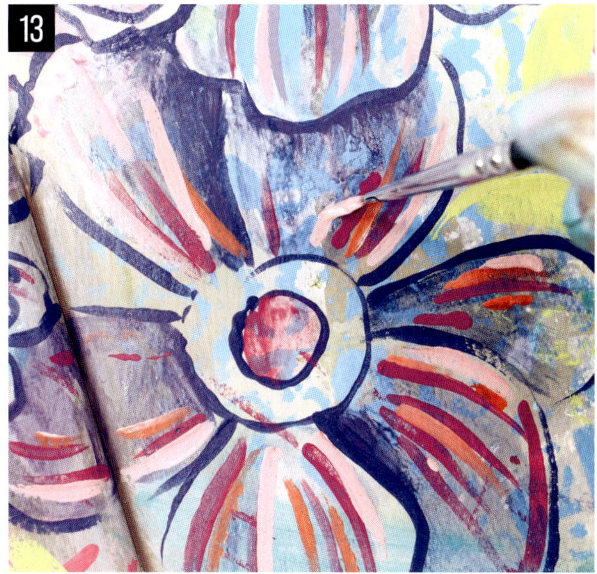

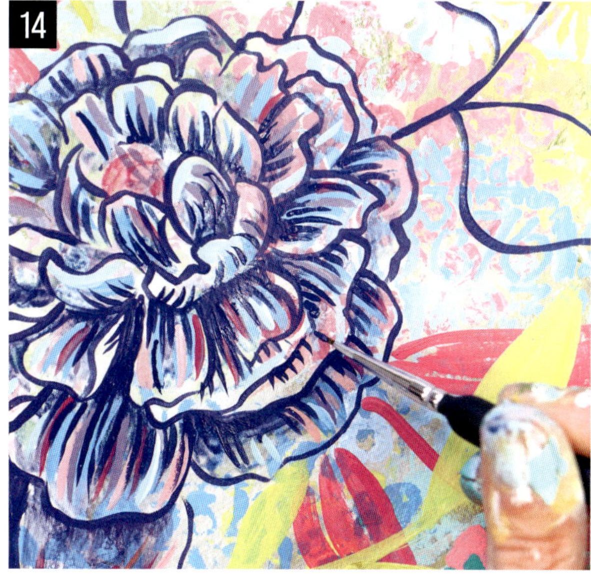

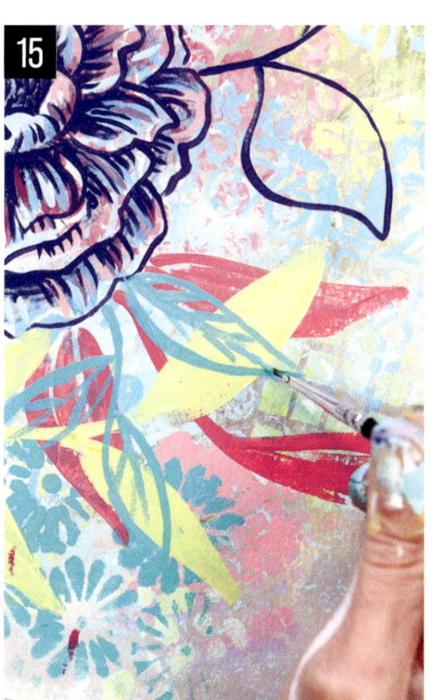

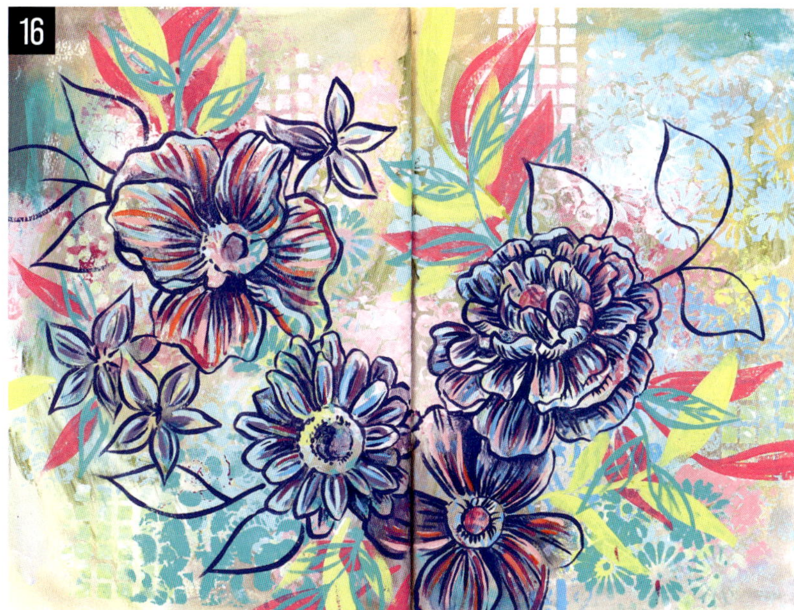

13 **Add lighter details next.** Now go in to add lighter linework details to these same flowers using brighter and lighter colors. This linework should be messy and free, creating highlights of these colors throughout the flowers. Do not put every color in every flower; instead, mix up the combinations.

14 **Add dark details last.** Now for the dark linework! Use the same color that was used for the outlines to add fine details to the flowers that emphasize the dimension in the petals, being more intentional with each stroke than you were when adding the previous colorful details.

15 **Add a third layer of background leaves.** The expressive leaves in the background are going to get one more layer in a third color, this time bright green. However, for this layer, draw them as outlines with loose details instead of as filled-in silhouetted shapes.

16 **Check your progress.** By this point your background should have a good bit going on and your flowers should be pretty heavy in detail. But we can bring the flowers forward to pop even more. Up until now, we've used deeper, darker colors to contrast with the flowers to bring them forward, but in the next step we will take the opposite approach and use white.

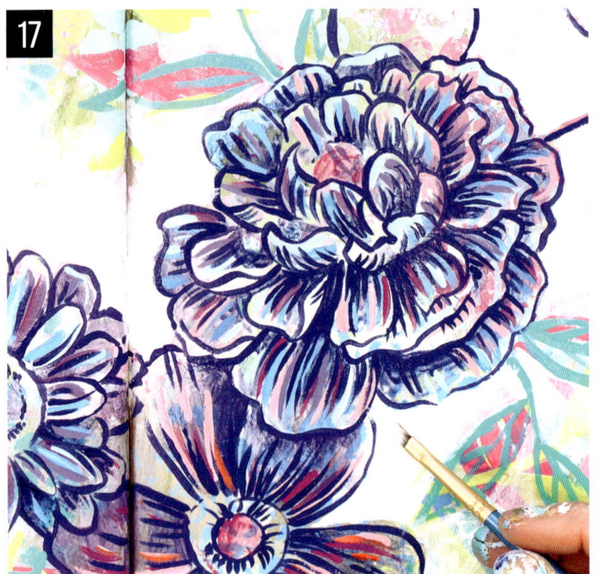

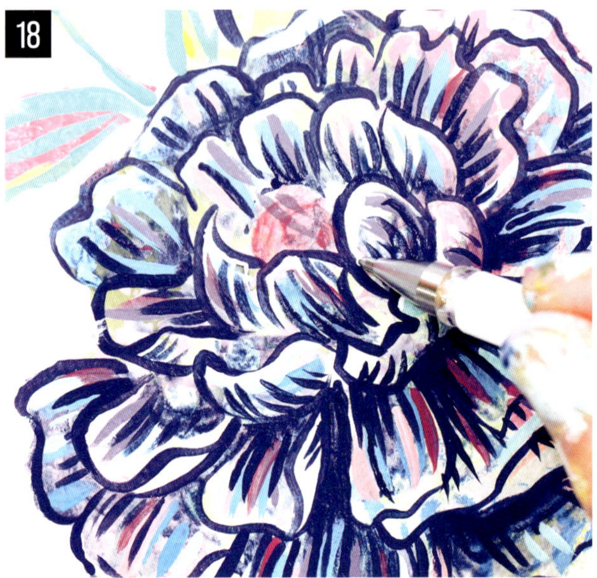

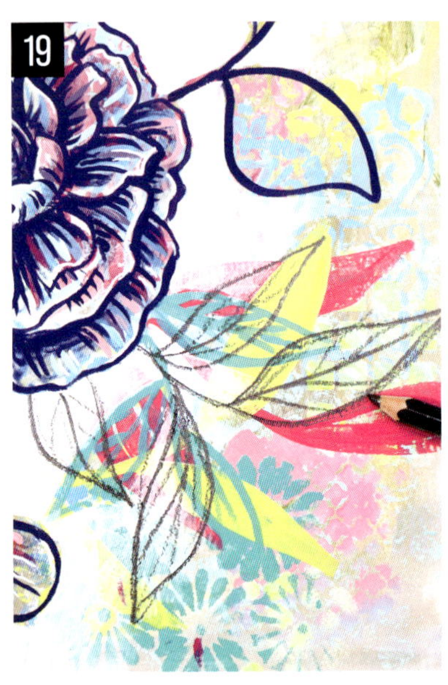

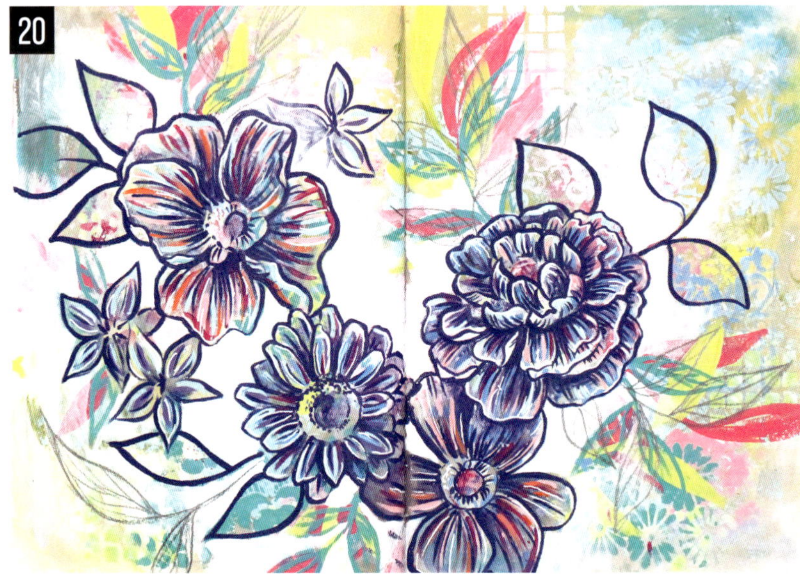

17 **Halo the flowers with white.** We'll use white to address the negative space around the flowers and leaves that has been left plain. Mix your white paint with some glazing medium (or matte medium, or water in a pinch) to create subtle transparency and to allow you to fade the white out into the background as you move away from the flowers. This will give the flowers the illusion of glowing.

18 **Add white highlights to the flowers.** Using your white gel pen, add white highlights to the flowers. Be selective in where you place these. A gel pen will typically bleed less on top of dried acrylics than it may on top of watercolors.

19 **Draw in one final layer of sketchy background leaves.** Using a dark pencil, draw in one final layer of messy leaves in the background. Not only will this add more interest by creating another layer, but the switch in supplies adds interest too. It's unexpected, and I like the unexpected.

20 **Make final tweaks.** The time to walk away has come. Step away, have a treat, and come back with fresh eyes to assess what more the piece needs. In my case, the piece was 99.9% complete; all I did at the end was use the deep-blue-violet paint to crisp up a few outlines that had gotten lost while I was painting the white in the negative space. I also made the linework in my leaves a bit thicker to give them a boost.

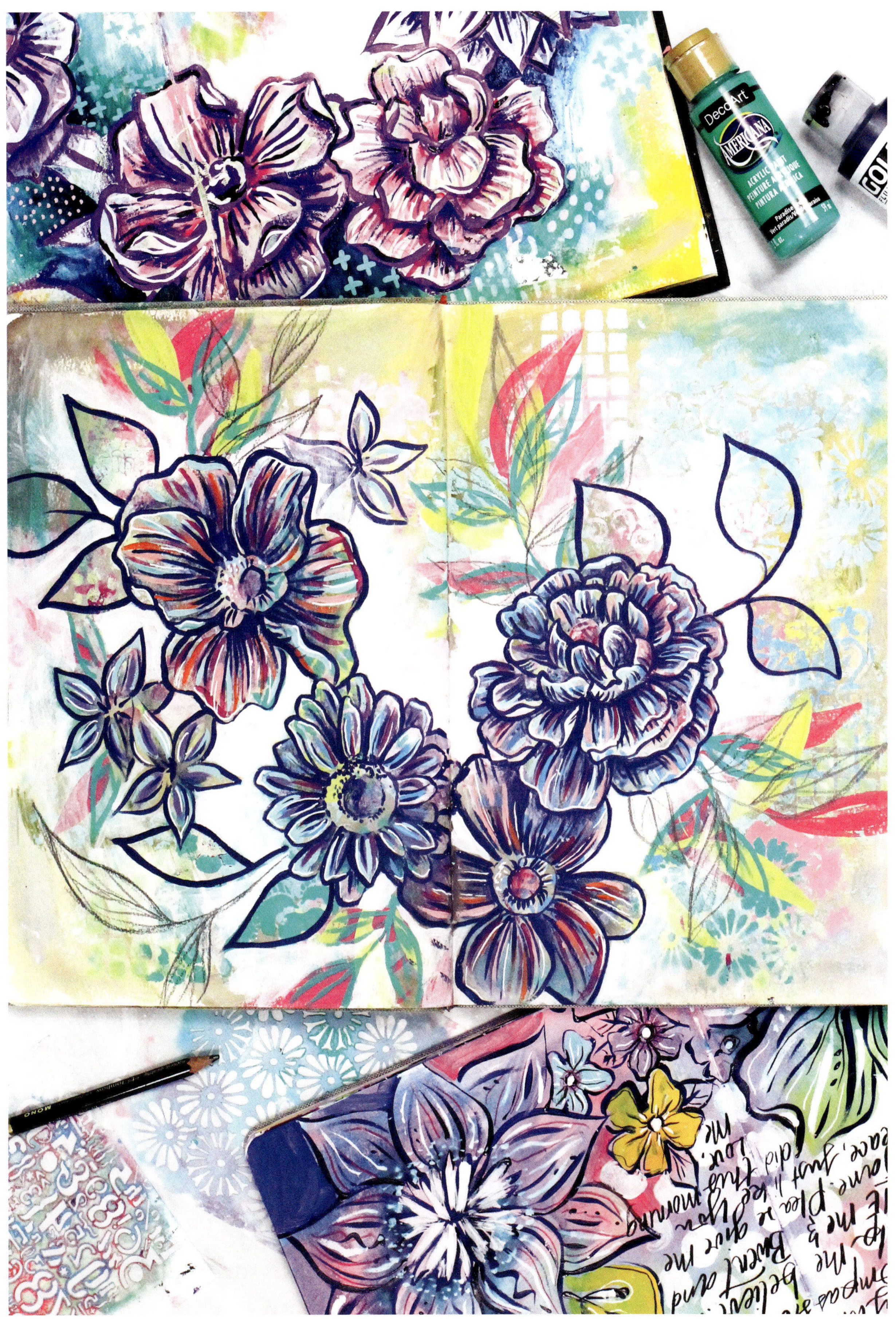

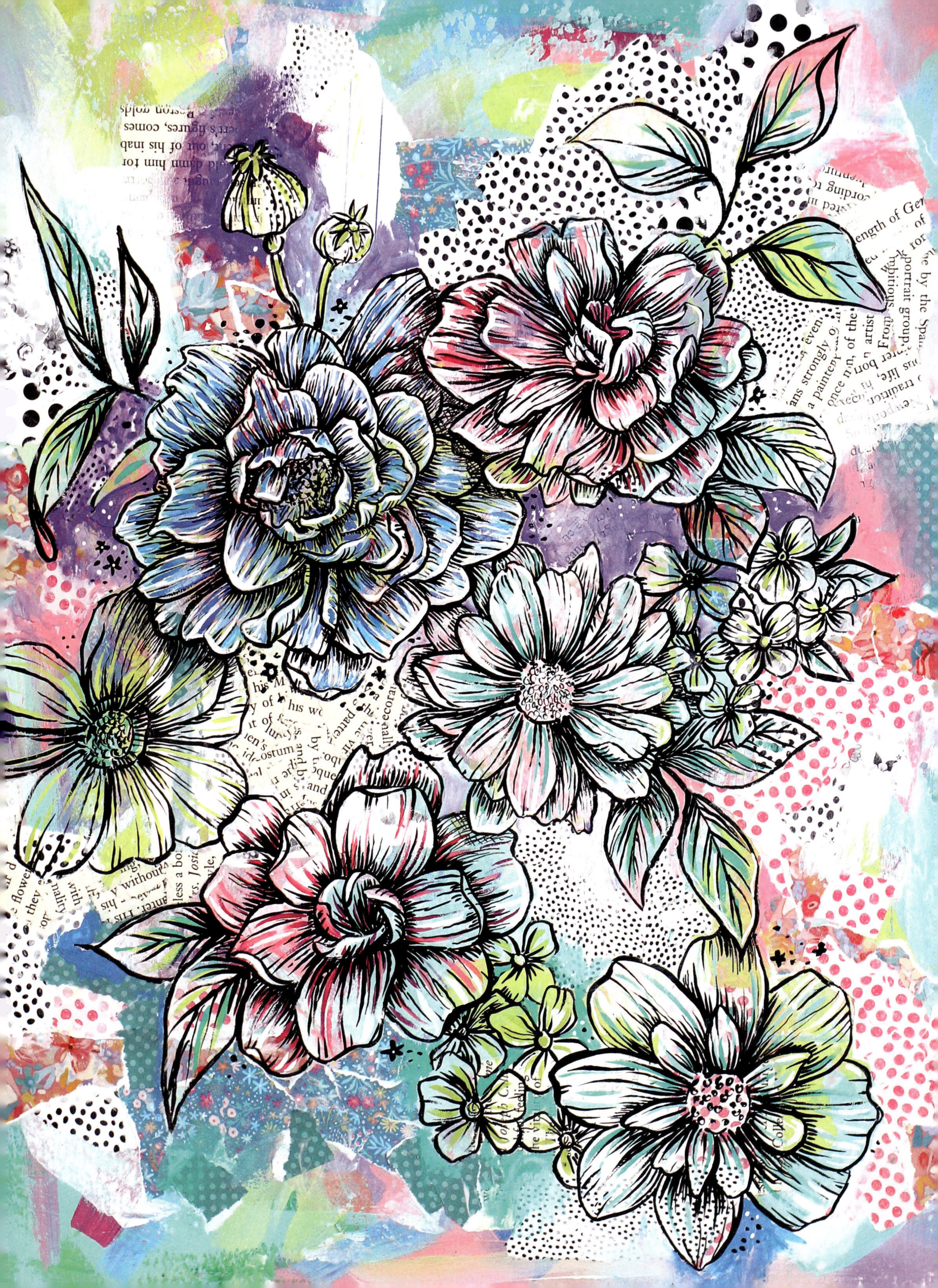

Collage Magic

*Learn to mix acrylics with collage elements
for a multilayered, dimensional look*

Is it just me, or is there something really enjoyable about ripping up paper and gluing it down? Perhaps it is because it reminds me of creating a construction paper mosaic in elementary school that gets displayed on the hallway wall gallery. (And, of course, once the piece was finished, I had the pleasure of picking all that dried glue off my fingers!) I know I love a good mess when I create, and a mess is sure to happen when I start ripping up bits of paper and gluing them down.

Just as much as I enjoy the process of collaging, I love the texture that it brings to a piece. When you combine this with quick and messy brushstrokes, textures from scraping paint across the page, and delicately painted floral linework, the results are mesmerizing. This piece will have a lot going on, but we'll rein in the chaos to create a cohesive work of art.

Tools & Supplies

- Acrylic paints
- A size 24 flat paintbrush, plus sizes 00, 1, and 6 round paintbrushes (or your choice of an extra-small, a small, and a medium brush)
- Old gift card or other disposable hard edge
- Scissors
- Collage elements such as scrapbook papers, personal patterns, notebook paper, old book pages, washi tape, etc.
- Matte medium/adhesive
- Watercolor paper, mixed-media paper, or Bristol board

What You'll Learn

SCAVENGING: For this piece, look around your house to find interesting papers, tapes, and other scraps to collage with. You may not have a box full of patterned papers like I do, but you can find patterns in your everyday papers as well—in notebook papers, paragraphs from magazines, washi tapes, etc. Look around and see what you have on hand; ordinary papers can be turned into extraordinary elements.

CONTROLLED CHAOS: Once again, we'll have a lot going on in this project. With all the paper scraps, paint scraping, and manic brushstrokes, it can feel a bit overwhelming. But we'll use that chaos intentionally and in a somewhat organized method to add interest and excitement. It's going to feel great.

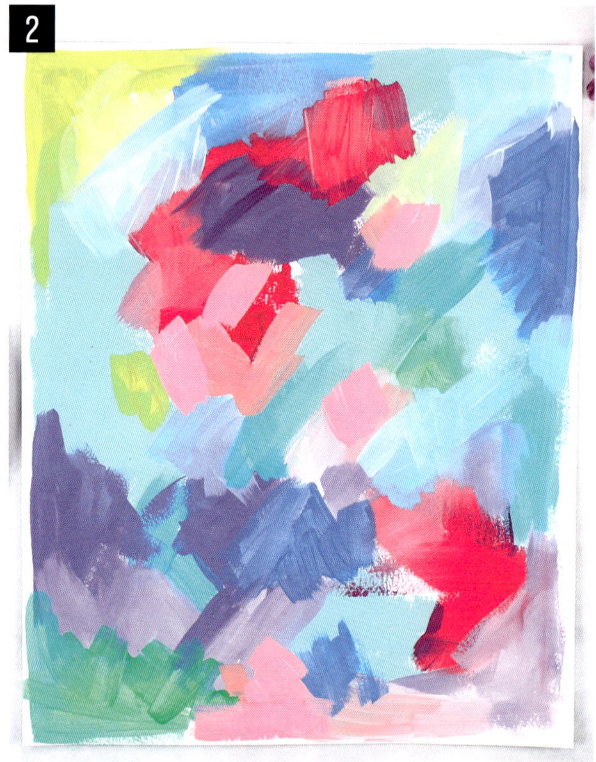

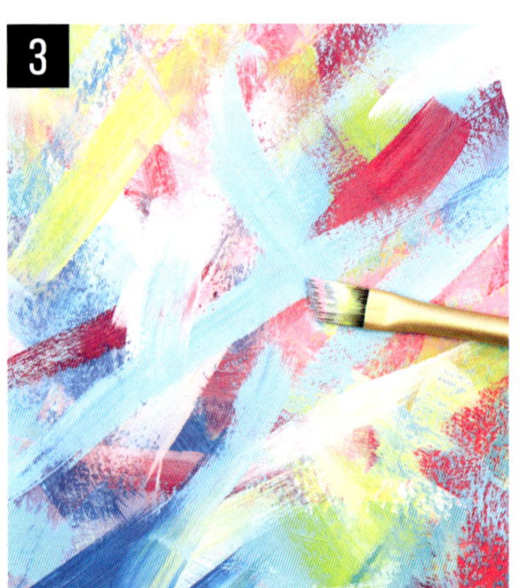

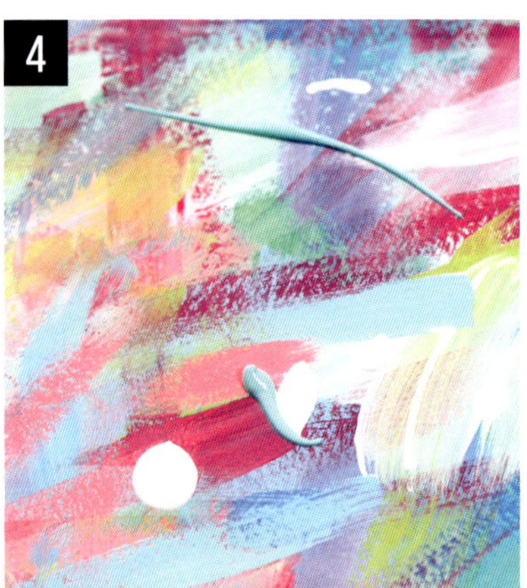

1 Choose colors for the background. Let's demolish that white space! Find a happy place and immerse yourself in freeing brushstrokes in whatever colors your heart desires. My color scheme is going to be tropical and beachy; I'm shaking off the rules I gave myself in the previous project and diving headlong into some comforting (for this ocean girl) colors. Start with just one color, adding some patches here and there. I often use a flat brush as opposed to a round one when adding my background layers in acrylic.

2 Finish painting the background. Repeat, adding patches of other colors on the paper, until the paper is completely filled.

3 Add messy brushstrokes. Once the first layer is complete, begin to break up your sections of color with layers of messy brushstrokes. Allow the first layer of paint to disappear in areas or barely peek through. Add as many layers as it takes to get you to sink into the piece, and do not concern yourself with how things look. Instead, concern yourself with how you feel as you make this mess. Try a dry-brushing effect as well, allowing the paint to wear off your brush and create imperfect streaks full of funky texture.

4 Add paint blobs and scrape. Now it's time for a new technique—paint scraping! Apply a few blobs of paint directly on the paper without

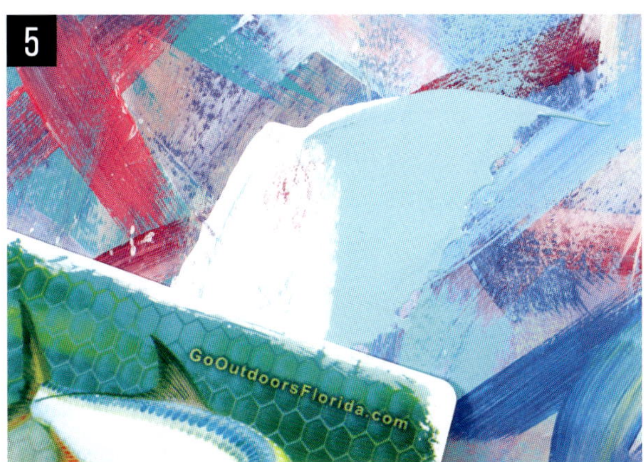

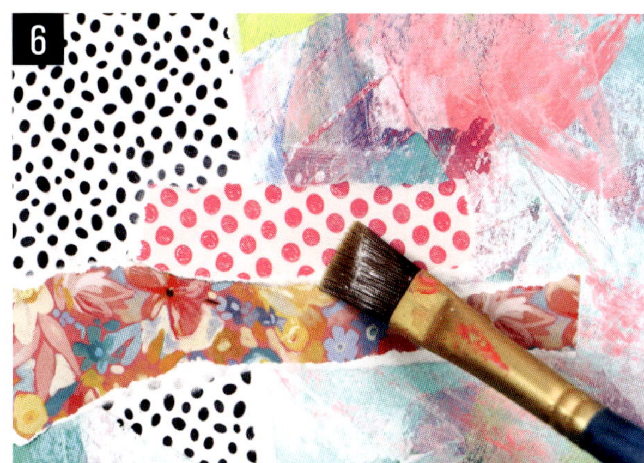

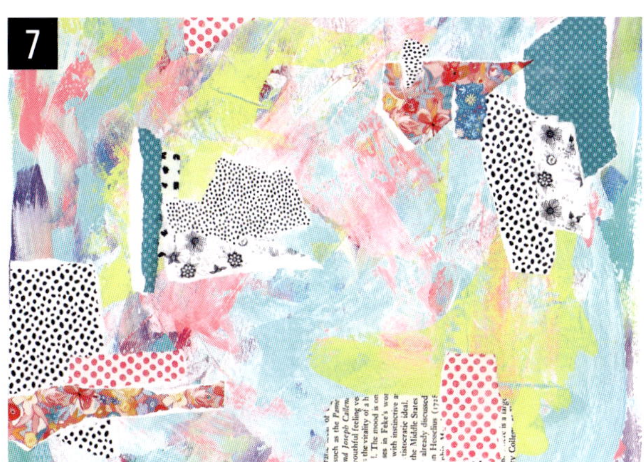

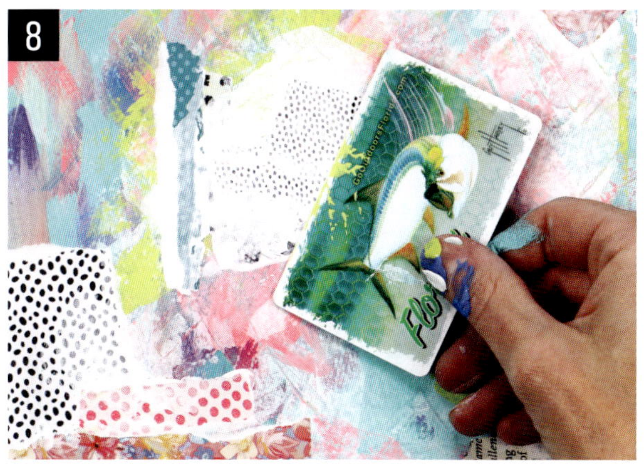

brushing it in. Then, using an old gift card or similar item (I'm using my expired fishing license!), scrape the paint across the paper. Look at the amazing texture that results (in the step 5 photo)!

5 Repeat all over the paper. Repeat this technique with a few different colors, moving in all different directions across the paper, until you're satisfied. There's no way you aren't having fun and feeling loosened up by now. (If you aren't, then just keep going until you do!)

6 Start collaging. Gather your scrap papers, washi tape, and whatever else you have and rip them up. When you're ready to start applying the elements, there are several ways to adhere them, and, depending on your papers, I recommend the following. For thinner pieces, I prefer to use a matte medium to adhere the piece and then to

coat across the top. For thicker pieces, I apply an adhesive to stick it down and then coat across the top with my matte medium.

7 Experiment with different approaches. There are no rules to collaging, but there are a few things I do recommend. First, tear your edges as opposed to cutting them with scissors, unless you are up against the edges of your surface. Also, create sections of collaged elements as opposed to separating tiny scraps all over the page.

8 Push some collaged bits back into the background. As you collage, leave plenty of background space visible around the collaged areas. Then use the scraping technique again to push some of the collaged areas into the background, allowing them to peek out partially from beneath the new layer of paint.

9 **Start painting flower outlines.** Once your workspace is a complete mess, it's time to paint some flowers! I'm using black acrylic and an extra-small round paintbrush to paint in my basic outlines, but you are free to use any color you'd like. Start with thin, delicate lines (as in "Party in the Background"), but let your composition develop organically, without a plan. Simply paint your first flower and see what unfolds from there.

10 **Finish composing the flowers.** Add flowers and leaves until you are satisfied with your composition. Try to leave some negative space between some flowers as well as around the flowers.

11 **Collage around the outlines of the flowers and leaves.** Get your collage materials back out and fill in the areas of negative space right up against your flowers and leaves, effectively outlining them in collage. Wherever the flowers themselves feature collage elements peeking through inside them, strive to put contrasting pieces up against those areas. For instance, don't use black dots in the negative space around a leaf that's filled with black dots. You may want to use darker papers against lighter florals and vice versa.

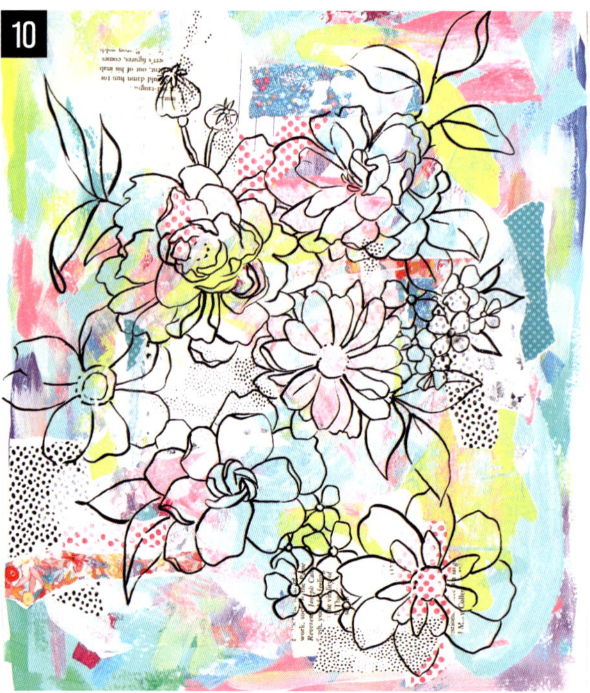

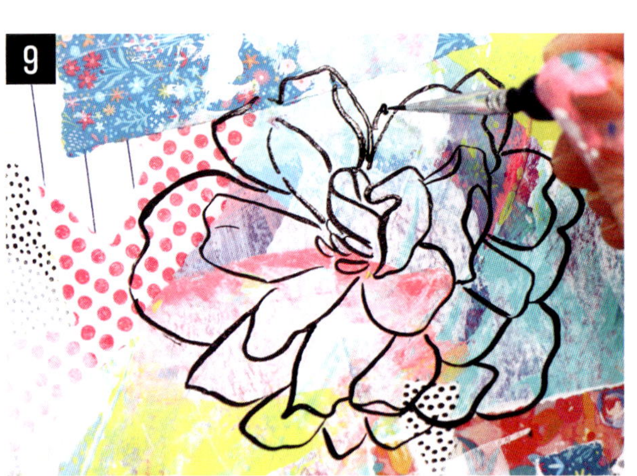

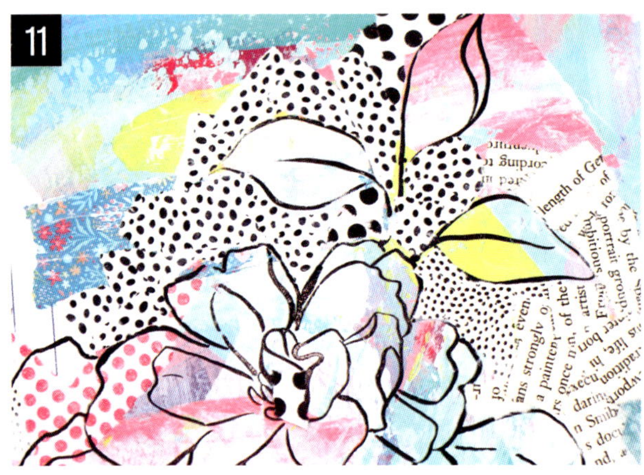

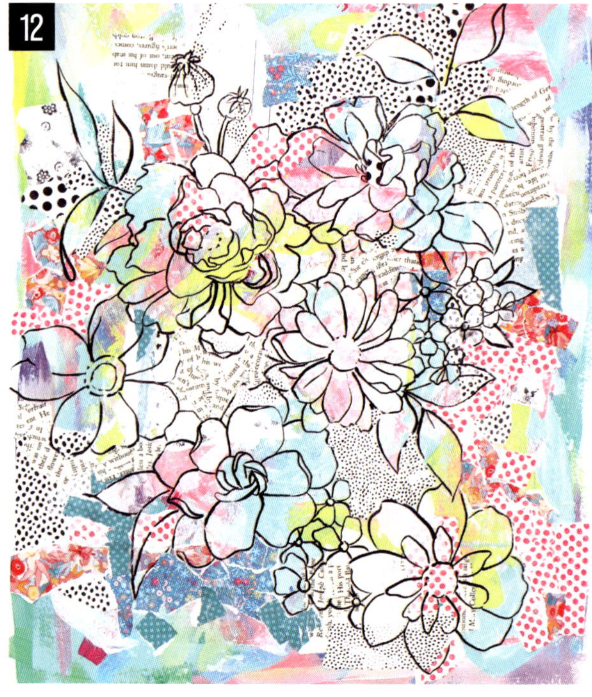

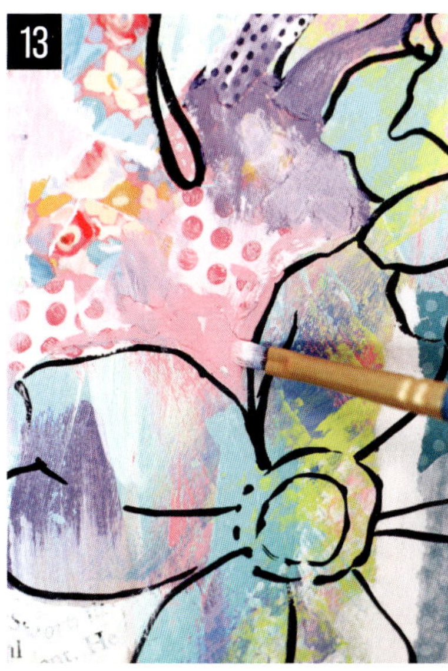

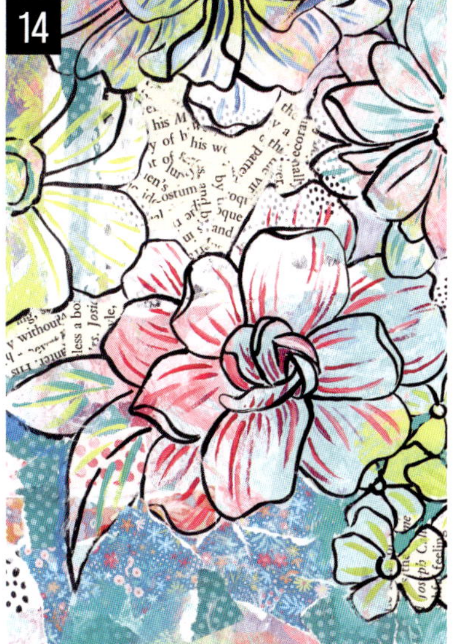

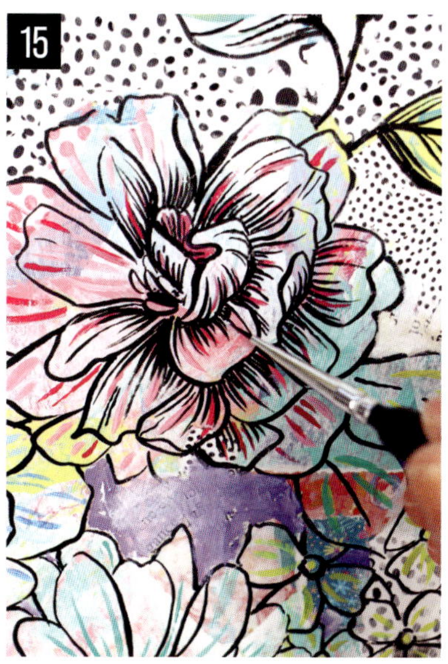

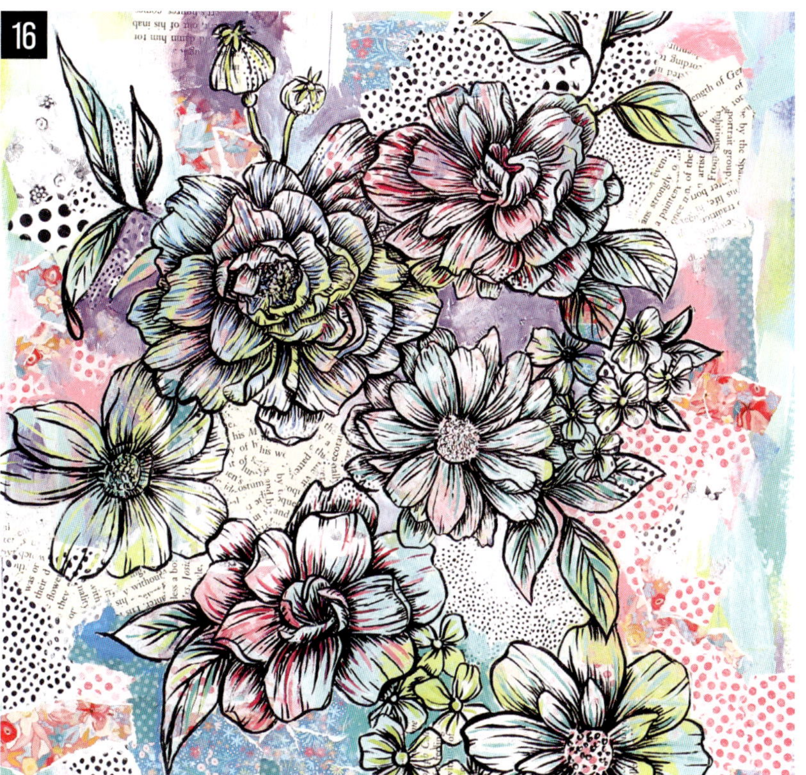

14 Add color to the flowers.
Let's revisit the flowers now. We will build these up in three phases. For the first phase, add line details in color in each flower. You want to preserve the interesting textures and collage elements in each flower, so do not go overboard here. Simply choose different colors in each flower to create a sense of separation, helping each flower stand out from the others.

15 Add black to the flowers.
For the second phase of enhancing the florals, add dimension using fine black linework details. Continue trying to preserve as much of the gorgeous, interesting background peeking through each floral as you can, but use black on a fine-tipped round brush to add dramatic depth in each flower and leaf.

16 Restore any lost outlines.
This is also the time to clean up any edges that were lost when you added collage elements to the negative space. Once you've finished, look at how thickly textured your flowers now are. They really stand out from the background!

12 **Finish the outline collaging.** Continue filling in the spaces between flowers and surrounding the flowers with collage. Use your matte medium to apply the elements, tearing tiny pieces in some areas as needed to fit into small nooks and crannies. If you go over the floral outlines a bit, you can always bring those back when it's time to work in the flowers again.

13 **Paint in the remaining corners.** At some point you'll probably be a little sick of sticking down tiny scraps of paper up against your flowers. Step back and take a look at what you've done; if there are areas where you did not fill in the negative space or you missed a nook or a cranny, paint it in with color instead. You can fade out the color or let it have a precise edge like the collage pieces do.

17 **Add white highlights.** It's highlight time! Use a white gel pen and/or white paint to add highlights to bring the petals even more forward. A gel pen is great for the thinnest white lines. Create the most dramatic contrast between shadows and highlights in the florals that you want to draw more attention to.

18 **Add black "sparkles."** Embrace the maximalism in this piece by going in and adding small dots and tiny flowers in some areas of the negative space. I like to tuck these into little nooks and crannies around the flowers that I have been focused on making most prominent. Although these are tiny additions, you'd be surprised how much of a difference they can make.

19 **Assess your work.** Now, instead of walking away and coming back after a few minutes for a fresh look, try something new: take a photo of your piece. Look at it through a different lens (literally) to see if there are any areas you'd like to address. One thing that I wanted to do was to emphasize where some flowers overlapped others just a bit more. I did this by adding more black lines in those areas, like shadows cast on top of the flowers underneath (for example, the "shadow" cast by the small pink flower onto the large blue flower, as shown here).

20 **Add finishing touches.** My last tweak was to bring more attention to my favorite flower, the focal point of the piece—the only blue flower. I wanted the viewer's eye to be drawn to this flower first. Even though it is behind a brighter pink flower, it's the largest flower, the only blue flower, and my favorite shape of all the flowers. So, to bring it even more to center stage, I applied more blue to it. Now the piece feels complete, and completely full of life and vibrance!

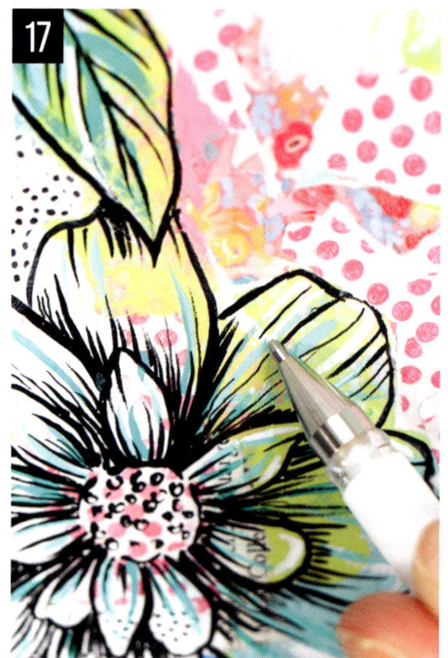

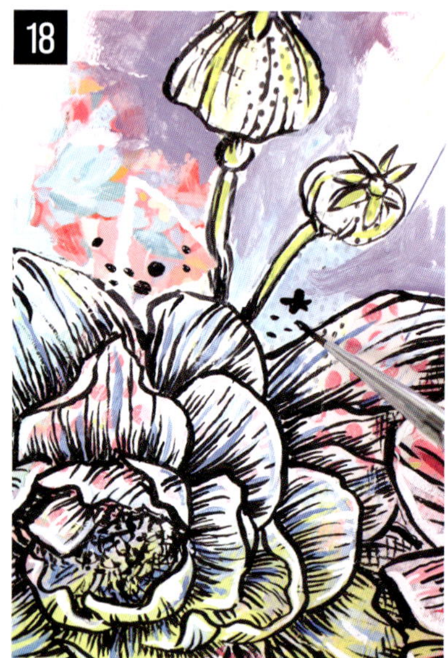

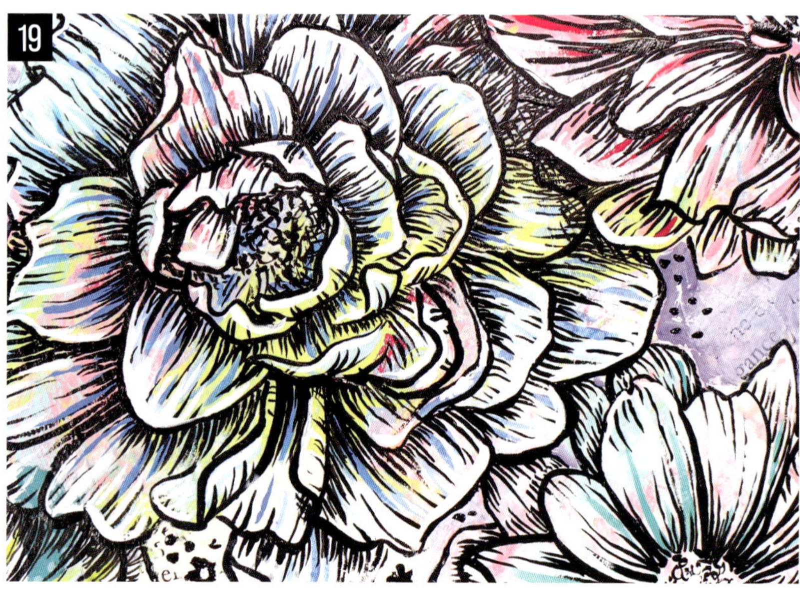

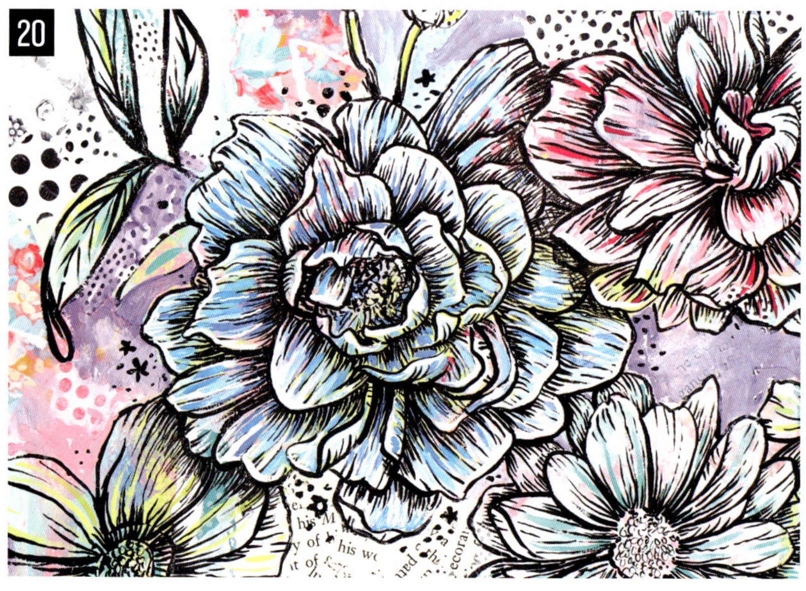

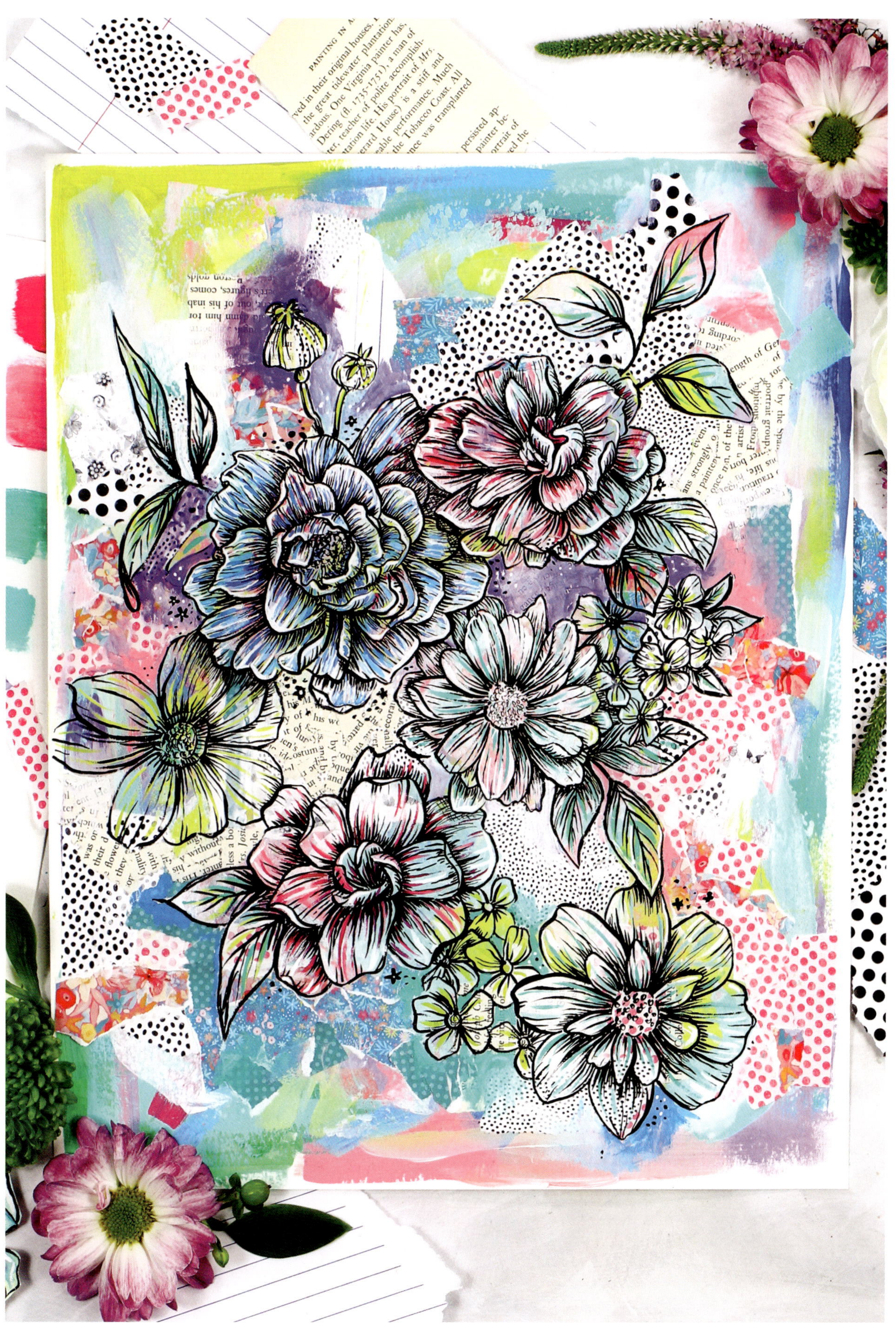

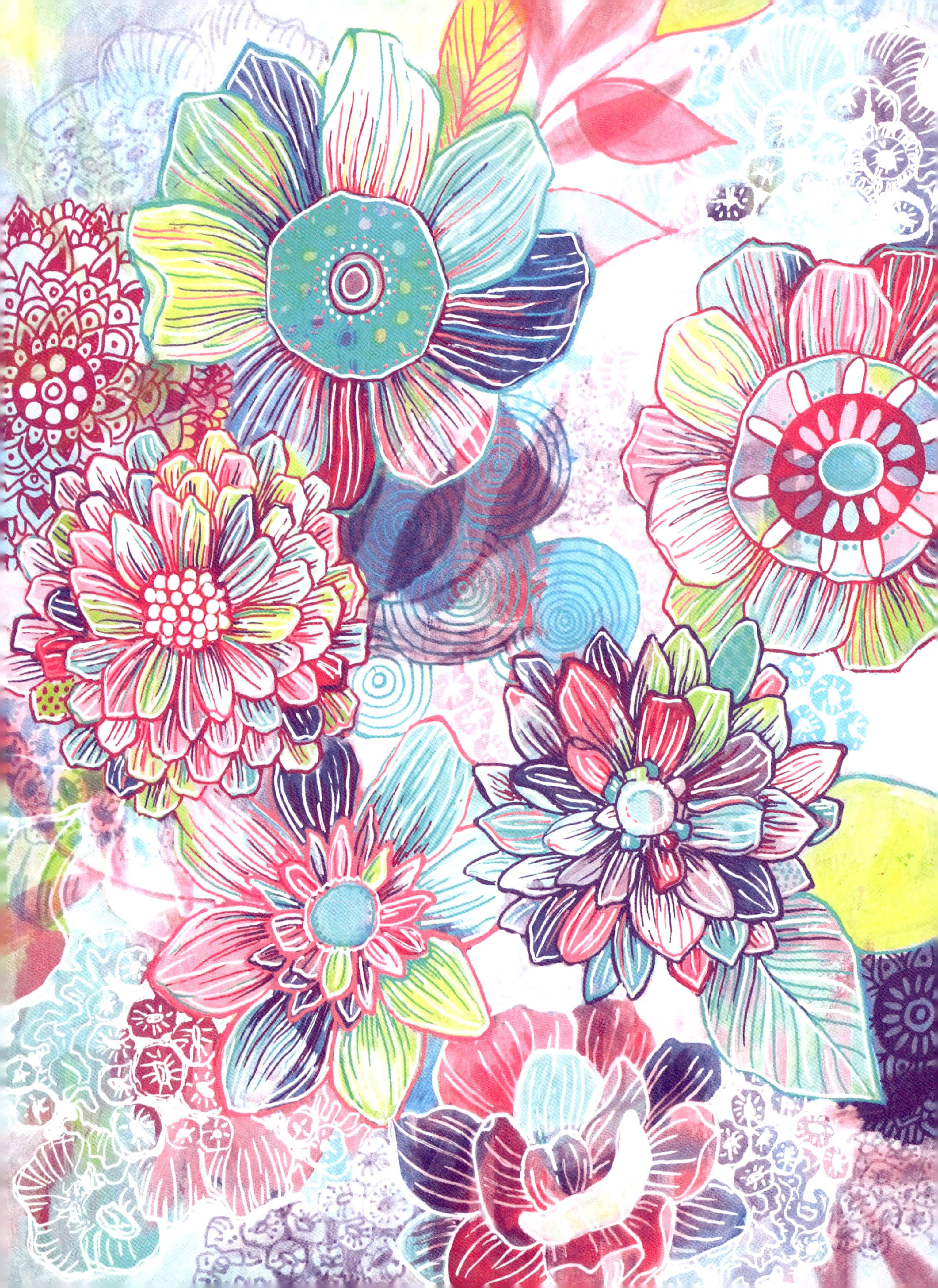

Pens, Markers, and Paint, Oh My!

*Learn to paint, draw, and highlight with color (no black!)
using acrylics, gel pens, and water-based markers*

So far, we've worked our way from water-based markers to watercolors and then on to acrylics. Watercolors and water-based markers make a logical combination, as we learned that they can produce very similar results and that they work very well together. But what about water-based markers and acrylics? Well, guess what—they love each other too!

In this project, we will begin with a mess of acrylics and then use colorful gel pens and markers to create some mesmerizing layers. In case you haven't noticed yet, I have a thing for layers. When I create a work of art, I like to hide a trove of treasures in it to be found when the piece is studied up close. After taking in the main shapes in my composition, I want to wander around, peeking through to discover things below the surface.

Just to mix things up, we'll also move beyond florals and look around at nature to discover other beautiful patterns and designs to incorporate in our funky florals composition. I'll be using designs found in my favorite place, the ocean, which is an underwater garden all its own.

Tools & Supplies

- ▶ Acrylic paints
- ▶ Water-based markers
- ▶ Gel pens
- ▶ Sizes 6, 8, and 10 flat paintbrushes (or your choice of a medium and a large brush), plus a size 1 round paintbrush (or your choice of a small brush)
- ▶ Glazing medium (or matte medium)
- ▶ Watercolor paper, mixed-media paper, or Bristol board

What You'll Learn

FINDING YOUR OWN WAY: At this point, you should start taking the techniques and processes you've learned and begin molding them into your own, personal methods of working. Feel free to work out of order, add techniques learned in previous projects that I don't include in this piece, and choose different supplies.

MOVING BEYOND FLORALS: Because florals contain natural patterns and organic shapes, it is hard to truly "mess them up." When I look closely at other elements in nature, I see this as well, and I find so much inspiration in the patterns, designs, and textures that make up creation. I hope with this project that you can also start to see beyond florals and incorporate different natural elements into your work.

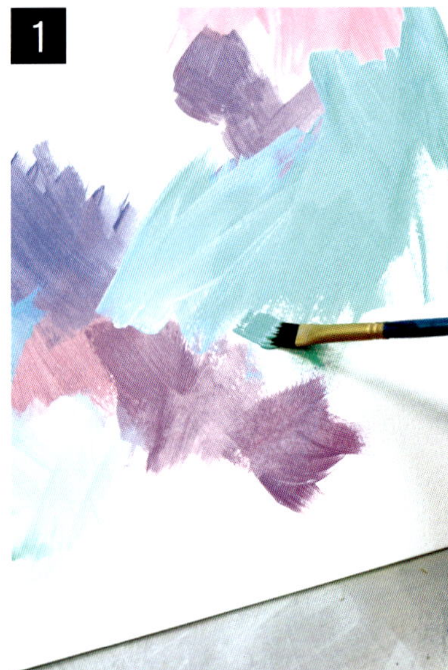

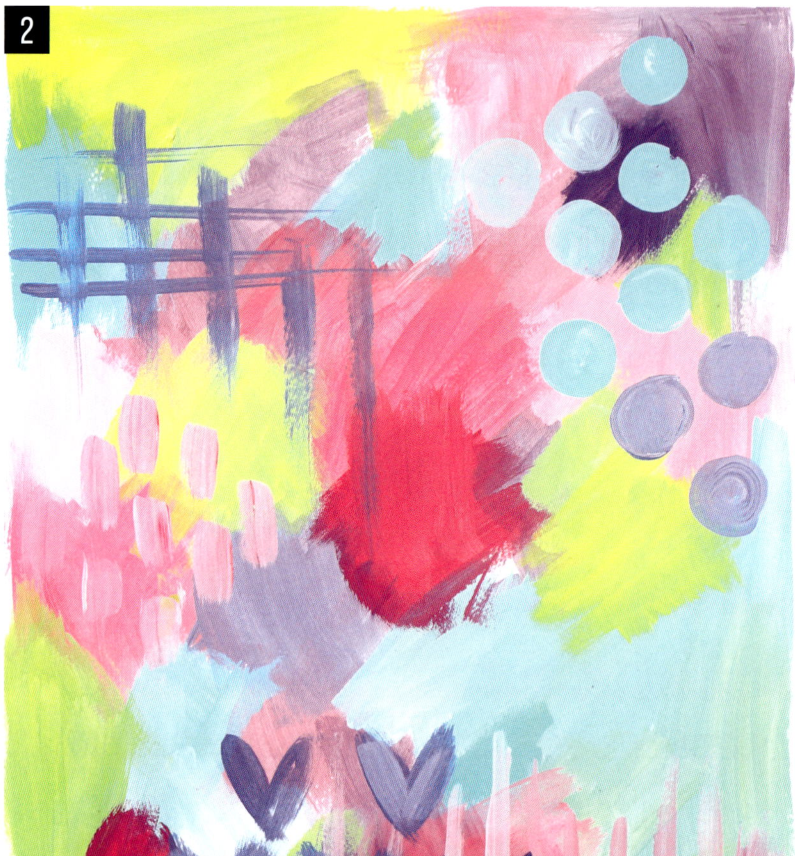

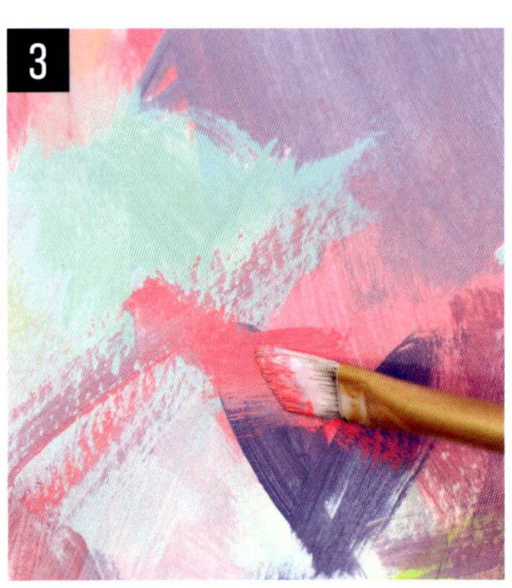

1 Paint a background. Off we go! To start this project, fill up the paper with color right off the bat. I've chosen a very light, pastel-ish color scheme, and although you can choose any color scheme you'd like, I recommend starting off on the lighter side of the value scale. Quickly put down patches of color throughout the piece, covering every bit of white space.

2 Add some basic patterns. Now that Easter has exploded on my paper, I'll create some fun, colorful marks and patterns all over the piece. Lines, dashes, and dots are great go-to designs because of their simplicity. Just scatter some of these across the background. Use a couple different colors.

3 Add messy brushstrokes. Put down another messy layer of color on top of these first two layers. You can cover some of your designs and then bring them back out if you choose to. I love to use the dry-brushing technique in this step to create interesting texture.

Remember that this is becoming YOUR own process. You may want to skip these designs or go even crazier than I have. Perhaps you want to bring in collage elements. Embrace what you are wanting to do in the moment and begin to make this process of creating your own.

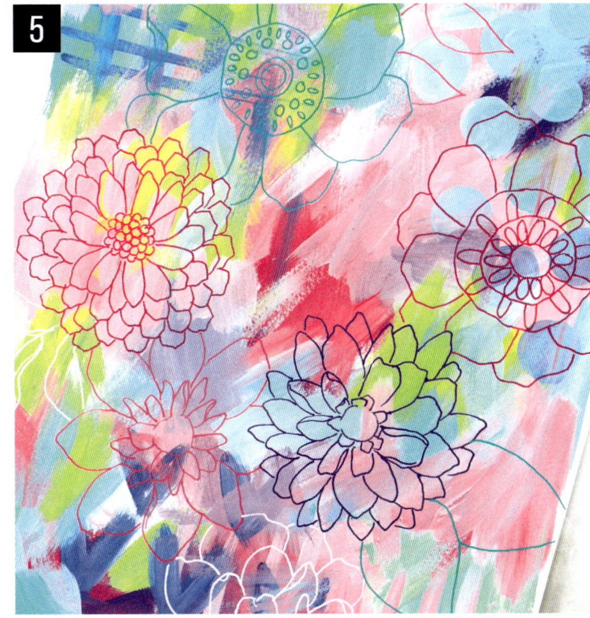

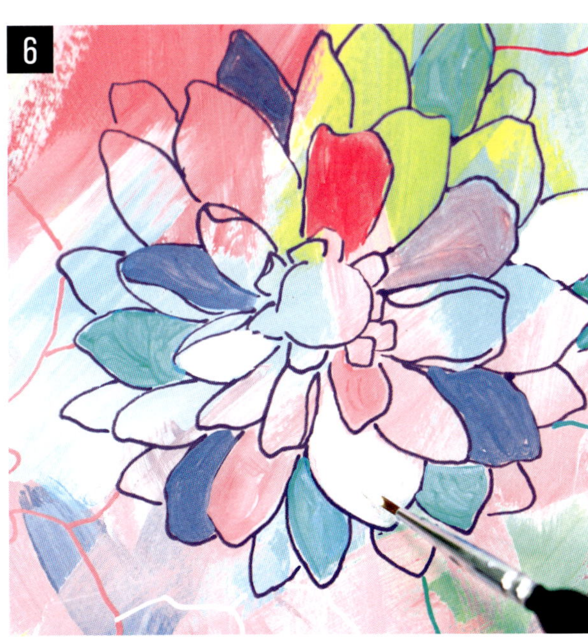

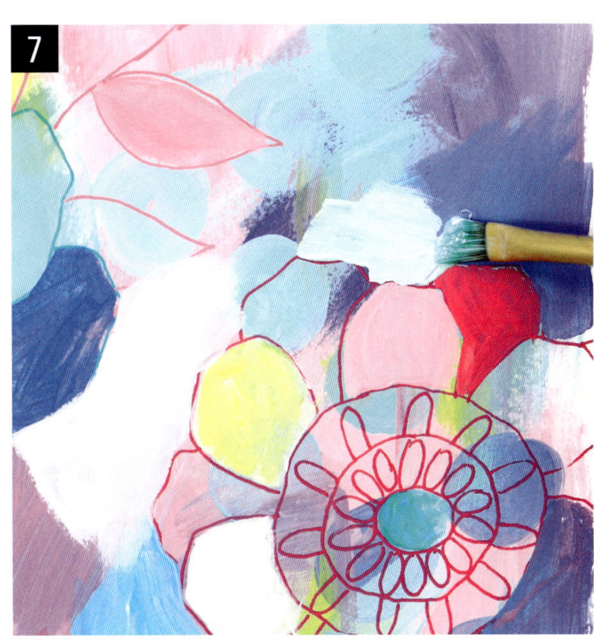

4 **Start drawing flowers with gel pens.** It's already time for florals! For the first time, we'll draw these florals using gel pens. Gel pens work wonderfully on top of matte craft acrylics. Use several different colors to draw the different flowers.

5 **Finish composing the florals.** Feel free to include florals drawn from references as well as others drawn more whimsically, from your imagination. Include some large leaves as well.

6 **Fill in some petals with color.** Now for a fun approach to coloring the petals that is different from every project before this. Use your acrylic paints to fill in some petals with various colors, including white, but use just one color per petal. Don't fill in every single petal; leave some as they are. Use different colors in each flower, mixing it up as you go.

7 **Paint around the flowers.** After giving the petal treatment to each of your flowers, move back to the negative space around them. You probably knew this was coming! Use solid colors to paint around the edges of your flowers, changing up colors as you go. This will start to create more separation between the positive and negative space.

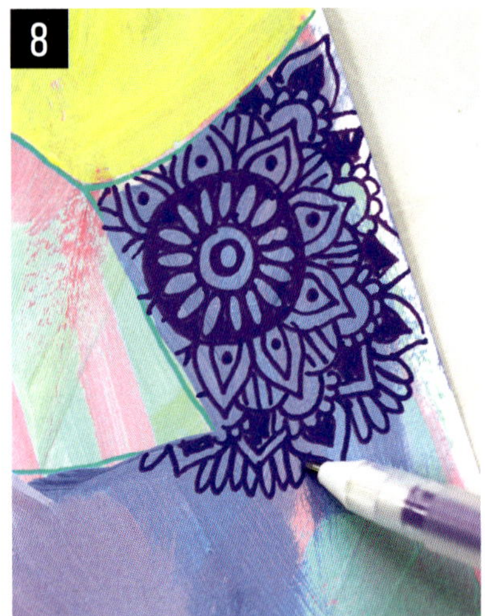

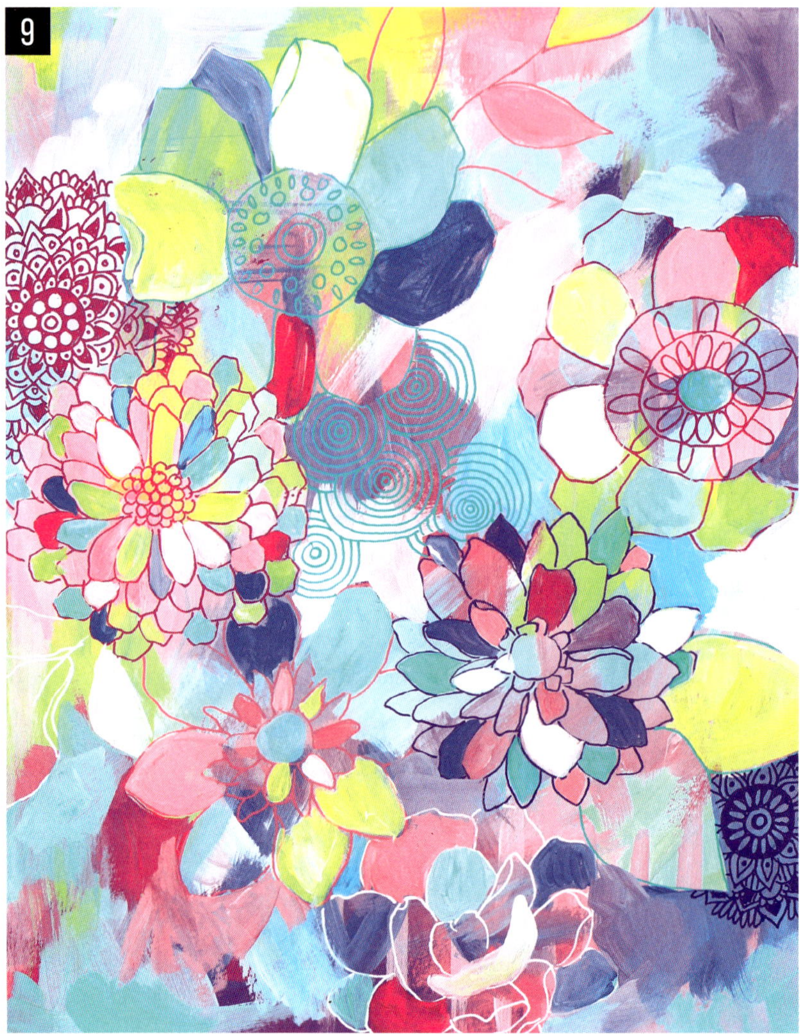

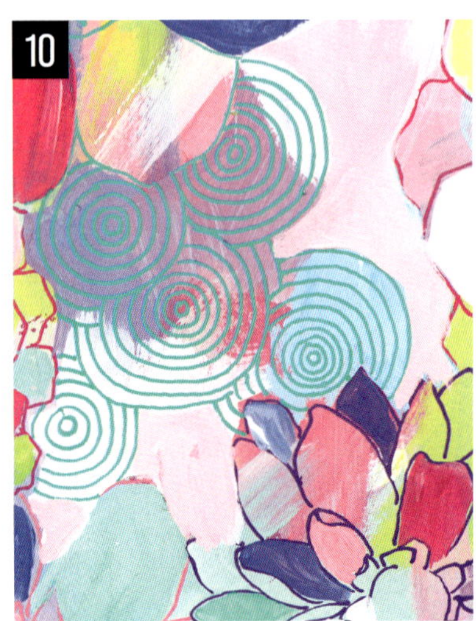

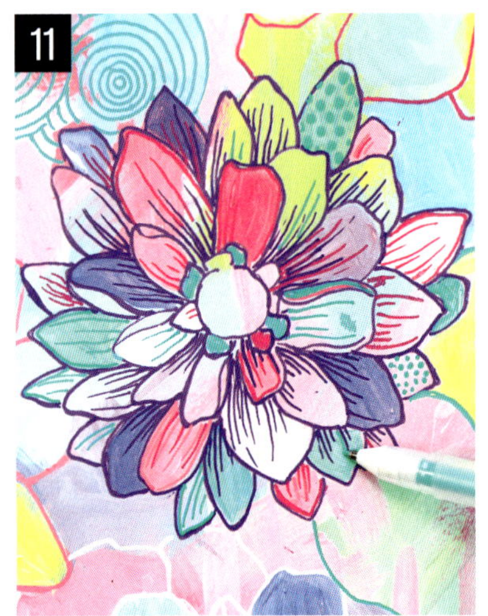

8 **Start adding mandalas.** As your new colors are drying, choose a spot that has already dried, and add a mandala in that negative space using a gel pen. Try matching hues in some places, like the dark purple on top of the medium purple here.

9 **Add other doodles.** In some places, add other patterns instead of mandalas, like the concentric circles in the center of this piece.

10 **Paint around the new doodles.** Next, add some solid areas of color around your new gel pen designs. This will help them pop more. These background designs become middle-ground designs, building up the layers in the piece.

11 **Add detail to the flowers.** Using your gel pens, go back into the flowers to crisp up all the linework, add details, and begin to add some solid areas of color as well.

12 **Continue adding dimension.** As you continue to work on the flower details, think about dimension. Add more and thicker lines in areas you want to push back. Add polka dots to some petals and outline other petals with a different color, creating a double-outline effect. Use several colors in some petals and just one color in others.

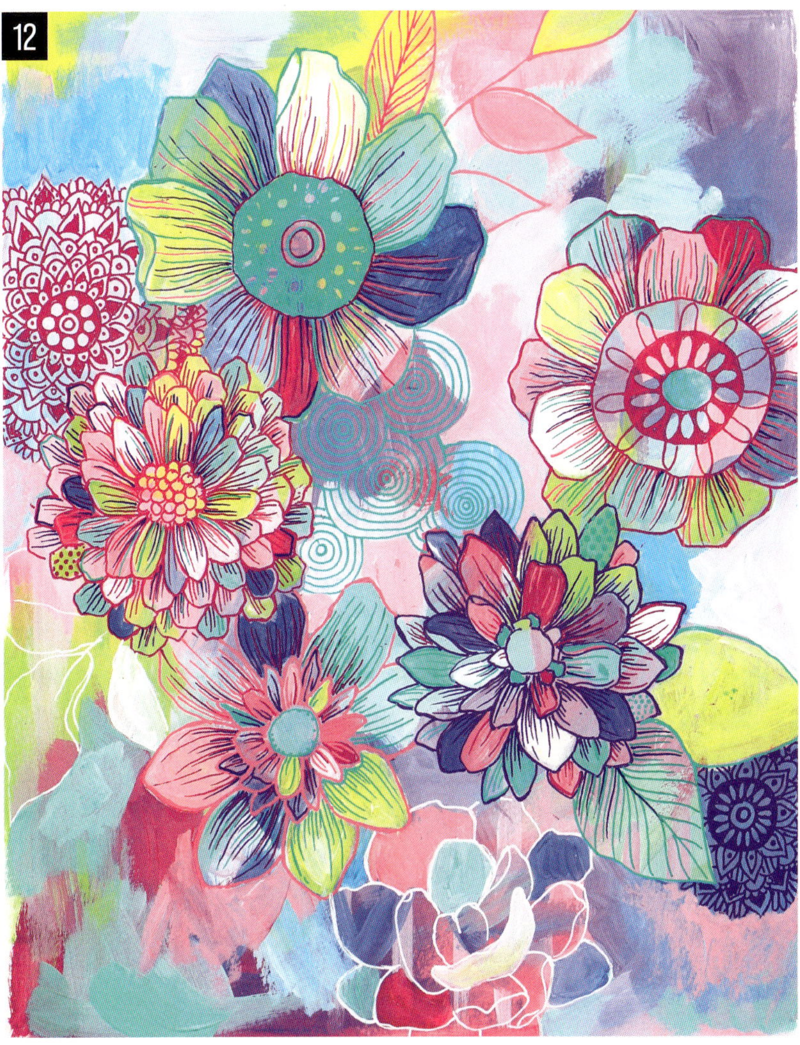

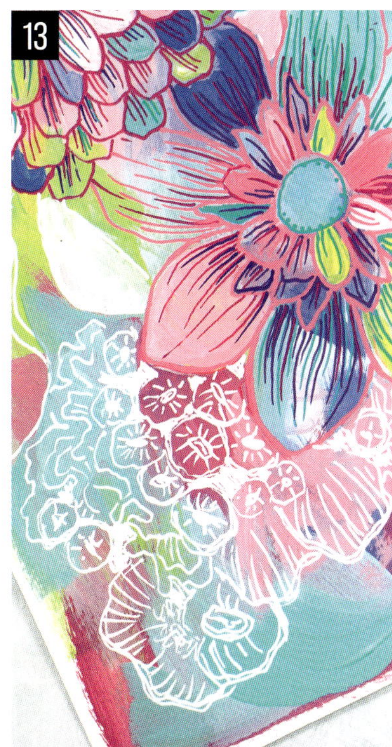

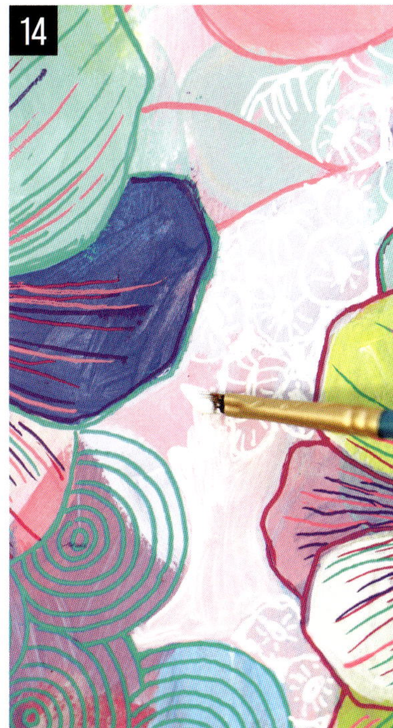

Use any color you'd like for adding these natural doodles! White is my favorite for this step, but you may want to go darker or brighter.

13 **Draw in other natural patterns.** Now for a very special phase of this project! Using your white gel pen, begin incorporating a few patterns from nature that are not florals in the negative space. I encourage you to look around and find patterns in creation—perhaps in tree bark, shells, or animal prints. As an ocean-loving girl, I tend to lean into an underwater garden vibe and love to incorporate coral designs. There are so many kinds of coral that the possibilities are almost as endless as florals.

14 **Add a white wash to empty areas.** Once you have filled a good amount of negative space with these designs, go back into the negative space that is not covered with designs and cover it with a washed-out white acrylic. The goal is to lighten these areas, not make them opaque white. You can mix your white paint with a glazing medium to get this washy effect or simply water down your paint.

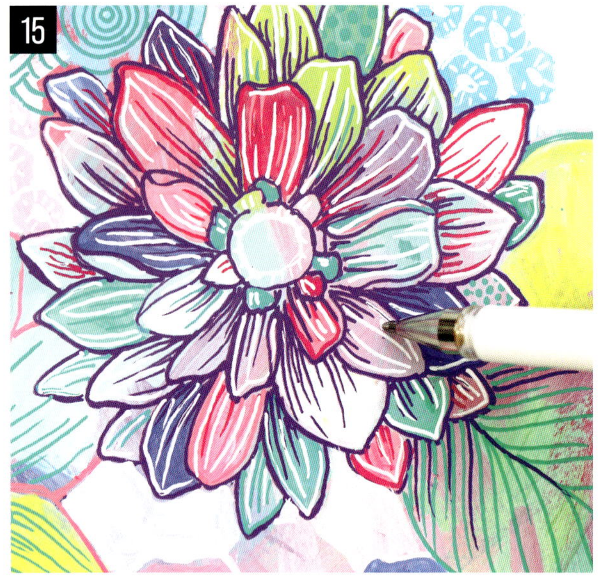

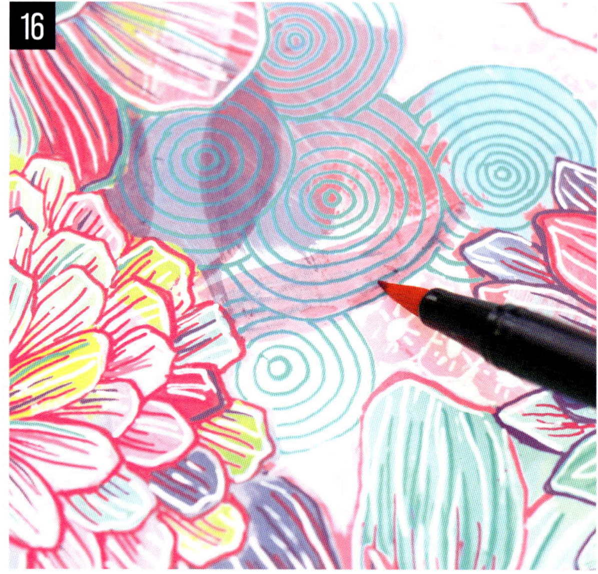

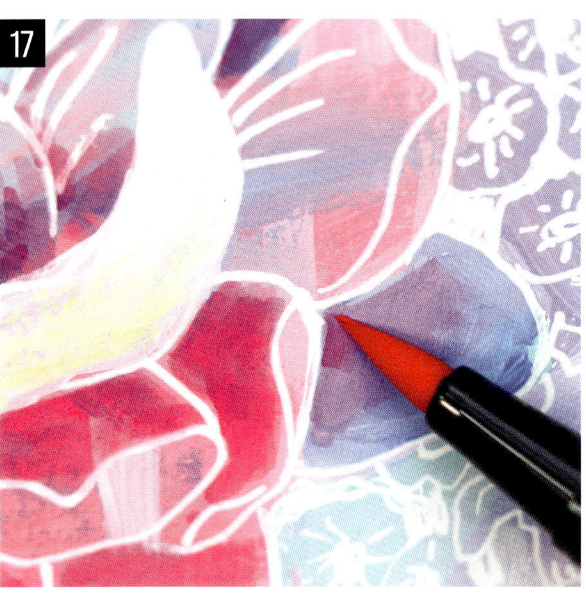

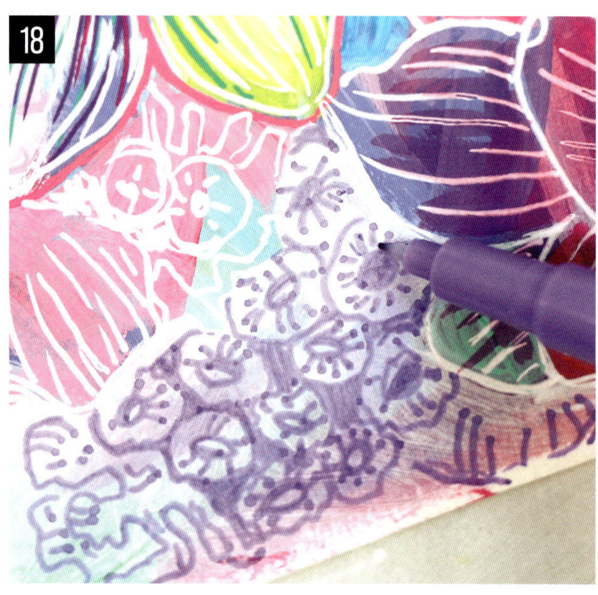

15 **Add white highlights.** While the washy white areas dry, go back into the flowers using a white gel pen (or paint) to add highlights and details.

16 **Add subtle solid leaves in the background.** Next, use a couple of very light water-based markers to add some faint leaves in the background space surrounding the white doodle designs. You can also layer these across some of the leaves you've left without linework, as well as the designs in the negative space done in color. These subtly transparent layers of marker will add another magical touch.

17 **Find any spots that need more attention.** In my piece, I have one flower that I outlined in white instead of color, so I decided to use my water-based markers to add a bit of dimension within this flower before adding white linework on top.

18 **Add finishing touches.** Step away, come back, and look at the piece with fresh eyes one last time. Does it need any more tweaking? In my case, I used another water-based marker with a fine tip to add the same coral designs I had done in white earlier in some of the remaining negative space that I had covered in transparent white. With that, I'm happy to call this one done!

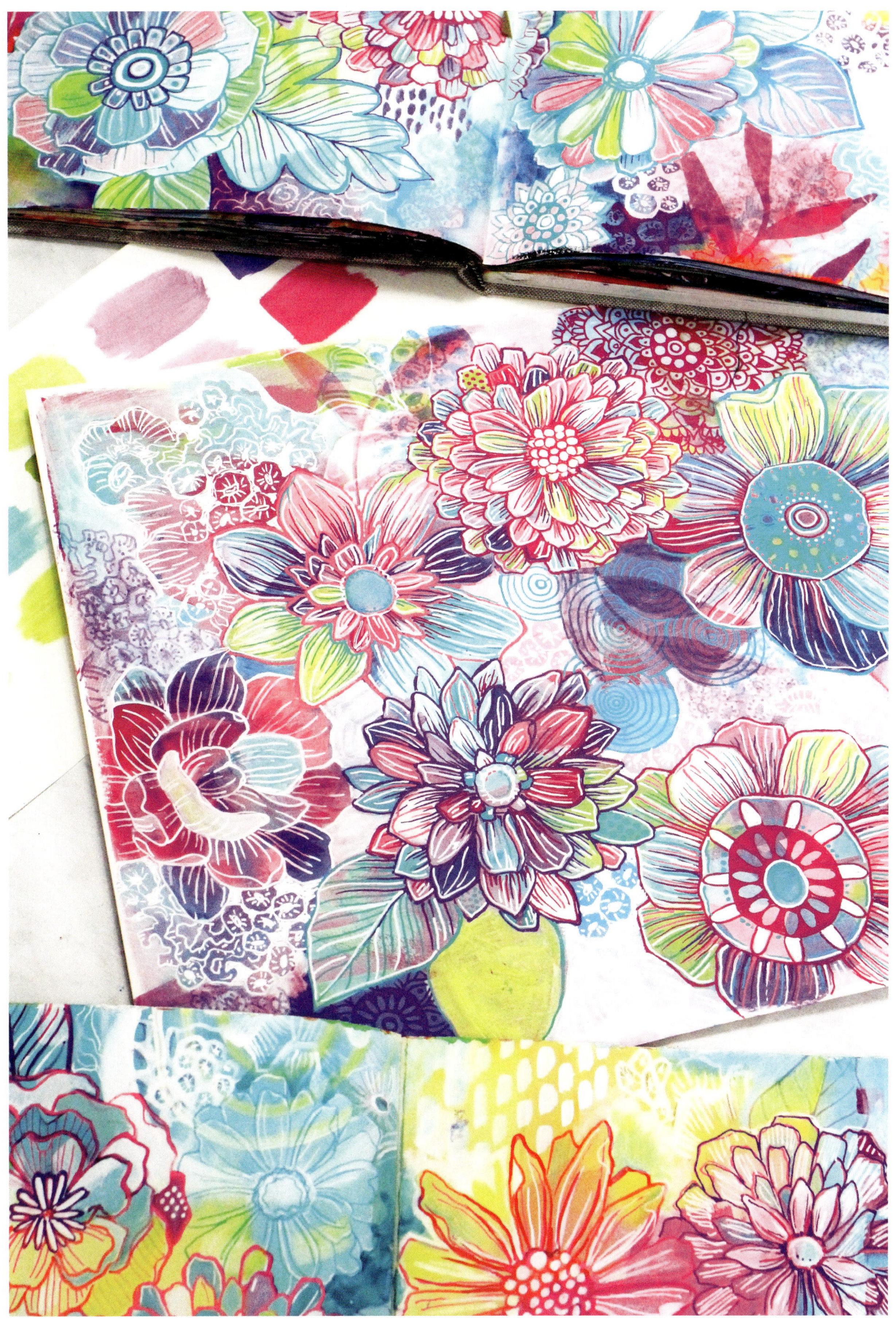

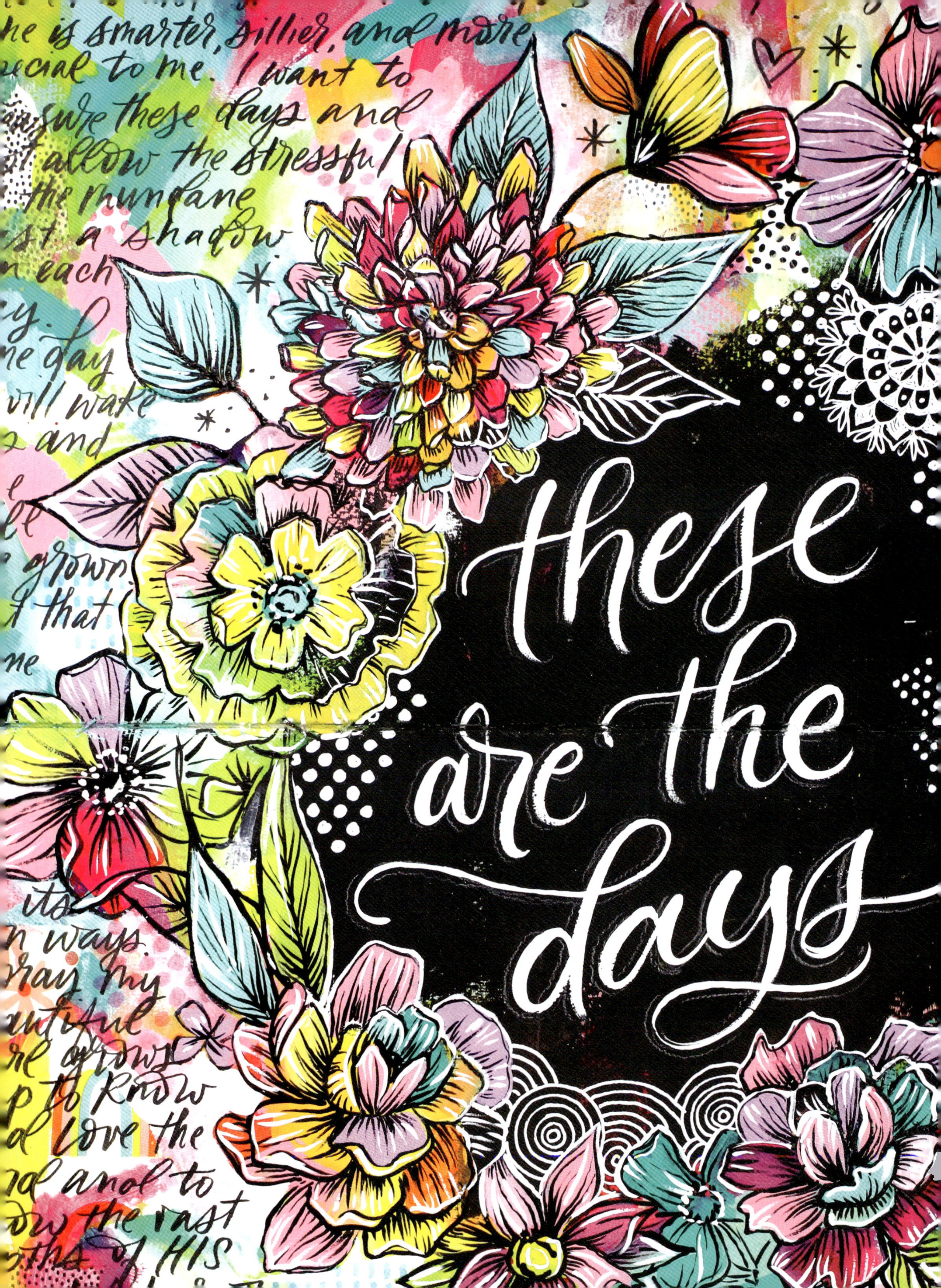
these are the days

Letter It Out

*Learn to incorporate journaling into your work
using acrylics and black pen*

I don't have a strict definition for what counts as "art journaling," and in fact don't think writing is required to consider something an art journal! Sometimes I am journaling just through the florals alone. I'm simply playing, wherever the paint happens to take me. I began keeping an art journal in my junior year of college. At publication date, that is 21 years ago. Yes, I do have a lot of art journals! Over the years, there have been times when I wrote more and other times when I wrote less. We all have seasons of creating, so I have gone where my ideas take me throughout the seasons of my life.

Often, when I'm creating, in my special little world, my thoughts spill over into my paintings. I may create an entire page with paints, markers, and pens and then return to add written journaling and lettering to it. Or I may incorporate my thoughts as I go, hopping back and forth between thinking visually and thinking through words.

For this project, we are going to begin by writing and documenting along with our funky florals. We will create pages intentionally designed to give us room to write and add lettering after painting in our floral composition. In this first project, we'll be focusing on acrylic paints.

Tools & Supplies

- Acrylic paints
- Chalk pencil or white colored pencil
- Black pen
- White acrylic paint or white gel pen
- A size 14 flat or size 12 round paintbrush (or your choice of a large brush), plus sizes 00, 1, and 5 round paintbrushes (or your choice of an extra-small, a small, and a medium brush)
- Watercolor paper, mixed-media paper, or Bristol board

What You'll Learn

USING LETTERS AS BACKGROUND DESIGNS: Besides the larger lettering we will do in this piece, which naturally becomes a focal point in the foreground, large areas of smaller letters and writing can also become their own unique pattern in the negative space. Try to view writing as a part of the art piece, not just an additional and separate part of your work.

INCORPORATING THOUGHTS: Losing yourself in the process of creating is a magical thing, but sometimes adding an intentional prompt to focus on can lead you to be even more free in your work. In this project we'll aim to straddle that line.

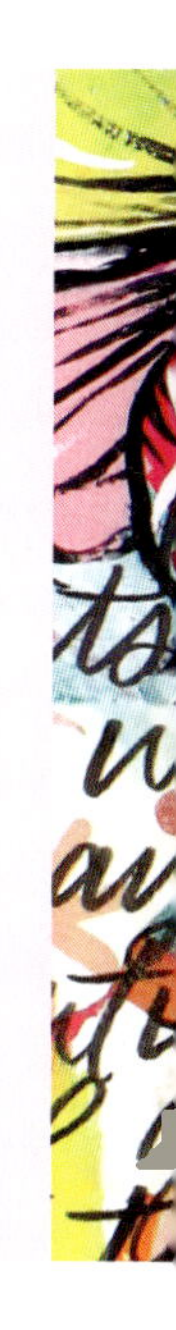

Journaling Prompts

Some days you may not know what to write when you sit down to art-journal. Most of the time, I choose to write about what is on my heart, but sometimes you just draw a blank. That's where this list of simple prompts comes in. When you want to journal but don't know where to start, take a peek at this list to get your thoughts moving!

Why not write about: song lyrics, bucket list, gratitude list, childhood memories, change, poems, daily routine, home, word of the year, dreams, favorites list, things to make, children, goals, Bible verse, places to visit, things that bring you joy, courageous acts, seasons, prayers, notes to your 10-year-old self, your ideal day, reading list, yearly or monthly review, family or spouse or children, health and fitness, any kind of top 10 list, current mood, dream vacation, happiest memories.

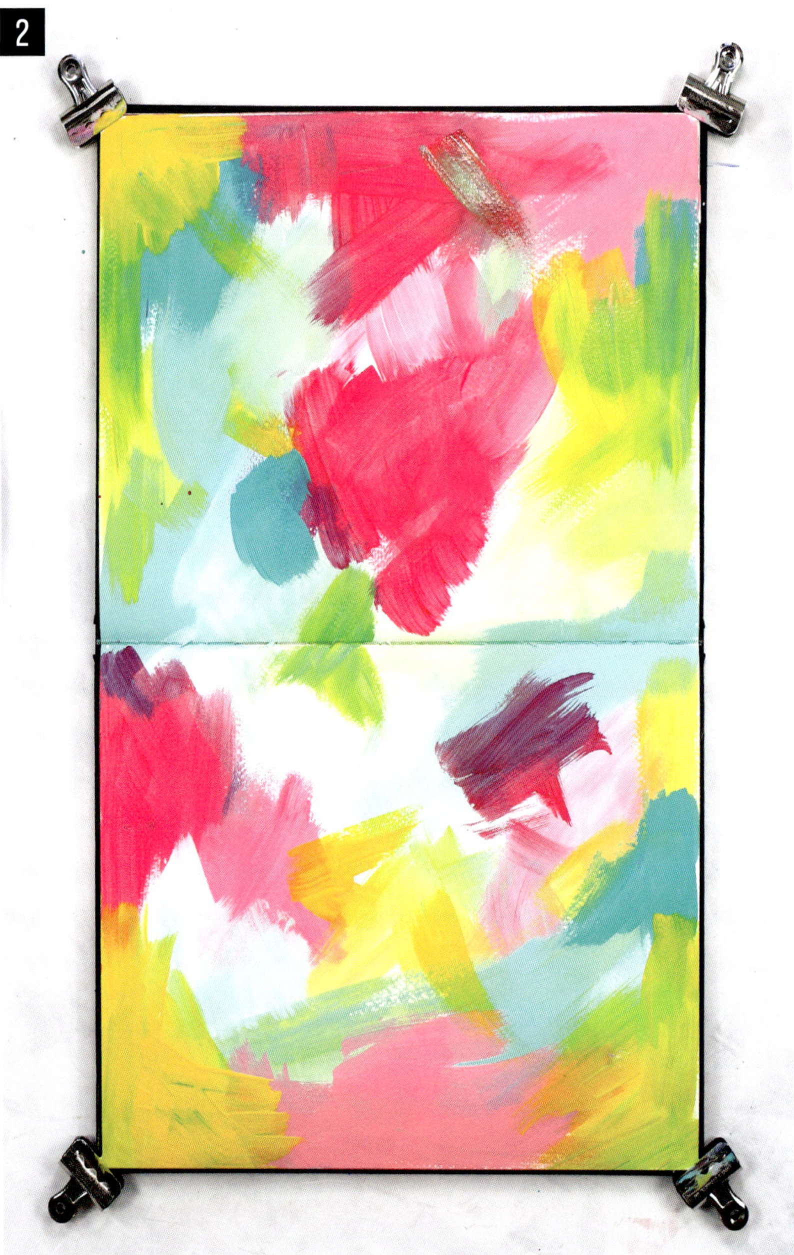

1 Start painting and thinking. Let's get started by giving ourselves a nice stretch and easing our way into this piece and this new addition to our creative process. While you begin laying down a first layer of acrylics all over your background, think about what you are thinking. Yes, I just said, "Think about what you are thinking" . . . but what I mean is, be mindful of the voice swirling around in your head. Let that lead you to a specific topic you want to reflect on while creating.

2 Finish your background and settle your thoughts. My first layer here is messy, a mix of washes and more-opaque areas of color. For this piece, we will be journaling as well as lettering a phrase in the center of the piece. My phrase is "These are the days." My journaling will revolve around this topic, and, although I know my thoughts will wander this way and that as I create, I'll keep this theme front and center in my mind.

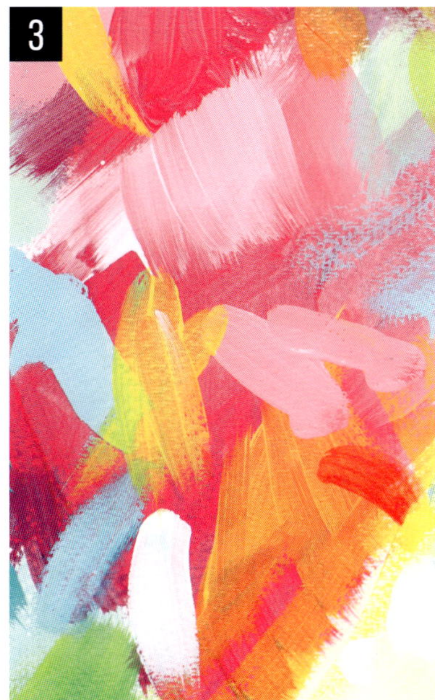

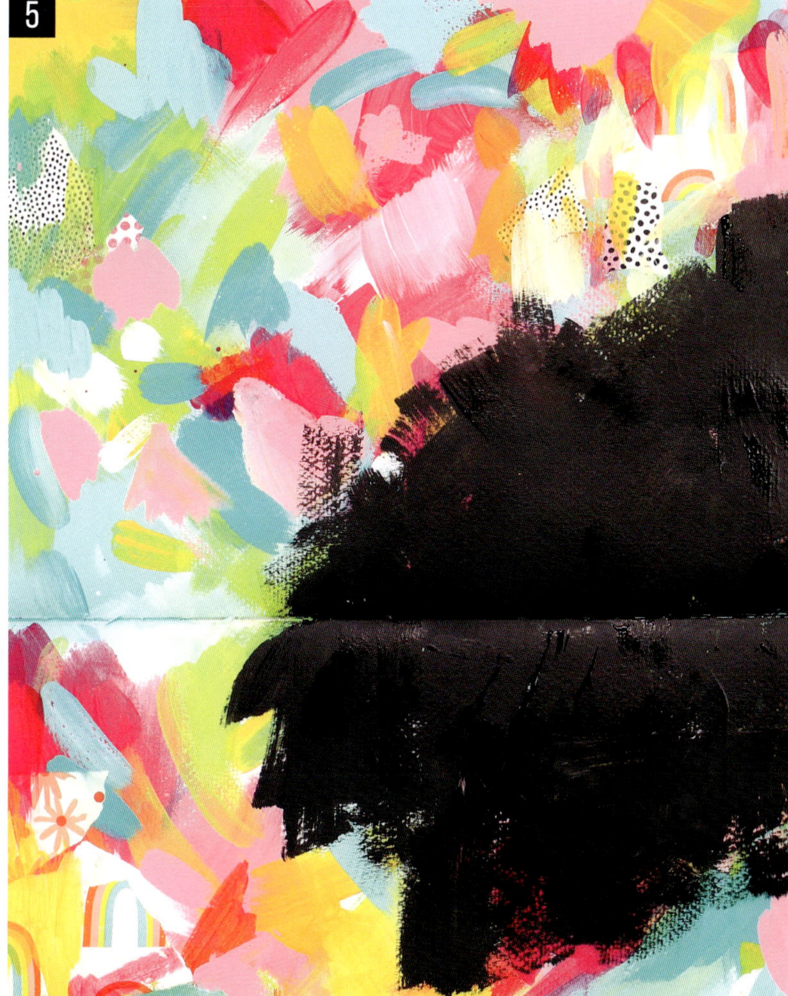

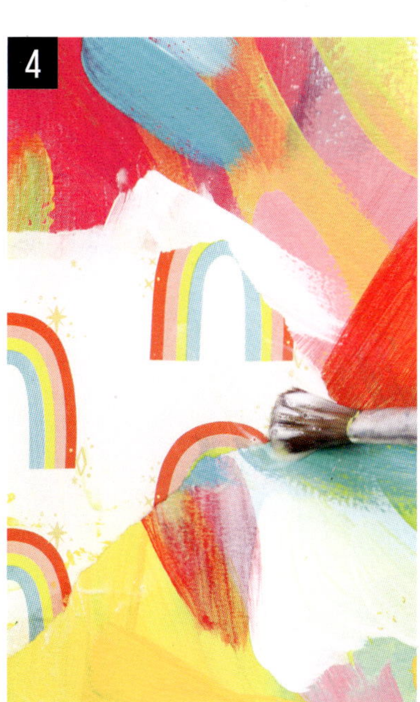

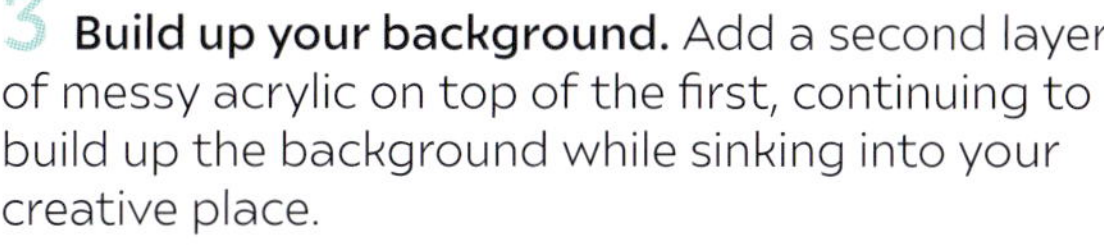

3 **Build up your background.** Add a second layer of messy acrylic on top of the first, continuing to build up the background while sinking into your creative place.

4 **Collage a few elements to the background.** Use matte medium to apply collage elements to the background. Then use more acrylics to fade these elements into the background again a bit. Take your background as far as you'd like, using the methods discussed in "Collage Magic." For this project, I recommend only adding a few small collage spots, not as many as in "Collage Magic."

5 **Create a black area on the background.** Now that you are warmed up, and once your background collaging and painting are dry, use black acrylic to paint a large black space near the center of the composition. This should take up approximately one-quarter to one-third of the space. Avoid smooth shapes; instead, let your brushstrokes create expressive edges.

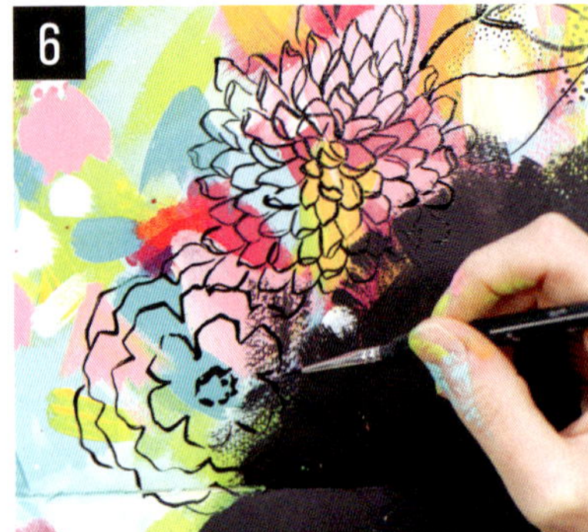

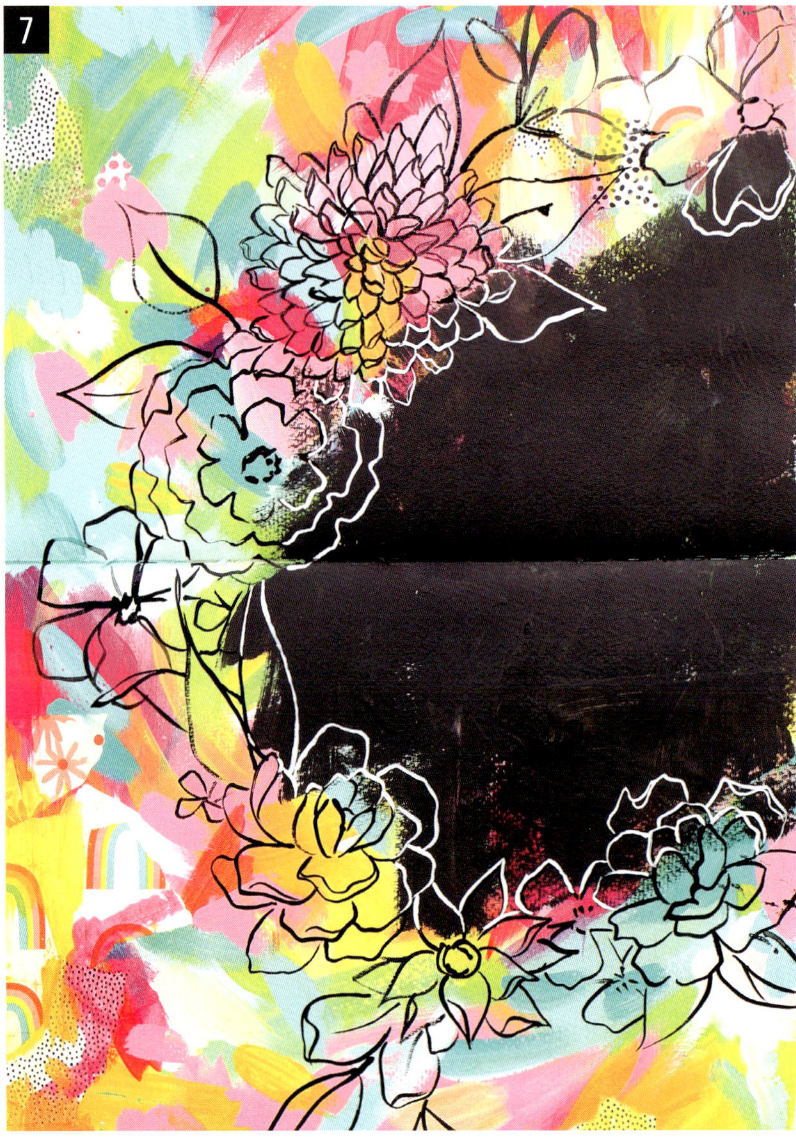

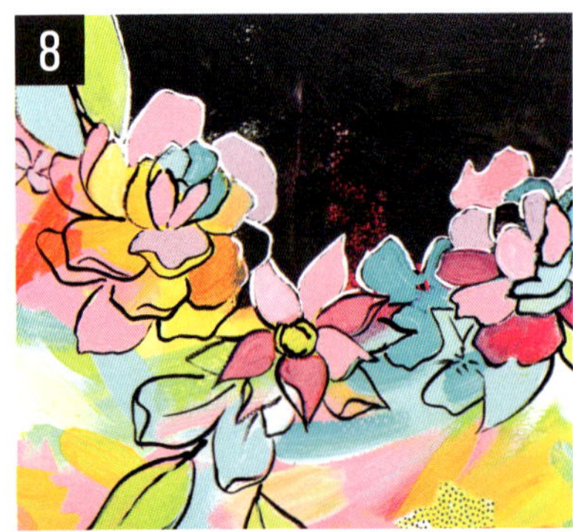

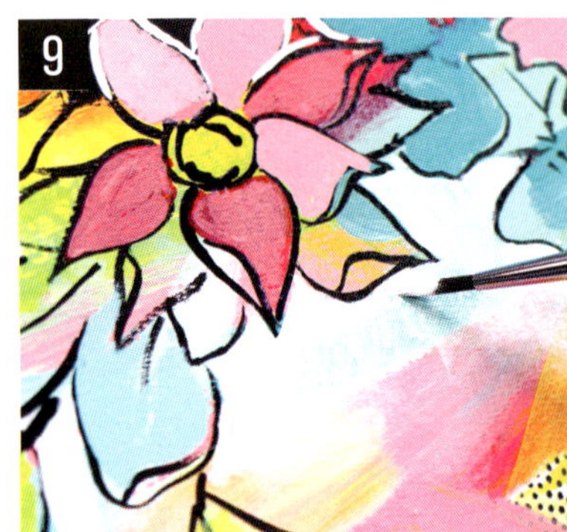

This is another one of those moments where you can choose your own path.
By this point in the book, I've given you a tool kit full of ways to paint your florals, so if this is
not the road you'd like to follow, go in the direction of your choosing.

6 **Paint black florals around the black area.**
Continuing with black acrylic, paint floral shapes
around the edges of the black patch, letting these
spill over into the patch. Overlap the florals as you
follow along the edges of the black patch, creating
a nice border all the way around the patch.

7 **Trace the black flower halves with white.** Make
sure the black patch is completely dry. Then, using
white paint (bleed-proof if you can, but normal
white acrylic will also work), finish the main shapes
of the florals wherever they overlap onto the black
patch—like a reverse color image.

8 **Fill the petals with color.** Fill most of the flower
petals with solid layers of acrylic color, giving each
flower a variety of colors within its petals.

9 **Add white haloing around the flowers.** The
flowers need a little help to stand out from the
background. Use a mix of white paint and glazing
medium to create a washy white shade, then add
this transparent white around the edges of the
flowers and leaves where they touch the colorful
background, fading the white into the background.

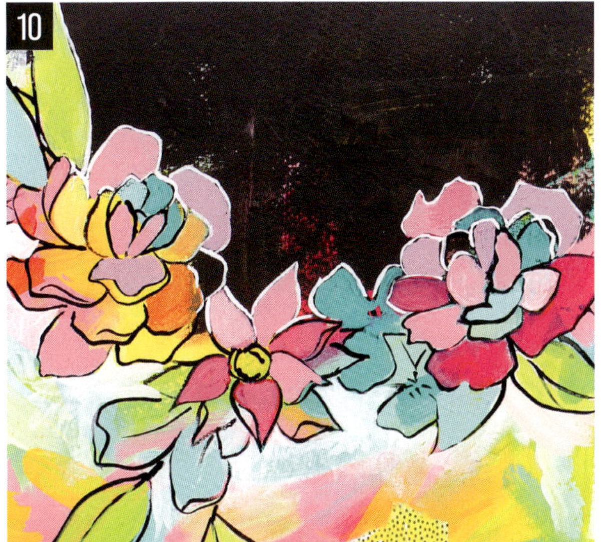

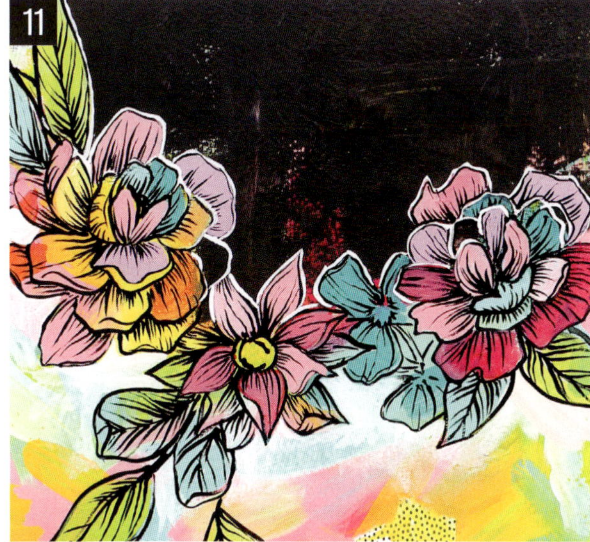

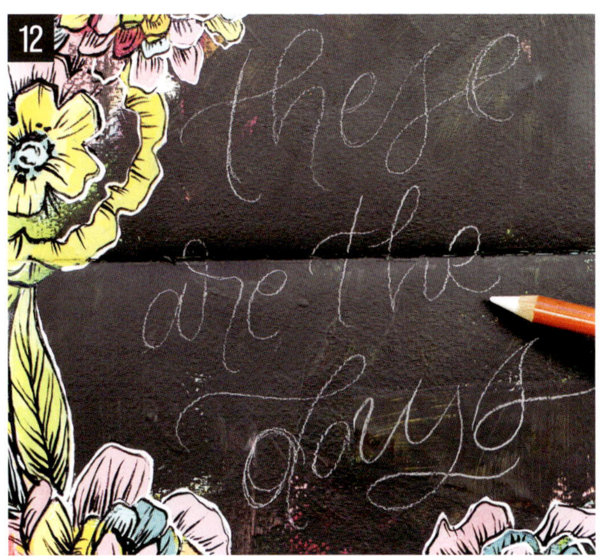

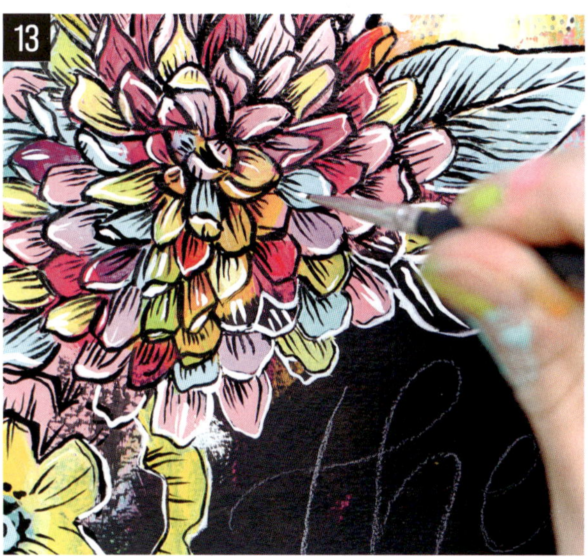

If you are not confident about your lettering, go back and take a peek at my tips on pages 52–55. Remember to slow down and approach lettering as "drawing letters." By sketching super lightly with your chalk pencil, you can easily erase things if you don't like your first shot at it.

10 Choose how much white to add. You can push this white border color as far as you want or hold back on it. For example, I focused the white up close to the flowers where they are near the black patch, but I did not add white haloing to the far-flung leaves, such as in the top left and bottom center.

11 Add black linework detail to the flowers and leaves. Return to the black acrylic. Tidy up the outlines of the flowers and add some detailed line work inside them, really focusing on using the lines to bring out the dimension in each flower.

12 Sketch the lettering. It's time to add the phrase to the large black patch. I chose a shorter phrase because I wanted to make this lettering a large, eye-catching focal point. Using a white chalk pencil, lightly sketch in your lettering.

13 Add white highlights to the flowers. Using white acrylics or a bleed-proof white paint, add white details to the flowers and leaves.

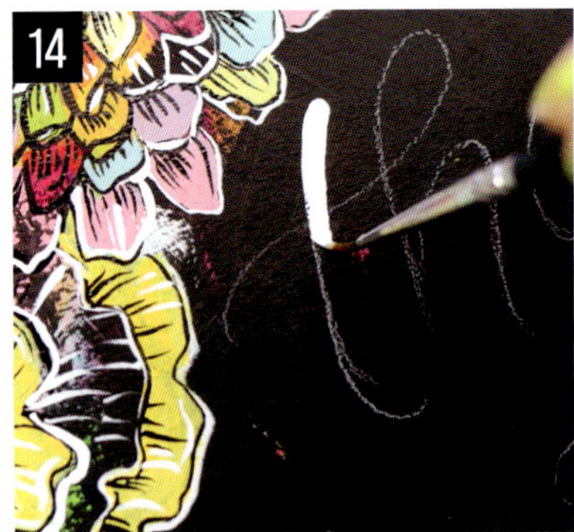

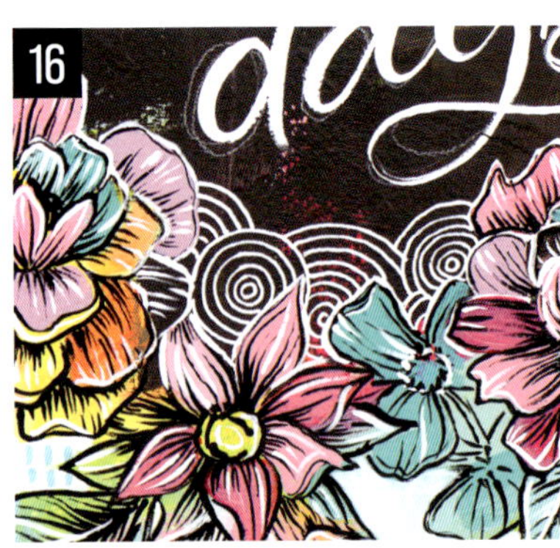

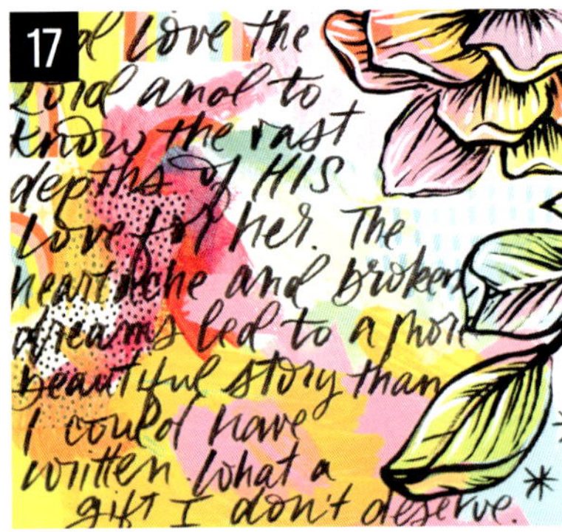

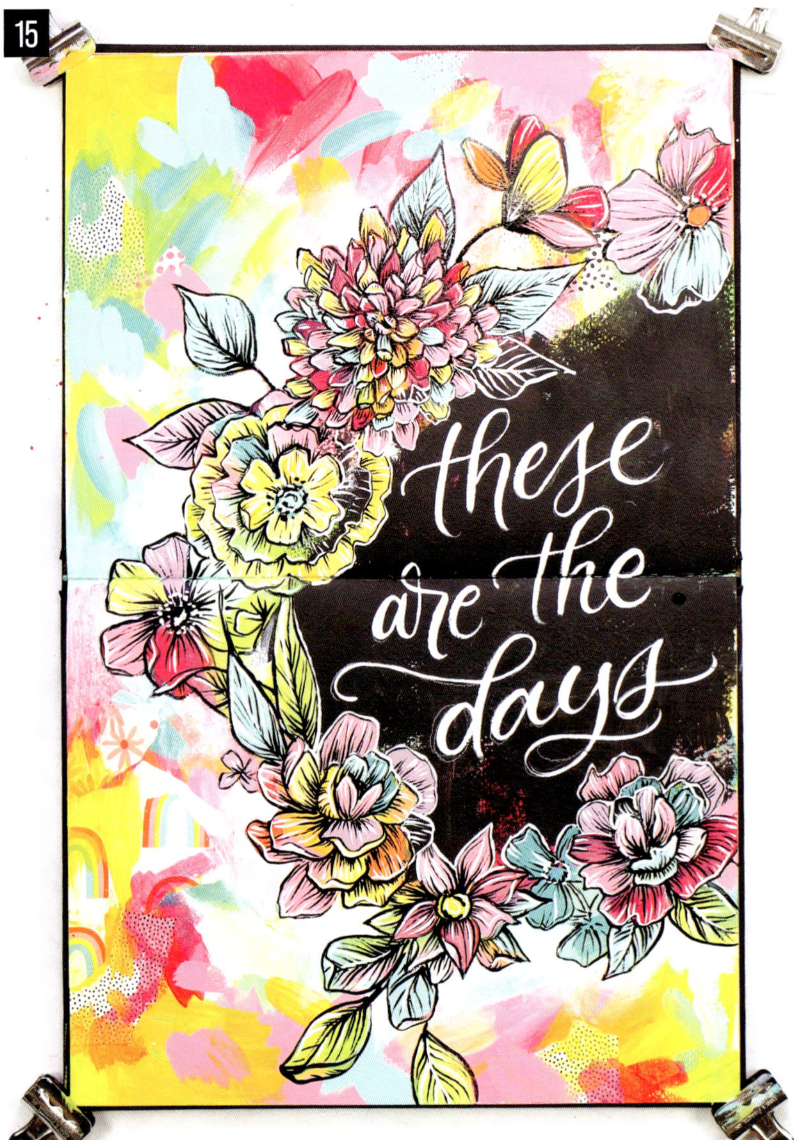

14 **Paint the lettering white.** Continuing with the same white, paint over your lettering sketch. While I tend to rely on brush pressure to make my thicker strokes, painting the skeleton of each letter and returning to add thicker downstrokes afterward can be just as effective. Do whatever works for you.

15 **Check your lettering.** Take a step back to make sure you are happy with your lettering. Once the lettering has dried, you can erase any stray bits of chalk pencil (such as the extra loop in my "y" here). At the very end of the project, I ended up going back in with the white chalk pencil again to add a faint drop shadow to the lettering in my phrase, giving the piece one extra-special touch; you can see this in the finished project photos.

16 **Add doodles.** Just because I'm such a maximalist, I returned to a few spots in my black area in the center to add some white designs using a white gel pen. I added some concentric circles, some polka dots, and a mandala. Then, just because I never know when to stop, I did the same around the edges of the journaling space using markers. Do this too if you like, or not!

17 **Add journaling.** It's time to add journaling to the background of this piece. As you journal, try to write quickly and let the words come to you, filling all the empty space. Remember to forget any apprehension you have about your natural handwriting—this is the moment to switch over from journaling visually to journaling through thoughts and words. I usually prefer to write using a calligraphy brush pen, since these pens make it easy to vary thick and thin lines even as I rely mostly on my natural handwriting. When you're done, don't forget to add the date!

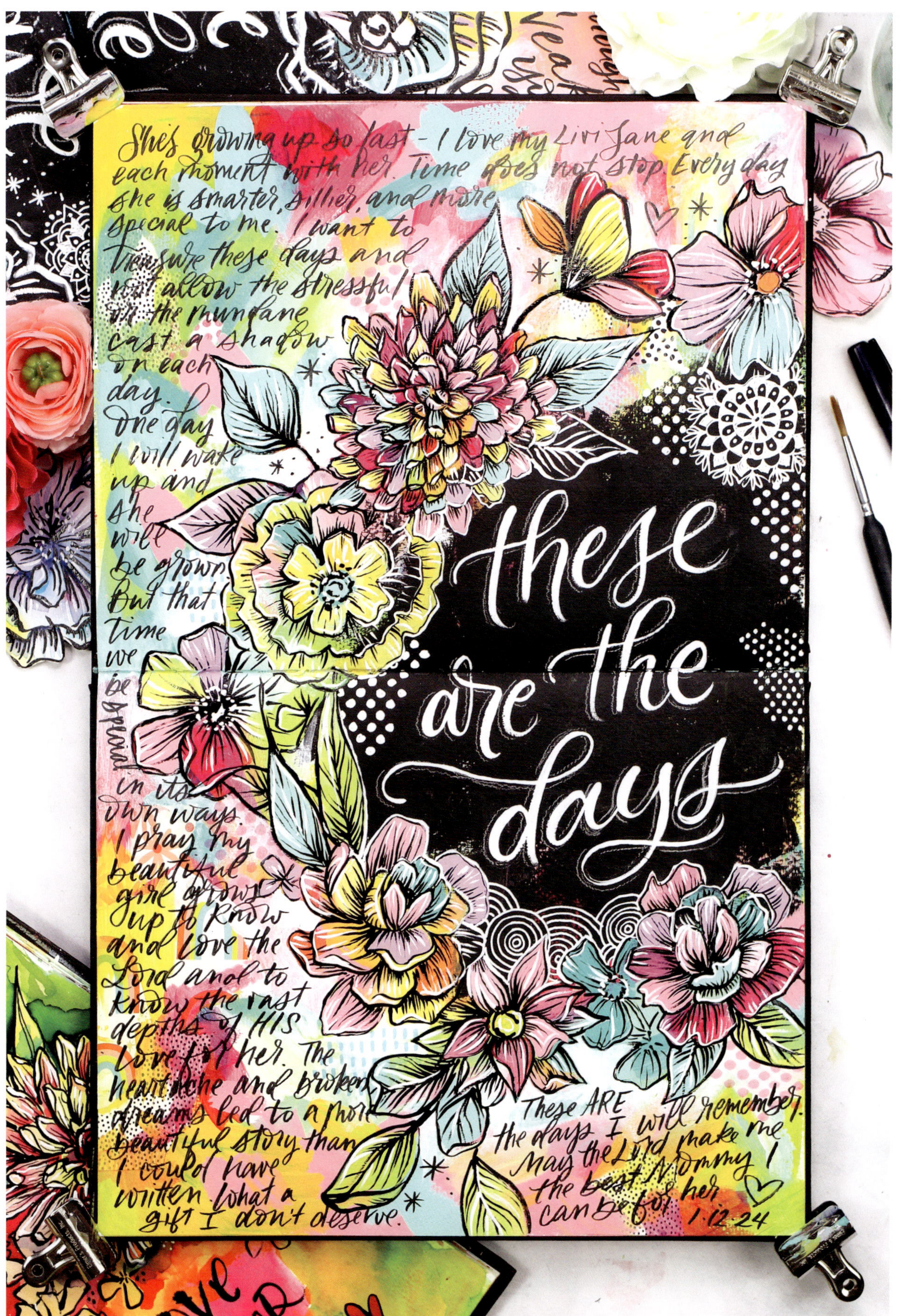
these are the days

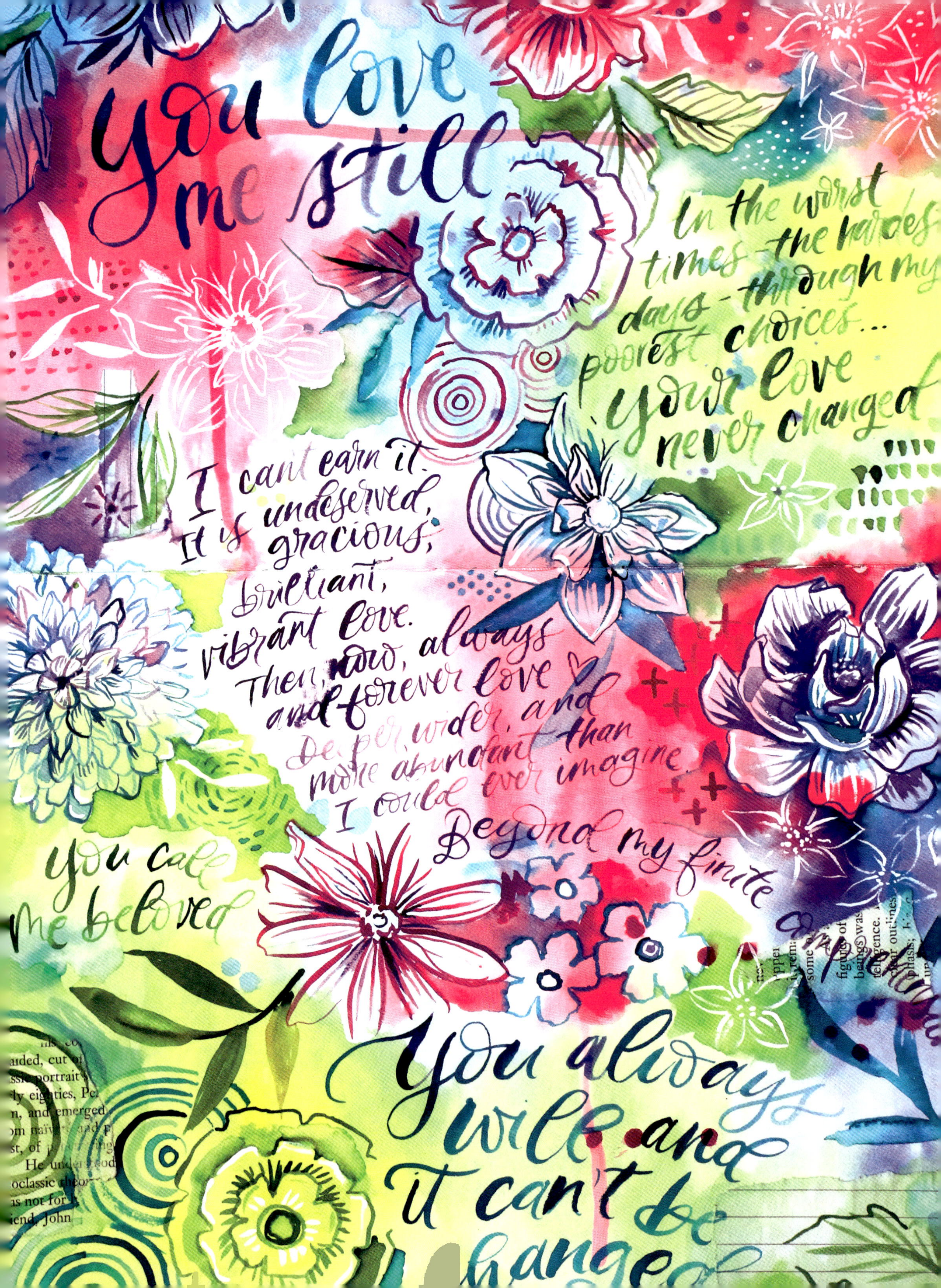

You love me still
In the worst times - the hardest times - through my days - through my poorest choices... your love never changed
I can't earn it. It is undeserved, gracious, brilliant, vibrant love. Then, now, always and forever love
Deeper, wider, and more abundant than I could ever imagine. Beyond my finite
you call me beloved
You always will and it can't be changed

Watercolor Words

*Learn to art-journal using watercolors
in a free-flowing approach*

Sometimes my visual journaling and my written, thoughtful journaling become more of a process that is one and the same. In our last piece, the process was more or less split into two: create the piece, then journal. In this project, the flow between painting beautiful florals with textures and washes merges with the writing to establish a rhythm that flows back and forth between the two.

I tend to wander more when working with watercolors. I work slower, and, because of this slowing down in my process, I enjoy the back and forth between painting and writing or lettering. So, in this piece, we will embrace this idea and alternate painting and writing as we go. This approach can also help keep my thoughts flowing. I usually don't begin this type of piece with a prompt but instead let my mind simply wander. As words come to mind, I can let them spill out at any time and then return to my flowers.

Tools & Supplies

- Watercolors
- White acrylic paint or white gel pen
- Sizes 000, 1, 5, and 8 round paintbrushes (or your choice of an extra-small, a small, a medium, and a large brush)
- Collage elements such as old book pages
- Adhesive
- Water
- Watercolor paper, mixed-media paper, or Bristol board

What You'll Learn

ESTABLISHING RHYTHM: Merging the process of painting and journaling will create a beautiful rhythm. Lean into allowing the two approaches to become one, and see how it affects your process.

STREAM-OF-CONSCIOUSNESS WRITING AND CREATING: Allow yourself to go where your thoughts take you instead of establishing a prompt or theme before starting. This is a very peaceful and tranquil experience that you may want to incorporate more frequently into your work.

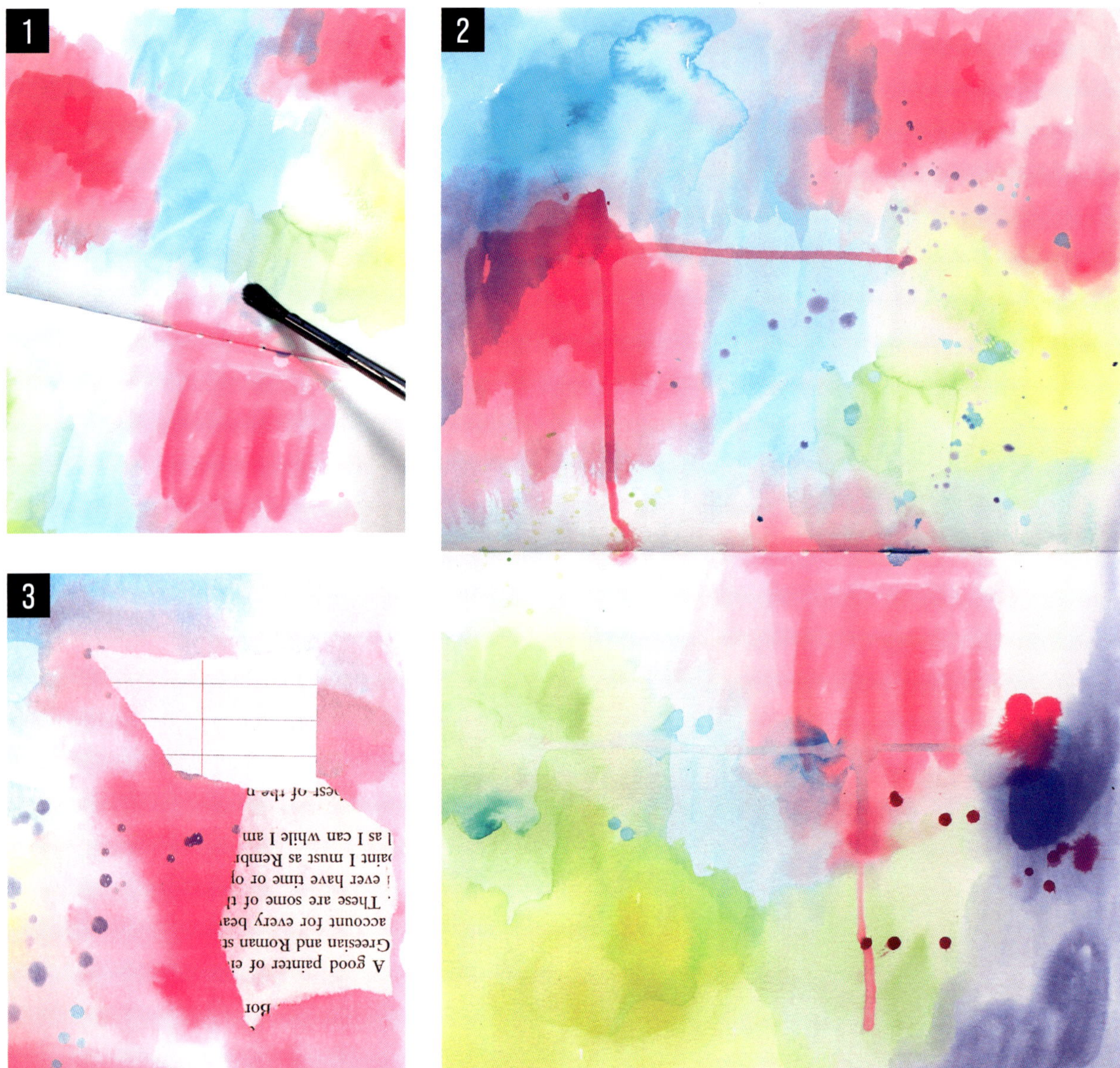

1 Paint a washy background. Let's start off by easing in slowly with a light wash of watercolors with a large round brush. I encourage you turn on some music as you create this project, selecting music with lyrics that you connect with. I often listen to my favorite worship music as I paint, as those lyrics stir my soul and prompt me to reflect on things close to my heart. Most often, I don't need to reference a prompt to know what to journal. As I get started creating, my mind begins to find its focus, and I go where it takes me.

2 Add some drips and splatters. Once the paper is covered in a light wash of color, add bit of fun to it with some pooling, splattering, and dripping, as you learned in "Party in the Background." These first few steps will warm you up before you begin to merge painting florals and painting words.

3 Add collage elements. If you are feeling spunky, add some bits of subtle collage. I used pages from an old painting book. Because we're using watercolor, avoid coating the papers with gel medium, as this repels the watercolor. Instead, add a generous amount of adhesive to the backs of the papers to stick them down.

This is one of those moments
where you need to assess your mood.
If you think adding collage is a step you don't
want or need, stick to just watercolors.

4 **Add a bit of color on top of the collage elements.** Use a light wash of watercolor over the collage pieces to push them back into the background space.

5 **Start painting florals.** Now, beginning in the top left (just as you would work if you were writing a paper), begin painting the first flowers. Start the shapes with linework and add a bit of shading as you go.

6 **Add another flower.** In the process we want to focus on for this project, there is less step-by-step structure. If you are painting your florals and something comes to mind to write down, feel free to leave the florals and come back. Or, if you're processing something mentally, you can work on each flower for a while, building up the details while you think over the things in your heart.

7 **Letter the first element or thought.** Now that you've eased yourself into your creative time, use a small round brush and a deeper, more opaque layer of watercolor to journal your first thought. Use brush pressure to create thick and thin strokes. Use this space to letter your topic or a quote or lyric that embodies the theme of your journaling.

8 **Switch back to florals.** Now add in more flowers, allowing them to fade out and stop before bumping into your writing. Give yourself time to work through these areas, adding detail and shading and even filling in some negative space. As you paint, continue to reflect and cycle through your thoughts. You may want to work quicker through your flowers and continue on writing sooner. Remember, this is your process—mine is just inspiration for you.

Try not to overthink what you want to reflect on. The first thought that pops into your mind is often just what your heart needs to write out.

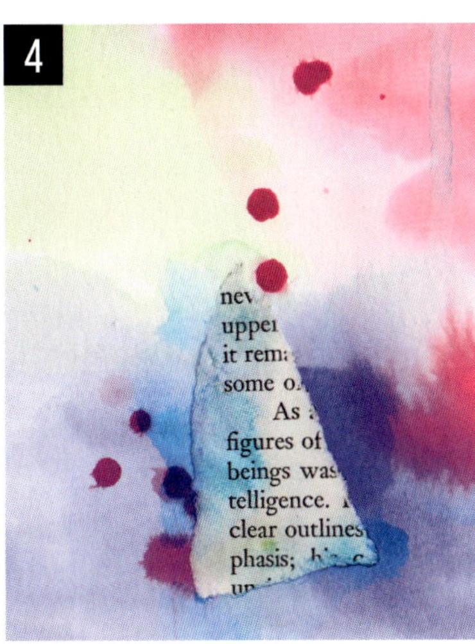

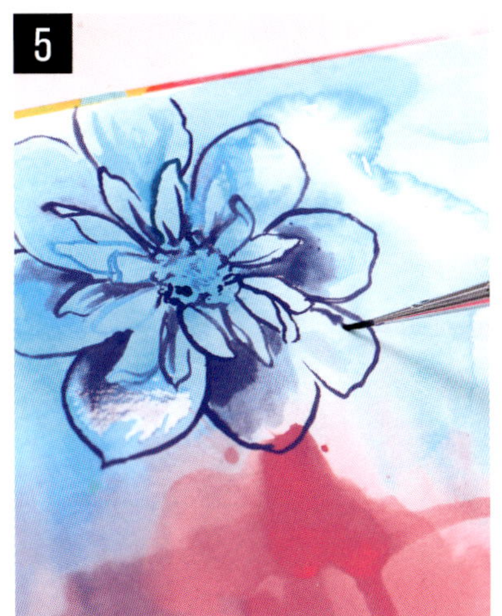

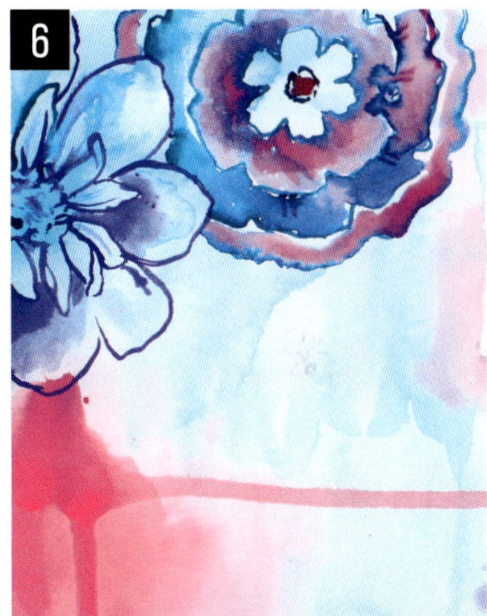

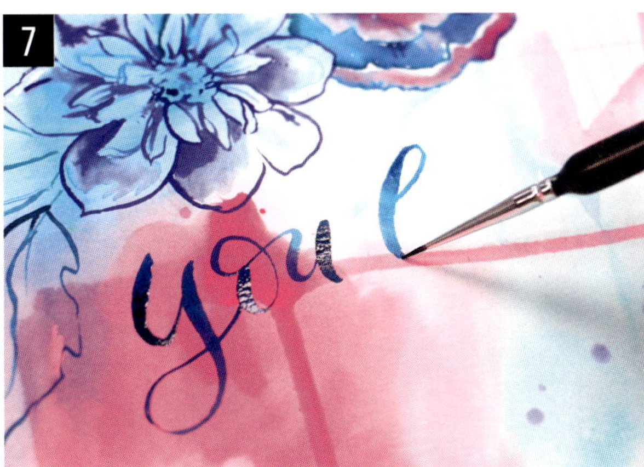

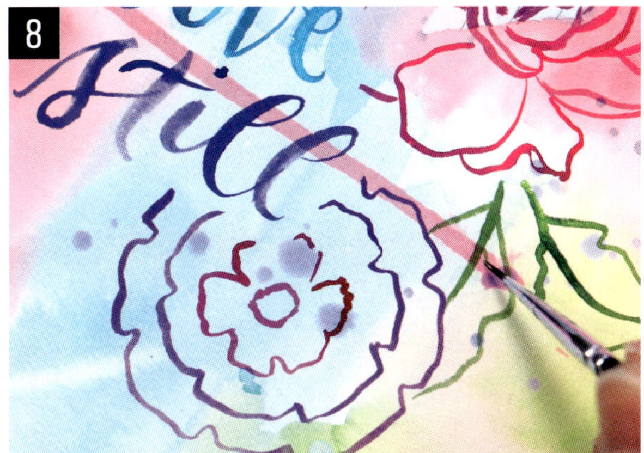

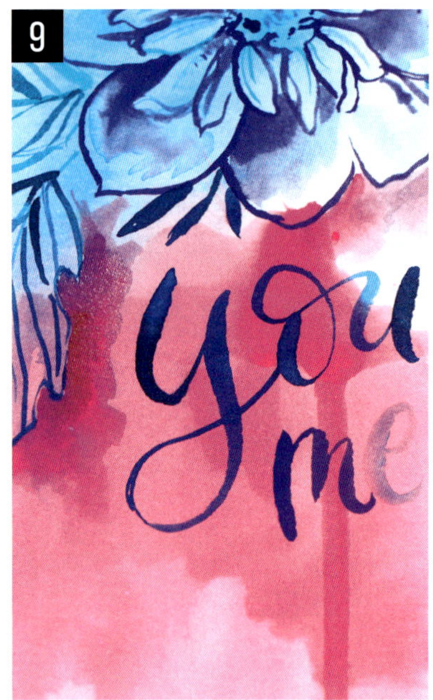

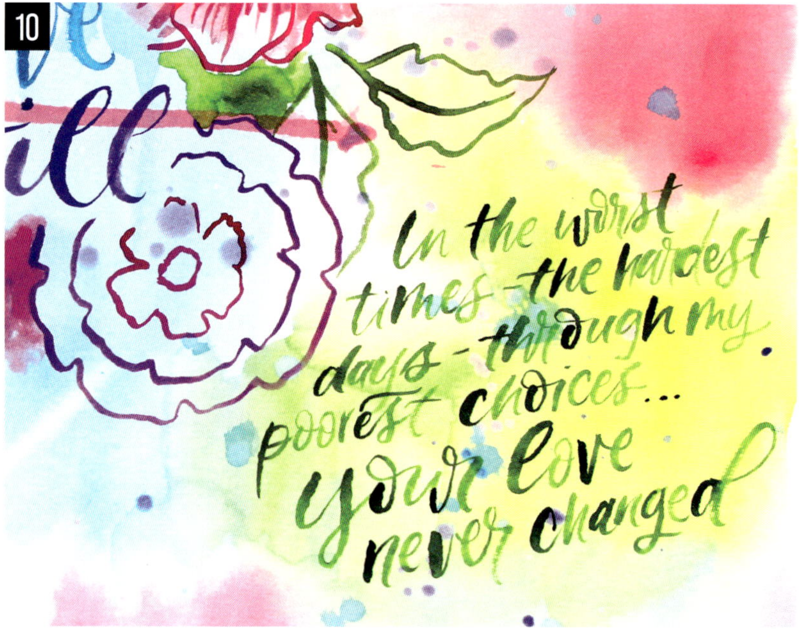

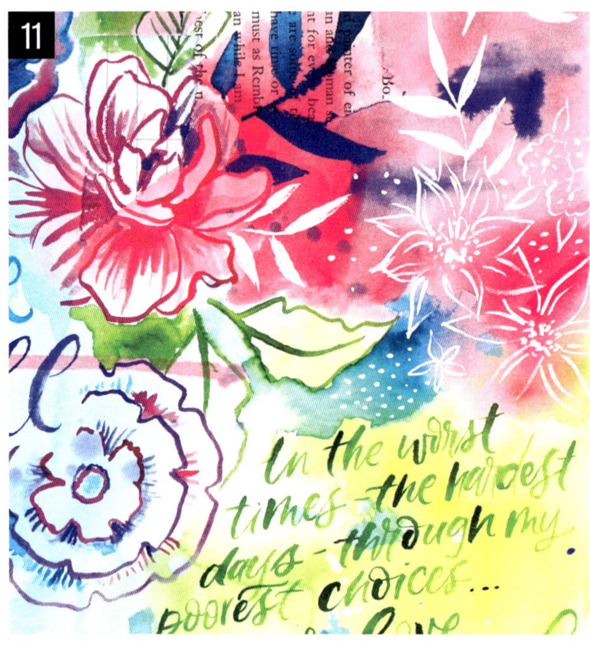

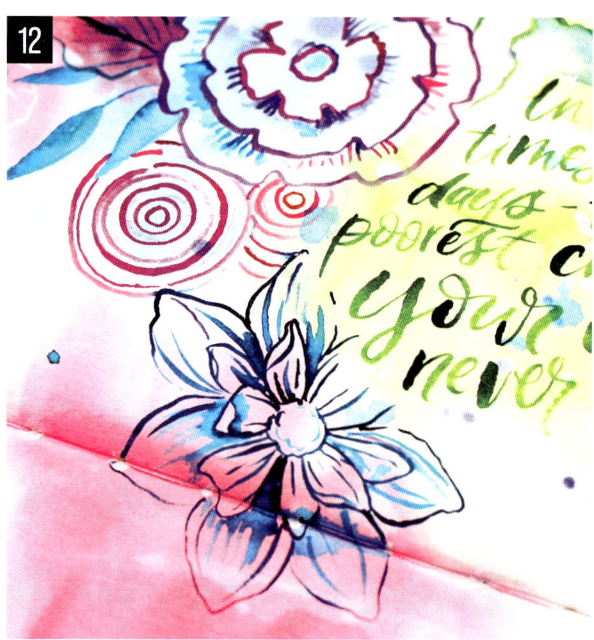

9 **Create contrast between the flowers and the background.** In the negative space that is left around the flowers and lettering, wash in some deeper colors to create even more of a separation between the illustrations and the words.

10 **Journal in a different spot.** Move to another area to journal more thoughts, this time writing smaller with a tiny brush. While I encourage you to give writing with a paintbrush a try, you can use any pen instead. I love to write with my paintbrush because it merges the words and flowers and washes into one. But if you are not comfortable yet with this method, use a brush pen or even a pencil and just let the words flow.

11 **Add more color and doodles.** As you continue to move back and forth between journaling with words and journaling with beautiful florals, play with adding some white florals into the mix. Here, for example, I first added deeper colors to the negative space, as explained in step 9, and then, once they were dry, I added white as well as color doodles and leaves on top. This contributes to the buildup of gorgeous layers.

12 **Keep moving down the page.** As you continue to move down the page from top to bottom and left to right, add more florals, designs, and details.

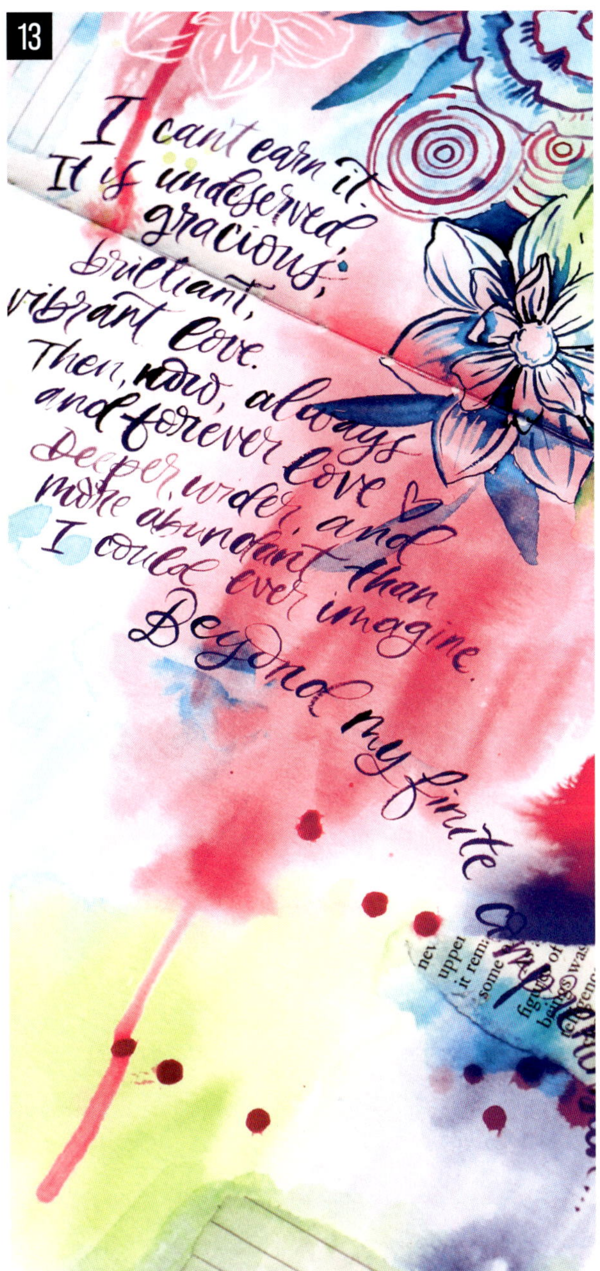

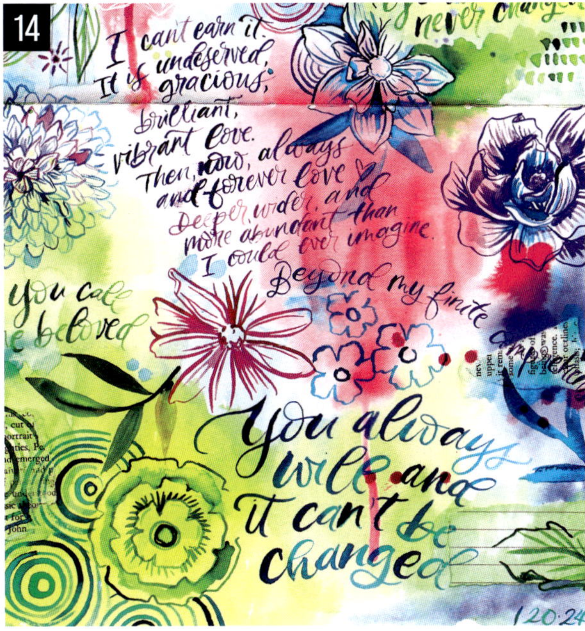

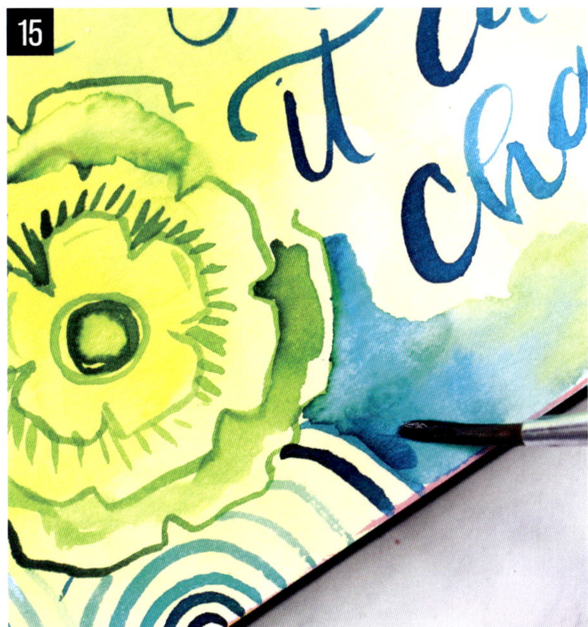

13 **Journal again and experiment with shape.**
Return to journaling, painting your letters in another
color and allowing them to flow down the page.
Don't feel like you have to write in straight lines!
You can follow the curve of nearby shapes or
completely strike out randomly into the available
negative space if you feel inclined.

14 **Keep filling the page.** This is truly your time.
Allow yourself to look away from my instructions
and just work through the entire piece using the
method we've established, flowing from your
painting to your writing and/or lettering and back
again. While you paint florals and reflect, switch

back to writing those thoughts down, creating
a rhythm and a balance between painting flowers
and painting words. This is a space to get lost
in what you are doing, a space in which you
treat your words and your florals with the same
thoughtfulness.

15 **Revisit areas that need more contrast.** Once
you have filled the page, return to any remaining
negative space to add in deeper washes that will
help your florals and designs stand out. This may
have already become part of your flow as you work,
or not—it's up to you how much time you spend on
each area as you go.

16 **Revisit your florals to add details.** It's time to give your flowers some final attention, going back in with dark, concentrated colors to add high-contrast line details. This is also a time to reflect on what you've written. I love to reread what I've written—the permanence of my words in paint reflects what my heart was truly saying in that moment, and I love to go back through these thoughts as I return to the florals.

17 **Add white highlights.** If you'd like, make a fresh pass across the entire piece again to add white details and highlights to your florals.

18 **Add white background doodles.** Last, add white designs in some areas of negative space, such as solid silhouettes of leaves or mandala-like doodled flowers. Allow yourself these last few moments to close out the time spent creating and reflecting. When you feel like the page is complete, step back and take it all in. Look at the piece as a whole first, and then look through it going from top to bottom, just as you created it.

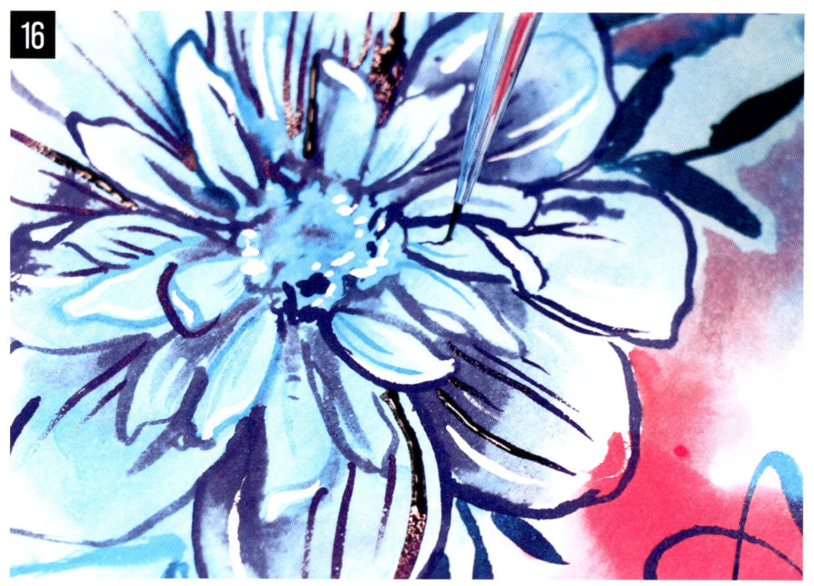

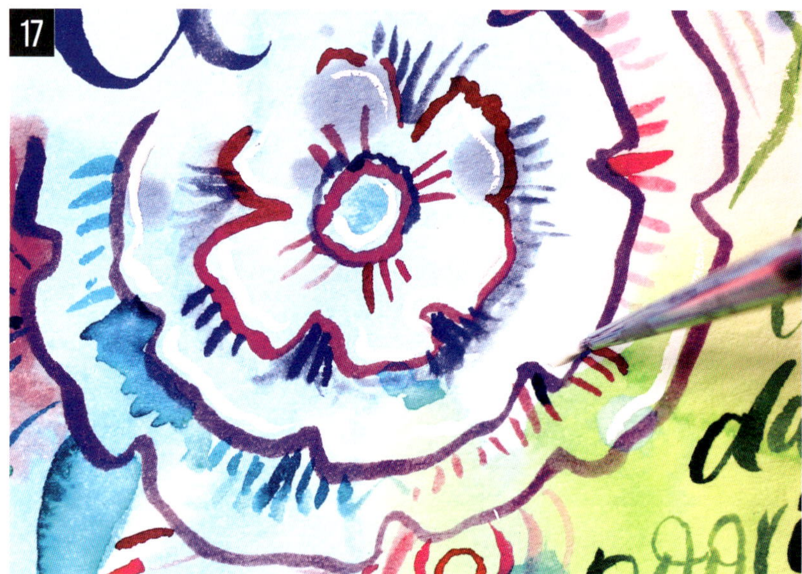

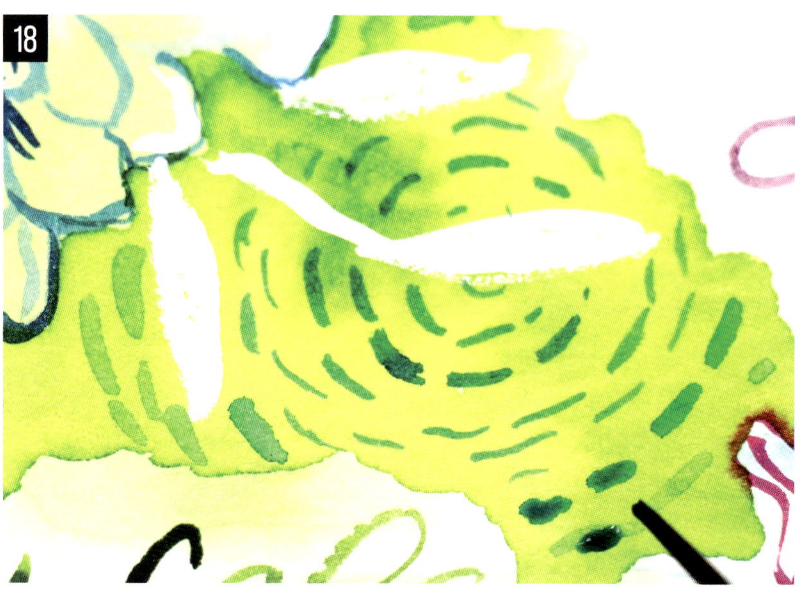

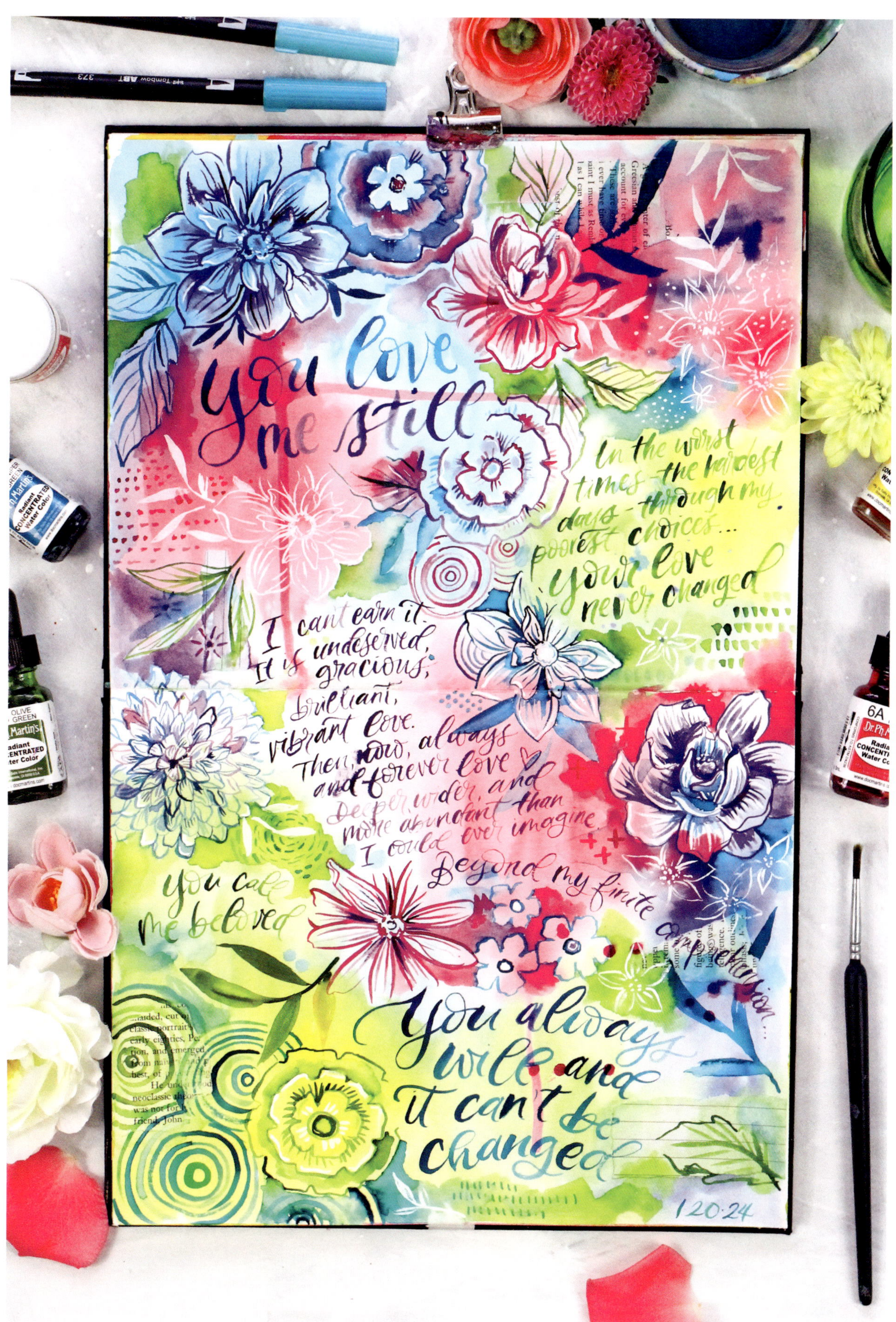
you love me still
In the worst times—the hardest days—through my poorest choices... your love never changed
I can't earn it. It is undeserved, gracious, brilliant, vibrant love. Then, now, always and forever love. Deeper, wider, and more abundant than I could ever imagine. Beyond my finite comprehension...
You call me beloved
You always will and it can't be changed
1 20:24

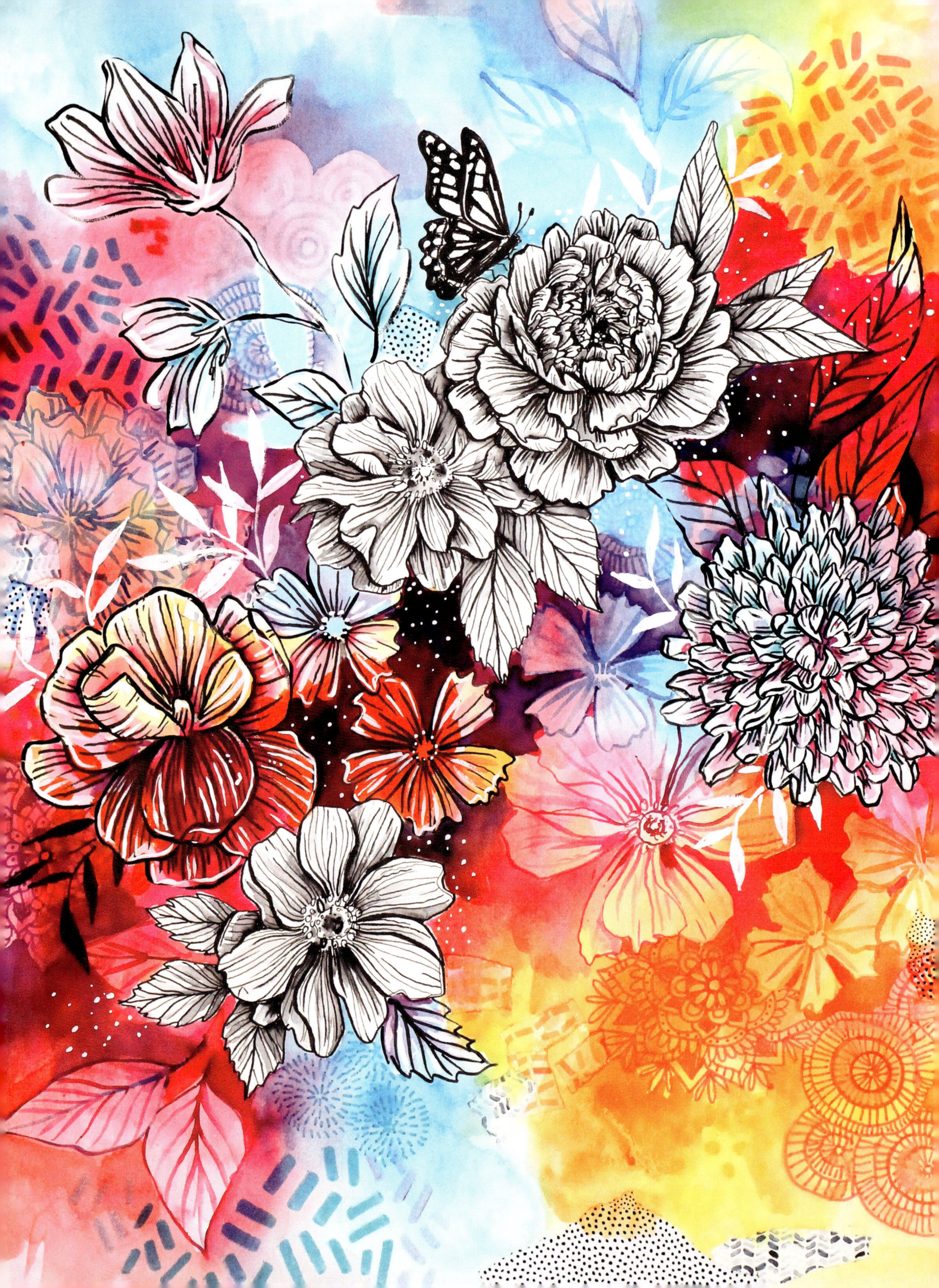

Abundant Garden

Learn to use every tool in your arsenal at once to discover new and exciting combinations

While this project is our last in the book, I can't even begin to count how many projects, techniques, tricks, and experiments my brain has left. Even as I've written these pages with step-by-step processes to teach you in mind, I've continued to learn and grow over the several months I have poured into this book. I've gotten to know my supplies better and how those supplies can interact with one another. I've stumbled upon new shapes and compositions to explore. I've spent days upon days experimenting with this last project, trying to find exactly what I want to leave you with.

And this is where I've landed—on a project that I personally have never tried until creating it for this book. Discovering it has been such a wonderful experience because I feel like I have been learning right alongside you.

In this piece, we're incorporating markers, pens, watercolors, and acrylics—you know, ALL THE SUPPLIES. We'll be combining several techniques that you learned up to this point, while using more whimsical, illustrative floral shapes to create something that I am sure will lead you toward even more ideas and creativity in the future.

Tools & Supplies

- ▶ Black pen with broader tip or calligraphy tip
- ▶ Fine-tipped black pen
- ▶ Water-based markers
- ▶ Watercolors
- ▶ Acrylic paints
- ▶ Sizes 00, 1, and 5 round paintbrushes (or your choice of an extra-small, a small, and a medium brush)
- ▶ Collage elements
- ▶ Adhesive
- ▶ Water
- ▶ Watercolor paper, mixed-media paper, or Bristol board

What You'll Learn

THERE IS ALWAYS SOMETHING NEW TO TRY: As I mentioned above, even I, after months spent writing this book and years spent developing my style, still stumble on new things. Some ideas may not work, but they never fail. There is no failing in trying something new and inventive. The joy is in finding out what happens when you make the attempt.

MIXING SUPPLIES IS FUN: In this piece, we use it all—pens, markers, acrylics, watercolors, and collage, all working in harmony to create a unique and cohesive work of art. Don't limit yourself to one medium in your work—use what you need and want to use to achieve the outcome you are looking for. Supplies can comingle in stunning and amusing ways.

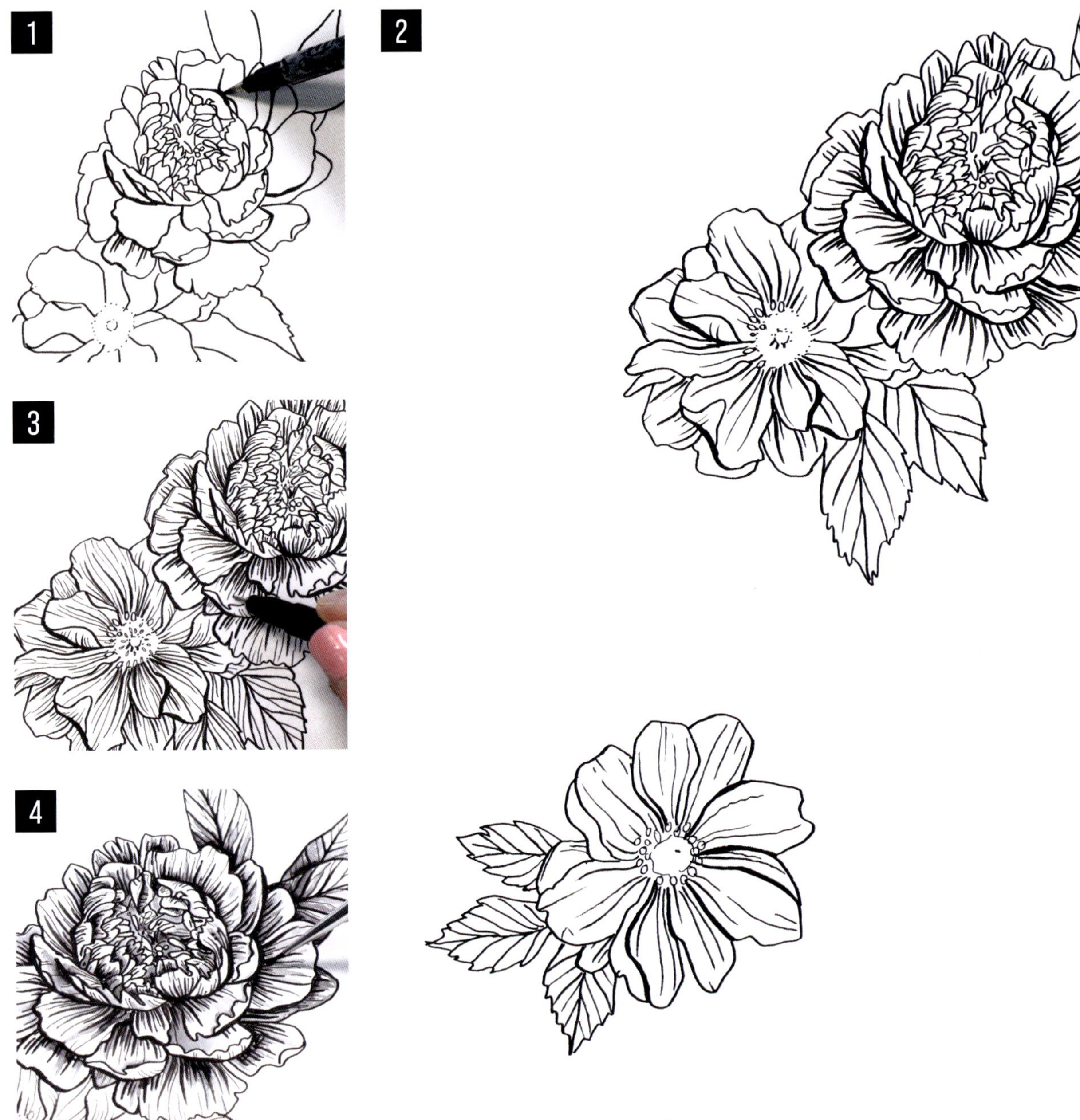

1 **Draw one group of flowers.** To begin, let's return to the only project in the book where we started out drawing in pen before eliminating the white space: in "Freestyle Floral Doodling," we drew our florals in black before adding color, and that's exactly how we'll start now. First, draw a small grouping of florals in an area near the top center of the piece.

2 **Add a second flower.** Add a single flower on its own lower down on the page. All these florals will remain without color for the entire piece. Add a good amount of linework as you go; if your pen tip is a calligraphy style, use it to create easy line variation.

3 **Add fine detail.** Switch to a very fine-tipped drawing pen, such as the size 01 that I'm using, to add even more detailed linework to your flowers. We're going big or going home on this last project, so push the detail as far as you can in these first three blooms. Don't neglect the leaves either!

4 **Add a gray wash to the flowers.** Let's take a familiar technique but push it in a new direction. Using a black water-based marker, add the slightest bit of shading in the flowers, then wash it out with a small, wet brush. The goal is NOT to cover the flowers entirely in gray. Be careful not to apply too much black at first, as you want to preserve the whites in the highlights and keep the florals from getting too messy or dull.

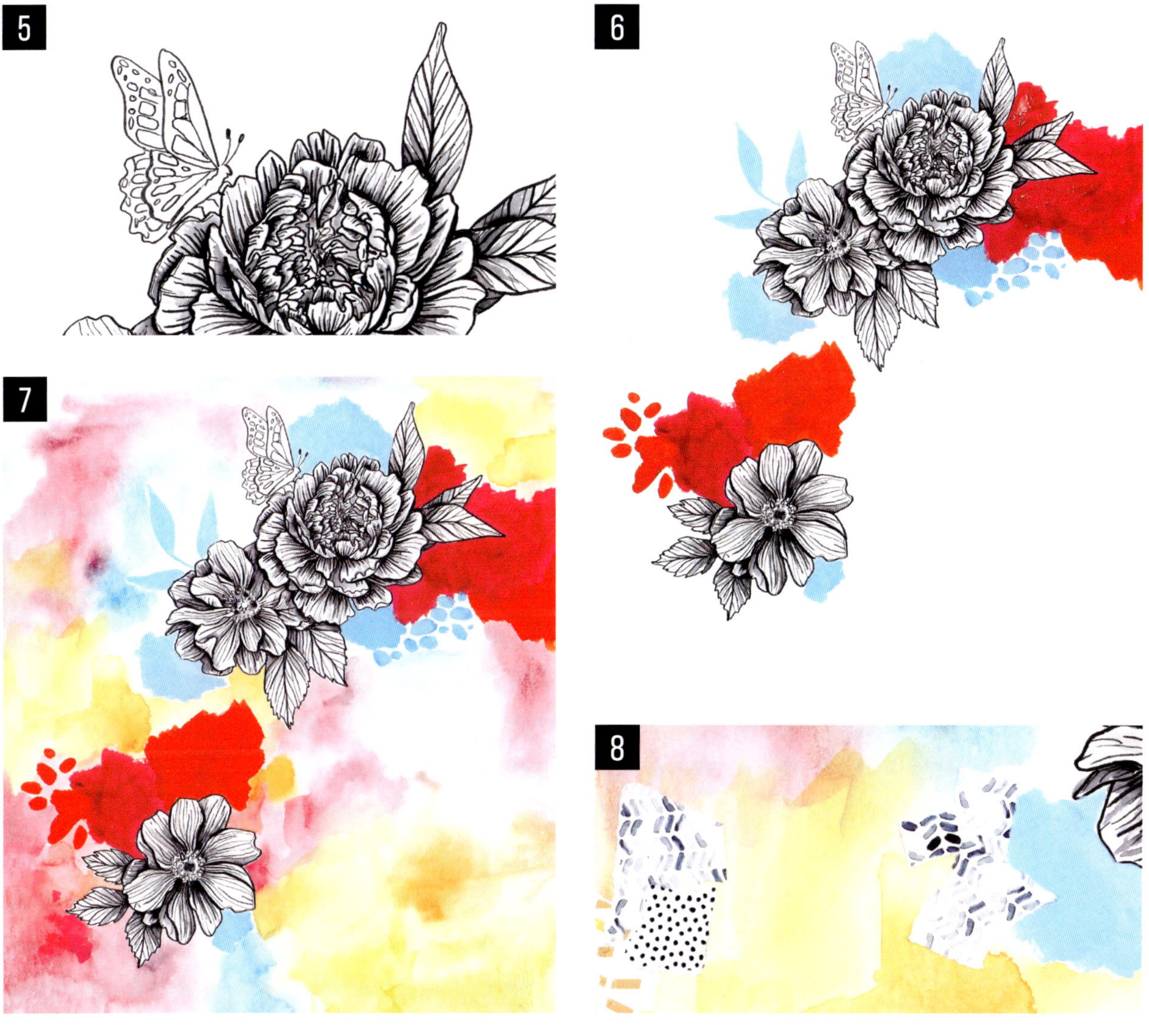

Is there something else you've been wanting to bring into your floral work? Stay in the bug world with a ladybug or a bumblebee or consider adding something weird that doesn't seem to fit! Perhaps you want to explore a different plant form, such as berries, cacti, or vegetables. Be open to your weird ideas and go for it!

5 **Add a butterfly.** I think it's time for a butterfly to make an appearance, don't you? Butterflies and blooms seem to go hand and hand, so draw a butterfly in black and leave it for now as a simple line drawing. We'll come back to it with some color in a later step.

6 **Start painting with acrylics in the background.** We're going to use both acrylic and watercolor on the negative space. I want to mention that the only reason I decided to do this is because it's something we haven't done yet (besides with black). That's the only reason I tried it! Start by choosing a few acrylic colors to add in your negative space.

Create a few patches of color, being careful to stay outside the flowers, and then add some abstract shapes and some leaf silhouettes.

7 **Switch to watercolors.** Staying in the negative space, get out your watercolors now and fill in the remaining space with a light wash of various colors, allowing areas to pool and adding bolder colors in spots as you go. Keep these values light in general.

8 **Add some collage elements.** I'll add just a bit of collage simply because it's fun! I've chosen papers with small patterns that fit in with the color scheme that I have developed. You can skip this collage step if it doesn't speak to you.

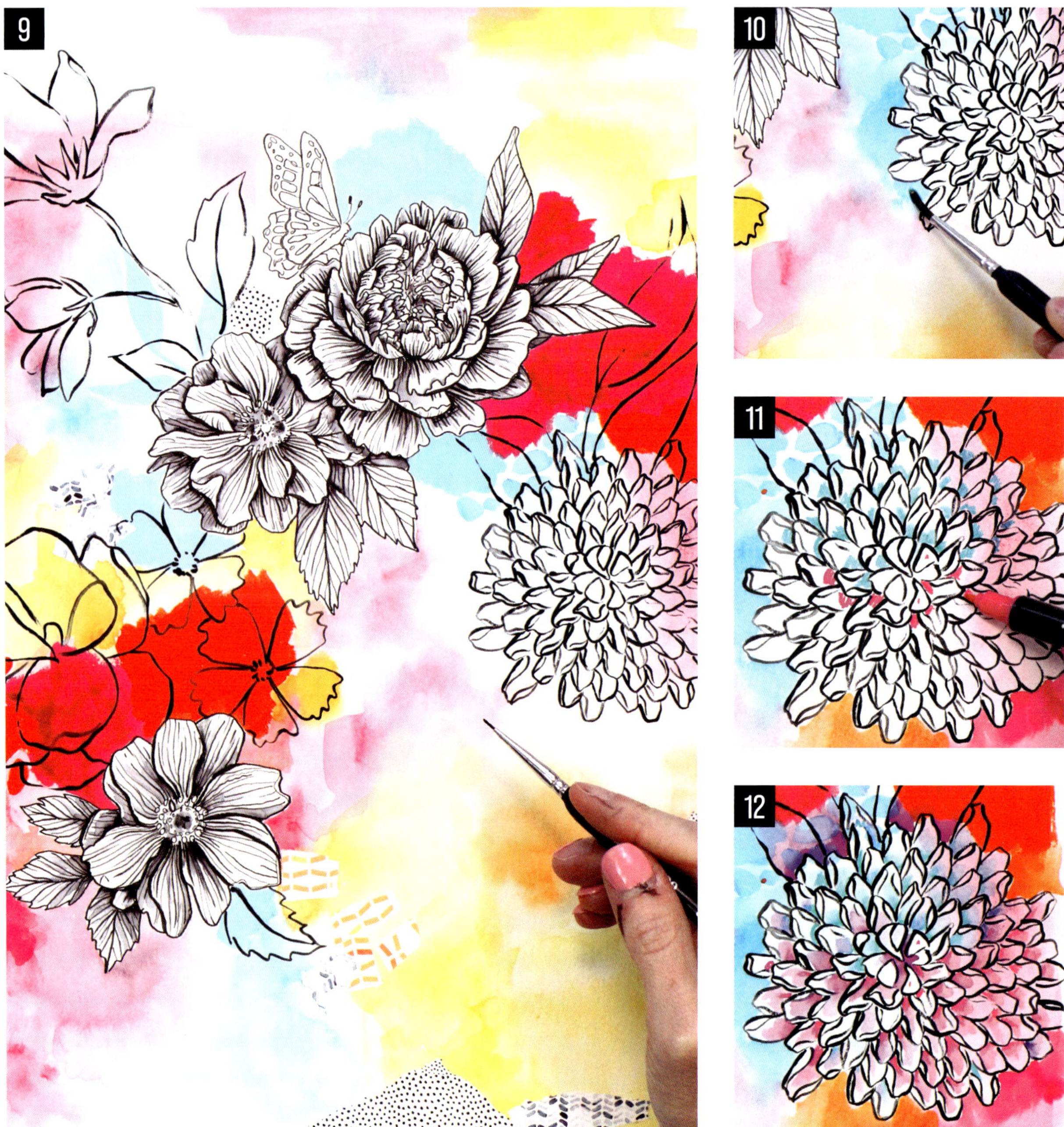

9 **Paint in some black florals.** Add in some more florals outlined in black acrylic. You can discover your composition as you go, like I have, allowing intuition to determine where each flower and leaf should fall. Because you have switched over to a paintbrush, your linework will naturally become a bit looser than it was with the initial marker-drawn flowers.

10 **Add deeper color around the newly drawn florals.** I am certain that you know what's next—back to the negative space! Use only watercolor to deepen the colors right around the edges of your newly painted florals to help them pop off the background. The areas of acrylic will resist the watercolor, so the acrylic color will be mostly preserved where the watercolor overlaps.

11 **Add color to the flowers.** Using water-based markers, add small patches of color within the new flowers, ready to be blended in the next step.

12 **Blend the flower colors.** Use a paintbrush and water to activate and blend the marker color, spreading it out nicely within each petal and flowers.

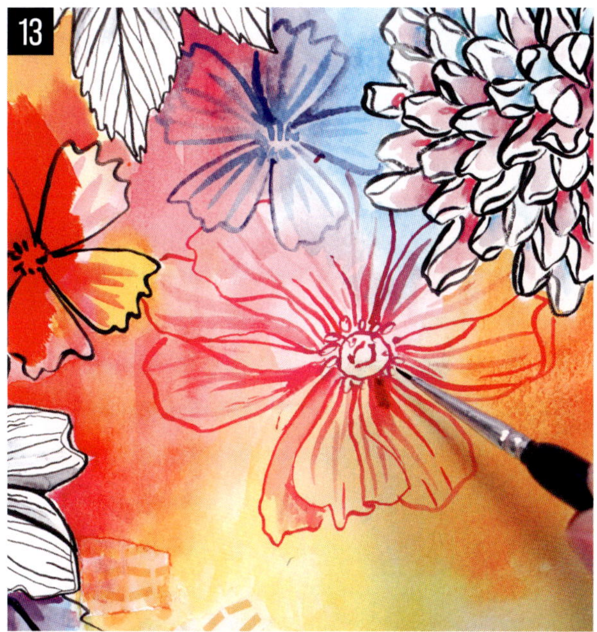

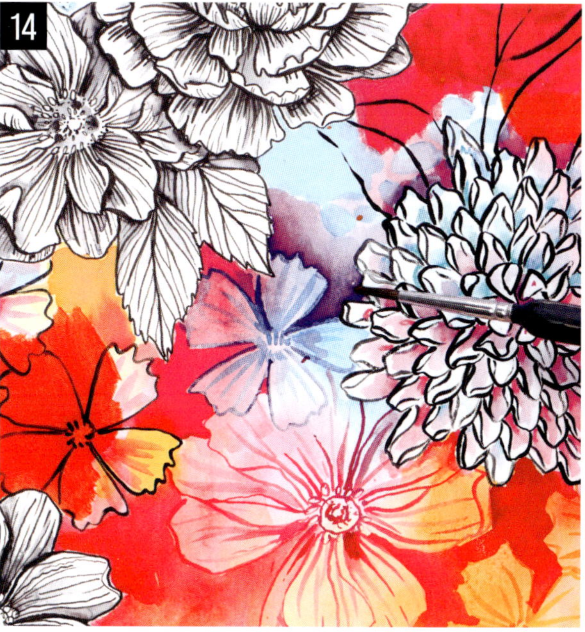

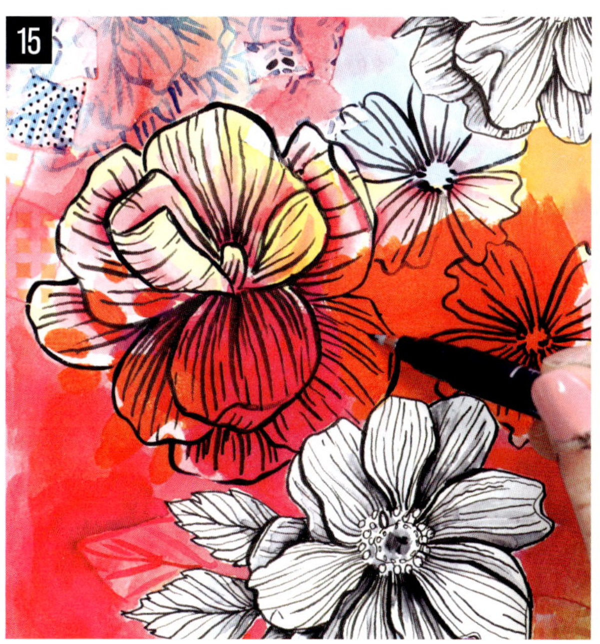

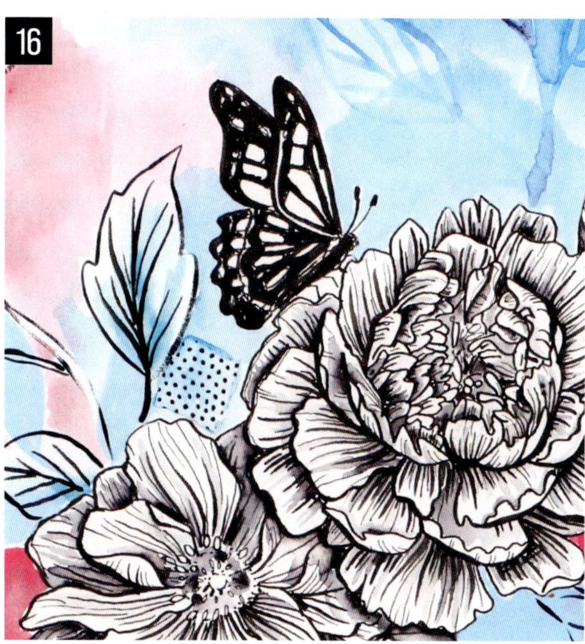

13 **Paint in color flowers.** While the previous step dries, draw some flowers in the remaining areas of the negative space using watercolors and a fine-tipped round brush. Go for a concentrated or saturated shade so the outlines are crisp and clear. As you create each flower, include linework and shading.

14 **Add deeper colors around the new flowers.** Use more watercolor to keep pushing the values in the background immediately around the newly painted flowers, helping them to come forward thanks to the contrast.

15 **Crisp up and add detail to the black painted flowers.** While the previous step dries, return to the flowers you painted in black to bring in linework detail. Although you outlined them in paint, use your black marker or pen to achieve a bit more precise variation in the linework.

16 **Add details to the butterfly.** It's finally time to return to that neglected butterfly! Fill in most of the butterfly with solid black, leaving the isolated shapes within its wings white.

17 **Doodle in color.** The negative space is still crying out for some added detail. Use the fine tip of your water-based markers to draw in mandala designs and other patterns. Sometimes these designs can match the hue below them (orange on orange); other times the designs can be a contrasting color (blue on magenta).

18 **Darken areas of the negative space one last time.** This will be our last trip to the negative space. Add your deepest values of watercolor around any areas that you feel need to be pushed further back. In areas that you want to darken that are acrylic, use your markers instead of your watercolors so the acrylic doesn't resist the color. Compare this photo to the photo for step 16 to see the change.

19 **Add white sparkles and highlights.** Get your best white paint out and add highlights to the flowers outlined in black. Then paint a few solid-white vines and sprinkle some dots throughout the piece. Although I want my initial black-and-white flowers and butterfly to stand out as the focal point, incorporating this white elsewhere now will help tie the piece together.

Congrats!

You've completed your 12th funky florals piece. I won't call this your final one, though, because I have a strong feeling that you are just beginning your journey.

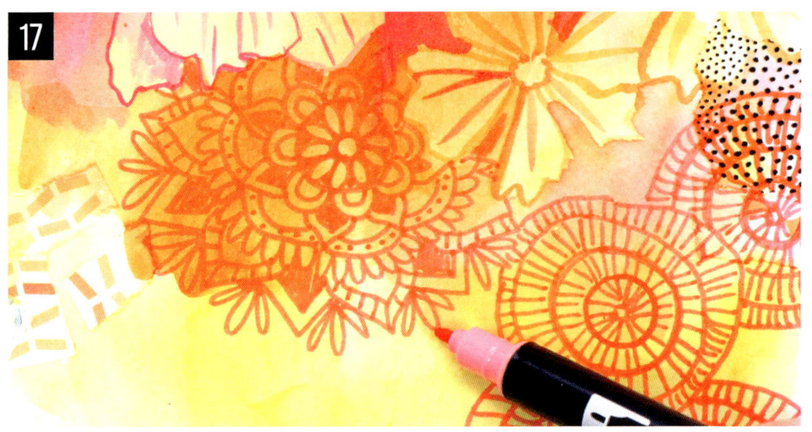

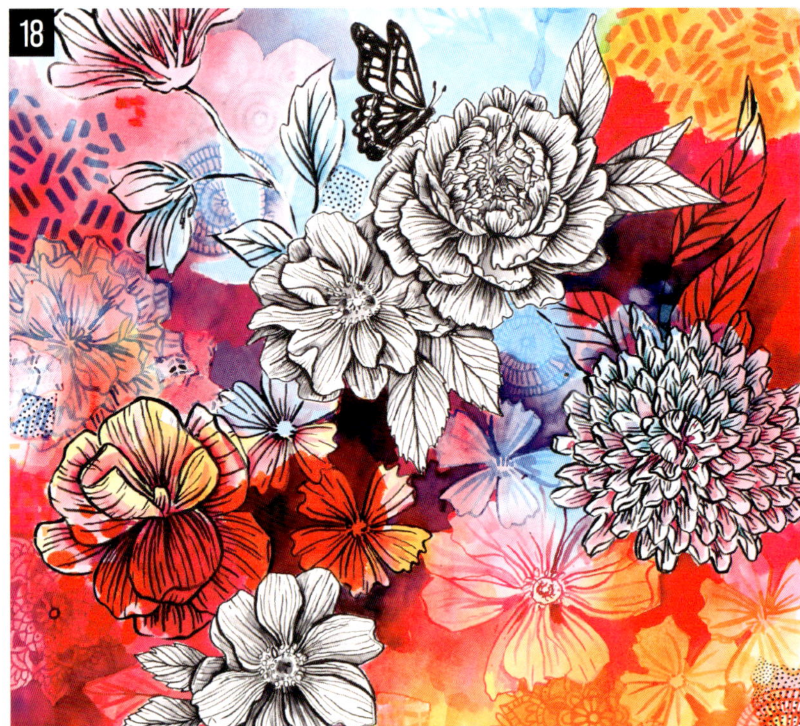

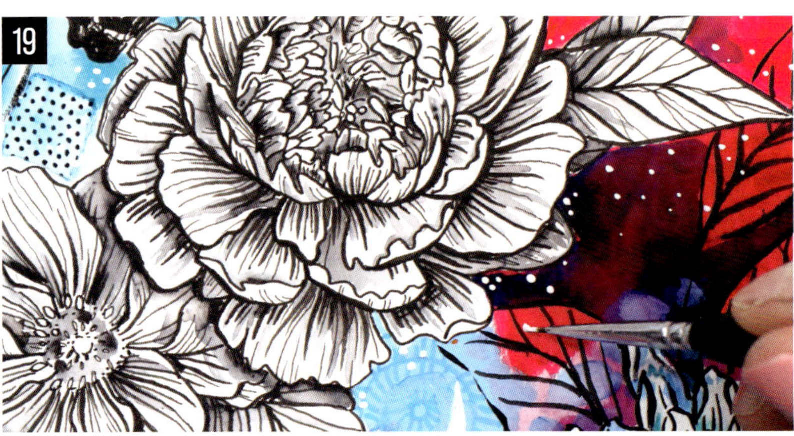

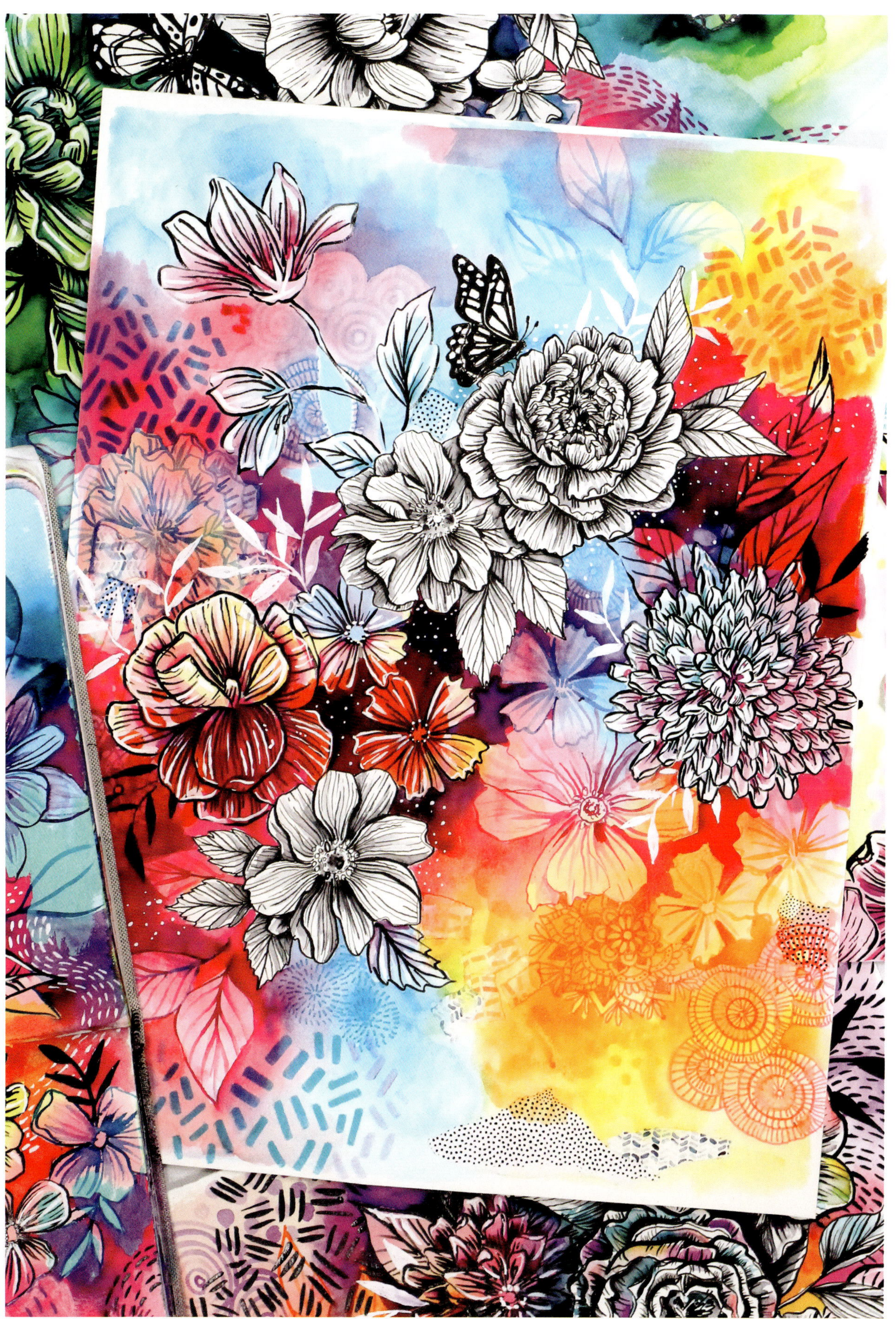

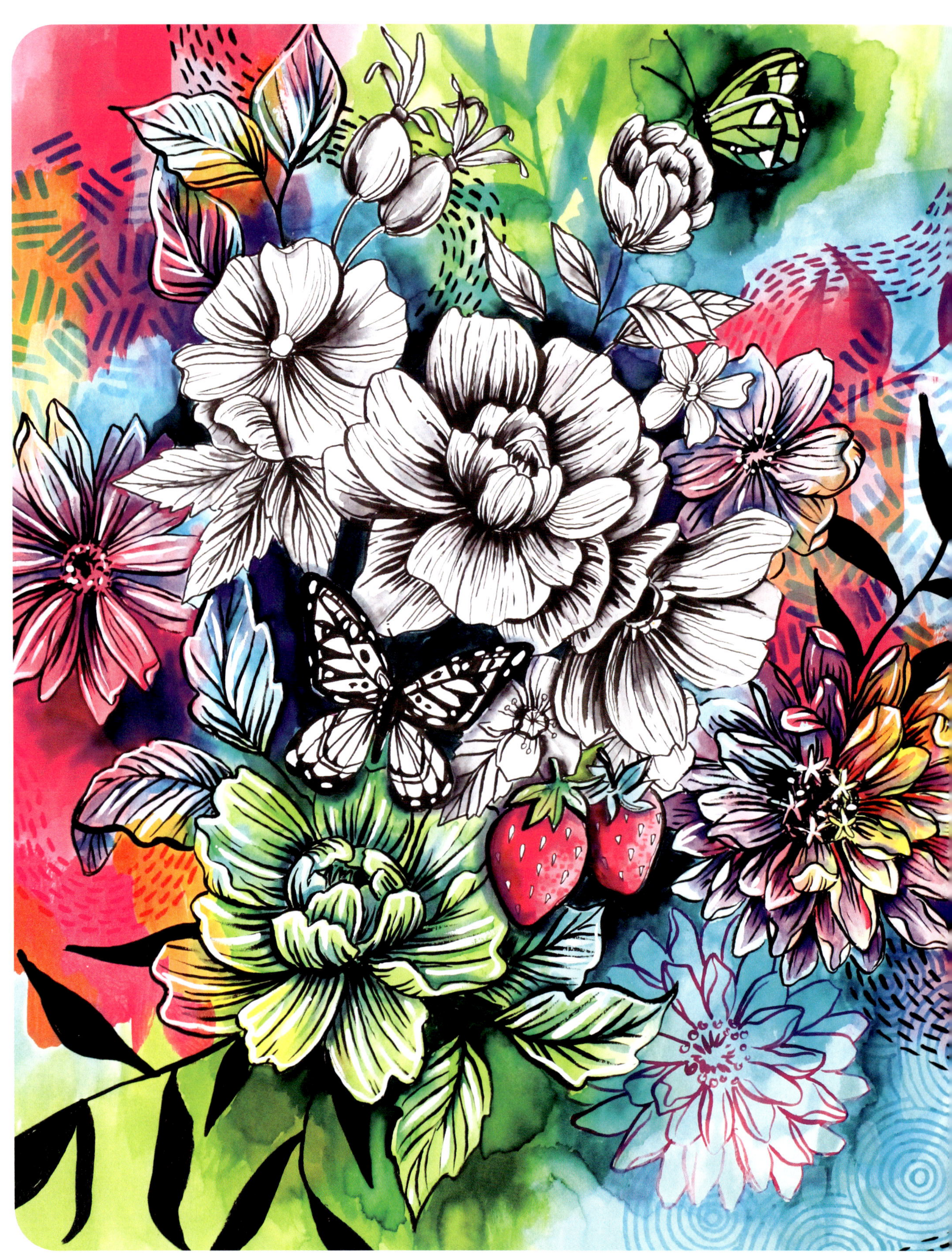

PART 3
Inspiration Gallery

Believe me when I say that I have so. many. funky. florals in my studio!
The projects you've seen up to this point in the book are just the tip of the
floral iceberg. In this final part of the book, I'd like to share with you some of
my favorite pieces in the hopes that they will inspire you to new and stunning
levels of creativity in your future funky floral work. I know your artistic journey
will be unique and fulfilling for you in a deeply personal way, so take what
you will from what I share, and go out there and create!

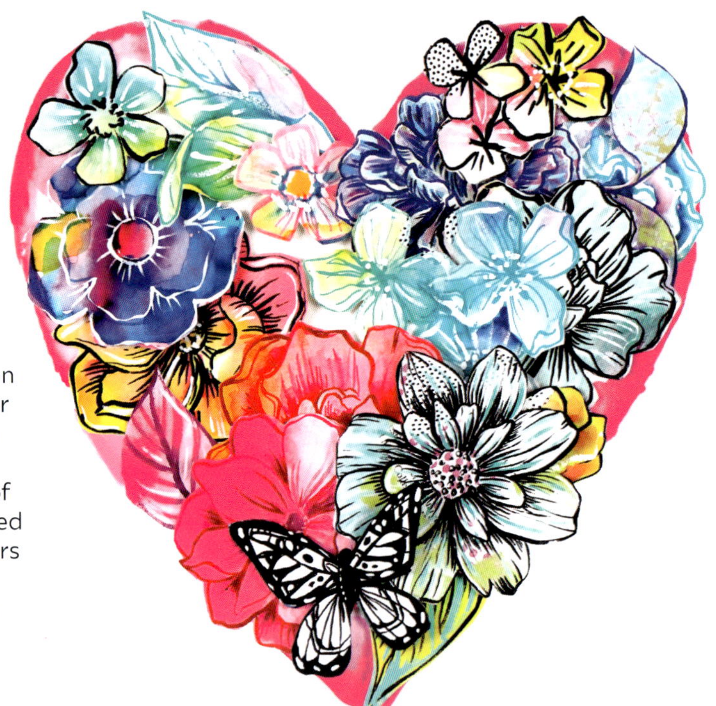

One thing I love to do is photograph my work and then cut out flowers to use in other pieces or to create new work altogether. The cover of this book is actually an example of this process! This heart-shaped piece was created with flowers using all types of media. The flower on the bottom right is from "Collage Magic"!

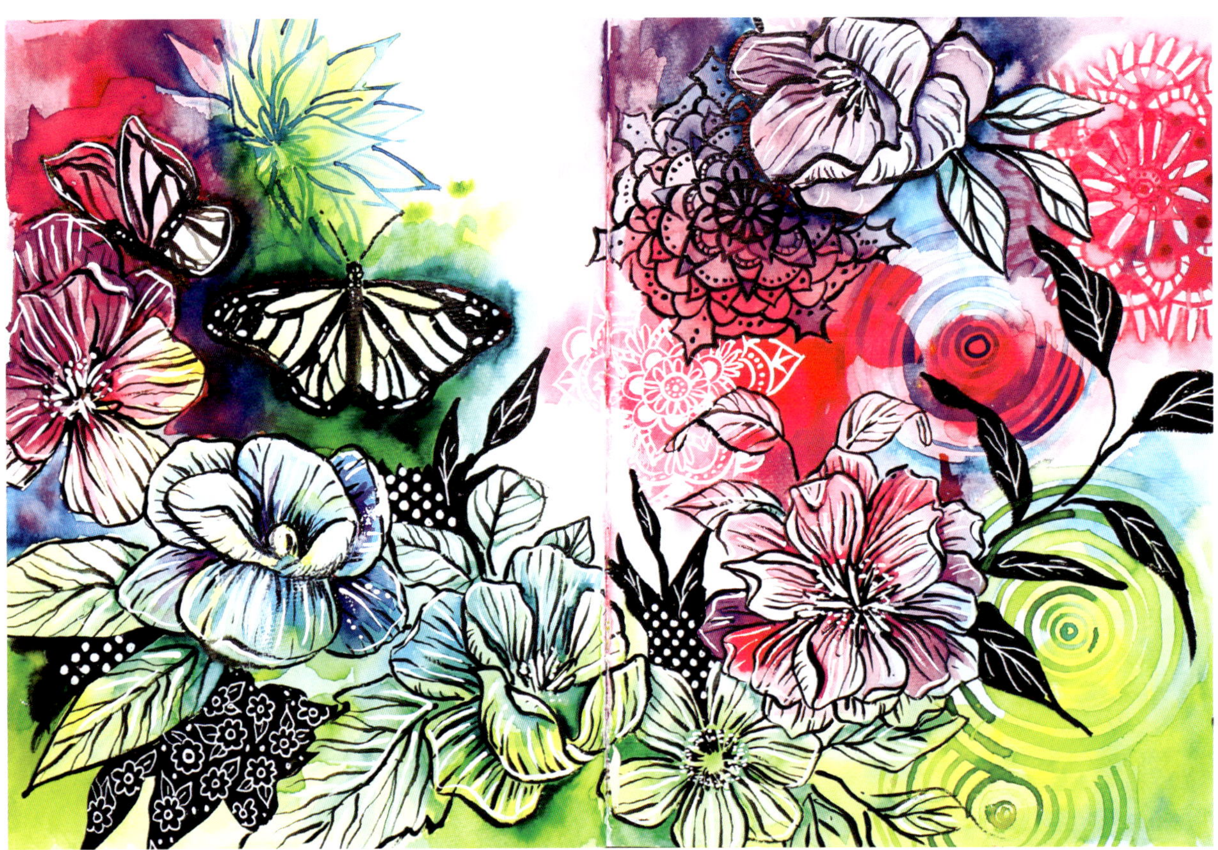

I often incorporate butterflies in my work when I'm wanting more than flowers in the composition. This piece uses watercolor, black acrylic, and water-based markers to create a sweeping composition. Small areas of black (like we created in "Risky Black") are filled with patterns, and the washy designs in the background are reminiscent of the process in "Party in the Background."

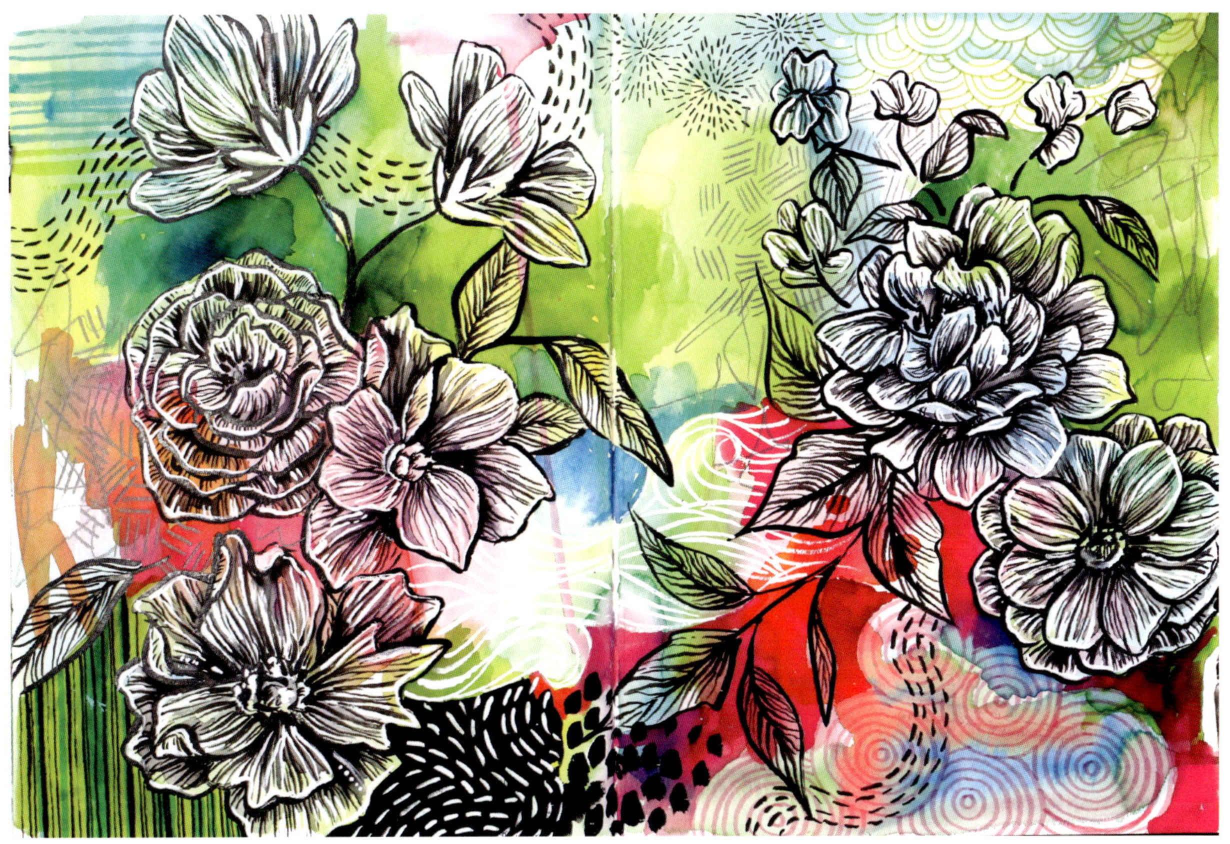

This piece was an exploration in negative-space designs. I used pencil (as I did in "Transformative Contrast") to add interesting texture and experimented with swirling linework that moves the eye through the piece.

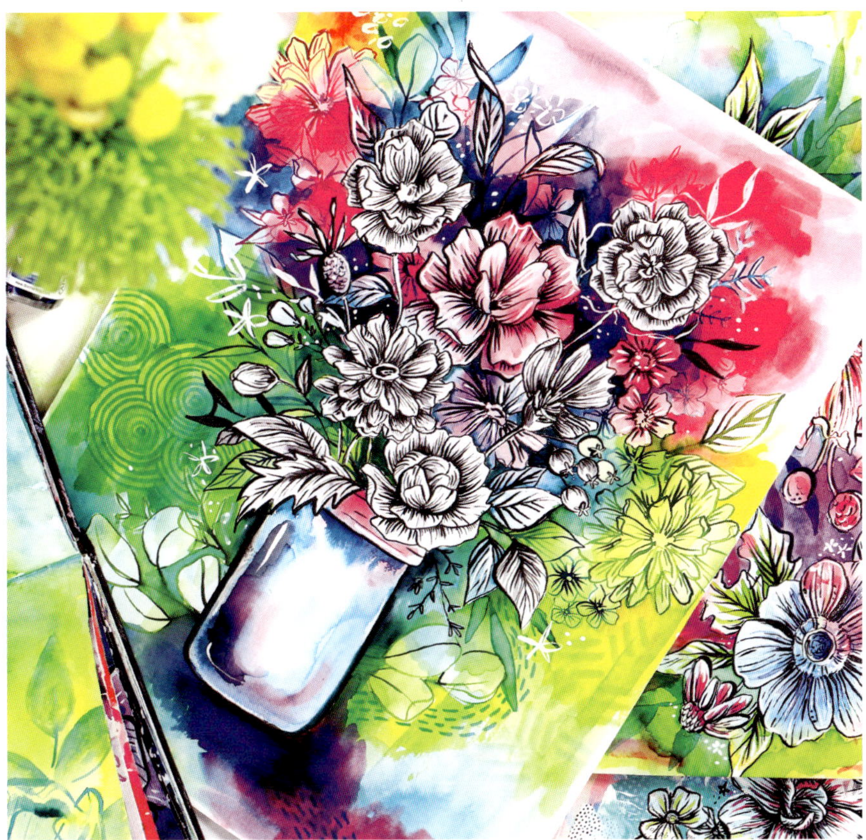

This piece was created while a real bouquet in a mason jar sat on my windowsill, although the flowers are from my imagination. My process here was the same as in "Abundant Garden," incorporating black-and-white flowers drawn with my calligraphy pen; layers of washy fun, created with water-based markers and watercolor, fill the background.

In this piece, I had fun exploring a complementary color scheme while incorporating one of my favorite elements: black acrylic patches with white gel pen doodles. The black-and-white sections create strong contrast, and the use of complementary colors (red and green) adds to that effect.

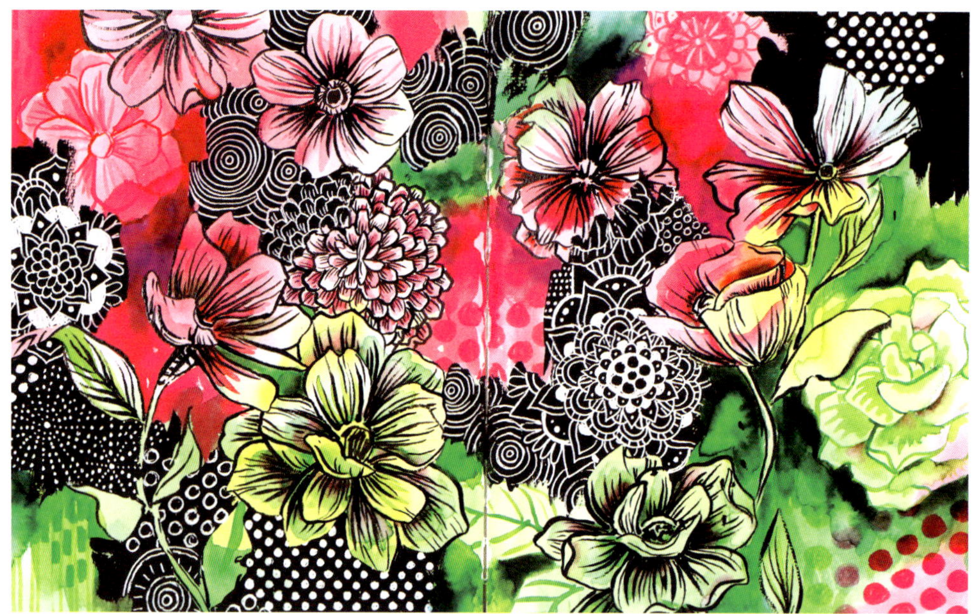

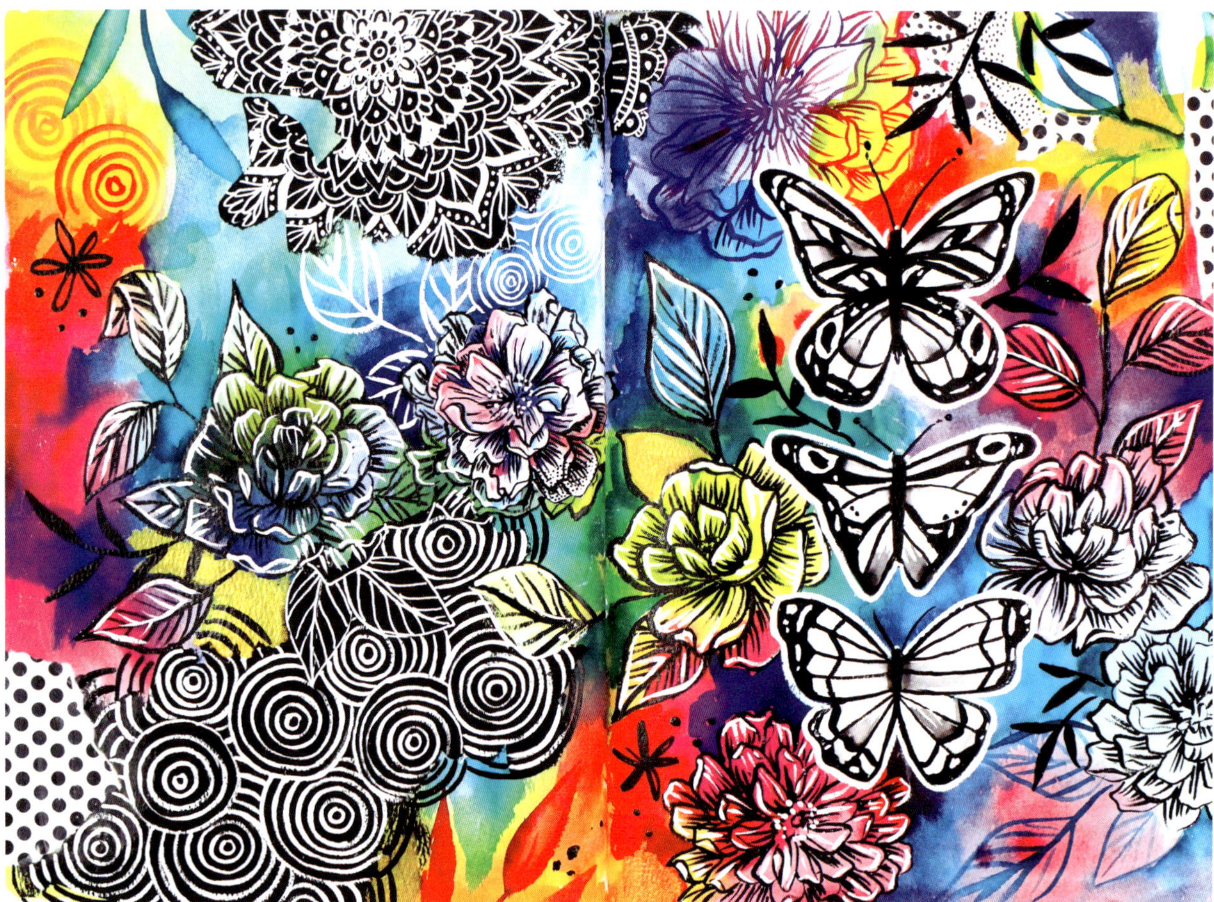

I love experimenting with new compositions, and this column of three black-and-white butterflies creates an organized structure in the midst of an otherwise chaotic composition. Large areas of black acrylic and white designs peek through the washy watercolor background, and I even used a sticker I printed for one of the flowers! Can you guess which one? (The answer is, it's the flower closest to the center on the left-hand page.)

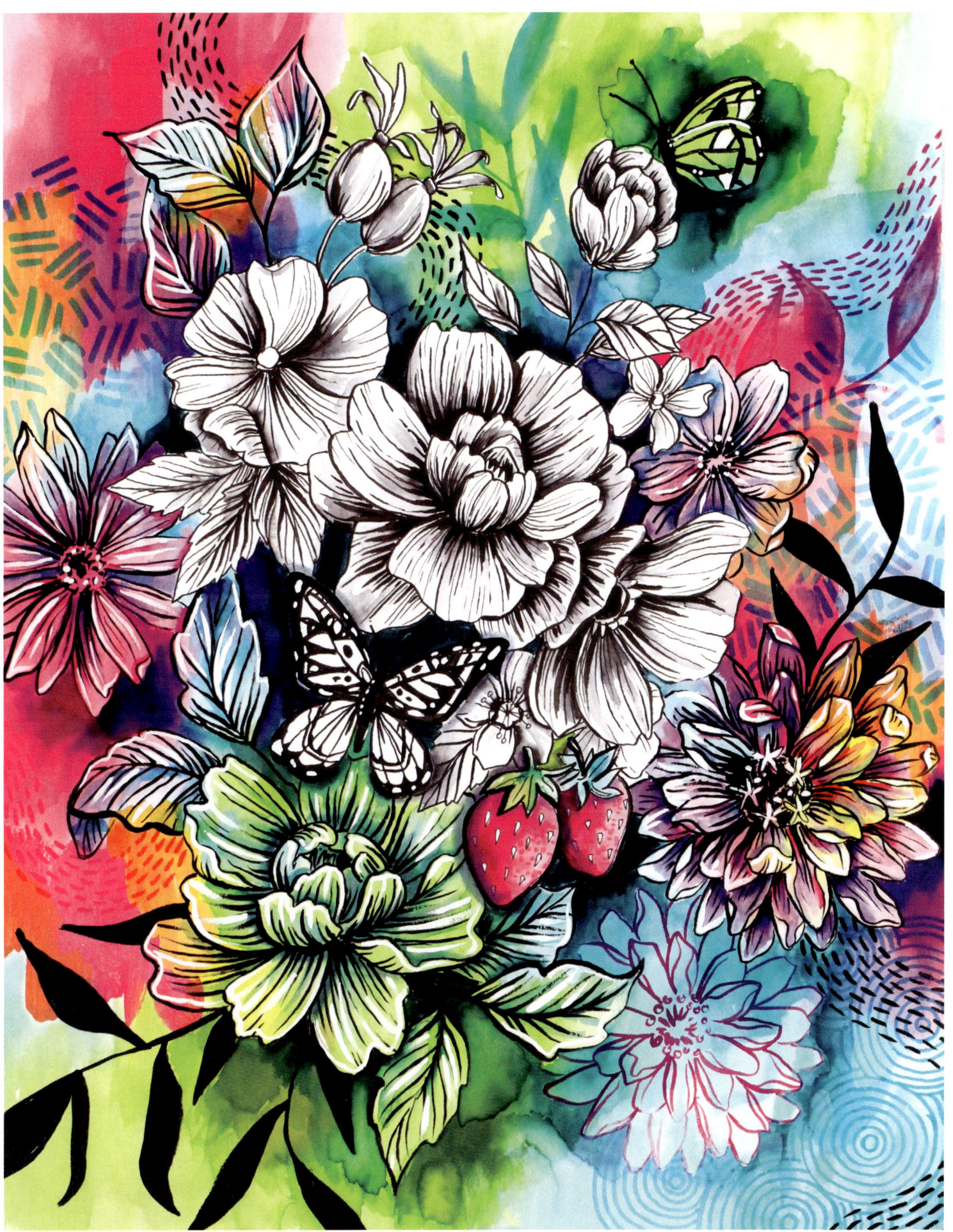

"Abundant Garden" was too much fun to create only once! Here I used the same process and supplies as that project, but the outcome is unique. Strawberries make an appearance for an element of surprise, while I also wandered through the negative space with my water-based markers to create movement through patterns.

Hello, happy accident! I began my lettering in black acrylic before my background was dry, and the bleeding letters, which started off as a big oops, ended up being my favorite part of this piece. The black flowers and fun details in the background remind me of the process for "Party in the Background."

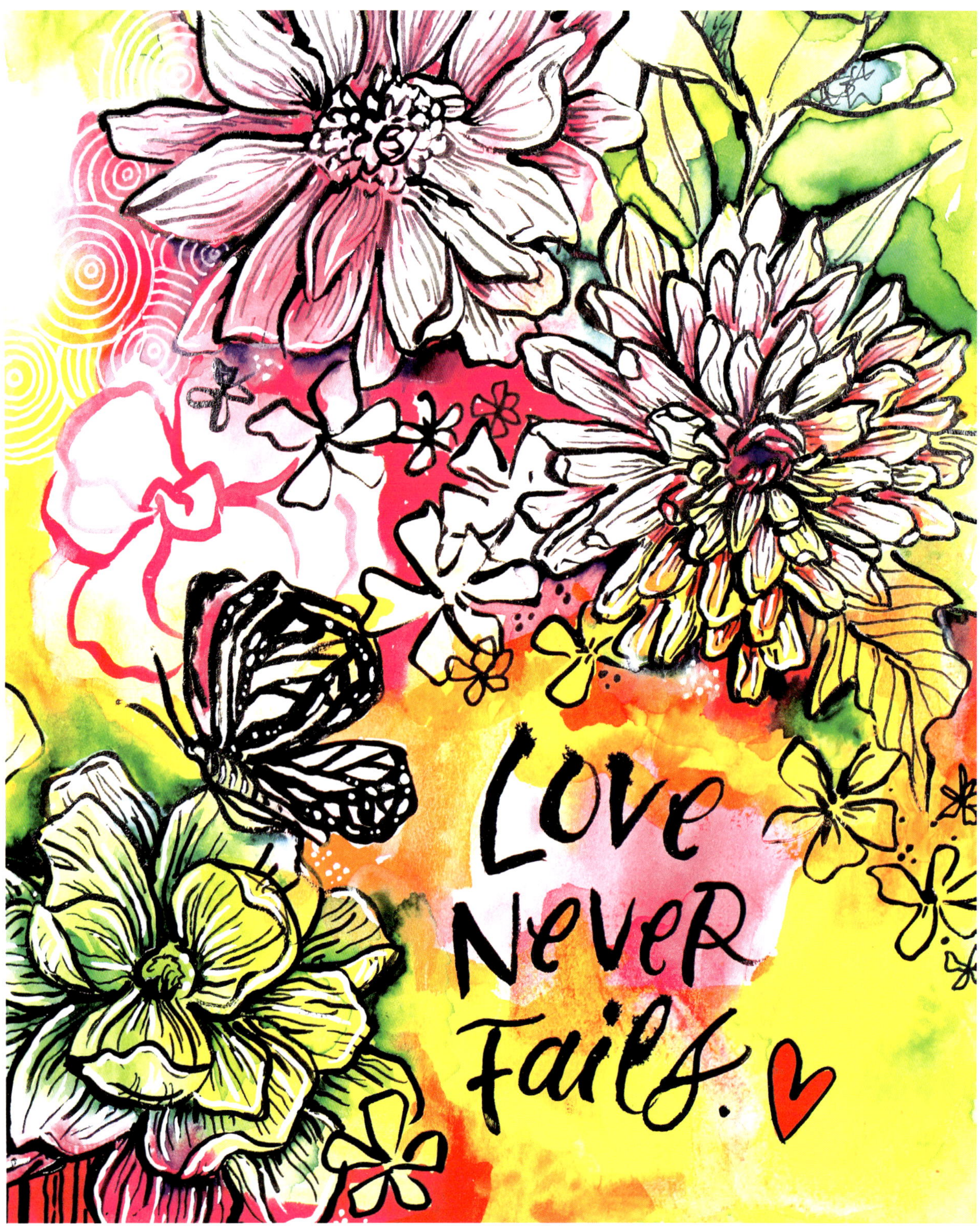

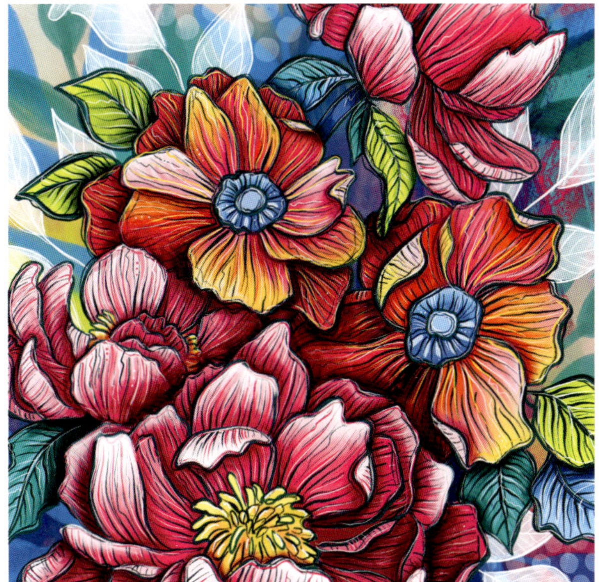

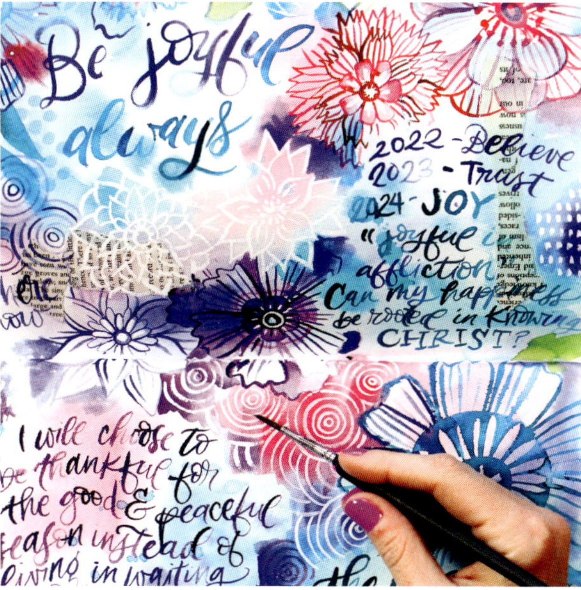

My funky floral process is also fun to create on my iPad using the Procreate app! By adding a messy background and layers of patterns and leaves beneath my floral composition, I can create in the same way even when I don't have access to all my normal art supplies.

Creating this piece ultimately led me to creating "Letter It Out," as I thoroughly enjoyed the process of using watercolors to paint the flowers and writing as I moved through the piece. This has become my favorite method of working while incorporating my thoughts, and I look forward to creating more pages in this style.

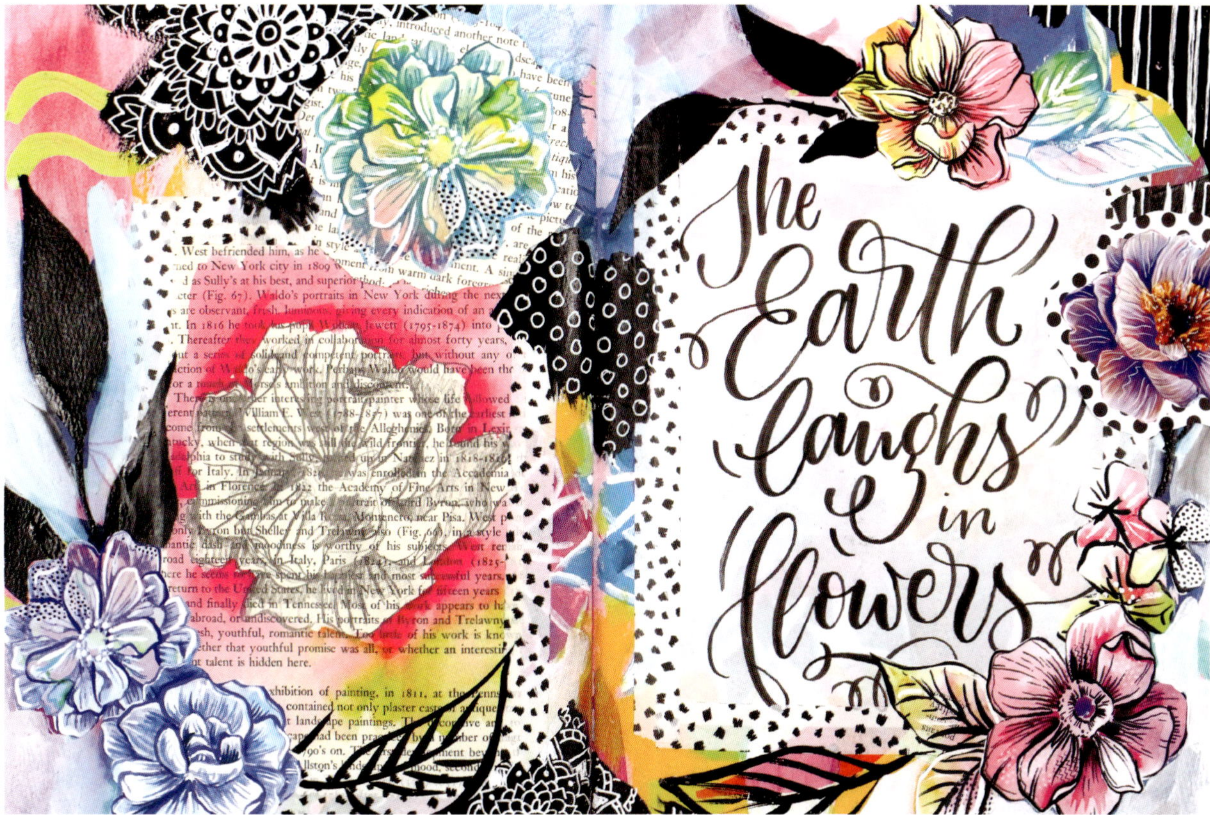

This spread in my art journal has just about everything happening. After a messy acrylic wash in the background, I used techniques from project #6 (black patches) and project #8 (collage) before taping down a lettering sketch, as well as a pencil-drawn flower on an old book page and my own floral stickers. It's a big mess of fun!

Just as I did in "Transformative Contrast," I avoided using black in these flowers and leaned heavily into a deep Prussian blue acrylic. The deep washy watercolor tones create a bit of moodiness, which is balanced out by the bright, happy flowers and funky patterns.

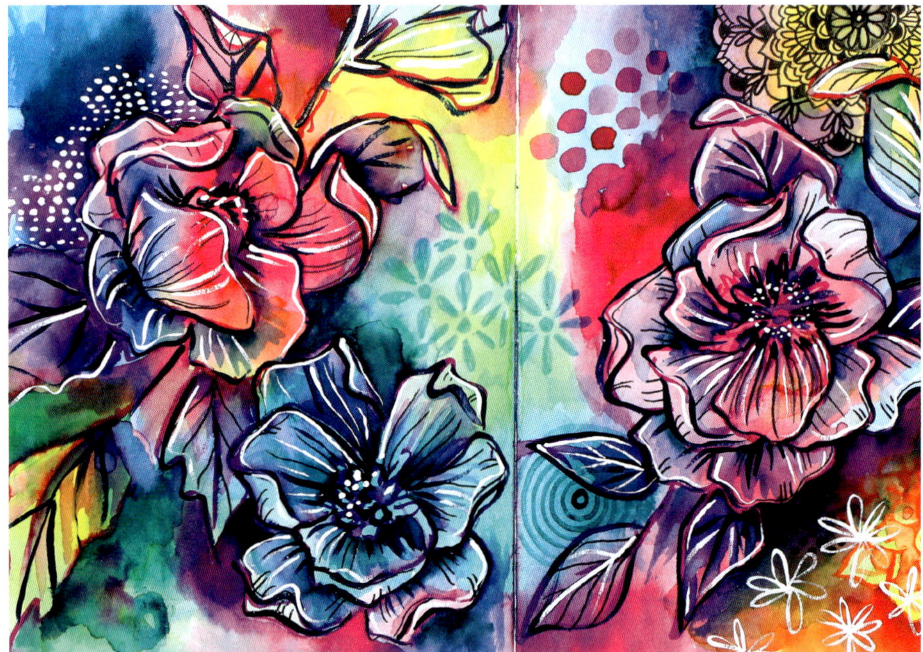

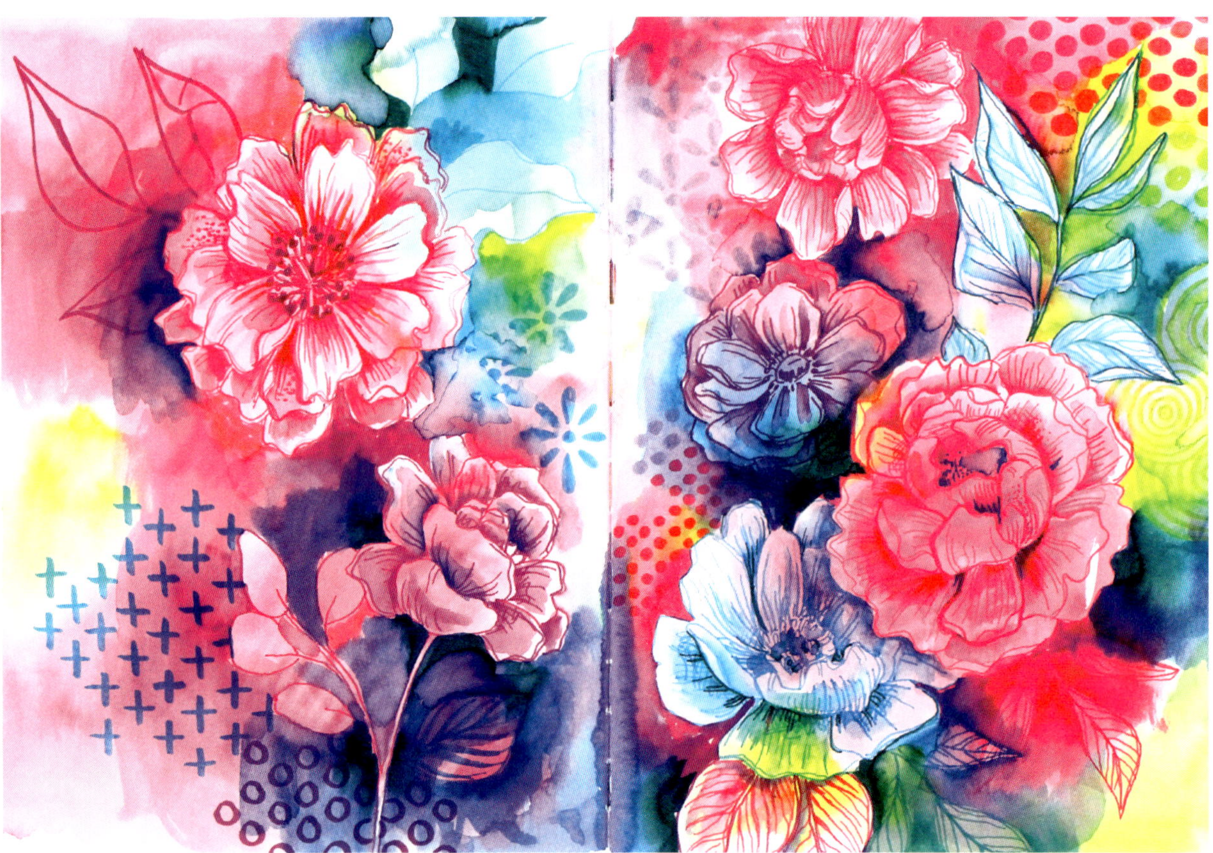

Oh, how I love this piece! It was created entirely with water-based makers and a water brush, and I incorporated stippling and loose linework as I did in "Washy Negative Space," as well as plenty of fun patterns in the negative space. This piece just makes me happy to look at, and I can still remember the day I created it—it was a good day!

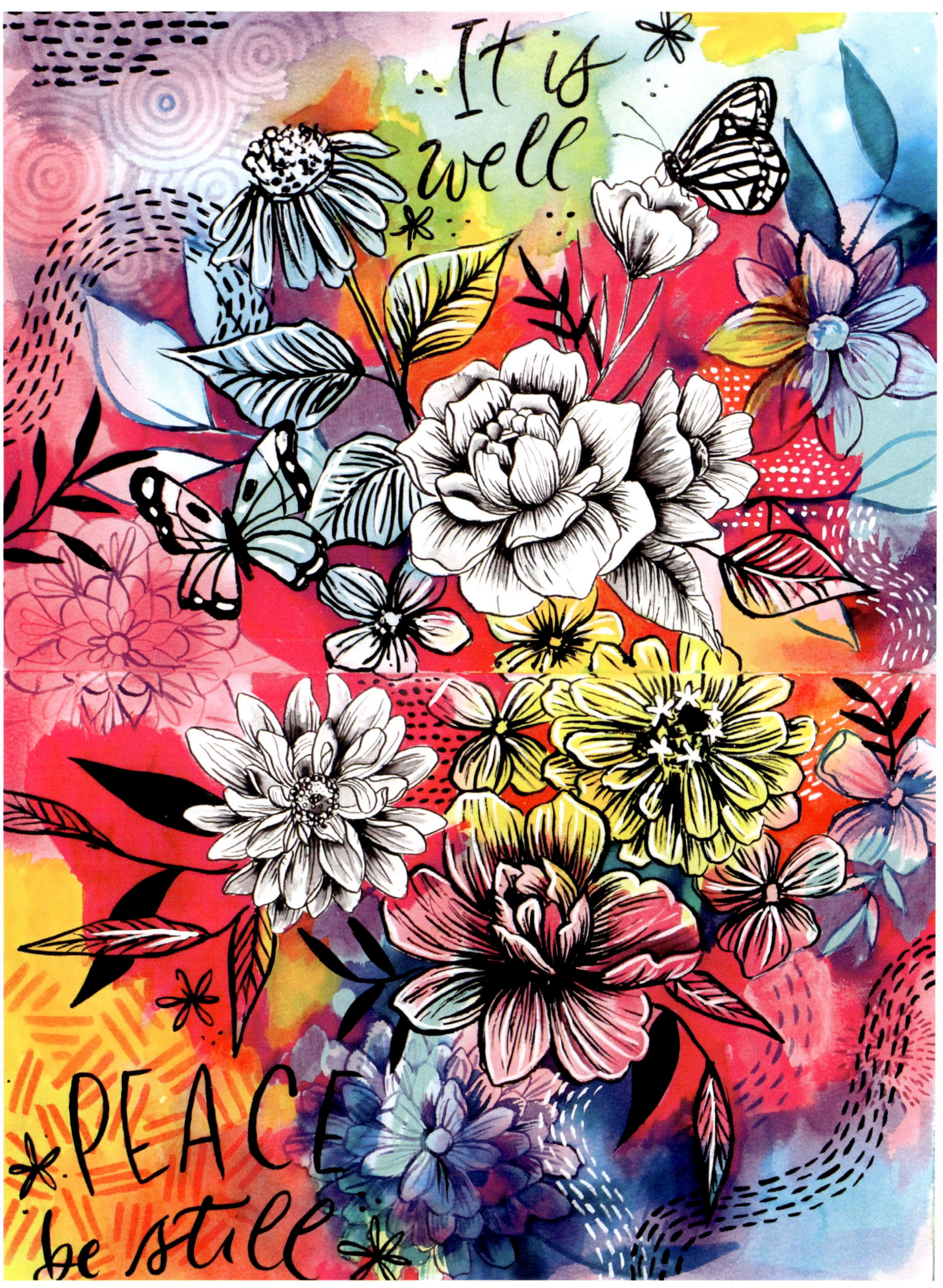

This is another piece inspired by the process from "Abundant Garden"—a project that uses ALL THE SUPPLIES. I hesitated before adding lettering in black acrylic, but the song the lyrics came from was playing, so I couldn't resist.

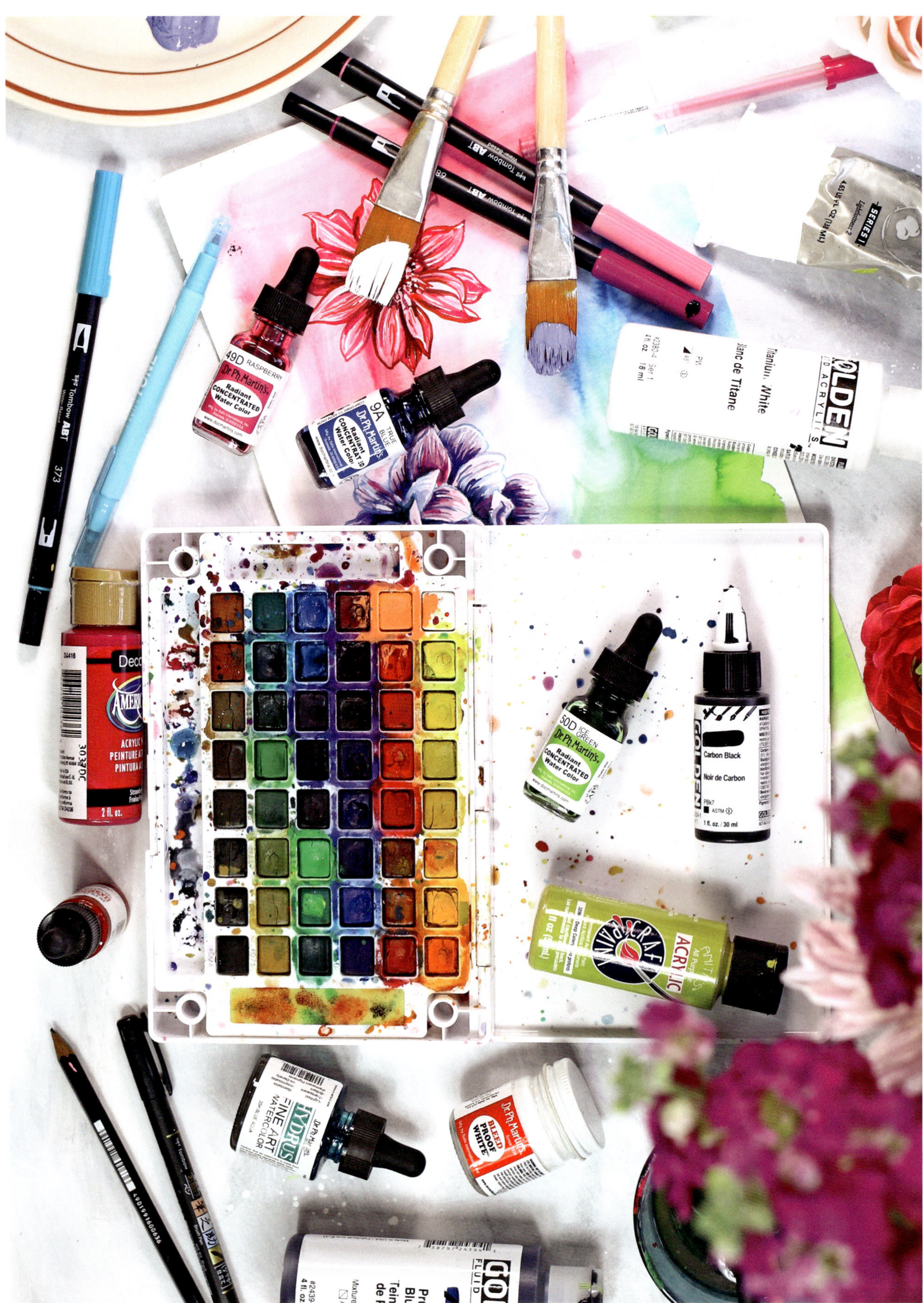

Supply Favorites

Here are some of the products I reach for again and again! When possible, I'll give you options for both stricter budgets or splurges. Remember that you are in no way obligated to use what I use—experiment on your own to figure out what works for you!

Painting Surfaces

- Strathmore 400 Series Watercolor Art Journal, 8.5" x 11" (22 x 28 cm): pricey and great for all media
- Arteza Watercolor Book, 8.3" x 11.7" (21 x 30 cm): affordable and better with acrylics than water-based media
- Canson XL Series Mixed Media Pad, 7" x 10" (18 x 26 cm): affordable and good for all media
- Canson XL Series Watercolor Pad: affordable and good for all media

Paintbrushes

- Royal and Langnickel Zen brushes: I like their large round brushes
- Vinonzi Miniature brushes: this is a 10-piece set of small round brushes that is extremely affordable and that I use for most of my linework and details

Watercolors

- Dr. Ph. Martin concentrated watercolors (both Hydrus and Radiant lines): pricey liquid watercolors that are unbelievably vibrant
- Sakura Koi watercolor pans: a great pan set

Water-Based Markers, Gel Pens, and Pens

- Tombow Dual Brush Pen water-based markers: pricey but great, and you can slowly build a collection of colors
- Sakura Gelly Roll gel pens: tons of colors, smooth, opaque, and reasonably priced
- Uniball Signo gel pens: I've yet to find a white gel pen that is more opaque
- Sharpie permanent markers: classic and reliable
- Tombow Mono permanent markers: a solid choice
- Tombow Fudenosuke calligraphy pens: a great calligraphy marker option

Acrylic Paints

- DecoArt Americana acrylic craft paints: tons of colors, affordable, and have a nice, matte finish
- Golden High-Flow and Fluid acrylics: my "splurge" paints that I typically purchase in black and white

Adhesives

- Liquitex Matte Medium: my go-to matte medium
- Tombow Permanent Adhesive: this feels like using a hybrid glue stick and tape; it's extremely sticky
- Folk Art Glazing Medium: a more affordable option to a fluid matte medium

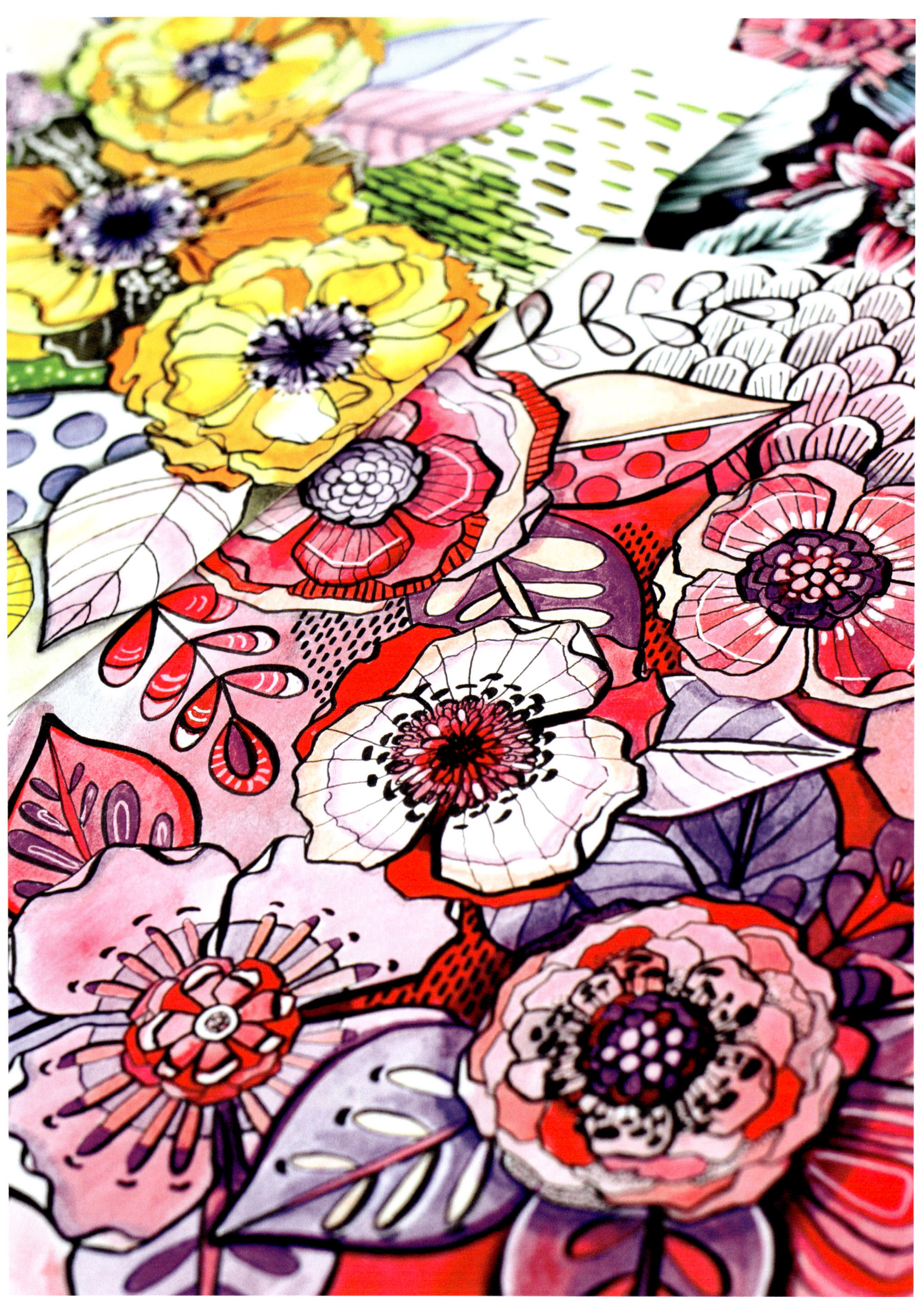

Index

Note: Page numbers in *italics* indicate projects.

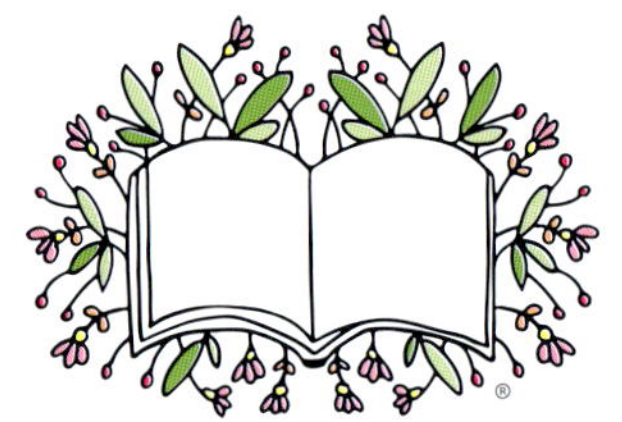

BETTER DAY BOOKS®

HAPPY • CREATIVE • CURATED

Business is personal at Better Day Books. We were founded on the belief that all people are creative and that making things by hand is inherently good for us. It's important to us that you know how much we appreciate your support. The book you are holding in your hands was crafted with the artistic passion of the author and brought to life by a team of wildly enthusiastic creatives who believed it could inspire you. If it did, please drop us a line and let us know about it. Connect with us on Instagram, post a photo of your art, and let us know what other creative pursuits you are interested in learning about. It all matters to us. You're kind of a big deal.

it's a good day to have a better day!®

www.betterdaybooks.com
better_day_books